DEAN JOHN COLET OF ST. PAUL'S

DEAN JOHN COLET OF ST. PAUL'S

Humanism and Reform in Early Tudor England

JONATHAN ARNOLD

BLOOMSBURY ACADEMIC
LONDON • NEW YORK • OXFORD • NEW DELHI • SYDNEY

BLOOMSBURY ACADEMIC
Bloomsbury Publishing Plc
50 Bedford Square, London, WC1B 3DP, UK
1385 Broadway, New York, NY 10018, USA

BLOOMSBURY, BLOOMSBURY ACADEMIC and the Diana logo
are trademarks of Bloomsbury Publishing Plc

First published in Great Britain by I.B. Tauris 2007
Paperback edition first published by Bloomsbury Academic 2020

Copyright © Jonathan Arnold, 2007

Jonathan Arnold has asserted his right under the Copyright,
Designs and Patents Act, 1988, to be identified as Author of this work.

For legal purposes the Acknowledgements on p. vii constitute
an extension of this copyright page.

All rights reserved. No part of this publication may be reproduced or transmitted
in any form or by any means, electronic or mechanical, including photocopying,
recording, or any information storage or retrieval system, without prior
permission in writing from the publishers.

Bloomsbury Publishing Plc does not have any control over, or responsibility for,
any third-party websites referred to or in this book. All internet addresses given in
this book were correct at the time of going to press. The author and publisher regret
any inconvenience caused if addresses have changed or sites have ceased to exist,
but can accept no responsibility for any such changes.

A catalogue record for this book is available from the British Library.

A catalog record for this book is available from the Library of Congress.

ISBN: HB: 978-1-8451-1436-7
PB: 978-1-4729-8116-5
ePDF: 978-0-8577-1198-4
ePub: 978-0-7556-2923-7

To find out more about our authors and books visit
www.bloomsbury.com and sign up for our newsletters.

For Emma, Katherine and Thomas

CONTENTS

Acknowledgements vii

Conventions viii

Introduction 1

1. The Early Years 17

2. In Search of Perfection: Colet's Written Works 30

3. Reform I: St. Paul's Minor Clergy in 1506 65

4. London Life: The Mercers and St. Paul's School 88

5. Preaching to the Converted: Colet's Convocation Sermon of 1511/12 108

6. Preaching and Controversy: The King, the Bishop and the Cardinal, 1512-15 136

7. Reform II: Colet's Final Reform Efforts of 1518 157

Conclusion 178

Abbreviations 186

Notes 187

Bibliography 229

Index 254

ACKNOWLEDGEMENTS

I would like to thank all those who have helped and encouraged the completion of this book. Special thanks go to the supervisor of my Ph.D. thesis, Dr. David Crankshaw, of King's College London, whose dedicated and meticulous guidance has been of supreme importance. My appreciation goes also to those who have helped me to develop my ideas by offering feedback on papers given in seminars: to Dr. Nicholas Tyacke and members of the Institute of Historical Research fortnightly seminar on Religious History from the fifteenth to the eighteenth centuries, and to the members of the weekly summer seminar on Late-Medieval and Early Tudor London convened by Professor Caroline Barron and Dr. Vanessa Harding. My sincere appreciation is offered to those who have assisted my research by reading extracts from work and offering helpful criticism and advice. In particular, I thank the late, and much missed, Professor J.B. Trapp of the Warburg Institute, Professor Christopher Harper-Bill of the University of East Anglia, the Rev'd Brian Mastin and Sally Dunkley. The monograph has also benefited from those who have brought my attention to relevant information or documents, especially Nigel Ramsay of University College London, and Dr. Anne Sutton. My particular thanks extend to Joseph Wisdom, of St. Paul's Cathedral and Guildhall Libraries in London, and to Ursula Carlyle, at the Mercers' Company, for giving of their time and expertise.

I wish to thank my parents, Brenda and Christopher, for their steadfast love and support over the years. Finally, I wish to express my heartfelt thanks to Emma, my wife, for her unfailing love, help and guidance, without whom this book would not exist. I dedicate the work to her, and to our two wonderful children, as a token of my esteem.

CONVENTIONS

(i) Dates

Until 31 December 1751, in England and Ireland, the new year began on 25 March. However, on the Continent, 1 January was increasingly treated as the beginning of the year of grace in the sixteenth century. That change began to have an influence unofficially in England in the seventeenth century, causing some English writers to use a split date in order to denote a particular year. To avoid confusion, therefore, when referring to dates from 1 January to 24 March in the sixteenth century, both years will be given; for example, '10 January 1500/1501'.

(ii) Editions Used

When more than one edition of a work is cited, the last given edition indicates the one to which I refer, unless otherwise indicated.

(iii) Latin Quotations

When quoting from Latin sources, the English translation will be given in the main text. Due to restrictions in the length of the book, it has not been possible to include the Latin original in the endnotes. Unless otherwise stated, translations are taken from the editions indicated.

INTRODUCTION

Taken at face value, the facts of John Colet's life appear to portray a successful, humanist clerical reformer, active in London on the eve of the English Reformation. Born in 1467, Colet was the son of the wealthy mercer, Henry Colet, and Christian Colet (born Knyvet).[1] He was probably educated in Cambridge.[2] The university Grace Books show Colet as a B.A. in 1485 and an M.A. in 1488.[3] He travelled to Italy between 1492 and 1496, becoming a devotee of the Florentine humanist Marsilio Ficino (1433-99).[4] Upon his return to England, he settled in Oxford, where he lectured on all of St. Paul's epistles;[5] his lectures on Romans and 1 Corinthians are extant.[6] The works are saturated with Neoplatonic and humanist ideas and, if we are to believe Erasmus, were well received.[7] Colet held several benefices, including Dennington, in Suffolk, from 1485;[8] Thurning, in Northamptonshire, from 1490; and Stepney, in Middlesex, which he resigned in 1504.[9] He was also a prebendary of York and Salisbury cathedrals.[10] In 1505, the chapter invited Colet, acting under Henry VII's mandate, to become Dean of St. Paul's Cathedral,[11] where he attempted a series of reforms and, in 1509, founded his famous school, which still exists.[12] He died in 1519.[13]

This book contends that, as a cleric, John Colet was neither successful nor a reformer. Just as he did not belong to a proto-Protestant movement in England,[14] nor can he simply be described with reference to a circle of Catholic humanist clerical reformers.[15] Colet is distinguishable from both categories in one important respect: he was dominated by a vision for Church perfection and it was the chief motivation for his life's work. As Dean of St. Paul's from 1505 to 1519, Colet sought to achieve Church reform by implementing his ecclesiological vision in the form of disciplinary procedure, cathedral administration, attempted statute reform, preaching, education, and even by use of his political connections.[16]

Evidence from the sixteenth century onwards suggests that Colet associated himself with the foremost Christian humanists of his day, headed by Desiderius

Erasmus (1467-1536) and Thomas More (1478-1535).[17] As Colet's Christian humanism differed significantly from that of other contemporaneous humanists, particularly with regard to classical authors whom he considered anti-Christian,[18] it will be helpful to define the term 'Christian humanism'.

As Dowling acknowledges, 'humanism' is a nebulous term, which derived from the Latin *humanitas*, as used by Cicero in classical times. The *Studia Humanitas* tended to involve the study of classical literature and languages, the rhetorical arts, such as debating skills, philology and the development of eloquent use of vernacular language, in order that civic virtue and common wealth should increase.[19] Thus the term *umanista* described a student or teacher of the liberal arts in late fifteenth-century Italy. The Christian branch of humanism encouraged the appreciation and study of languages such as Hebrew, Greek and Latin in order to gain a proper understanding of Christian texts (scripture and patristic writings), which thus underwent the humanist scholarly and philological treatment.[20] Christian humanists were particularly concerned with Church reform, the provision of an incorrupt, educated clergy and a preaching ministry.[21] Colet's Christian humanism, which formed the basis of his ecclesiology, was developed as the result of his engagement with an eclectic selection of intellectual fields, including Pauline theology;[22] Pseudo-Dionysian spirituality;[23] the Augustinian and Franciscan traditions of thought;[24] as well as Platonism and Neoplatonism, which perhaps also needs some definition.[25]

The Platonic ideals that Colet assimilated into his work emphasized ethics, the cultivation of the mind and will and the goodness of the soul.[26] For Plato (429-347 B.C.), the Demiurge (or, for Colet, God), who brought the world into being, enabled it to share in His perfection by putting the image of the eternal into the human mind.[27] The body of thought generated by Plato's Athenian Academy, and by the middle Platonic schools that followed, was expanded into a philosophical movement by Plotinus (205-70 A.D.), who stressed the transcendence of 'the one', who was the highest principle and above human understanding; in Christian terms, a transcendent God. However, the human soul, according to Plotinus, was by its nature divine, even though it had fallen into a human body, and longed to return to 'the one'.[28] Platonism was revitalized in the late Renaissance, most famously embodied in Ficino's Florentine Platonic Academy in the late fifteenth century. For Colet, following Plato, Plotinus and Ficino, every Christian's destiny was to be reunited with divine perfection. However, human failings remained an obstacle in the journey from humanity to divinity, and Colet's public wrestling with the problem led to his failure in the practical administration of his cathedral.

Thus, various theological and philosophical influences helped define the chief characteristics of Colet's outlook: a hierarchical, perfectionist, strict code of Christian moral virtue, the aim of which was to unify the Church and enable it to ascend to the Divine.[29] The motivation for writing this monograph has been a desire to bridge a gap in Colet scholarship by focusing attention on a previously underexplored area of Colet's thought, namely his ecclesiology, and on one specific period of his life: his tenure as Dean of St. Paul's, 1505-19. This work argues that, despite his qualifications, connections and credentials, Colet's failure was directly attributable to his overly idealistic expectations of what it was possible to achieve, to his unrealistic view of the Church, and to the inappropriate manner in which he expressed his idealistic ecclesiological vision.[30] I examine several episodes during Colet's life as dean, episodes in which he attempted to apply his ecclesiology. It is hoped that a greater appreciation of this ecclesiology, which motivated his attempted clerical reforms, may help to promote a better understanding of those reform endeavours and, therefore, of Colet's role within pre-Reformation Church administration.

Ecclesiology has been described as 'the science of the Church';[31] it is Colet's understanding of this science that is the concern of this work: specifically, his intellectual development, his vision for the Church, and how his ideas were expressed at St. Paul's. I shall argue that, although several scholars have made either direct or tangential contributions to the study of the dean's ecclesiology, much has been misrepresented or ignored.[32]

In order to justify the present work, this introduction begins with a description and evaluation of five centuries of Colet scholarship, of what insights have been gained into his life and of what omissions remain. This analysis and justification is followed by an exposition of the outstanding questions regarding Colet's life. The answers suggested will be fully explored in the remainder of the work. Finally, the shape of the book is outlined by a summary of the contents of each chapter, its relevance to the work as a whole, and its significance for our understanding of the Church in pre-Reformation London.

Scholarship

For theologians, historians and antiquaries, discerning Colet's significance within English history used to be simple. He was a heroic reformer, a 'great forerunner of the Reformation', a proto-Protestant who heralded the new Protestant age[33] – the evil and despicable pre-Reformation Catholic Church, which Colet had so rightly criticized, and which had barbarically accused him of heresy, was doctrinally reformed according to his wishes, albeit posthumously, in the English Reformation.[34] Thus, writers repeated for centuries John Foxe's (1516-87) polemically distorted version of Erasmus's first-hand recollections of Colet's life.[35]

Colet's portrait was given subtler colour by subsequent insights into his intellectual, educational or administrative significance,[36] yet his place within history was not seriously reconsidered until revisionist historians of the last thirty years 'collectively recognized that the pre-Reformation Church was both a dynamic and well-loved institution and the object of fierce criticism by lay and clerical writers'.[37] Above all, in 1989, Gleason rightly reclaimed the dean as a traditionalist pre-Reformation Catholic, a pious Christian humanist, who preached, worked and wrote for his beloved Church. Gleason's Colet sought no structural or doctrinal change to the existing order, but the renewal of people's minds and a perfected Church for the glory of God.

Following his reclamation into traditional Catholic territory, Colet has been the focus of little post-revisionist scrutiny until now. Yet his relegation to a minor role in the English Reformation, and Gleason's detailed assessment of Colet's thought-world, and of his educational and political activities, has left outstanding questions. There are two main omissions in scholarship which this book addresses: firstly, the nature of the relationship between his intellectual life and the Church; and secondly, the nature of Colet's decanal administration of St. Paul's Cathedral. The process of filling the historical gaps will begin by assessing the earliest available sources.

Historians investigating Colet can refer to two early accounts of his career, written by Erasmus and by Foxe, Erasmus portrayed him as a devout Catholic; Foxe portrayed him as a proto-Protestant. Nearly everything written about Colet, from the mid-sixteenth century until the mid-nineteenth century, followed Foxe's misplaced assumptions about, and assessment of, the dean. I shall examine Erasmus's account first.

The earlier of the two accounts, penned by Erasmus in 1521, forms part of a letter to his friend Jodocus Jonas, which also deals with the life of Jean Vitrier.[38] The purpose of the letter was to persuade Jonas against converting to Lutheranism by relating *exempla* from the lives of two men who had been critical of the Church without resorting to apostasy.[39] Thus, Erasmus was characteristically flattering of his subject and it is largely due to Erasmus's portrayal, as well as to Colet's school foundation, that the dean's fame was preserved. Indeed, when reading Erasmus we must remember that 'one should never place too much faith in individual writings of Erasmus, who wrote a great deal for effect, a great deal for money and a great deal to curry favour.'[40] Therefore, whilst the Colet scholar cannot ignore Erasmus's biography, it is to be approached with an element of caution.

Erasmus portrayed Colet as an example of true Catholic piety.[41] Unlike his Protestant successors, Erasmus focused on the dean's considerable intellect, relating that Colet had lectured in Oxford on all of St. Paul's epistles.[42] Erasmus also described the influences upon Colet's thought world, and therefore upon his ecclesiology, by relating that Colet was a devotee of St. Paul, Pseudo-Dionysius and Neoplatonic humanism.[43] Although Erasmus was absent from England at crucial stages of Colet's life, nevertheless his account is the longest and earliest narrative account of his career. It is ironic, therefore, that other extant sixteenth-century references to Colet portray him as a Protestant in spirit, if not in fact. The present work makes discriminating use of Erasmus's account of the Catholic Colet, but also reveals characteristics of his ecclesiology.

Colet's Catholic allegiance was quickly forgotten, or perhaps ignored, as some sixteenth-century writers portrayed him as a persecuted hero: in 1529, William Tyndale wrote that Colet was making anti-Catholic gestures when Bishop Fitzjames of London (1506-22) 'would have made the old dean of Paul's a heretic for translating the *Pater Noster* in English, had not the Bishop [*sic*] of Canterbury holp the dean.'[44] In the 1540s, John Bale wrote that Colet's offence had been 'reading Paul's Epistles by his life',[45] presumably referring to the idea that Colet used literal interpretation in his biblical exegesis, influenced by his Italian travels, which was a departure from traditional medieval allegorical exegesis – an argument used for Colet's alleged Protestant attitudes well into the nineteenth century.[46] In 1552, Hugh Latimer recalled that Colet would have been burned as a heretic had it not been for the king's protection.[47] Thus, Latimer misleadingly portrayed him as a herald of the king's established Church. In 1562, John Jewel, Bishop of Salisbury, listed Colet among the forerunners of the Reformation, but was rebuked by the Catholic Thomas Harding in 1566, who argued that there was no evidence for Jewel's assertion because 'as for John Colet, he hath never a word to show, for he wrote no works', referring to Colet's lack of published work.[48] Remarkably, this is apparently the only acknowledgement of Colet's Catholicism extant from the sixteenth century, except for Erasmus's biography. To Matthew Parker, Colet was the Oxford divine who imposed 'the [Protestant] rule of sacred scripture' at St. Paul's.[49]

Following Colet's posthumous transformation from Catholic to Protestant, Erasmus's letter was used as the basis for Foxe's account of the dean's life in the 1570 edition of his *Acts and Monuments*,[50] also known as the 'Book of Martyrs', even though Colet was not a Protestant Martyr.[51] Foxe made much of Colet's battle with Fitzjames, viewing it as one of a proto-Protestant against a conservative Catholic. Based upon the evidence of Colet's 1511/12 Convocation sermon, Foxe enhanced Colet's supposed proto-Protestant status by emphasizing his criticism of the clergy, his evangelistic preaching, and the fact that Lollards travelled to St. Paul's in order to hear him preach.[52] Therefore, only five decades after Colet had died a devout Catholic, in 1519, Foxe had claimed him as a forerunner of English Protestantism. Foxe's version became very influential upon subsequent Colet biographers over the next four centuries. The significance of these misrepresentations is their crystallization into assumptions that have been perpetuated for generations since, only recently being dismissed. One example of this kind of false assumption is Dawley's assertion regarding Anglicanism:

> In its appeal to Scripture the evangelical spirit of John Colet triumphed over the narrow biblicism of Thomas Cartwright ... The line of spiritual continuity is clear – from Colet to Cranmer to Jewel to Hooker, and then to the Caroline divines.[53]

Therefore, the first objective in this book is freshly to appraise Colet's devout Catholicism and his intellectual and clerical life, but also to recognize his distinctive contributions to those Catholic and intellectual traditions by means of an investigation of his life and works.

Little written about Colet remains extant from the seventeenth century, but clearly he was not forgotten: Pitts listed a dozen Colet works extant in 1619, some of which are now lost;[54] Donald Lupton described Colet as a Protestant Divine whose 'nature was against those which persecuted the professors of [Protestant] truth.'[55] Dugdale drew attention to Colet's reforming efforts of 1518 by reproducing his *Exhibita* of statute proposals of that year in his 1658 history of St. Paul's.[56] Henry Wharton wrote of the dean in similar terms in 1695.[57] Colet evidently did not escape the proto-Protestant label in the seventeenth century.

In the 1720s, Bishop White Kennett (b.1660) made extensive notes on Colet's life.[58] His interpretation of Foxe's material was that Colet was Protestant in spirit, a harbinger of a much-needed Reformation, and an evangelical.[59] Although Kennett did not convert his notes into a published biography, which was surely his original aim, he passed on his ideas to Samuel Knight, a man 'at the Protestant end of the Anglican spectrum', who published the first full-length Colet biography in 1724.[60] The illusion of a Protestant Colet was perpetuated in the nineteenth century by a reprint of Knight's text in 1823.[61] However, in the 300 years after Colet's death, there appeared no significant analysis of his biblical lectures, his Pseudo-Dionysian commentaries, or his treatises; in fact, his thought, except for his Convocation sermon of 1511/12, remained unexamined until 1867.[62] Historians from Foxe to Knight had concentrated on Colet's reform endeavours rather than on his intellectual life. This lack of scholarly engagement with the intellectual origins of Colet's actions has led to misrepresentations of his motives for attempted reform. The present monograph suggests that a close examination of the dean's ecclesiology is the key to a correct explanation. This investigation is assisted by, and conducted in the context of, the growing interest in Colet's intellectual life that was first rejuvenated in the nineteenth century.

Colet scholarship was transformed in 1867 with the publication of Frederick Seebohm's *Oxford Reformers*. Seebohm's Colet remained a proto-Protestant divine, but the Victorian antiquary contributed a further invention: the fantasy of a group of Oxford-based humanists consisting of Thomas More, Erasmus and Colet himself. In fact, the evidence for contact between these men in Oxford is virtually nil, Seebohm's theory being based on mistaken chronology.[63] However, his work was significant in that he recognized, for the first time since Erasmus, an important aspect of Colet's life: Italian humanism.[64] This revelation was soon seized upon by enthusiastic followers, such as Green, who in 1874 proclaimed that 'the awakening of a rational Christianity, whether in England, or in the Teutonic world at large, begins with the Florentine studies of John Colet.'[65] Seebohm asserted that Colet had inaugurated a new kind of exegesis, using literal rather than allegorical interpretation of scripture; that he had possessed a sound knowledge of Greek; that he had scorned Catholic 'superstition' and left no money for prayers to be said for his soul; and that he had been the single greatest influence upon Erasmus.[66] As Gleason was later to argue, all of these assertions are untrue.[67] Nevertheless, Seebohm's recognition of the significance of Colet's humanism was a small step towards a wider investigation of his writings and thought, which prepared the way for this author's investigation of one aspect of Colet's intellect: his ecclesiology.

Whatever its insights, Seebohm's work was only a prelude to a greater work written by the surmaster (second master) of St. Paul's School, Joseph Lupton. Lupton's biography of Colet was the most comprehensive of its time, using material drawn from Erasmus, Foxe, Kennett, Knight and Seebohm.[68] Lupton traced Colet's life from his London childhood, family, school, university, travels in Italy, to Oxford, and back to London. Like Seebohm, Lupton placed a strong emphasis on Colet's skill as a biblical interpreter, giving him the accolade of being the first modern exegete.[69] A whole chapter is devoted to 'Incidents of Life at the Deanery' – the facts of each episode examined in this thesis were all well narrated and described by Lupton, although not in relation to Colet's ecclesiology.[70] Lupton possessed a keen interest in Colet's intellectual life, being the first scholar so far to translate and publish editions of most of Colet's extant works.[71] Indeed, Lupton was also the first man, after Erasmus, to take seriously the influence of Pseudo-Dionysius upon Colet's thinking, but unfortunately did not relate this aspect to Colet's life as dean.[72] Lupton failed to link Colet's intellectual life with his working life in general, focusing mainly upon the sermon preached to the Convocation of the Province of Canterbury for evidence of his thought in action, and upon the foundation of St. Paul's School for evidence of his practical humanism.[73] Both Seebohm's and Lupton's works, therefore, were significant in drawing attention to aspects of Colet's life that had previously been ignored. The two authors emphasized Colet's humanism, exegesis, preaching and educational reforms.

The twentieth century has seen more written about Colet than any other.[74] However, in the first half of the century, Colet scholarship moved slowly, advancing little in substance, with writers such as Marriott persisting in categorising Colet as a 'harbinger of the reformation'.[75] Significant works relevant to this work from that period include Allen's article on Colet's relationship with Archbishop Warham,[76] which took the unprecedented step of trying to understand Colet's life from a pre-Reformation perspective, rather than from a post-Reformation viewpoint. In addition, P.S. and H.M. Allen's editions of Erasmus's letters, which appeared in the first few decades of the century, provided an invaluable source for the Colet scholar by providing wide access to the texts of the correspondence between Erasmus and Colet, and to Erasmus's 1521 biographical letter on Colet.[77] This access helped to strip away the layers of Protestant gloss that had built up. Allen's work, therefore, enabled a more objective historical analysis to emerge in the subsequent decades of the twentieth century, and is work to which this thesis is indebted. From the 1940s onwards, research about Colet was published mainly in the form of articles. Insight into his intellectual life was taken to a new level of scholarship in the 1950s by Rice,[78] who offered a perceptive reassessment of Colet's thought within the context of medieval ideas. Rice was the first to examine the dean's life from his writings rather than from biographical accounts. This book builds upon Rice's observation of Colet's Augustinian 'annihilation of the natural':[79] Colet's intellectual tendency to ascribe great significance to the celestial and no significance to humanity and earthly things. This annihilation of the natural was also an aspect of his ecclesiology: for Colet, God was everything; humanity was nothing. Therefore, Rice has unwittingly contributed to our understanding of Colet's ecclesiology,[80] acknowledging that the dean's low view of humanity was the starting point for his ecclesiology. However, the views expressed in other articles, such as one published by Miles in 1951, were retrograde, returning immediately to post-Reformation Protestant assumptions.[81] Of more positive significance was Hunt's 1952 mini biography,[82] which examined Colet as a reformer, preacher and exegete,[83] but also entertained the idea that he may have been a mystic, a contention based upon his love of the writings of Plato and Pseudo-Dionysius.[84] Hunt's intriguing suggestion has proved significant in this study of Colet's intellect. Although reading devotional texts and being an idealist does not make one a mystic, Hunt highlighted Colet's employment of certain mystical formulae, such as Pseudo-Dionysius's three-fold formula for the ascent to God, in the development of his vision for the Church.[85]

By the mid-twentieth century, therefore, various aspects of Colet's intellectual life had been analysed, including his humanism, biblicism, piety and anti-naturalism.

Platonism was also deeply embedded in Colet's ecclesiology, and several authors made significant examinations of this facet in the 1960s.[86] Miles's 1961 study of Colet's Platonism was quickly superseded by Jayne's introduction to, and edition of, Colet's marginalia to a 1495 copy of Marsilio Ficino's *Epistolae*.[87] Jayne observed that Platonism pervaded Colet's written work, but concluded that his compositions were imbued with a Christian moral fervour of his own.[88] Additionally, Jayne recognized Colet's Augustinian view of humanity, an acceptance of St. Paul as central, and a religious zeal combined with an Aristotelian pragmatism.[89] While Jayne overstated the dean's Hellenism and linguistic skills in Greek,[90] his study was nevertheless a breakthrough in Colet research: Christian moral values mixed with Italian Neoplatonism were shown to be strong elements in Colet's thought. This monograph further argues that these characteristics shaped both Colet's ecclesiology and his activity as dean. Porter, also writing in the 1960s, focused on another of Colet's intellectual characteristics.[91] Examining Colet's legal fixation, as expressed in the sermon preached to Convocation in 1511/12, he observed that the dean wished to curtail the power of the Church courts.[92] Porter also acknowledged

> ... the eclectic, almost eccentric, cast of Colet's mind, with its diverse ingredients: the primacy of Paul; the platonic tradition of the Pseudo-Dionysius; and also the contemporary Florentines, Marsilio Ficino and Pico della Mirandola.[93]

In addition, Porter convincingly argued, from Colet's own Convocation sermon and other works, that he was anti-litigious, noting his absolute rule that '... it is not the part of Christians to dispute at law ...'.[94] Porter plausibly suggested that Colet was a prophet, concluding that, in the Parliament of 1529, lay grievances against the ecclesiastical courts had grown to damaging proportions, in accordance with Colet's fears, although Haigh subsequently demonstrated that anticlericalism, and grievances against the ecclesiastical courts, were limited to specific interest groups in specific locations.[95] Significantly for Colet scholarship, Porter examined how the dean's thought was applied to a single ecclesiastical event: the Convocation sermon of 1511/12. This thesis seeks to build upon Porter's insights, and Gleason's subsequent assertions concerning Colet's work within a traditional Catholic setting, by suggesting that Colet's emphasis upon canon law was one of several aspects of his ideology, which he tried to apply not once, but throughout his tenure as dean.[96]

Porter's and Jayne's insights set the pace for accelerated progress in Colet research thereafter. Trapp's contribution has been particularly valuable, not only in expanding upon Colet's association with Italian humanism and upon his devotion to the work of Pseudo-Dionysius, but also with regard to the palaeographical identification of the penmanship in Colet's manuscripts.[97] Trapp convincingly established Colet as a faithful, if unorthodox and indiscreet, member of the pre-Reformation Catholic Church and a passionate Christian humanist, devoted to St. Paul, Pseudo-Dionysius and Ficino.[98] Trapp did not explicitly deal with Colet's ecclesiology, but, by his work on Colet's intellectual life, he laid the foundation of this study of how the dean sought to put his ecclesiological thought into practice.

Progress was made in the 1970s and 1980s concerning another important influence upon Colet: Erasmus. A number of articles compared Colet's thought with that of his friend. Kaufman refutes Harbison's opinion that Colet was 'more than any other human being ... the source of Erasmus's vision and sense of calling'.[99] Not only does Kaufman rightly observe that Colet owed an intellectual debt to Erasmus, but also that Erasmus's *Enchiridion* was far more influential upon the initial stages of the English Reformation than anything that Colet had produced.[100] Jarrott's comparison between Colet's Pauline commentaries and Erasmus's *Annotationes* highlights several similarities between the scholars and suggests that Colet's humanistic fervour eclipsed any characterisation of him as 'gloomy.'[101] By the 1980s, therefore, several main characteristics of Colet's intellectual make-up had been identified: Pauline theology, Pseudo-Dionysian spirituality, Platonism and Neoplatonism, humanism, a high opinion of the priesthood, a low view of humanity, a Christian moral fervour and a pious Catholicism.

Important revisionism in the past three decades has reassessed the origins and impact of the Reformation, by a more sociological approach to the evidence, and by a reconsideration of the popularity of the Catholic Church on the eve of the break with Rome.[102] Revisionism has discovered that the Church, in the late-medieval period, was not as corrupt as has previously been asserted.[103] It was, rather, a healthy, devotional, and self-critical institution. Thus, scholars have been able to put the revised Colet portrait into a more realistic pre-Reformation context than that managed by the Victorians and their followers. In discussing Colet, revisionists have adopted humanism as their theme: Rex rejects Seebohm's idea of a circle of Oxford reformers in favour of a humanist Catholic reform circle centred on Fisher.[104] Brigden also ranks Colet amongst the 'brightest and best of the English humanist community' that 'were gathered in London on the eve of the Reformation', although her description of Colet as 'the reforming Dean of St. Paul's' is an exaggeration.[105] Harper-Bill declares that Colet's preaching was 'merely ... a new humanistic variation on a traditional theme', a sentiment echoed by Haigh, whilst Kaufman concludes from Colet's treatise *De Sacramentis*, and an observation of parts of his career as dean, that he stopped short of being anticlerical, but was nevertheless an uncompromising idealist – an observation elaborated upon in this thesis in relation to the practical application of Colet's ecclesiology.[106] Revisionist histories of the

English Reformation and pre-Reformation Church stimulated renewed interest in Erasmus and humanism; this, in turn, brought Colet to the forefront of scholars' attention, if only by default. However, the most recent scholarship to appear echoes rather the Victorian idealised view that Colet 'must have brought a welcome breath of reform' to St. Paul's and that he was 'an energetic reformer'.[107] As I have argued in this introduction, and will do so throughout the thesis, Colet only **attempted** reform. Moreover, those attempts were not particularly welcome. One important work is Trapp's article on Colet in the *Oxford Dictionary of National Biography*.[108] Though it is a mainly factual and conservative portrait of Colet's life, the article demonstrates Trapp's great depth of knowledge about the dean, and will be referred to at relevant points in this book.

The most important monograph so far on Colet's life is by Gleason. Although it is not a full biography, it is the most comprehensive and valuable revisionist work on Colet to appear in recent years. Examining several episodes in Colet's life, Gleason offers a reassessment of his education, the dating of his extant works, his intellectual life, the foundation of his school and his brief flirtation with politics.[109] Gleason was the first scholar to deal with what he called Colet's 'mistaken identity': he tackles the erroneous notion that Colet was a proto-Protestant and convincingly replaces him in conservative Catholic territory.[110] Gleason refutes Seebohm's claim that Colet was an immense influence upon Erasmus and seeks to correct a defect in Lupton's account, which had divorced Colet's life from his writings, by connecting his 'world of thought' with his '*Vita Activa*', if only in the realms of education and politics, rather than attempted clerical reform.[111] Gleason's work is significant in that he understands Colet's complex intellectual make-up and therefore refuses to portray Colet one-dimensionally; he examines Colet's written works and the foundation of his school in detail.[112] However, such a detailed work obviously necessitates some omissions. Consequently, Gleason almost entirely ignores Colet's administration of St. Paul's and, like all preceding Colet scholars, does not attempt an assessment of his ecclesiology, although he suggests in passing that the argument of Colet's *De Sacramentis* was 'in effect Colet's personal ecclesiology.'[113] My own work departs from Gleason considerably on the issue of the dating of Colet's written works and, therefore, arrives at a fresh conclusion concerning how and when Colet's intellectual life affected his cathedral administration. Gleason suggests that Colet composed many of his works late in life; the present reinterpretation considers Colet's written works, apart from sermons, to have been largely completed by the time of his appointment as dean.[114] This study is dedicated to answering questions that have not been addressed to date: how Colet's intellectual life and career as dean were linked. His life and work present a significant example of the relationship between late-medieval thought and ecclesiastical reform in pre-Reformation England. Colet's well-informed, highly developed idealism was indicative of the care, devotion and vision evident in the Church on the eve of the English Reformation.

Outline

The object of this work, as has been stated, is to reassess Colet's thought and life by means of a study of his ideological vision. First, we must establish whether or not Colet possessed a distinct idealist ecclesiology. If he did possess one, then we must examine its nature and elucidate its formation. Why and when he developed it; how it was put into practice; and how it was received are all important issues to be addressed. These issues will be discussed by means of an examination of Colet's intellectual and working life. Colet's written works, lectures and sermons, in which his ecclesiology was expressed, will be related to his administration of St. Paul's Cathedral and the foundation of his school. The nature of his ideology, and the issues of when, where, why and how it was formed, will be explained in the first two chapters, which concern his education, written works and thought. The matters of how, as dean, Colet put his humanist and reformist vision into practice, how it was received at St. Paul's, and what impact it made, will be addressed in the remainder of the book, which is concerned with Colet's attempted reforms of 1506; his London life as a mercer and his grammar school; his sermon delivered to the Convocation of the Province of Canterbury of 1511/12; the impact and significance of his preaching in the wider Church between 1512 and 1515; his involvement in royal politics between 1515 and 1518; and his final attempt at reform in 1518. A close investigation of these events, or clusters of events, forms the evidential basis for the argument that Colet's efforts were overly idealistic and thus ineffective. The conclusion will include a summary of the solutions offered to the problems surrounding Colet's ecclesiology, an assessment of the significance of his life and work for our understanding of the late-medieval Church, and a restatement of the my main argument based on the evidence provided.

The first two chapters, therefore, lay the essential foundations upon which the rest of the work is built. Firstly, an examination of Colet's early years, his schooling, university education, travels on the Continent and move to Oxford, where he began to write in earnest and where his ideas were fully formed in his written works.

Secondly, the ideology emerging from his written works is examined. This has significance as documentary evidence for the argument that his theoretical humanism, theology and ecclesiology, rather than merely his ministerial experience at St. Paul's, were the driving force behind much of his practical action. Thereafter, the remaining chapters explore Colet's ideals in action, by examining several events of ecclesiological and secular interest from Colet's decanal career; each of these chapters relates to a different event and its significance assessed. It is worth outlining the contents and significance of each chapter now.

Although little is known concerning Colet's schooling, it is clear that his early years were dominated by the increasing status of his father, Henry, as a London mercer, which became a significant factor in Colet's return to the capital as dean. Chapter one follows Colet's progress from his merchant family background to Cambridge University, and thus to France and Italy, where his love of humanist and Neoplatonic ideas was established. Thereafter, having settled in Oxford, Colet's newly acquired sensibilities were transferred to the page, and his humanist and reformist tendencies were further entrenched by the arrival of, and friendship with, Erasmus.

The fact that Colet possessed a highly developed ecclesiological vision is evident in his written work, which I examine in the second chapter.[115] That chapter, therefore, discusses scholarship concerning Colet's ecclesiology and demonstrates its nature, as well as why and how it was developed. Discussion of the main influences upon Colet includes an evaluation of the influence of Pseudo-Dionysius in Western medieval thought until the sixteenth century, followed by a demonstration of how this Pseudo-Dionysian tradition was received by Colet and influenced him. Other influences, including Pauline Theology, Platonism, Neoplatonism, Augustinianism and the Franciscan tradition are also examined. Drawn from his commentary on the *Ecclesiastical Hierarchy* of Pseudo-Dionysius, examples of Colet's written work are analysed, in order to illustrate his distinctive interpretations of the Pseudo-Dionysian texts and to establish the chief characteristics of Colet's ecclesiology itself. Examples from his other works are assessed for the purposes of highlighting some of his ecclesiology's sub-themes and to demonstrate how his ecclesiology was central, in terms of his characteristic interpretation of Pseudo-Dionysius, to his work as dean. I also argue that the motivation for Colet's ecclesiological theory grew from his discontent with the perceived state of the Church and was developed in an attempt to heal the Church of moral disease. Finally, I contend that Colet's ecclesiology was distinctive from contemporaneous humanist thought.

Chapter three analyses the dean's first attempt at clerical reform, its level of success, the reception it was given and its significance. Undertaken in 1506, following his visitation in June of that year, Colet's first reforming action as dean was to propose the manufacture of little books containing collected statutes and fresh injunctions, to be available to the cathedral's junior clergy.[116] The lives and duties of minor clergy at other secular cathedrals are appraised in comparison to the vicars-choral, chantry priests and minor canons – the minor clergy – at St. Paul's. I investigate why Colet wished to compile these statutes and compose new injunctions for the minor clergy. Three reasons are suggested: firstly, his desire to improve standards, which will be revealed through a consideration of clerical discipline and behaviour of the minor clergy, in order to establish whether or not there was a genuine need for improvement; secondly, his desire to control finances; and thirdly, his desire to follow a trend of statute reform, which was common in English secular cathedrals. Colet had five chief ecclesiological concerns in 1506, which are explored in turn: clerical learning; doctrinal error; Godly conversation; Christian morality; and clerical behaviour during the offices. The chapter concludes with an observation of the austere nature of Colet's approach to cathedral administration, as exemplified in his withdrawal of decanal hospitality.

The fourth chapter traces Colet's increasing reformist aims in the following years, with the revival of the Guild of the Holy Name of Jesus, in the crypt of St. Paul's in 1507; the restoration of the Hospital of St. Thomas of Acre; and of course, the foundation of his great legacy, St. Paul's School, in 1509-12. These episodes were all closely linked with the Mercers' Company. Thus, an examination of them presents the opportunity of analysing the dean's credentials in the more secular environment of the city, as a Londoner and a mercer.

Chapter five concerns the second documented incident in Colet's decanal career in which his perfectionist vision was expressed: his sermon preached to the Convocation of the Province of Canterbury in 1511/12. As the most public statement of his clerical concerns, the text is an important example of how Colet addressed his ecclesiology to the wider Church. The chapter includes a summary of the sermon, which is contextualized in terms of the late-medieval homiletic tradition, in order to ascertain how unusual Colet's preaching was and whether he can be said to have been part of a well-established tradition or not. Therefore, medieval forms, styles and thematic schemes will be considered. I compare Colet's sermon with certain works by another contemporary English preacher: John Fisher (1469-1535). A comparison is also made with Continental contemporaries, including Jacques Lefèvre d'Etaples (c.1460-1536), Johann Geiler von Kaysersberg (1478-1510) and Girolamo Savonarola (1452-98), all of whose reform ideals bore some similarities to Colet's own, but whose ecclesiological emphases on the issues of individual sin, repentance, penance and purgatory were not shared by the dean. Moreover, Colet's call for more general councils is compared with the views of fifteenth-century Continental conciliar radicals. In conclusion, the sermon is reassessed as part traditional reform sermon and part conciliarist tract. However, I further argue that the sermon fits best into Colet's own ecclesiology because it belonged uniquely to Colet as an intense vision of a Church in perfect communion with God.

Chapter six assesses the impact of the dean's preaching in London. The chapter begins with an examination of the king's reaction to his sermon on war and of the subsequent discussion between the two men on that subject. This section is followed by a consideration of Fitzjames's reaction to Colet's preaching, starting with a brief description of the dispute between them; a narrative explaining how the antagonism arose; an outline of the allegations made against the dean; an assessment of those allegations; and an analysis of whether or not he was guilty of them. Having appraised the significance of the attack, I analyse reactions to Colet's preaching from his cathedral clergy and the wider Church, along with the social and political activities that affected his sermon output between 1513 and 1515. Finally, the significance of his sermon preached at Thomas Wolsey's installation as cardinal in 1515 is assessed. I conclude that Colet's notorious reputation as a preacher earned him hatred, but also respect, and that this mixed reception compromised his chances of succeeding in his projected reforms.

The seventh chapter concerns the significance of Colet's final attempt at clerical reform in 1518 when, following his entrance into political life as a royal councillor and ally of Wolsey (1472-1530), he proposed amendments to the existing cathedral statutes concerning residence and the behaviour of the cathedral clergy and other staff, including lay virgers. The nature of Colet's political involvement between 1515 and 1518 is investigated, an involvement that provides the background to his attempt at cathedral statute reform in 1518. I analyse the sixteenth and seventeenth-century reactions to his proposed emendations in order to demonstrate how contemporaneous and subsequent generations of clergy perceived Colet's ideals. Finally, the significance of Colet's last clerical reform attempt is assessed by means of a comparison with previous statute reform at St. Paul's and with Wolsey's own cathedral statutes of 1518. This investigation leads to the conclusion that Colet's reform efforts were invested with little significance at the time, but that they are very significant for historians as evidence of pre-Reformation clerical activity.

If the significance of Colet's life is to be assessed in a proper perspective, as it is in the conclusion to this study, then his vision must be contextualized in terms of his overall contribution to early sixteenth-century religious society. His greatest achievement, and lasting legacy, was the foundation of his school. Thus, in the sphere of Christian humanist education, Colet was a success. He also achieved some fame at Court as a regular preacher, as a royal councillor and as Wolsey's ally.[117] However, in all his dealings, Colet considered the spiritual life to be of paramount importance. In this respect, although Colet's ecclesiology may not have effected any significant change in the early sixteenth-century Church, it nevertheless pointed, in a prophetic way, to the possibility of a more spiritual, unified and holy Church.

This investigation of Colet's life, in word and deed, reveals a passionate and pious man whose aim was the deification of sinful humanity, not just for a few exceptional individuals, but for the entire Church as a single unit. Even allowing for his similarities with other humanists, such as Fisher, and other would-be reformers, such as William Melton,[118] Colet does not fall easily into any historical, intellectual, or ecclesiastical category. He was not part of a humanist club, but he was a humanist; he was not a proto-Protestant, but he was critical of the Church; he was not a Lollard, but he was suspected of heresy; he was not an Oxford reformer, but he was, for a time, an Oxford intellectual; most importantly, he was not a reformer who actually changed things, although he dearly wished to be. Ultimately, Colet escapes identification with any other set of contemporaneous idealists because his vision was his own. His ecclesiology set him apart because it combined a huge and eclectic range of ideas into an individualistic vision of perfection.

1

THE EARLY YEARS

Birth, Childhood and Education

Due to a scarcity of documentary evidence, Colet's parental background, birth, childhood and education can be dealt with quite fully in one chapter, even once certain inaccuracies of previous scholarship have been corrected.[1]

Colet spent the first seventeen years of his life, and the last fourteen, in London;[2] we can thus name him a Londoner with confidence. However, his family background is to be found in the Chiltern hills, forty miles west of London, in Wendover, near Aylesbury in Buckinghamshire. It was here that his father, Henry Colet was born, the third, or fifth, son of Robert Colet.[3] Henry's birth date is unknown, but we may guess that he was born somewhere between 1430 and 1440, given that he was Alderman in the Ward of Farringdon Without in 1476, and Sheriff the following year, at which time he was presumably middle-aged, and his will is proved 20 October 1505.[4] Henry had two elder brothers, Thomas and William and a younger brother James. According to a monument once in Blythborough Church in Suffolk, William Colet, a merchant, died in January 1503-4. There was also a John Colet, apparently another of Henry's brothers, as well as a citizen and mercer of London, whose will was dated 5 May 1461 and proved 27 October 1461.[5] In the will he names a brother Thomas, a wife Alice, and sons Robert, John and Jeffrey.[6]

As for Henry, it is probable that he left Wendover for London around 1450-55. Gleason suggests that Henry preferred duties, as a mercer, that others avoided, such as riding out to greet the king on his return to London after a victory.[7] For instance, on 5 June 1461, Henry Colet was one of twenty-four 'goodely horsemen' in the coronation procession of Edward IV.[8] Therefore he was a 'conspicuous and faithful member of the company'.[9]

Henry was a Warden of the Mercers' Company in 1476 and Alderman of Farringdon Ward Without from 15 November 1476, moving to be Alderman of Bassishaw Ward. As Sheriff in 1477, alongside a John Stokker as fellow-Sheriff, he may have undertaken a great burden, given that, in 1476, the Lord Mayor, Humfrey Heyford was a 'sykley man, ffeble and weke, wherfore he had not his mynde so fresshely' etc.[10] In 1480 he was elected a Master of Mercers' Company for the first of five times.[11] On 1 February 1483, Henry was elected Alderman of Castle Baynard and on 13 October 1486, he was appointed Lord Mayor, and subsequently knighted on 13 January 1487.[12] He was made Alderman of Cornhill on 7 March 1487.[13] In the same year he was elected to parliament, representing London (on 9 October 1487) and re-elected on 2 December 1488.[14] The mercers were very wealthy by this time, as a comparison of money given in compulsory loans to the Crown indicates: on 19 January 1489 the Mercers' gave £740, compared to £455 by the Grocers, £420 by the Drapers, and £280 each by the Fishmongers and Goldsmiths.[15] Henry's personal wealth can be gauged by his above-average donations to the Crown.[16]

As Lord Mayor, his sheriff's were John Percyvall and Hugh Clopton.[17] Henry would again be mayor in 1495-6, in which year he would offer King Henry VII good service within the context of rebellion from Cornwall, reaching as far as Blackheath and from Perkin Warbeck arriving at Deal.[18] Owing to the support given to the rebel Warbeck from Flanders, commercial dealings between that country and England had ceased and trade had begun to suffer. In order to restore commerce a treaty was created called *magnus intercursus*, between the king and the Archduke of Flanders. This treaty required the seal of the Corporation of London, which for some reason, they refused to give. Henry Colet intervened and gave his personal seal, as Lord Mayor in lieu of the Corporation's guarantee, thus enabling the treaty to be enforced.[19] Of Henry Colet's other accolades, John Stow mentions him as a benefactor of St. Antolin's Church, Watling Street, and in 1505 he is mentioned as a contributor towards Great St. Mary's Church in Cambridge.[20]

Whilst Henry Colet largely created his own fortunes, his wife was born into aristocratic wealth. Henry married Christian Knyvet (d.1523), or Knevet, of Allwelthorp in Norfolk, Buckinghamshire in 1465.[21] Her father, Sir John Knevet, married Alice (Lynn), daughter of Reginald, Lord Grey of Ruthyn. Upon her death, John remarried to Joan, daughter of Humphrey Stafford, Duke of Buckenham. Sir John and Joan's daughter, Christian, was educated at a Benedictine priory at Carrow, Buckinghamshire.[22] She married Henry Colet and became known as good Dame Christian, after her husband's knighthood. Christian was very well connected: her brother was son-in-law to the Duke of Buckenham, Norfolk; her father was Sheriff for Norfolk and Suffolk and had acquired, by marriage, extensive property including Buckenham Castle.

In London, moving from their first home in Budge Street to 'Great Place' in Stepney, Christian became a great favourite of Erasmus.[23] She was also visited by the German theologian and physician Henricus Cornelius Agrippa, in 1510. In

December that year she was granted letters of fraternity by Christ Church Convent in Canterbury.[24] Correspondence between Colet and Erasmus in 1512 and 1516 suggests that Dame Christian was spending a happy old age in the country (Stepney). Being co-executor of her husband's will and those of her sons, Robert and John, she remained wealthy until her death in 1523.[25] Of her many children only one survived to maturity, past 1503: John, almost certainly born in the parish of St. Antholin, Watling Street, was the eldest of eleven sons and eleven daughters, according to Erasmus,[26] although John Stow's *Survey of London* (1598) describes a stained glass window in the church of St. Antholin as showing Henry and Christian with ten sons and daughters. Whatever the case, Christian managed to survive them all, including her son John, by four years. On her death, she was buried, according to her will, near her husband in St. Dunstan and All Saints, Stepney.[27]

Whilst the details of Colet's birth and parentage are sketchy, those of his childhood and education are even more so. It cannot be ascertained with any certainty where he was schooled, although it is possible that it was in London. In the Victorian period it was assumed that he attended St. Anthony's (or Antholin's) Hospital, Threadneedle Street, a feeder school for Eton.[28] This is based upon the conjecture, found in Anthony á Wood's *Athenae*, of 1691-2, and a statement in Knight's biography, who asserted that he was taught 'in that school which bare the name of his parish'.[29] However, this conclusion is far from satisfactory, for the parish of St. Anthony, in which Sir Henry and Dame Christian lived, had no connection with the Hospital of the same name in Threadneedle Street.[30]

Another possibility, which is also conjecture, would be that Colet attended the school attached to St. Thomas of Acre (or Acon), because of its connection with the Mercers' Company. Other great schools, such as St. Paul's (1509), Westminster (1560), Merchant Taylors (1561) and Charterhouse (1611), had not yet been founded. At the end of the fifteenth century, good schools were few and ill-supported in London with perhaps only St. Paul's Cathedral School, St. Peter's Westminster and the School of St. Peter's Cornhill flourishing. This lack of good schools prompted, in 1447, a petition presented to parliament by four London clergy, including Sir John Neel and William Lichfield, pointing out the lack of decent teachers and asking permission to establish their own schools in their respective parishes, namely, All Hallow the Great, St. Andrew Holborn, and St. Mary Colechurch. They wrote:

> For wher there is grete nombre of lerners and few techers, and al the lerners be compelled to go to the few techers, and to noon others, the maisters waxen riche of monie, and the lerners pouerer in connyng, as experience openlie shewith, agenst all vertue and ordre of well publik.[31]

However, there was a particular connection between St. Thomas of Acon School and the Mercers' Company: apparently the sister of Thomas á Becket, Agnes, helped found a hospital and chapel in her brother's name with the mercers appointed as patrons.[32] The name Acon is a corruption of Acre, the Syrian town, from where it was traditionally thought that St. Thomas had taken a Saracen bride.[33] By the time of Stow's survey of London in 1598, only four schools are mentioned: St. Paul's, Westminster, St. Thomas of Acon and St. Anthony's.

At school, whichever one he attended, Colet would have learned his ABC and his Latin Grammar: either the *Doctrinale* of Alexander Dolensis or the *Editio Secunda* of Aelius Donatus's *De Octo Partibus Orationis*, who was teacher of St. Jerome, and commonly called *Donat*.[34] Written years later, Colet's own *Aeditio* was a short practical prose manual in imitation of *Donati editio secunda*. Another of his school books might have been Cato's *Disticha de Moribus*. It consists of a number of short adages in prose followed by four books of 'distichs', pairs of hexameter lines, filled with moral precepts. Polydore Virgil attests that Colet's holy and pious nature lent him towards the study of the scriptures, with St. Paul being his lifelong hero.[35]

With regard to Colet's University education there has been much mistaken scholarship printed suggesting that he went up to Oxford. This is based upon Wood's 1691 assertion that Colet was a student at Magdalen College and graduated with a B.Th. in 1501 and D.Th. in 1504. Lupton devotes a whole chapter to Colet's Oxford days[36] asserting: 'That it is Oxford that Colet went is beyond question' and yet admitting that he was 'without any certain knowledge of the college or hall at which he entered.'[37] However, Godfrey rightly corrected this error with his 1974 article, which argues convincingly that Colet gained his degree at Cambridge.[38] The Cambridge University Grace Books show Colet as a questionist (B.A.) in the Lent term of 1485 and an M.A. in Lent of 1488/9.[39] Gleason and Rex have assimilated this revision into more recent scholarship.[40] It was in Cambridge that Colet was most likely to have come into contact with humanistic ideas and Neoplatonism, which was to become such a huge influence upon him.[41] As Erasmus relates:

> During his younger days, in England, he diligently mastered all the philosophy of the schools, and gained the title expressive of a knowledge of the seven liberal arts. Of these arts there was not one in which he had not been industriously and successfully trained. For he had both eagerly devoured the works of Cicero, and diligently searched into those of Plato and Plotinus; while there was no branch of mathematics that he left untouched.[42]

During his university career Colet may have come into contact with the works of Priscian, the 'major' and 'minor' Latin grammars, whose sixteen books covered the eight parts of speech and construction. In the area of rhetoric, Colet would probably have studied Aristotle's treatise *De Rhetorica*, the fourth book of Boethius on the *Topica* of Cicero; as well as Cicero's *Nova Rhetorica*; the *Metamorphoses* of Ovid; and Virgil's *Poetria*. On the subject of logic, Aristotle's *De Interpreatione, Analytica Priora* and *Topica* would have been on the syllabus. Under Geometry he would have read Euclid and Vitellio's *Perspectiva*. Finally, in the last of the arts, Astronomy, he may have studied *Theoretica Planetarum* (Gerard of Cremona, 1472) and Ptholomaeus in *Almaiesti*. With regard to the three philosophies – Natural, Moral and Metaphysical, Aristotle would be paramount yet again.[43]

Before he had left full-time education, and even before his ordination to the deaconate on 17 December 1497 and his priesting on 25 March 1498, Colet had already been admitted as Rector of Dennington in Suffolk (6 August 1485).[44] This benefice was in the gift of his mother's family. He held the post until his death in 1519. In 1486 he was also made Rector of the free chapel of Hilberworth in Norfolk. From 1490-94 he became Rector of Thurning, Huntingdonshire, a parish in the gift of his father, and he became a Canon of York Minster and Prebendary of Botevant from 1499-1519. He was a Canon of St. Martin's-le-Grand and Prebendary of Goodeaster by 1497 until 1504. He held the richest living in England, that of Stepney, from 1499-1505, was Canon of Salisbury Cathedral and Prebendary of Durnford from 1502-19, Rector of Lambourn, Berkshire in 1505 and Treasurer of Chichester in Sussex from after 1508 until his death. Lastly, he was, of course, Dean of St. Paul's Cathedral, 1505-19, and collated prebendary of Mora on 5 May 1505 and elected dean on 2 June 1505.

Colet's grounding in the humanistic skills, which began in his university education, would be continued and intensified by his travels in France and Italy to come (1492-6), and developed further upon his return to England, this time to Oxford, where he would expound his Neoplatonic and Pseudo-Dionysian perspective on the Pauline epistles. It is to his travels and his period as an Oxford resident that we turn next.

European Travel

All we know for certain about Colet's travels is that he left England around 1492/3, returning in 1496 and that Erasmus tells us '... like a merchant seeking goodly wares, he visited France and then Italy'.[45] Archbishop Parker simply asserted: 'He studied for a long time in foreign universities'.[46] Although Colet is not mentioned in the University records of Orléans or Paris, he is known to have stayed in Orleans.[47] In a letter of 1516 to Erasmus the jurist Francois Deloynes recalls that he was impressed with Colet's piety and intellect when they studied together at Orléans. We know from Colet's own words that he stayed in Paris on his return.[48] With regard to his travels in Italy there is little evidence. However, Hook suggested that:

> He [Colet] was at Rome, and there he probably met with Grocyn and Linacre, with William Lilly, who had lately arrived from Rhodes, and they all went to Padua, where William Latimer was perfecting himself in Greek.[49]

Although there is no direct evidence of the truth of this statement, it does point towards an explanation for why Colet might have wished to travel on the Continent: firstly, because his contemporaries were doing it and, secondly, to further his humanist education. For an example of such travellers, there is William Tilly, or de Selling (d.1495), prior of Christ Church Convent, Canterbury, in 1472. Selling was in Bologna in 1485, receiving tuition in Greek from Politian (d.1494). Selling's pupil, and Colet's friend, Thomas Linacre (1460?-1524), then at All Souls' College, Oxford, visited Bologna on his way to Florence, staying in the latter city for a whole year before travelling to Rome. He also visited Venice, Padua, Vicenza, Verona, Brescia, Milan and returned to England *via* Paris. Thus, Linacre, travelled between 1487 and 1492.[50] William Grocyn (1446?-1519), of Magdalen College, went to Italy from 1488 to 1491, heading for Florence, where he studied Greek with Chalconydes and Politian.[51] Grocyn's godson, William Lily, later to be the first highmaster of Colet's St. Paul's School, stayed at Rome on his return from Palestine and also studied Greek with Sulpicius and Pomponius Sabinus.[52] Colet's friend, Erasmus, visited Italy in 1506, taking in Turin, Venice, Bologna and Rome.

From the evidence above, it would be tempting to conclude that Colet, like his humanist friends, might have learned Greek whilst in Italy. If this was his aim, he did not manage to achieve it, being less than accomplished in the language even at the end of his life.[53] Nevertheless, Colet immersed himself in the Neoplatonic ideas of Marsilio Ficino.

Colet was in Rome by September 1492[54] and on 13 March 1492/3 he was admitted into the English Hospice there, along with his parents and his brother Richard in the *Fraternitas Sancti Spiritus et Sanctae Mariae de Urbe*, conferring on them all the spiritual benefits of the fraternities good works. On 1 April 1493, Colet wrote to his old friend Christopher Urswick (1448-1522) and sent him a gift of Aeneas Sylvius's history of Bohemian heretics (*Historia Bohemica*) in the Hussite wars.[55] Colet was admitted into the confraternity of the Hospice, enrolled as *confrater*, on 3 May 1493.[56]

The most pressing question regarding the travels, considering Colet's subsequent writings and ministry, is whether he visited Marsilio Ficino in Florence at his

Platonic Academy in Careggi.[57] Colet, as we shall see, was enormously influenced by the Neoplatonic thought of Ficino,[58] and therefore one might expect the two men to have met, especially when we know that they corresponded with each other.[59] Lupton, Marriott and Ferguson believed Colet to have travelled to Florence,[60] as does the most recent authority, J.B. Trapp: 'It is likely that Colet followed Grocyn's, Linacre's and Lily's example in spending time in Florence.'[61] However, other twentieth-century scholarship is persuasive that Colet and Ficino never met, but that the correspondence took place once Colet had returned to England in 1492 with a copy of Ficino's *Epistolae* of that year in his possession.[62] Colet would not, therefore, have had the opportunity of meeting or hearing the great preacher Girolamo Savonarola (1452-98), as Lupton conjectures.[63]

The most we know about Colet's travel is the knowledge with which he returned. Unaccomplished in Greek, unlike his English humanist colleagues Linacre and Grocyn, he was nevertheless, entranced by the humanism and Neoplatonism of the Italian philosophers Pico della Mirandola (1463-94) and Ficino. Armed with this new philosophy, he returned to Oxford and began his writing.

Oxford

According to Erasmus, Colet's learning from the Continent was devoted to the sacred writers, including Dionysius, Origen, Cyprian, Ambrose, Jerome, Augustine, Scotus, and Thomas.[64] He also read non-Christian writers, such as Catullus, Vergil, Ovid, ' ... screening out what was un-Christian'.[65]

However, his piety appears to have tainted his opinion of university education, according to Erasmus.

> He did not attach much value to the public schools on the ground that the race for professorships and fees spoilt everything and adulterated the purity of all braches of learning.[66]

Indeed, Gleason suggests, 'It seems that even before he set out for the Continent at the age of twenty-five he had a fixed agenda – to preach Christ'. This inflexible otherworldliness maybe, in some part, due to his upbringing.

At Oxford, Colet was not formally employed by the university to teach, nor was he officially registered to study for a doctorate in theology. Nevertheless, in his nine years there, he reportedly lectured on all of St. Paul's Epistles and left for St. Paul's Cathedral in 1505 as a Doctor of Divinity. To study for the Doctor of Divinity degree was long process of nine or ten years. If Colet had researched for this degree conventionally, it is possible that he began his doctoral studies in the Michaelmas term of 1490 and resumed them after his Italian travels in 1496 and finished it in

1504. However, this seems unlikely.[67] According to Erasmus's 1521 recollections, by the time he and Colet first met in Oxford in the late summer of 1499, Colet had been giving popular free and public lectures on Paul for several years. How this came about is not certain. Lupton suggests that Colet would have returned to begin the degree of Bachelor of Divinity, which required candidates not only to attend lectures but also to give lectures. However, Erasmus tells us that Colet 'had neither obtained nor sought for any degree in Divinity' even though the D.D. was given to him upon his departure for London, perhaps as an honorary gift in acknowledgement of his appointment as Dean of St. Paul's. If Erasmus is correct, then Colet's lectures would have been an unorthodox occurrence, being offered gratuitously for anyone who wished to attend. This may be an indication of the touch of audaciousness in Colet's character, which became more evident in his London ministry, as we shall see in later chapters.

It was in Oxford that Colet and Erasmus met, the latter being an important life-long influence upon the former. Twenty-three letters between the two men survive, dating from 1499-1517, seven of which are from Colet. To give an example of the nature of their relationship, a letter from Erasmus to Johannes Sixtinus, of November 1499, serves to illustrate the heated discussion they had concerning the scriptures. One discussion concerned the sacrifices of Cain and Abel from Genesis chapter four. According to Erasmus, Colet's opinion was that Abel's offering had been more acceptable than Cain's 'by Faith', a typically Pauline view.[68] Erasmus, as he himself relates in the letter, apparently attempted to cool down the debate with a light-hearted fable. Two further letters of 1499, published in *Lucubratiunculae* (1503), give an account of a further argument, which took place in the Augustinian College of St. Mary, Oxford on the subject of Christ's agony in the garden of Gethsemane just before his capture, trial and crucifixion. Erasmus had apparently argued that Christ's human nature were evident in his plea to his Father that the 'cup should pass from him'. Colet's indignant response was that this argument was a denial of Christ's divinity. Colet's interpretation of the Gospel text was that Christ's agony was due to his foreknowledge of Jewish guilt for His death.[69]

These disputes (*disputatiuncula*) did not weaken the strong bond of friendship between Colet and Erasmus. Erasmus's affection for the dean is evident in his biographical letter, about his friend, of 1521.

Oxford Writings

Colet's works, mostly written in Oxford before his time as dean are entirely in Latin, and consist of lectures, commentaries and treatises. As a biblical interpreter, he had a homiletic, anti-scholastic style with an emphasis upon literal/historical interpretation into which he assimilated Platonic and Neoplatonic ideas of hierarchy and the achievement of perfect union with God. His weaknesses of employing an unsystematic treatment of the text and his lack of Greek did not preclude him from being one of the most prominent Christian humanist writers of his age.

Colet's influences include Florentine Neoplatonism. His heavily annotated copy of Marsilio Ficino's *Epistolae* (Venice, 1495) proving the point.[70] He also knew Ficino's *Theologica Platonica* (1482) as well as his translations of Plato and Plotinus and the *Corpus Hermeticum*. Of the other Italian Neoplatonists Giovanni Pico della Mirandola's *Heptaplus* (1490), *Apologia* (1482) and *Opera Omnia* (1496 and 1498) were also known to Colet. From Pico he learned of the Hebrew Cabbala, augmented by his reading of Reuchlin's *De Verbo Mirifico* (1494) and *De Arte Cabbalistica*, although he later departed from Reuchlin's ideas, preferring 'love and imitation of Christ' as the path to God.

Colet's knowledge of the Pseudo-Dionysius may have come from Ficino's Latin versions of 1496 and certainly from Ambrogio Traversari's edition, overseen by Jacques Lefèvre d'Etaples (Paris, 1499) for the *Ecclesiastical* and *Celestial Hierarchies*. Colet probably continued to believe that Pseudo-Dionysius was Dionysius the Areopagite (Acts 17:34) despite Lorenzo de Valla'a 1505 treatise demonstrating that the author was not the convert of St. Paul but a much later writer.

Erasmus was a considerable influence on Colet, both in his works and as a person. Colet would probably have possessed Erasmus's *Lucubratiunculae* (1503), including the *Enchiridion Militis Christiani*, along with Erasmus' later works.

Of the patristic writers, Augustine is most highly favoured in Colet's works. Others include Jerome, St. John Chrysostom, Ignatius of Antioch, Lactantius, the 'Christian Cicero'[71] and Polycarp of Smyrna. He also quotes the Pseudo-Clementine and Origen as well as several pagan writers, of whom he was so suspicious: Cicero, Ovid, Suentonius, Terrence, Varro and Vergil. From the medieval he knew Thomas Aquinas, Anselm and Scotus amongst others.

The extant Colet works are: his lectures on 1 Corinthians; a treatise on the Mystical Body of Christ, the Church; a treatise on the Hierarchies of Pseudo-Dionysius, specifically on the *Celestial Hierarchy*; another treatise on the Hierarchies of Pseudo-Dionysius, specifically on the *Ecclesiastical Hierarchy*; a letter addressed to Richard Kidderminster; a copy of Marsilio Ficino's *Epistolae* (Venice, 1495) containing Colet's marginalia and transcripts of three letters: two from Ficino to Colet and one from Colet to Ficino; four letters addressed to Radulphus on the Mosaic account of Creation; lectures on Romans; an exposition on Romans, chapters one to five; and a treatise on the sacraments of the Church: *De Sacramentis Ecclesiae*. The extant Colet manuscripts are to be found in Oxford, Cambridge, and London.[72]

Of the works listed above the lectures on 1 Corinthians and Romans, the separate commentary on the first five chapters of Romans and the commentary on Genesis (addressed to an unidentified Ralph) comprise the surviving biblical work, except for the commentary on 1 Peter and maxims extracted from other Pauline epistles, found in a manuscript held in Trinity College, Cambridge. However, the authorship of this latter work is very doubtful.

Colet's exegesis was unique for its time. He was prolific, if we are to believe Erasmus, lecturing on all of St. Paul's Epistles at Oxford, regardless of the fact that he was not neither requested nor employed to do so. His style is homiletic, rather than scholarly, showing a particular distaste for the work of scholastic biblical interpreters. In contrast to Aquinas, for instance, Colet's Pauline commentaries and lectures appear to be intended for a wide audience, in an attempt to make scripture accessible and not just strictly academic; he is more concerned with soteriology than the schoolmen and with exploring the personality of St. Paul as a real human being. Moreover, Colet gives more attention to the historical circumstances surrounding St. Paul's life, comparing St. Paul's portrait of Roman society, for instance, to that of the historian Suetonius. No scholastic is quoted in Colet's works. However, Platonic ideals were assimilated into his biblical interpretation, emphasising ethics, the cultivation of the mind and will and the goodness of the soul. For Colet, following Plato, Plotinus, Pseudo-Dionysius (sixth century A.D.) and Marsilio Ficino, every Christian's destiny was to be reunited with divine perfection. However, human failings remained an obstacle in the journey from humanity to divinity, and Colet's public wrestling with the problem led to his undistinguished practical administration of St. Paul's Cathedral.

Although Colet was familiar with the traditional medieval ways of interpreting scripture: historical/literal; allegorical; anagogical; and moral, for him the Bible, and particularly the New Testament, was to be interpreted almost wholly in the literal, historical, sense. Colet's insistence upon the unity of biblical meaning was a source of contention between he and Erasmus. From this literal starting point, Colet's interpretive style took an erratic form by not commenting on every verse, but often using the text as a springboard to exhort his readers or hearers to holiness – his one consistent aim was to bring humanity into closer union with God.

Colet's skill as a biblical interpreter, though fresh in its outlook, suffered from his personal limitations. He was not an accomplished linguist, failing to learn Greek by the end of his life in contrast to his humanist contemporaries. His ideas concerning the utter hopelessness of humanity in comparison to the perfection of divinity add a touch of pessimism to his works. Colet's encounters with Ficino and the works of Pseudo-Dionysius (whom he believed to be Dionysius the Areopagite from Acts 17:34) led to a Neoplatonic gloss in his biblical lectures and commentaries; and his treatment of biblical text was unsystematic and uneven, choosing to dwell on sections that support his attempt to persuade his readers and hearers to strive towards greater diligence in their faith, thus combining their wills with God's and drawing closer towards the perfection required of the Church.

Colet was not embarrassed to use literal interpretation of the text, believing that the scriptures were the only resource required to access God's grace. Grace, for Colet could lead not only the individual, but also the whole Church, as a communal body, through the Pseudo-Dionysian process of purification and illumination to ultimate perfection and union with God.

Colet was a visionary. His vision, which he developed whilst resident in Oxford, was characteristic to him alone and was the dominant force behind his ministry. The basis for his biblical interpretation was his engagement with Christian humanism as well as with a wide variety of theologians and philosophers. Consequently, the aim of his work was to promote a hierarchical, perfectionist, morally strict and ascetic code, the aim of which was to achieve unity, and therefore order and beauty, within the Church, thereby facilitating a communal ascent towards union with God. Having given a general overview of Colet's works I shall now highlight some of the particular characteristics that contributed to Colet's peculiar works.

One of the most striking characteristics of Colet's works is the number of digressions he takes. Sometimes these are to explain grammar or vocabulary, such as the derivation of the word 'prevaricate'[73], and sometimes they are to elaborate on issues of his own day:

> Like the Apostle whose writings he comments on, he is apt to be carried away from his immediate argument by some passing word or allusion. The thought of some abuse in church or state, suggested by a passing expression in the text before him, calls forth at times a passionate outburst of invective.[74]

As far as Lupton was concerned the clergy of Colet's acquaintance deserved the scorn heaped upon them, (an 'Atrocious race of men ...' according to Colet[75]). Colet's main concerns were the corruption involved in conferring Holy Orders, or Simony, and the use of litigation.[76]

Another theme in Colet's writings is that of the use of Classical authors. In his commentary upon 1 Corinthians, 10:21, he distinguishes those who are 'partakers of the Lord's table' (those who read only the Holy Scriptures) from those who eat 'at the table of devils' (those who indulge in reading secular, or pagan, authors).[77] He writes: 'Do not become readers of philosophers, companions of devils. In the choice and well-stored table of Holy Scripture all things are contained that belong to the truth.'[78] This opinion is in contradiction of Colet's own practice of reading philosophy and classical authors, as well as recommending classical authors for the St. Paul's School syllabus.

One other striking opinion that appears in Colet's works is his unwavering views on marriage as a concession to human frailty or 'as a remedy for his [man's] passion',[79] which should, ideally, not exist at all. For Colet, marriage

> ... contained ... a sacramental principle having respect to Christ and His bride the Church ... But now that the Bridegroom has come, the truth of spiritual marriage is fulfilled, there is no longer any necessity for the married state to exist as a figure of that which is to come.[80]

In answer to the inevitable problem that, if Colet's ideal were employed, the world population would die out, he argues that there would still be enough heathen to populate the world (and converted to Christianity). However, if the whole world becomes faithful and celibate, married only to Christ, then all will die, and the world will end in a state of blissful sanctity.

Of the more ordinary, and less eccentric, characteristics of Colet's works, the Neoplatonic is one of the most prominent. He uses figures of speech, terms, metaphors and ideas from Plotinus, Pseudo-Dionysius, Pico and Ficino. For instance, 'the theory of emanations from the Divine Being, materialized and distorted by the successors of Plotinus, had been taken up by the writer of the 'Hierarchies' and adapted to the divisions of the angelic host'.[81] So, for instance, in his commentary on the *Celestial Hierarchy* of Pseudo-Dionysius, Colet explores the idea of the nine-fold hierarchy of angels, which is reflected in the nine-fold ecclesiastical hierarchy.[82] There are two main problems resulting from a Neoplatonic approach to theology: firstly, how can evil exist if everything emanates from a first cause? Secondly, what place do redemption, incarnation and atonement have when radiating hierarchical orders linking God to humanity fill all possible space? Colet answers these questions by emphasizing the work of Christ and grace:

> By the death of Christ men are retained in life by the marvellous grace of God; that their sins may be blotted out by the death of Christ, even as by their own, and that all the rest of their life they may strive after virtue and aspire unto God.[83]

Thus, the Church is a city of light and perfection 'made luminous by the light of the divine sun, and ... perfected by the crowning love of God in Christ, in heaven.'[84]

Regarding the sacraments, on which Colet wrote a whole treatise, influenced by Pseudo-Dionysius, he groups together Holy Orders and Matrimony as distinctive of the *vir*, the masculine or sacerdotal element in the Church. The remaining five, of which Penitence is paramount, is assigned to the *uxor*, the feminine or lay element.

One last, and general, characteristic, which cannot be ignored is Colet's mixture of passion and piety regarding humanity's sinfulness: 'O how dreadful in the sight of God are sins!'[85] Like Augustine, Colet's disgust for human frailty and weakness derived from observation of his own sins:

> Here do I, helpless one, conscious of my own sins, and blushing at them in secret, cry suddenly and lift up my voice to Thee, most loving God and Father, saying 'Impute not unto me my sins'.[86]

Colet's main theme of how sinful humanity can be reconciled to a perfect God is derived from the acute awareness of his own frailty and therefore of all human weakness. Colet took solace in the truth that 'there is nothing that conquers evil but good'.[87]

To summarize Colet's writing one must point out its variety: the mixture of lecture, exposition, commentary, treatise, and letter; the use of Pseudo-Dionysian mysticism and Neoplatonic philosophy; the scholastic terminology combined with a contempt for the schoolmen; the 'grammatical' interpretations and the indignant outbursts against the Church and society; the shaking off of traditional forms of exegesis and the desire to change the readers' hearts and minds; above all, his passion and piety for the text and for transforming the way people thought in order that they may strive for greater purity. Thus, Colet's written works offer us an enormous source of evidence for his character and thought. In order to investigate the works more fully, and to put them into their proper historical context, the next chapter will examine the characteristics of Colet's written work in more detail.

2

IN SEARCH OF PERFECTION: COLET'S WRITTEN WORKS

The foundation of Colet's thought was built upon a Christocentric and hierarchical scheme, the aim of which was to reconcile a sinful Church to God by a process of cleansing, illumination and perfection.[1] It was a system characterized by the pursuit of order and beauty. The hierarchical order consists of Christ at its head, above the angelic hierarchy, which in turn is superior to the ecclesiastical hierarchy – the Mystical Body of Christ on earth and the only hope for a depraved humanity. The existence of proper order enables a process to take place: the diffusion of God's love, which emanates through the hierarchy of the sinful Church. With the aid of God's facilitative grace, humanity is slowly able to conform to God's loving will and is thereby transformed from disorder to union with God. The Mystical Body is thus transformed from multiplicity to unity, united in love for a single purpose: the attainment of perfection. Colet's theology is, therefore, otherworldly, celestial and cosmic in its scope; it is absolutist (one is either wholly in or wholly out); it is also public in its nature, concerning an institutional, rather than an individual, relationship with God. The ecclesiological scheme elevates the role of human will above intellect because it is this will that conforms to God's loving will and thereby enters into the process of ascent, and return, to God. Therefore, it departs from scholastic, and even humanist, considerations of the triumphs of human reason and achievement. The will is conformed to God's will by grace, not by the use of reason – the only route to God is through the hierarchical order. Thus, Colet's scheme is highly clericalist and limited to a two-tier secular ecclesiastical hierarchical structure of priesthood and laity.[2] Nevertheless, the maintenance of the hierarchical order is essential for the attainment of perfection; therefore, priests must be as virtuous as the angels in order to save the Body of Christ. Out of this restrictive hierarchy, dependent upon the obedience of all, arises order and beauty. It is the purpose of this chapter to explain this concept, how it developed and how it was distinctive.

Colet loved the Church and strove throughout his life to improve it by bringing it closer to God. Hence, he created an obsessional perfectionist vision for the Church by selecting aspects of theological and spiritual thought from an eclectic range of sources, and combining them with ideas of his own. From St. Paul, he took his Christocentricity and emphasis on love and unity within the Body of Christ;[3] from Pseudo-Dionysius, he extracted mystical ideas of order, hierarchy, cleansing, illumination and perfection;[4] from the Platonists, and Neoplatonists, he inherited the notions of the emanations of God's love, through which humanity (for Colet, the Church) returns to God (or the One);[5] from Augustine, he adopted an anti-Pelagian stance by choosing to emphasize both the depravity of humanity and the utter dependency of humanity upon God's grace;[6] and from the Franciscan tradition, he accepted the primacy of the loving will over intellect.[7] To the foregoing elements, Colet added his own characteristics: an obsession with order and beauty in the Church; a fixation with the cosmic and otherworldliness of that order; a limited imagination with regard to metaphor; and a tendency towards the literal application of his ecclesiology. This latter characteristic became influential in Colet's work at St. Paul's Cathedral: it was Colet's expectation that the Church was literally to achieve perfection that provoked an unrealistic ambition for his clergy and contributed to the thwarting of his projected reforms.

Just as Colet was selective in the sources for his ecclesiastical vision, so also was he selective about which ideas he chose to reject: he shunned Aquinas's ordering of the intellect over will; he rejected the works of classical and secular authors as anti-Christian;[8] and he ultimately differed from other humanists on matters of Aristotelian and Thomist thought, the nature of humanity, will and intellect, and grace.

This chapter argues that there were many more aspects to Colet's ecclesiological thought than are currently recognized. In order to engage with current thinking on the subject, we must first analyse existing scholarship and demonstrate which aspects of Colet's ecclesiology have, rightly or wrongly, been identified and on what basis. The second section of the chapter explores the range of ideas in Colet's ecclesiology, including those drawn from Pseudo-Dionysian, Pauline, Platonic, Neoplatonic, Augustinian and Franciscan thought, and explains the significance of each concept, or cluster of concepts, for Colet's ecclesiology. Conversely, concepts that Colet chose to exclude from his ecclesiology will be identified and an explanation for their exclusion will be given. Part three explores, by means of a detailed examination of one of his texts, how the various aspects of Colet's ecclesiology were presented in his written work. All of Colet's treatises, commentaries and lectures are permeated with his ecclesiological vision. However, in order to show the densely ecclesiological nature of Colet's works, I have chosen, in that section, to examine in detail his commentary on the *Ecclesiastical Hierarchy* of Pseudo-Dionysius, although any of his other works would suffice as examples. Thus, Colet's other works will be examined in less depth in part four, in which I argue that Colet's works also possessed a number of sub-themes, not as important or prominent as the main themes outlined above, but nevertheless contributory elements of his overall thought. These sub-themes will be identified and analysed. Colet's ideas were therefore not only characteristic to him alone, by virtue of his acceptance or rejection of existing theological and ecclesiological ideas, or by the addition of his own ecclesiological emphases, but also, as part five argues, by its distinctiveness from contemporaneous Christian humanist thought. Although Colet was a Christian humanist himself, the characteristic nature of his ecclesiology is apparent when compared to the ideas of such humanists as Ficino, Erasmus, Fisher and Lefèvre.

Scholarship

Colet's ecclesiology was the backbone of his intellectual and active life. Until now, however, scholars have wrongly viewed it as a small and insignificant part of his overall theological outlook. The limited amount of existing scholarship on Colet's written ecclesiology, and the implausibility of some of that scholarship, means that a thorough re-examination of his output is now required. Contrary to existing understanding, I argue that Colet's ecclesiology was not restricted to his exegesis, nor was it contained only in one or two works; rather, it ran through the entirety of his known literary work and consequently affected the whole of his working life. Once the deficiencies of current thinking on the dean's ecclesiology have been identified, then the task of contributing a fuller picture of his vision can proceed through the remainder of this chapter.

From the Victorian period to the mid-twentieth century, the ecclesiological content of Colet's work went unnoticed due to a concentration upon his literal method of exegesis.[9] Porter first identified ecclesiological themes in Colet's thought, yet failed to acknowledge them specifically as constituting ecclesiology. For instance, he recognized Colet's emphasis upon the diffusion of the deity from higher to lower orders of the celestial and ecclesiastical hierarchies; he noted that, for Colet, priests, of whom bishops were most exalted, stood between God and humanity, as guardians of the hidden treasure of God's truth; and he emphasized the importance of order, for Colet, in fighting the disorder of this world by illuminating it with God's light.[10] Thus, Porter rightly recognized three important aspects of Colet's ecclesiology, but without necessarily realising their full significance within the proper context of his life and works. Likewise, Alden's consideration of Colet's interest in

Platonic and Pseudo-Dionysian thought failed to further scholarship beyond the misconception that Colet was a transitional figure between late-medieval humanism and the English Reformation.[11]

More recent scholarship concerning Colet's ecclesiology has either been inferential, such as Trapp's tantalizing reference to his 'Neoplatonic search for reform and perfection', or has limited itself to the examination of one Colet treatise: *De Sacramentis*.[12] However, various characteristics of his ecclesiology listed above have been touched upon, such as its cosmic otherworldliness and the absolutist position arising from it.[13] It has also been described as both clericalist and anticlericalist; and, most importantly, the features of perfection and order have been noted.[14] Such contributions are worth evaluating here.

The otherworldly nature of Colet's ecclesiology was implied by Rice's observation of Colet's 'annihilation of the natural'.[15] Although not writing about Colet's ecclesiology specifically, Rice highlighted the fact that Colet relied upon a cosmic view of a universal hierarchy, headed by Christ and the angels and mirrored by the ecclesiastical hierarchy on earth. This important point was also recognized, over three decades later, by Gleason: 'He [Colet] grossly undervalued everything this-worldly and set a correspondingly extravagant valuation on everything renunciatory and otherworldly.'[16] Similarly, Trapp observed that Colet 'eliminated the world of man, the mortal, corruptible world, and added the divine world'.[17] However, like their predecessors, Trapp and Gleason omitted to contextualize this characteristic into the body of Colet's ecclesiological thought. The consequence of the dean's other-worldliness was his tendency to take an absolutist position on Church membership: because the Mystical Body of Christ is part of a cosmic order, the members have the potential to become 'in a sense Christs.'[18] Rice, followed by Gleason, contributed to the idea that Colet's ecclesiology is cosmic and eternal in its scope.[19]

Colet's ecclesiology has wrongly been portrayed as anticlerical. Kaufman misrepresents Colet by alleging his 'clerical anticlericalism', a phrase suggesting overt criticism of the clergy from within clerical ranks.[20] For instance, he suggests that Colet 'advocated the rights of righteous laity and expanded their role in the reform of the Church',[21] implying that his ecclesiology of reform encouraged layfolk, such as Richard Hunne,[22] to challenge the authority of the clergy. As we shall see below, this suggestion cannot be substantiated. Colet's ecclesiology was extremely hierarchical and it exalted the priesthood above all other human vocations, including the monastic.[23] He was naturally disappointed when clergy misbehaved, but he is perhaps better described as a discriminating clericalist, rather than an anticlerical one. Therefore, Kaufman was wrong in his basic assertion that Colet was anticlerical and that he wished to redesign Church policy so that 'laypersons and clerics were placed on equal footing with respect to the institution's primary purpose, the proliferation of righteousness.'[24] As will be explained in this chapter, Colet's main desire for the Church was not equality amongst its members, but unity of purpose, order, beauty and perfection.[25] Despite Kaufman's misunderstanding of Colet's ecclesiological thrust, he nevertheless correctly stated that 'Colet's 'perfectionism' ... gives his ecclesiology in *De Sacramentis* ... a radical edge',[26] referring to Colet's demand that one enter the Church fully or not at all. Thus, according to the dean's absolutist stance on ecclesiology, one is either wholly in, or wholly out, of the Mystical Body of Christ at any one time; his ecclesiology is a theology for the Church alone, not for the whole of humanity.

In contrast to Kaufman, Haigh challenges overstatements concerning the alleged rise of late-medieval anticlericalism and Colet's part within it.[27] Moreover, he observes that, far from wishing to level the status of priests and laity, Colet wished to sustain the existing order and reinforce the privileges of the clergy:

> Colet ... had a high view of the priesthood and its privileges ... he believed that only the ministrations of a virtuous priesthood could bring the laity to Christ and through him to salvation.[28]

Likewise, MacCulloch recently added that Colet's 'apparently anti-clerical outpourings are in fact the highest form of clericalism.'[29] Rex makes the same observation and, in addition, correctly identifies Colet's use of the hierarchical language of Pseudo-Dionysius:

> Colet himself was anything but anticlerical. He was an avid disciple of the late classical 'Pseudo-Dionysius' whose writings on the heavenly and ecclesiastical hierarchies coined the concept of 'hierarchy' (rule by priests) and put it into circulation. Colet regarded ordination as the paramount sacrament of the Church and was unhesitating in his elevation of spiritual authority and dignity over the temporal.[30]

Moreover, Rex notices Colet's exaltation of the priesthood:

> The high place accorded to the priesthood in late medieval theology (for example by Colet) was indeed reflected in popular attitudes, and it was above all the priestly power to consecrate the body of Christ in the mass that set priests apart.[31]

As we shall see, Colet did not base the superiority of the priesthood solely on their ability to celebrate the Eucharist, but upon the fact that they were different in nature, according to their rank within the hierarchical order, to the rest of humanity: they were *'primarii homines'* – the highest ones.[32] The difference between the priesthood and the laity was qualitative; priests were simply closer to God by virtue of their exalted position, and therefore greater recipients of God's love.

The most important challenge to Kaufman's anticlerical Colet comes from Gleason, in his excellent assessment of *De Sacramentis*. Gleason demonstrates that the argument of the treatise, upon which Kaufman's essay is based, is as follows: God is priesthood and order; priesthood is sacrifice, the purpose of which is the diffusion of justice, by which Colet means the act of mediating God's love: 'a work most just'.[33] Colet goes on to make a connection between priesthood and matrimony, the latter being an earthly representation of the marriage between the Church and Christ. Through cleansing, illumination and perfection, the Church becomes ready for the marriage to Christ. Just as Eve was formed from Adam's side, so the Church was born from the blood from Christ's side. Therefore, true matrimony has now been established: the Church is to be married to Christ, and the priests are the head of the Church, implying, incidentally, that, in a perfected world, carnal matrimony should disappear. 'This ingenious argument', Gleason says, 'is in effect Colet's personal ecclesiology.'[34] Thus Gleason rightly dismisses the notion of an anticlerical Colet who desired the reform of Church structures by the exaltation of the laity. Any study of Colet's ecclesiology must recognize the importance of Gleason's insights into Colet's emphasis upon the highly clerical and Godly role of the priests in the process of ascent. Gleason opens up the possibility that, for Colet, the concepts of priesthood, sacrifice and justice (God's love) were connected, although imbued with many layers of meaning in the late-medieval Church.[35] For just as a human priest offers the sacrifice of the Eucharist, so the ultimate priest, God, offers the sacrifice of His very nature, the just work of love, which is diffused to the Church through the hierarchy of angels and earthly priests, by which the Church is cleansed, illumined and perfected, and thereby made fit to return to God.[36]

However, whilst Gleason's contribution to the study of Colet's ecclesiology is valuable, it is limited in its description, relying, as it does, upon the evidence of one treatise only. I shall argue in this chapter that Colet's other works show several further characteristics of his ideology. Gleason's analysis of Colet's thought, regarding the Church's creation and purpose, is merely the starting point for an exploration of Colet's theology, which concerns not a fixed description of that in which the Church consists, as Gleason suggests, but an obsession with the process of purification and illumination towards perfection and deification.

Moreover, Gleason calls Colet's argument his 'personal ecclesiology'.[37] It is important to clarify, however, that his ecclesiology was personal only in the sense that it was distinctively his, but not in the sense that he kept it to himself. Colet's thought was the basis for public action. His entire ministry was built upon his desire to achieve perfection, which required the full commitment of the priesthood, in order to disperse God's just love throughout the Church. As this book demonstrates, his ecclesiology was most publicly expressed at St. Paul's Cathedral.

Although Gleason recognized *De Sacramentis* as part of Colet's ecclesiology, he also unwittingly put his finger on the nub of the dean's vision when he briefly referred to his 'deep rooted and pervasive concern for order', which 'assigns a place to each thing depending on its participation in a single agreed-on value.'[38] This is in fact the heart of Colet's vision because *ordo* is not the organic growth of society, as in Erasmus's *In Praise of Folly* or More's *Utopia*, but is equated with the *hierarchia* of heaven and earth, where everything, and everyone, has a specific place. Such restriction of freedom, in both Church and society, leads Gleason to suggest that Colet suffered from a 'limited imaginative reach.'[39] Colet yearned for simplicity (order) rather than multiplicity (disorder) in his life, exemplified by his desire for retirement amongst Carthusian monks. As Trapp observes, Colet transformed Paul's command to 'avoid that which is evil, cleave to that which is good' (in Romans 12:9) into a desire to 'avoid multiplicity, confusion and tumult; seek simplicity, tranquillity and peace'.[40] Colet desired this ordered simplicity, not just for himself, but also for the whole Church. Thus, Gleason's insightful aside regarding Colet's obsession becomes the springboard for a fresh examination of his ecclesiology.

Other recent scholarship has also noticed Colet's obsession with Pseudo-Dionysian order. MacCulloch, for instance, suggests that

> ... the passion which fired the Dean of Paul's [*sic*] was not disgust with the Church structures of his day; it sprang from his fascination with mystical writings from ... 'Pseudo-Dionysius' [who] had written in ecstatic detail about the hierarchical ordering of heaven, but he had gone on to emphasize that the hierarchy of the clergy on earth was a direct reflection of the orders of angels, and its divine purpose was to reunite fallen humanity with God. For Colet, this meant that clergy had a solemn and inescapable duty to be as pure and effective ministers of God as the angels themselves.[41]

MacCulloch expresses certain truths about Colet's ecclesiology: the obsession with priestly hierarchical order, reflecting angelic order with the purpose of reconciling humanity to God by means of effective purity. Moreover, Hankey has argued that this ordering is not consistent with contemporaneous humanism. For Colet, he writes, the angelic hierarchy determined 'the structure for everything below it from the planetary spheres to the material elements. In this regard, there is no basis for humanism here and ... John Colet found none.'[42] Therefore, as we shall see below, Colet's ecclesiology set him apart from his fellow Christian humanists.[43] Hankey rightly understands Colet's obsession with cosmic hierarchy, but misunderstands the objectives of his ecclesiology:

> In Colet's universe, the angelic hierarchy certainly provides the system through which all else is understood. But, in addition, the angelic nature is so much the highest and best that humans exist for the sake of the angels and with the hope of being transformed into their nature.[44]

Thus, Hankey wrongly suggests that the angelic hierarchy is both the source and goal of the Church, whereas the hierarchy is the means by which humanity can return to the real source and goal: God.

Trapp, Rex, Gleason, Hankey and MacCulloch offer mere glimpses of the huge scope and significance of ecclesiology for Colet's life and work. Trapp is keen to acknowledge Colet's Neoplatonism, but not in relation to his ecclesiology; Rex recognizes the importance of the priesthood in Colet's thought, but for the wrong reasons; Gleason explores several aspects of Colet's ecclesiological thought, but only in relation to one treatise, thus neglecting several other aspects of Colet's thought contained elsewhere; Hankey focuses on Colet's Augustinian and Pseudo-Dionysian thought and MacCulloch manages, in his characteristic way, to perceive the essence of the subject, but both scholars refrain from elaborating upon it further. This chapter seeks to bridge those gaps by building upon the insights of these writers in order to contribute to a fuller understanding of Colet's ecclesiology. Although Gleason and MacCulloch, amongst the above-mentioned historians, most particularly imply that Colet possessed a highly developed ecclesiology, neither scholar explains its full content, scope, context or significance. In order to begin such an explanation, the following section traces the various aspects of, and contributory factors to, Colet's complex thought.

Colet's Ecclesiology and its Sources

This section argues that Colet's ecclesiology derived from his discerning selectivity regarding pre-existing theological and spiritual material, as well as from his own imagination. The areas of theological and philosophical thought employed by Colet in his own ecclesiology are: Pseudo-Dionysian and Pauline theology; Platonism and Neoplatonism; Augustinianism; and the Franciscan tradition. There are also several aspects of his ecclesiology peculiar to himself. Each area of thought will be examined with regard to its place within the dean's Church vision, beginning with the main external contribution to Colet's ecclesiological outlook: Pseudo-Dionysius.

Colet believed Pseudo-Dionysius to be Dionysius the Areopagite, St. Paul's first Athenian convert, and therefore of great theological authority.[45] Until the fifteenth century, it was assumed that this same Areopagite was the author of such treatises as *The Ecclesiastical Hierarchy*, *The Celestial Hierarchy*, *Mystical Theology* and *Divine Names*.[46] Along with some letters, these texts comprise the totality of this author's known *oeuvre*. Colet drew upon two interpretative traditions of the works of Pseudo-Dionysius: the devotional (private) tradition and the political (public) tradition. Each shall be considered in turn.

As a guide for private devotion, Pseudo-Dionysius had a strong influence in Europe, particularly within early-medieval monastic communities. Hilduin, the ninth-century Abbot of St. Denis (near Paris), made translations of the Pseudo-Dionysian texts, from Greek to Latin, in 838. John Scotus Erigena (c.810-77), the Irish philosopher, made further translations in 862, which were updated by Anastasius in 875. John Sarrazin, a twelfth-century monk of St. Denis, wrote a commentary on the *Celestial Hierarchy* in 1140 and executed a translation of it, which was dedicated to Master John of Salisbury (c.1115-80) in 1165.[47] Thomas Gallus (d.1246), Abbot of Verceil, made Pseudo-Dionysius known at Chartres. It seems that Pseudo-Dionysian thought was less appealing to both the Cistercians, such as William of Saint-Thierry (1075/80-1148) and Bernard of Clairvaux (1090-1153), and the Carthusians. Nevertheless, Pseudo-Dionysius's thought permeated scholasticism: Hugh of St. Victor (d.1142) wrote two commentaries on the *Celestial Hierarchy* in 1125-37, while Richard of St. Victor (d.1173) was also familiar with the works of Pseudo-Dionysius.[48] In *The Twelve Patriarchs* and *The Mystical Ark*,[49] works written between 1153 and 1162, Richard taught Pseudo-Dionysian thought to the regular Augustinian canons at St. Victor, where he became prior in 1162.[50] Like those who were to follow him in interpreting Pseudo-Dionysius devotionally, Richard of St. Victor concentrated on individual, rather than communal, experience. He used the Pseudo-Dionysian understanding of the 'unknowability' of God to express the idea of ascension to God as being a process of introversion:

> Just as we understand the supreme point of the mind by the peak of the mountain, so we understand the innermost part of the human mind by the Holy of Holies. But in the human soul the supreme point is undoubtedly the same as the innermost part, and the innermost part the same as the supreme point.[51]

As we shall see, Richard's interpretations of Pseudo-Dionysius were admired by St. Bonaventure (1214-74) and those following in the Franciscan tradition, who regarded Richard as a master.[52] One aspect of this Franciscan legacy passed on to Colet was an emphasis on the primacy of the will over the intellect as the greatest human faculty for comprehending God.[53] In contrast to other humanists, such as Ficino and Erasmus,[54] Colet combined this view with the traditional use of Pseudo-Dionysian texts for personal and private devotion, which he expanded into a theory whereby the whole Body of Christ, as an institution, became devoted to God's loving will.[55] Just as humanity is 'wicked, unwise, impure, nothing',[56] so it was the duty of each member of the Church to devote him or herself to becoming more Godlike through the mediation of Christ, 'whom we must love and worship with all our love.'[57]

The second interpretative tradition concerning Pseudo-Dionysius was closely linked with political and religious power; this can be described as the political (public) strand of interpretation. It has recently been plausibly claimed that political ideas, in the period 1250-1350, relied as much upon Pseudo-Dionysius's *De Caelestis Hierarchia*, and Augustine's *City of God*, as upon Aristotle's *Nichomachean Ethics* and *Politics*.[58] Therefore, in the high middle ages, Pseudo-Dionysius's works were amongst the most important political guides. The essence of Pseudo-Dionysian political theory is twofold. Firstly, it involves the Platonic idea that society is the result of the emanation of multiplicity (the disparate many) from unity (God or the One). Secondly, it espouses the

> ... ascent of individual elements within this multitude back towards union with the One by virtue of being ranked or ordered such that those individuals which occupy a superior grade direct or mediate those immediately below them towards their ultimate end.[59]

Therefore, the journey of all creation back to the creator can only be realized through strict ordering, forming a kind of ladder of ascent back to God, because the whole universe is a 'single, articulated hierarchy.' Thus, the metaphysical principle of universal order translates into a political principle for Government (of Church or state). Evidence of Colet's use of this theory is found throughout his works, particularly in his conviction that the hope for humanity lies in the divine order of the Mystical Body of Christ, in which bishops play the crucial role of assisting those below them back towards God. However, Colet added a particularly devotional flavour to this essentially hierarchical theory, by stressing that the means by which the episcopate can achieve their aim is by conforming to the loving will of God.[60] Bishops, therefore, must discern the will of God and declare it to those below them.[61] In this way, the Church finds its true vocation within the universal hierarchy. Thus, the role of the will was also an integral part of this aspect of Colet's ecclesiology.

Pseudo-Dionysian theology was one of the largest contributory components of Colet's ecclesiological scheme,[62] partly due to the authority invested in Pseudo-Dionysius by virtue of his alleged status as the Areopagite.[63] The main Pseudo-Dionysian texts used by Colet to support this public, political and institutional interpretation were the *Ecclesiastical Hierarchy* and the *Celestial Hierarchy*. Colet found this interpretation fascinating because it appealed to his belief, essential to his ecclesiology, that order equated to beauty.[64] Leclercq pointed out that politics and hierarchy were integral to Pseudo-Dionysius's ecclesiological thought:

> In any survey of Pseudo-Dionysian influence, we cannot bypass ... ecclesiology, and all its links with politics, for in this realm the impact of Pseudo-Dionysius was very strong from the thirteenth century on. One of Pseudo-Dionysius's principles, often applied to political power both civil and religious, maintains that God's gifts are bestowed from on high through intermediaries who can guide others to the extent that they themselves are enlightened. What is deemed to be the case with the celestial hierarchy is considered to have a counterpart in the structure of the Church. Supporters of a pontifical theocracy concluded, therefore, that the Pope held power over all.[65]

Likewise, politics became an important factor in Colet's ecclesiology when he became an ally of Cardinal Wolsey. Colet's interpretation of this ecclesiological emphasis, however, was not one of pontifical absolutism.[66] Indeed, he could be said to have had conciliarist tendencies; although he referred to the Pope as 'a weighty authority', he did not consider him to be the only, or necessarily the greatest, authority in the Church.[67]

Colet's own interpretation of the works of Pseudo-Dionysius combined the two existing interpretative traditions (the devotional and the political) to produce a characteristic aspect of his own ecclesiology: not solely concerning either hierarchical authority or personal devotion, but as concerning the responsibilities of every individual member of the Church, graded according to their positions, with particular emphasis placed upon bishops:[68]

> Every hierarchy is a system and summary of things sacred. In the Christian hierarchy the office and duty of the Bishop is, to comprise in himself and possess all things sacred.[69]

As we shall see,[70] bishops, rather than the Pope (although he was Bishop of Rome), became Colet's focus of attention in the hierarchy of the Church because they were endowed with the ultimate ecclesiastical responsibility of passing on God's love to the lower orders of the Church hierarchy. I shall now explore the many other intellectual influences that contributed to Colet's thought,[71] demonstrating how his ecclesiology was affected by his engagement with Pauline theology, Italian Neoplatonism, Augustinianism and the Franciscan tradition.

Colet's work on St. Paul was prolific.[72] The most famous example of his use of Pauline theology to attempt reform within the Church is his quotation of Romans 12:2 in his 1511/12 Convocation sermon: 'Do not be conformed to this world, but be transformed by the renewal of your mind, that you may prove what is the will of God, what is good and acceptable and perfect'.[73] In his sermon, Colet implored the clergy attending Convocation to eschew the world and its vices. Likewise, Colet's commentary on this Pauline passage, found in his Oxford lectures, shows how much Colet incorporated Pauline concepts into his ecclesiology. In interpreting the passage, Colet wrote that the Church was to

> ... draw together and collect themselves; that is, to withdraw themselves wholly from the defilements of this world ... and submit themselves, as matter fit and cleansed, to the divine reformation; that every one, being seized by divine grace, and inspired by the divine Spirit, may become wholly new and divine; and that there may be reared, and stand forth visibly on earth, formed of all thus renewed, a new and heavenly City of God.[74]

This passage is packed with Colet's ecclesiological thought: the ideas of drawing together and collecting reflect his desire for Church unity; the otherworldliness of his ecclesiology is expressed in the notion of withdrawal from the world; the characteristic idea of being cleansed is mentioned as preparation for being divinely reformed; grace is essential to the process of reformation, but not just to some, it must be to all – bringing out the absolutist nature of Colet's vision; for his ecclesiology, as for Paul's theology, the Church becomes divine or perfected, not just in heaven, but now on earth. This passage serves well to demonstrate how Colet interpreted theological material in order to express his own ecclesiological views.

Another important Pauline theme in Colet's thought is that of Christocentricity. He takes Paul's theology of incarnation and places it within the Pseudo-Dionysian and Neoplatonic ideas of the diffusion of God's love and humanity's return to its source:

> Jesus Christ ... came down to bring the human race to a wise and good way, order and society, by infusing into men wisdom and power; that they might have in common the heat and light that tend to life ... and might be collected and drawn as one to God from whom he came forth.[75]

Alongside this Christocentricity, therefore, Platonism and Neoplatonism, to which I now turn, were also characteristics of Colet's thought.[76]

It is because of Colet's fundamental Christocentricity that one must be wary of Erasmus's revelation that Colet 'both eagerly devoured the works of Cicero and diligently searched those of Plato and Plotinus', for we are also informed that the dean was suspicious of secular authors.[77] Nevertheless, it is clear from Colet's works that he was influenced by Platonism, Neoplatonism and by Ficino's interpretation of Pseudo-Dionysius.[78] As Hankey rightly observes, Platonism affected his interpretation of other authors:

> In consequence of reading Paul through Dionysius, whose Platonism he finds equally in Augustine, Colet can strongly oppose, on the one hand, the mixing of philosophy with Christianity and, on the other, simultaneously embrace, even magnify, after the manner of Ficino, the Platonism of Augustine and Dionysius. For Colet, such Platonism is simply Paul's philosophy.[79]

In his Florentine Platonic Academy, Ficino championed Pseudo-Dionysian thought; his Platonic approach to the Church is seen particularly in works such as his *Theologica Platonica* of 1482.[80] In his commentaries on the *Divine Names* and *The Mystical Theology* of Pseudo-Dionysius, printed in 1492, Ficino expounded this mixture of Platonic and Christian thought with a resulting emphasis upon the primacy of intellect, as pure and refined will, over love, which is secondary, and upon the stages of ascent to union with God.[81] As we shall see, unlike Ficino and Erasmus, Colet gave primacy to the loving will over intellect.[82] Nevertheless, evidence of Colet's admiration for Ficino's works can be found in his manuscript marginalia, and transcribed letters, on a copy of Ficino's *Epistolae* (Venice, 1495).[83] Colet adhered to Ficino's emphasis on Pseudo-Dionysius's mixture of Platonism with Christianity and took a characteristically Christocentric approach to Florentine Neoplatonism.[84] In this marginalia, he translated Ficino's classical ideas and expressions into moral, Christian terms.[85] In contrast, Luther rejected Pseudo-Dionysius's teaching on the grounds that it lacked spiritual authority and was overtly pagan.[86] In his *De Captivitate Babylonica Ecclesiae* (1520), Luther wrote that 'Dionysius is most pernicious: he Platonizes more than he Christianizes.'[87] One could justifiably argue that, in contrast to this approach, Colet's understanding of Pseudo-Dionysius was of one who Christianized more than he Platonized.[88] Pseudo-Dionysius's Christian use of the Platonic idea of emanation became a major influence upon Colet's ecclesiology.[89] Colet concurred with Pseudo-Dionysius that God's love was radiated to humanity through the celestial beings and subsequently *via* the teaching of Church hierarchies.[90] Platonism and Neoplatonism for Colet, however, could only be relevant if built upon the rock of biblical theology and Patristic doctrine. For example, Origen's phrase '*extra hanc domum, id est extra ecclesiam nemo salvatur*'[91] was a sentiment with which the dean would wholeheartedly have agreed.[92] As well as Origen (*c.*185-254), Colet referred to several other patristic writers throughout his works, including St. John Chrysostom (*c.*347-407), Ignatius (*c.*35-*c.*107) and Jerome (*c.*342-420). As Gleason rightly observes, Colet built upon this 'solid erudition' of Christian classics.[93] However, the patristic authority most used in Colet's ecclesiology was Augustine, to whom this section now turns.

With medieval theology so steeped in Augustinian and Pelagian ideas,[94] it is hardly surprising that Colet's thought also reflected them, especially with regard to the doctrine of justification.[95] Oberman argued that

> ... all medieval theologians attempted to be as faithful as possible to St. Augustine's teaching with regard to man's justification and final salvation, and, in this sense, all were Augustinians.[96]

Likewise, Rorem asserts that: 'The medieval doctrine of the Church was developed within Augustinian parameters.'[97] However, soteriologically, Augustinianism had largely been replaced by Palagianism, hence Luther's reaction. Within this late-medieval context, Colet was deeply interested in the problem of how a sinful Church could be justified to God.[98] Augustine's use of the terms 'faith' and 'grace' were part of Colet's soteriological vocabulary, in which he mixed Platonic and Pseudo-Dionysian formulae with Pauline theology.[99] This mixture of ideas had precedent in medieval thought:

> Aristotle's *Politics*, Pseudo-Dionysius's *De Caelestis Hierarchia*, and Augustine's *City of God* were sources shared by, and authorities common to, all scholastic theologians.[100]

However, Colet was extremely sceptical of Aquinas's melding of Augustinian theology and Aristotelian philosophy. According to Erasmus, he despised Thomas's arrogance in defining everything and considered Scotists 'dull and stupid and anything but intellectual.'[101] The consequence of Colet's dismissal of scholasticism, and its attempt to understand God's word by the power of human reason, was his emphasis, in contrast to Erasmus, upon the Augustinian idea that scriptural truth is understood by grace.[102] Indeed, Hankey suggests that all of Colet's works involved 'a thorough blending of Dionysian and Augustinian elements',[103] although this expresses only two truths concerning his thought, which consisted of many elements. One concept apparently adopted by Colet, from Augustine, was that of double predestination – pre-election by God either to eternal paradise or to hell – as evident in a passage from his lectures on Romans:

> ... how marvellously just and merciful at once is God in the choice of those men who are fore-ordained to complete the number of the angels, so that, whether he elects or repudiates, there is no basis for quarrel from any and there is the rejoicing of many.[104]

However, there is little evidence that double predestination was a frequent element in Colet's thought. In fact, Colet chose to reject parts of Augustinian thought, such as 'the Trinitarian image of God in the human mind, that by which the human immediately mirrors God' because, for Colet, it would have been inconceivable that 'the human should be the place of the Divine self-creation.'[105] Thus, Colet chose to include as much Augustinian thought as suited his own ecclesiology, and no more. The same was true for his inclusion of Franciscan thought, which I consider next.

The Augustinian tradition, as received by Colet, was transmitted *via* Franciscan writers, such as St. Bonaventure (1182-1226). As Gleason succinctly notes:

> In the Franciscan school, represented for Colet ... by Bonaventure, the quest of the divine exemplar is driven by love and therefore ultimately by will, whereas Aquinas's system gives the central role to intellect. Colet's position is stated crisply and briefly: 'It is not knowledge but love (*charitas*) that leads to life'[106]

Colet's works therefore bear some resemblance to those of Bonaventure, especially with regard to the ideas of will; humanity's nothingness; the need for humans to be part of the Mystical Body of Christ; and the journey towards God.[107] For instance, in his *Itinerarium*, Bonaventure sought to move beyond the sensible world to a contemplation of the soul as God's image, but it was also said that humanity was bent away from God by ignorance of mind and temptation of the flesh:

> Man, blinded and bent over, sits in darkness and does not see the light of heaven, unless grace comes to his aid with justice to fight concupiscence, and with knowledge and wisdom to oppose ignorance.[108]

This passage is close in content and expression to the beginning of Colet's treatise on the Mystical Body of the Church:

> Mankind, of whom the Church is composed, are, of their own fallen and carnal nature, in a state of utter dismemberment and dispersion ... For what shall we say of this lowest region, the earthly one, where all is black and cold.[109]

Like Bonaventure, Colet suggested that the remedy for humanity's weakness was Christ.[110] Christ crucified offered humanity His grace of justice, knowledge and wisdom. Grace rectified human will and enlightened human minds, thus giving the opportunity for ascendancy to God. As Bonaventure wrote:

> We must first of all pray. Next, we must live holily. Then we must gaze at the spectacles of truth, and by gazing at them, rise step by step until we reach the mountain height where the God of gods is seen in Zion.[111]

In his first sermon on Holy Saturday,[112] Bonaventure suggested various possible routes for the ascent to God. There was, he preached, the path taken through an admiration of God's majesty and a sense of his judgement;[113] there was the six-fold contemplative programme of Richard of St. Victor, consisting of spontaneity, ordering knowledge, reason, pure reason, that which is above reason and, finally, opposition to reason (i.e. union with God).[114] Another Franciscan, Giles of Assisi, suggested pathways to the Divine involving a forgetting of self, consolation by the Holy Spirit, ecstasy, contemplation of eternal light, refreshment, an embracing of God, and, ultimately, rest.[115] All these Franciscan ideas were an expression of private, devotional exercise, which could bring an individual soul into union with God. Brown summarizes thus:

> The mind reaches highest perfection in contemplating the communicative life of the triune God, and especially in contemplating God's Son, Christ, the perfect image of the invisible God.[116]

Colet shared the intimate Franciscan ambitions for personal union with God, but also wished for an institutional harmony with the Divine.[117] Love of the divine, for the Franciscans, as for Colet, was paramount over knowledge of God. As Gleason rightly suggests, for Colet, 'the whole duty of the higher clergy ... is simply to ascertain God's will and proclaim it. Man's duty, correspondingly, is to conform his will to the ascertained will of God.'[118]

To conclude this section: Colet's contribution to late-medieval thought was his combination of the devotional and personal elements of Pseudo-Dionysius, expressed in his emphasis upon humanity's need to conform to God's loving will within the Mystical Body of Christ, with an institutional and political interpretation, used to express the corporate journey of the Christian community towards God. This ecclesiological synthesis resulted in Colet's obsession with otherworldliness, order and hierarchy, thus creating his characteristic ecclesiology: union with God was not only possible for an individual who, through contemplation of Christ, might be filled with grace by the Holy Spirit, but it also represented the aim of the Church, and was the realisation of the Church's true essence as the Body or Bride of Christ. Colet's ecclesiology was, therefore, fundamentally Pauline and Pseudo-Dionysian. However, it also contained Platonic and Neoplatonic ideas of emanation, diffusion, and return to the source of love; Augustinian, and therefore anti-Pelagian, notions of grace, predestination and the sinfulness of humanity; and Franciscan ideas of the primacy of will over intellect. Colet's own ideas included his obsession with order; his absolutist stance on membership of the elect; and his uncompromising perfectionism, which was reflected in all his thought.

In order to demonstrate how these ecclesiological ideas were expressed in his written work, I propose to analyse in detail one of Colet's ecclesiological texts: his commentary on Pseudo-Dionysius's *Ecclesiastical Hierarchy*

The Ecclesiastical Hierarchy

In his commentary on the *Ecclesiastical Hierarchy*, Colet imbued the Church with the order, or hierarchy, that emanated from God *via* the angels:

> And so, that which flows from God in a pure, simple and unmixed state upon the angels, to promote their stability, order and perfection when it further proceeds to men, declining, from its purity and simplicity, becomes, by the ministration of angels, to some degree perceptible to their senses.[119]

From the beginning, Colet drew out the fundamental Pseudo-Dionysian concept of how God communicates to humanity: light from God, he wrote, was mediated to humanity through the angels; light promoted order amongst the angels and drew humanity towards perfection:

That same Jesus now, as Light unspeakable, at the right hand of the Father, shines more brightly and more fully upon the angels, beings of far higher nature than man, and bestows on them a more abundant revelation.[120]

This process is a movement from darkness to light, which is Christ, the 'Sun of Righteousness'.[121] The Church, which, for Colet, was the Christian equivalent to Moses's synagogue, is part light, part dark, which is 'colour'.[122] The light shines through the angels to humanity: this was a Platonic and Pseudo-Dionysian characteristic taken up by Colet.[123] He examined the Pseudo-Dionysian explanation of how humanity should aim to be closer to God and the three-fold stages of movement towards God. Perfection, for Colet, was the mystical union with God.[124] Colet's ideas of the three-fold steps to God were based on several sources: Platonic purification as the prelude to knowledge, wisdom being the basis for right action; Pauline purification, followed by illumination through infused faith; and the Augustinian doctrine of God as light, who infuses the light of knowledge to humanity.[125]

How then, was the Church to be perfected? Each hierarchy is split into three divisions (i.e. Heavenly, Christian and Mosaic); every sacred order is distributed into *Teletae* (or perfections): those who are in the process of perfecting; those perfecting *and* being perfected; and, finally, those simply in the process of being perfected.[126] Colet followed the Pseudo-Dionysian triads in order to explain how the earthly hierarchy followed the Heavenly hierarchy, moving from most illumined and perfected, nearest to God, to the less well enlightened below. The heavenly hierarchy was the luminous truth, the Christian hierarchy was a bright image of the truth and the Mosaic hierarchy was a shadowing of the image.[127] As regards the hierarchy in the Church, Colet pointed out that there were three ecclesiastical orders according to Pseudo-Dionysius: bishops, priests and deacons (i.e. *Hierarchai*, *Hiereis* and *Leitourgoi*). It was inherent in the system of perfecting, which both Pseudo-Dionysius and Colet advocated, that those with the highest positions should be closest to perfection.[128]

This hierarchical understanding of the earthly Church, which corresponded to the celestial hierarchy, was also expressed in Colet's exploration of the role of the bishop. Scripture, wholly revealed by Christ to his disciples, was transmitted to the Church *via* the Holy Spirit, from angels to humans, so that the Church was purified, illuminated and perfected.[129] Everyone's goal was to be perfected by the divine agencies, and, as far as possible, to be brought into union with God. In this scheme, Colet accepted the bishop's role as evangelist:

> He that attains this [Holy Spirit] in the highest degree is the bishop, and rightly holds the first place in the ministry, to the end that he should transmit that which he has received.[130]

Colet explained the significance of a bishop in terms of a 'sacrament':

> Every hierarchy is a system and summary of things sacred. In the Christian hierarchy the office and duty of the Bishop is to comprise in himself and possess all sacred things. For the Bishop is a veritable sacrament, and a summary of all that follows after him in the Church. He apprehends and represents fully and clearly in himself the whole priesthood; so that there is nothing in any inferior minister given by God that exists not in Christ our Bishop more substantially, and clearly, and in a yet more perfect manner.[131]

Here, Colet compares the duty of an earthly bishop with that of the supreme celestial bishop, Christ. The language used to express this idea is so powerful and uncompromising, and appears so early in the text, that the reader is left in no doubt as to the importance that Colet placed upon the episcopal office. There are similarities between this discussion and his 1511/12 Convocation sermon, in which he placed a great responsibility on the shoulders of bishops. His fervent idealism, as expressed in his commentary, deepened his disappointment with his own bishop, canons, minor canons and chantry priests at St. Paul's in 1505, when coming to terms with his own position as dean. He made it clear that if a person could not accept the high demands of the job, then he should not hold the position:

> For in truth if he were wanting in anything proceeding from God that is found in any inferior person, such as holiness, wisdom, justice, he assuredly is not the one to occupy the seat of the Bishop.[132]

For Colet, the Church's earthly hierarchy was based on the heavenly one: Christ is at the head of the Church and has given sacraments and ceremonies which are important in the process of purifying, illuminating and perfecting, that is to say, the *scala perfectionis*.[133] There was an unwritten secret as to the reasons for sacraments and ceremonies known only to bishops:

> The reasons of them [sacraments and ceremonies] were committed not to writing, but to the minds of the holy bishops; that, just as the signs follow their course among the common people, so the reasons of them should follow in the minds of the bishops.[134]

Colet, therefore, concurred with Pseudo-Dionysius's hierarchical ordering of the Church, with the result that the minds of bishops were of paramount importance, a sentiment later to be expressed in his St. Paul's ministry at his 1511/12 Convocation sermon: 'be ye reformed by the renewal of your minds'.[135] This was not the optimistic exaltation of human reason, as expressed in Erasmus's, Ficino's and Pico della Mirandola's humanism,[136] but the hope of a mystical union with God, through the Augustinian reception of grace and love, and the Platonic return, *via* emanation, to God (the One). Based upon the order and beauty of Pseudo-Dionysius's own ecclesiology, Colet's vision became the basis for his London ministry.

Colet embellished Pseudo-Dionysius's work by dwelling much more heavily on the doctrine of Atonement and used several scriptural passages to reinforce the hierarchy. For example, Romans 8:3-4 is employed here:

> This was the eternal Son of God, whom the Father 'sending in the likeness of sinful flesh, and for sin, condemned sin in the flesh; that the righteousness of the law might be fulfilled in us, who walk not after the spirit' in the acknowledgement and worship of the true God. His office on earth the Bishops everywhere discharge, and in Him act as He acted, and with zeal strive for the purification and illumination and salvation of mankind, by constant preaching of the truth, and the diffusion of gospel light, even as He strove.[137]

This was the first mention of what bishops could practically do to facilitate the three-fold path to God: preach. Therefore, the act of preaching became essential to Colet's ecclesiological outlook. Preaching was necessary because of the example of Christ:

> Whilst he lived as mortal man in the flesh, he performed the office of Bishop himself, teaching the duty thereof in actual practice.[138]

Colet set out in full the hierarchy in the Church:

> Every Bishop accordingly in the Church ... acts the part of God himself. Under the Bishop, priests occupy the place of the Apostles. Under these, deacons are ministers for the faithful people. The office of the Bishop is, like Christ, to preach constantly and diligently the truth he has received. For he is as it were a messenger midway between God and men, to announce to men heavenly things, as Christ did; to render others such and suchlike as God has

rendered him; to proclaim unceasingly that precept of the Apostles: 'be ye followers of me, even as I also am of Christ.'[139]

This emphasis on preaching became crucial in 1514, when Richard Fitzjames (1467-1522) made accusations against Colet concerning the dean's alleged views on images, hospitality and preaching.[140] The latter allegation was that Colet had spoken against the practice of reading pre-prepared sermons from written notes or a book, something that the Bishop of London was apparently well known to do.[141] Erasmus reported that the bishop had taken Colet's words personally as referring specifically to him.[142] Colet may have thought that the effectiveness of preaching was being stunted by the act of reading pre-prepared sermons. He further asserted that the object of preaching was to bring people to repentance. The task therefore required a more spontaneous approach:

> The Bishop, exhibiting in himself the form of Christ, and preaching and exhorting and admonishing all men to desire to be fashioned after that form ... must needs move some, by reason of the power of the word of God.[143]

Having been moved to re-formation, the congregation was then, supposedly, ready to receive more preaching:

> That which is preached by the Bishop is a new thing, and requires vessels thoroughly new, with the old flavour scoured away; lest like new wine poured into old bottles, it should burst them and itself be spilled.[144]

Thus, the cleansing of the mind was a prerequisite to its illumination. Another analogy upon which Colet drew was that of an army fighting a battle against evil: the bishop is the captain to whom one should give obedience. A description of the ceremony of Baptism (here performed by the bishop) is followed by the third part of the chapter, which concerns the spiritual contemplation of Baptism. Using the metaphor of light to describe the experience of illumination in Baptism, Colet described an almost ecstatic state through which the bishop travelled in order to illumine others:

> The Bishop who is illumined by Christ, like the sun, shines from the pulpit with the light of truth, and makes the word of the gospel to stream forth alike on all. He cries 'Awake, thou that sleepest, and arise from the dead, and Christ shall give thee light.' His words are 'pure words, even as the silver, which is tried, and purified seven times in the fire.' The Bishop himself is made fire by

God; he has the light of truth, the warmth of goodness; in loving-kindness he teaches all.[145]

In writing upon the Eucharist, Colet continued this theme of the high standards required of those who perform the Mass.[146] The idea of keeping high standards was constant throughout Colet's life and can be found in his 1506 compilation of statutes and fresh injunctions for the government of the St. Paul's chantry priests;[147] his Convocation sermon of 1511/12; his sermon preached at Wolsey's consecration as cardinal in 1515;[148] and his *Exhibita* of 1518,[149] which proposed reform concerning the canons' residency at St. Paul's. Here, in his commentary on the *Ecclesiastical Hierarchy*. Colet explained how bishops came to exist and emphasized that they had duties as judicial arbitrators:

> Still, from the number of the priests, though equal in office and rank, the first disciples and followers of the Apostles, immediately after the apostolic age, made choice of one, and placed him at the head, for the settling of disputes and appeasing of strifes, and for putting an end to contentions by his opinion and sentence; that the Church might abide in harmony. To him an authority was deputed by the universal Church ... He then began to be specially called Bishop; a name which under the Apostles belonged to all priests, until there was chosen the one whom I have just mentioned [i.e. bishop], and for the reason above given.[150]

It is ironic that Colet stressed the role of the bishop as a settler of disputes, because, in 1513/14, Colet's bishop was far from conciliatory. Indeed, Colet did not follow his own advice and obey his bishop when accusations were made against him; rather, he turned to the higher episcopal authority of Archbishop Warham for arbitration in his case.[151] Colet believed that bishops should be obeyed, but only if they conformed to the high standards that were set for them. In the tone of this passage, there are signs of dissatisfaction with the episcopate. The reader senses that he was building up to an attack on the clergy, which indeed he was:

> Oh! Priests, Oh! Priesthood, Oh! The detestable boldness of wicked men in this our generation, Oh! The abominable impiety of those miserable priests, of whom this age of ours contains a great multitude; who fear not to rush from the bosom of some foul harlot into the temple of the Church, to the altar of Christ, to the mysteries of God. Abandoned creatures! On whom the vengeance of God will one day fall the heavier, the more shamelessly they have

intruded themselves on the divine office. Oh! Jesu Christ, wash for us not our feet only, but our hands and our head.[152]

This passage contains the characteristic phrase '*O sacerdotes, O sacerdotium, O hujus nostrae tempestatis detestabilis audacia hominum sceleratorum*', which is paraphrased in his Convocation sermon.[153] This phrase was not mere 'rhetorical phraseology', as Dean Hook described it,[154] but proceeded from a deeply held ecclesiological conviction that the clergy should be perfect in their piety.

Further on in the text, Colet builds up to another attack on the Church. This outburst deals with spiritual contemplation of the highest sacrament of Holy Orders. It appears that Colet was outraged at the practice of temporal rulers selling benefices. According to Colet, Pope Sixtus IV (d.1484) started the abuse:

> Wherefore one may here express an abhorrence of the detestable custom, which has a blindness whether more to be had in derision or wept over I know not, now for a long time ... growing in the Church, and is at the present time deep-rooted, almost to the destruction of the Christian commonwealth, whereby temporal princes, void of reason, and, under the name of Christians, open enemies and foes of God, blasphemers of Christ, overthrowers of his Church, not with humble and pious, but with proud and rash, minds; not in consecrated and holy places, but in chambers and at banquets; appoint Bishops to rule the Church of Christ; and those too (heinous crime!) men ignorant of all that is sacred, skilled in all that is profane; men to whom they have already shamelessly sold those very bishoprics. Out upon this wicked generation! These abandoned principles! this madness of princes! This blindness and folly of ecclesiastics![155]

Colet never shrank from speaking his mind, even concerning 'abuses' of which he was not entirely innocent himself. For instance, in his Convocation sermon he preached against pluralities, even though, before he became Dean of St. Paul's, he had held several benefices concurrently, one of which, at Dennington in Suffolk, had been bought for him by his father.[156] It could also be argued that it was largely due to his father, Henry, that Colet was appointed Dean of St. Paul's in 1505. In 1496, Henry Colet had pledged his entire fortune to King Henry VII, 'for the faithful observance of the treaty' with the Low Countries, which was known as the *Magnus Intercursus*.[157] This gesture apparently found great favour with the king and, although John Colet had only been ordained six years, he was appointed dean.[158] We can therefore conjecture that Colet was promoted to the deanery in grateful recognition of his father's help to the king and that such an appointment would probably have been unpopular with the cathedral clergy; the dean's unpopularity will be discussed in due course.

Colet expounds his high-clericalist views a little further on: firstly, the reader learns that, even in death, a priest has a superior status to a layperson:

> The diversity and order here in the Church militant is an image of that order which the Church triumphant is destined to have in heaven. And so, because the priest is esteemed more righteous than the layman, he is placed after death, during the obsequies, in the midst of the choir among the priests. A layman deceased, or the holier monk, is set among the lay people outside the chancel rails, and in front of the choir, in the quarter of the people; that we may by this arrangement be admonished and believe that another and far holier place is assigned in heaven to the priests than the laity.[159]

Colet made it clear that he did not believe in equality either in this life or the next: everyone has his or her rank.[160] He held that the bishop attained a closer relationship to God, closer to perfection and, presumably therefore, assigned a far holier place in heaven than even the other clergy. For instance, in mentioning prayer, Colet wrote thus:

> The prayer of the Bishop over the departed, that he may be in glory, is not so much a petition that it may be so, as a declaration that it is so. For the Bishop, as Malachi calls him, is 'the messenger of the Lord of hosts' and the interpreter of the will of God, moved by the divine spirit[161]

However, Colet also warned bishops against presumptuousness:

> They that are chief in the Church, as are the bishops, receive by revelation what has been there loosed and bound, and declare that they have received, and by their words execute the design of God, not their own.[162]

If they do not, then

> ... are they of necessity foolish and mad of themselves, and abuse the power given them, both to the blaspheming of God and the destruction of the Church.[163]

As Colet's opinion on this matter developed, he emphasized that a bishop must act lawfully,[164] a matter that became particularly important in the context of Bishop Fitzjames's allegations:

> If he be a lawful Bishop, he of himself does nothing, but God in him. But if he do attempt anything himself, he is then a breeder of poison … This has now indeed been done for many years past, and by this time so increased as to take powerful hold on all members of the Church.[165]

Thus, Colet related lawfulness to purity – a characteristic of his ecclesiology. Colet ends his work with an indictment of the Church, writing that it had degenerated from the days of Pseudo-Dionysius and that he intended to reform it:

> Thus much I have written in the track of Pseudo-Dionysius, on our Ecclesiastical Hierarchy; from the fair fashion of which we have far degenerated. But I pray God, the framer of all things Himself, to reform, of his own great goodness, what has become deformed in us; through Jesus Christ our Lord.[166]

In his career as dean, Colet attempted to bring about this transformation of an allegedly deformed Church.

Colet's commentary on the *Ecclesiastical Hierarchy*, therefore, demonstrates how he responded to the perceived problems in the Church. For Colet, the Church needed constant reformation. Pseudo-Dionysian ideas, interpreted so as to apply to the whole institution of the Church, gave Colet the ammunition both to criticize and encourage the higher clergy, who had ultimate responsibility for enlightening the body, in order that a return to God, by ascension of the ladder of perfection, was possible. Colet's method was to convince bishops of the seriousness of their responsibility as intermediaries of God's love to the lower parts of the Mystical Body of Christ. They were to ascertain God's will and proclaim it to the lower orders of clergy and to the laity. Access to God was available to all, facilitated by grace, but activated by a conformation of human will to Godly will. Bishops, and to a lesser extent lower clergy, were responsible for the diffusion of God's light through the hierarchical order, though not everyone would receive it in equal measure. In Colet's working out of this ecclesiology, his commentary covers the themes of order, hierarchy, purification, illumination, perfection, sacrament, will, intellect, and law. In doing so, he draws upon Paul, Pseudo-Dionysius, Augustine, Plato, as well as Neoplatonic and Franciscan thought. Having examined in detail the density of ecclesiological content within one of Colet's works, I now touch upon the ecclesiological content of his other extant texts, in order to discern further themes.

Other Themes in Colet's Works

Not only has existing scholarship failed to take account of the main themes of Colet's ecclesiology from the full range of his extant written work, but it has also failed to recognize that underlying the most apparent features of Colet's thought are a number of ecclesiological sub-themes, which became significant at different points of his life and thereby contributed to his overall vision, such as obedience; justification; incarnation and atonement; law and litigation; and money and possessions.[167] Thus, an analysis of some of Colet's other works brings to light, for the first time, these contributory components.

One important sub-theme of Colet's ecclesiology, found throughout his works, is that of obedience, necessary for the achievement of the ultimate goals of order and beauty. The dean's criticism of bishops, and other clergy, was driven by an ambition for unity, through obedience, in the Church. He saw no contradiction, therefore, between unity and conflict in a changing Church striving for perfection. Evidence to support this interpretation is found in various works. For instance, in his commentary on 1 Corinthians, he saw the Church as the Mystical Body of Christ:

> For all who are in this mystical composite are in God, who, beginning His deification in the manhood taken from Mary, through him thence as through the head has distributed to the rest for the fashioning of the whole.[168]

The Mystical Body was, for Colet, the Body of Christ on earth functioning by virtue of the Holy Spirit. Members were anointed ones: 'one unity under God, from many and varied members.'[169] In a letter to his friend Radulphus, Colet stated that mankind was fallen and could not, of its own accord, achieve unity or holiness:

> ... from the effects of the first fall we are inevitably born with a tendency to separate ourselves, each one from his neighbour, and to follow our own private interests.[170]

Such a quotation hints at the conflict that was to emerge as part of Colet's ecclesiastical career. However, despite this negative view of humanity, Colet sought for the transformation of all into the elevated position of unity with God; this meant being unified as a Church. Therefore, his desire for clerical discipline, and for a well-disciplined Church, was a reflection of the divine desire for unity. Doctrinally, Colet had no doubts about how a sinful collection of people could become a Holy Body:

> This society of men in Christ Jesus; this spiritual City, formed anew in the form of Christ, and happily begotten again by the Spirit of God; is an homogenous whole in itself. And it is so through the form of Jesus Christ, and through the existence of the one Spirit in the whole and in the parts, and His being present to the whole and to the parts.[171]

This acknowledgement of Christ's spiritual presence within the Church introduces another important theme in Colet's ecclesiology: grace.

For Colet, the people of the Church were united by Christ and justified by grace:

> Now we are thus righteous when justified by grace, being made righteous by God, to the end that we should live righteously ... Of our own human and carnal nature we are all unrighteous, confessedly powerless to do anything aright, though righteous deeds are enjoined upon us.[172]

Colet emphasized justification by grace through faith not only in his treatise on the Mystical Body, and in his commentary on 1 Corinthians, but also in his commentary on Romans, chapters one to five, where he espoused the Augustinian doctrine of predestination:

> Those whom God has ordained to be made true will be made true and righteous. No wickedness of men will interrupt the course and purpose of the will and grace of God.[173]

However, in the same commentary, he stressed that this included everyone, a characteristic of Origen:[174]

> Order there is in the Church, but not respect of persons. For this takes place when one person is admitted and another rejected. But God rejects no-one. Whomsoever and from whatsoever race a man may be sprung, if only he has come to God by Christ, he is admitted into the Church.[175]

Nevertheless, as we have seen, Colet was more of an Augustinian than a follower of Origen.[176] Using the Augustinian metaphor for the Church of a city,[177] Colet was clear that a healthy Church was one of order and, therefore, of beauty:

> And when the members that have been united to Him, are arranged in order and thoroughly adjusted to one another, there ensues, from the variety of

those who are thus fittingly united in the Spirit, a pleasing beauty in the Church, and in the members of Christ. By these I mean *men*, the citizens and household of God in Christ Jesus. He is the ruler of the City: by His wisdom and command the whole City is governed and directed.[178]

Colet, therefore, was willing to combine differing elements of theological thought in order to establish an ecclesiological theory that spoke of order and beauty.

Another sub-theme of Colet's ecclesiology is that of the incarnation. Although ideas of hierarchy and ascent to God were prominent in his vision, he did not ignore the incarnation as the means by which grace and the Holy Spirit could work among such evil human beings: 'God, made man, was the means whereby men were to be made gods. By His Godhead all are made godlike.'[179] Colet emphasized the atoning work of Christ more strongly than Pseudo-Dionysius, in order to explain how the disparate nature of humanity could be unified.[180] This did not mean that all would have to lose their individuality, but that diversity of gifts could be incorporated into the Church:

There are many diversities of gifts, but one Spirit. And though that Spirit infuses itself with varying intensity into different men, yet is it everywhere, and in all of them in its oneness and entirety, that all should sympathize and concur together.[181]

Again, the discussion returns to the theme of unity, for it is through unity that order can be achieved.

A further ingredient in Colet's ecclesiology is law, both secular and ecclesiastical. Colet developed his ecclesiology in order to solve the problem of how a sinful humanity could become the Holy Body of Christ. Paramount to his vision was a sense of order created out of nothing by the incarnation and the Holy Spirit and grace. This ecclesiological sub-theme was less theological or doctrinal than other sub-themes, but more concerned with the practical question of how to achieve his vision, given the problems facing the Church. For Colet, one means of unifying the Church was the application of canon law.[182] In his Convocation sermon, he suggested returning to the 'old laws', meaning canon law, as a way of bringing discipline back to the clergy:

Wherefore in this your assembly let those that are made all redye be called before you and rehersed: those lawes, I say, that restrayne vice, and those that furder vertue.[183]

Colet wished to remind the clergy of what canon law consisted, because he believed that they were ignorant of it and, therefore, had failed to apply it. Colet respected canon law as the basis for a sense of order needed in the Church. However, he found disputes over possessions and tithes particularly distasteful:[184]

> If you cast your eyes around, and survey the whole field with care, pondering well each single object, you will find nothing that has befallen the Church to have done more mischief, than possessions, and tithes of *meum* and *tuum*, and power of claiming property.[185]

He abhorred litigious clergy, begging Christians to avoid going to court and heavily criticising the ecclesiastical courts on the grounds that they perpetuated a grasping litigious spirit within the Church that was alien to the Spirit of God. Colet's views are strongly expressed at the end of his exposition on Romans, chapters one to five:

> How I wish that the ministers of ecclesiastical affairs, and those who call themselves expounders of pontifical law, would understand that, without the grace of Christ, they in vain administer laws for Christ's people.[186]

In the same passage, Colet explained that such litigation damaged the Church:

> For all they heed is, where they may punish with the law's scourges and wound with its knife, so as to drain the golden blood of the laity.[187]

Thus, those who practise avarice through the law are no less than evil:

> Atrocious race of men! Deadliest plague to the Church of Christ! Very devils transformed into angels of light![188]

Their acts are seemingly innocent, yet made with impure motives:

> Aye, and in their rebukes they would be acting the part of worthy lawyers, did but they proceed with holy and clean hands, grieving that there should be any cause for punishment, and inflicting punishment at last only for that honourable end, to be desired of all men, the emending of our evil ways.[189]

For Colet, there were no circumstances in which going to law was correct for a Christian:

> Let us plainly conclude, therefore, that it is not the part of Christians to dispute at law before any judge about any matter, whether of property or of person, or to seek their own rights, since for a Christian man there can be no greater justice, nothing more equitable, than to suffer and put up with wrongs.[190]

This last example demonstrates Colet's purist nature, which perhaps helped him to obtain his reputation at St. Paul's as a harsh and unbending clergyman.[191] However, one has sympathy with his protest against litigious excess, which brought disunity and dispute to the Church. All the laws of the nations, civil law and common law, were wicked to Colet. As Gleason rightly points out, for Colet, laws were of no help to society; his alternative, and absolute, remedy to humanity's hopelessness was each individual's absorption into the Mystical Body of Christ.[192] In contrast to human law, therefore, Colet saw the shining light of divine law as perfect and human law as corrupt: '... there ought to be one law and right of living, even the divine canonical law, wherein is the rule of Christian life.'[193] This quotation emphasizes Colet's rejection of the secular world, and the otherworldliness of his ecclesiology. Wicked doers were to be expelled:

> Beyond this circumference, He prohibits and forbids. And hence the Church excommunicates transgressors; is satisfied with those who do not overstep the circumference of precepts; praises those who strive to reach the centre, Christ; admires those who are perfected in the very centre.[194]

This passage serves as an example of Colet's obsession with regard to Church purity. Although Colet would ideally include everyone,[195] once someone is excommunicated, they must be 'driven off' until they are cleansed through penance and reconciliation.[196]

Another sub-theme of Colet's ecclesiology was money. In the same work, Colet expressed his disappointment at the grasping spirit of some clergy with regard to tithes. He scorned

> ... these lost little men - and our age is full of them, and among them are those who least ought to be, churchmen, and those who are given first rank in the Church – these men, I say, profoundly ignorant of the teaching of the Gospels and of the Apostles, ignorant of the divine justice, ignorant of Christian truth, have the habit of saying that they must defend the cause of God, the rights of

the Church, the heritage of Christ, the property of the priesthood, that they cannot without sin not defend them.

O the narrowness, the blindness, the wretchedness of these fools! Undertaking a course that brings the loss of everything, not only these worldly things, but of those that are everlasting also, they still think, even while they are losing them, that they are acquiring, defending, and saving them.[197]

It was this ecclesiastical discipline that characterized Colet's paradoxical attitude to money. He was rich, and yet held money in no esteem; he was frugal, and expected his clergy to be so too, regardless of wealth – he emphasized this necessity in his comments on Romans 14:17:

Now, what St. Paul says in this passage about meat and drink, that they neither are, nor constitute the kingdom of God, may also be said with the greatest truth about money, possessions, tithes, oblations and whatever else is of an earthly nature – I mean that they are not the kingdom of God, nor do they constitute it.[198]

As Rice crucially observed in the 1950s, for Colet, the kingdom of God was to be found in spiritual, rather than material, wealth.[199] Colet's own money was spent in supporting charitable and educational causes.[200]

This outline of several sub-themes in Colet's ecclesiology demonstrates the breadth of his knowledge and intellect. Not only was Colet extremely well read, but he was also adept at deploying his knowledge in the creation of his own vision for the Church. He was concerned with individuals only as part of the structured community of the Church. When he used the word *individuum* it was always in the sense of an 'undivided' part of the whole body, rather than 'individual'.[201] Therefore, he dealt not only with the personal and devotional aspects of their spiritual lives, but also with the institutional (political) and the hierarchical, here equated with order and beauty. He drew upon the work of St. Augustine, Plato, Ficino, Origen and many others in the moulding of his ideal. The wide variety of influences upon his ecclesiology is reflected in the diversity of themes and sub-themes. All these ideas were combined for a single purpose: the search for perfection in the Church. In the next section, I argue that, comparing Colet with contemporaneous humanists, this search for perfection was distinctive.

Colet and Christian Humanist Thought

So far, we have seen that Colet's ecclesiology, which has not been examined fully until now, was highly developed and complex; that many of the theological and philosophical elements were extracted from Pauline, Pseudo-Dionysian, Augustinian, Neoplatonic and Franciscan thought, but also that Colet added ecclesiological emphases and ideas of his own. It has also been argued that Colet was a Christian humanist. However, I also wish to argue that Colet's complex ideas were distinctive from contemporaneous Christian humanist thought, which can be demonstrated by means of a brief comparison between his ecclesiology and the thought of three of the leading Christian humanists of his time: Erasmus, Fisher and Lefèvre.

It has already been noted, by Jayne, that Colet parted company with Ficino on the subjects of will and intellect, and that Colet tended to Christianize Ficino's Platonic concepts with a moral fervour of his own.[202] However, the key features of Colet's ecclesiology are also highlighted when compared to the beliefs of the greatest Christian humanist of the age, and Colet's good friend, Erasmus. Colet admired the mystical theology of Pseudo-Dionysius, whereas Erasmus was distrustful of mysticism; Colet found the Augustinian soteriology of grace and predestination attractive, whereas Erasmus considered Origen's more inclusive soteriology to be more palatable; Colet was fundamentally pessimistic about humanity, in an Augustinian sense, whereas Erasmus, like most humanists, was optimistic concerning the potential of the human mind; Colet despised classical authors, whereas Erasmus honoured and extolled them;[203] Colet hankered for the simplicity of the ordered life, deciding to retire amongst Carthusian monks, whereas Erasmus was suspicious of the cloister and had left it;[204] Colet considered the Church, as the Mystical Body of Christ, to be the most important entity in creation, whereas, for Erasmus, the Church was 'chiefly important to him as one of his main sources of cash';[205] most crucially, Colet considered that the will held primacy over the intellect, whereas Erasmus considered reason and knowledge to be paramount.[206] Thus, although Colet and Erasmus were united in their humanism, they were at odds in their relationships to the Church.

Colet's ecclesiology was also distinct from that of other highly clerical humanist clergy, such as John Fisher, Bishop of Rochester. For instance, unlike Colet, Fisher had 'immense respect for medieval scholastic learning.'[207] Moreover, whereas Colet and Fisher were united in their use of St. Augustine's works, Fisher placed more emphasis upon the work of prevenient grace in reconciling humanity to God. Prevenient grace, or 'grace which goes before', has the value of recognising sin and opening the eyes of the sinner to it, thus provoking the sinner to receive the sacrament of penance and to go out and practise good works: a doctrine lacking in Colet's ecclesiology. Thus, Colet's thought was distinctive from Fisher's English clerical humanist stance.

Another humanist's thought, with which Colet's ideology can usefully be compared, is that of Lefèvre d'Etaples (c.1460-1536), one of the most notable

Christian humanists of the period.[208] Influenced, like Colet, by Italian humanism, scripture, Pseudo-Dionysius and the Fathers, he sought reform in order to recapture the purity of the gospel and the early Church.[209] Travelling from his native France in 1491-2, he visited Italy and made contact with Ficino and Pico, devoting himself thereafter to humanistic textual scholarship, editing and commenting on Aristotle, the Hermetic corpus[210] and Pseudo-Dionysius. His *Quincuplex Psalterium*, published in 1509, showed an exegetical approach comparable to Colet's lectures on Romans.[211] In 1521, he joined Bishop Guillaume Briçonnet in Meaux and attempted religious reform on humanist principles as Briçonnet's vicar-general.[212] Lefèvre inherited the medieval mystical tradition *via* Nicholas of Cusa (1401-64), who had been a keen exponent of scriptural exegesis in the humanist mould.[213]

Colet and Lefèvre were similar in some ways. For instance, both were interested in Pseudo-Dionysius, Lefèvre making Latin translations of all Pseudo-Dionysius's works and including some of them in a collection of patristic texts printed in Paris under the title *Theologia Vivificans Cibus Solidus* (1498/9).[214] Although Lefèvre does not discuss the Pseudo-Dionysian texts in this volume, his other works are infused with a Pseudo-Dionysian and Neoplatonic philosophy.[215] Not only was Colet aware of Lefèvre's translation of Pseudo-Dionysius's *Celestial Hierarchy*,[216] but he also used Lefèvre's Pseudo-Dionysian ideas of 'Christoformity' in his own commentary on the *Celestial Hierarchy*.[217] In order to illustrate Pseudo-Dionysius's point that angels learn divine knowledge from Christ and mediate it to the lower orders of life, Lefèvre invented a conversation, using dialogue taken from scripture, between the Church, Jesus and the three highest angelic orders (Seraphim, Cherubim and Thrones), which Colet incorporated into his commentary on chapter seven of the *Celestial Hierarchy*.[218] The political (public) interpretation of Pseudo-Dionysius, as espoused by Lefèvre, appealed to Colet enough for him to include it within his own ecclesiology.

However, there are also several differences between Colet's and Lefèvre's thought. Firstly, although Lefèvre considered the works of Pseudo-Dionysius to be 'most sacred', he was also an Aristotelian, a position not shared by Colet.[219] Secondly, Lefèvre was also fond of the works of Aquinas, who was despised by Colet.[220] Thirdly, Colet and Lefèvre took differing stances on the nature of humanity: Colet considered humanity to be hopelessly depraved,[221] whereas Lefèvre exalted the dignity and abilities of humankind.[222] This antithesis led directly to the fourth difference, which concerned will and intellect. Praising human reason, like Erasmus and Ficino, Lefèvre considered intellect superior to the human will. For Colet, however, the reconciliation of humanity to God was achieved by conforming the human will to that of the loving will of God, not by the achievements of human reason.[223] The fifth difference was the two men's opposing views on divine grace. For instance, in exegetical practice, Lefèvre favoured philological and historical interpretative methods, whereas Colet was 'violent and suspicious' of such methods, preferring to rely upon God's grace to reveal the truth of the text.[224]

To conclude this section: Colet differed from Erasmus ecclesiologically. Both men were passionate about the Church, but for very different reasons: Colet because he loved it, and Erasmus because he was suspicious of it. Fisher and Colet shared many ecclesiological characteristics; indeed, Fisher was a model bishop according to Colet's ideals. However, they parted company in their doctrinal emphases upon the sacrament of penance. For Fisher it was central, but it was of little importance to Colet's ecclesiological vision. Lefèvre and Colet were united in their love of the works of Pseudo-Dionysius, but they did not share an appreciation of Aristotle and Aquinas. Moreover, they had opposing views on the nature of humanity, on will and intellect and on exegetical technique. Colet's ecclesiology was, therefore, distinctive not only from that of his English humanist colleagues, but also from the ideas of Continental Christian humanists. It was this characteristic ecclesiology that became the basis for a life-long pursuit of clerical perfection.

Conclusion

To conclude this chapter, two quotations, one from Colet's treatise *De Sacramentis* and the other from his commentary on 1 Corinthians, demonstrate the scope of his vision and help to summarize both his attitude to the Church and the motivation behind his attempted reforms:

> If the lower world were not lifted up and supported by the higher and spiritual part, the downward tendency of all things toward evil and ugliness would, because of men's utter powerlessness, bring him to nothing.[225]

> Jesus himself came into the world to the aid of the angels, to purify, enlighten and perfect the world.[226]

The first quotation encapsulates Colet's obsession with humanity's depravity and hopelessness – his otherworldliness. The second quotation expresses his hope in the cosmic order, of which Christ is the head. The chief question in Colet's ecclesiology, therefore, was this: how could a sinful body of people be justified to God and reach the required perfection for union with God? Colet found an answer in order: Pseudo-Dionysius's three-fold process of ascent to God: purification, illumination and perfection.[227] These were not simply stages of personal spiritual development, but concepts lying behind the most important aspect of the Church: hierarchy, for

> The goal of hierarchy ... is to enable beings to be as like as possible to God and to be at one with him. A hierarchy has God as its leader of all understanding and action. It is forever looking directly at the comeliness of God.[228]

For Colet, as for Pseudo-Dionysius, every sacrament entered into was part of a progressive return towards God; every member of the Church hierarchy had a place in communicating the love of God, which emanated from the deity *via* the celestial hierarchy to the world.[229] The Church's goal was to be nothing short of perfection, which was union with God. Colet loved the Church and yet, since it was composed of sinful people, it had constantly to reform itself in order to make the ascent to heaven *via* the teaching of the earthly hierarchy of the Church, helped by the spiritual hierarchy of saints, angels and Christ:

> Moreover for the work of founding a church of Christ for a time beneath the angels, out of men that shall be purified, illumined and perfected under Jesus Christ, the angels are ministering spirits.[230]

The motivation for Colet's attempted ecclesiastical reform arose, therefore, from his view of the stark contrast between the ugliness of humanity and his vision of God's will for the Church, which was union with Him, made possible by the support of celestial beings. The discernment of God's will, by the higher clergy, therefore became crucial to Colet's ecclesiology, because it is they who were responsible for passing on God's love to the lower clergy and laity.[231] The result of Colet's ecclesiological thought was a hard rule for those falling under his authority, because of its otherworldliness. However, it was born of a love for the Church, which sought the best for it. Humanity was nothing to Colet; God was everything. Ultimately, however, the perfection desired was not merely the logical consequence of humanist optimism, but was love, which was higher, in Colet's opinion, than knowledge. Towards the end of his life, Colet planned retirement in a monastic community.[232] Just as simplicity was indicative of goodness and multiplicity of evil, so Colet desired a life of simple beauty for the whole Church. His dealings with the clergy, and his attempts to put his ecclesiology into practice, will therefore be the subjects of the remainder of this study.

3

REFORM I: ST. PAUL'S MINOR CLERGY IN 1506

In this chapter I argue that Colet's first documented attempt to implement his perfectionist ideals at St. Paul's was a failure because his practical ecclesiology was based upon the following concept:

> In Christ's Church it is most especially fitting, and ought, surely, to be kept as an established and fixed custom, that disciples should obey their teachers, and that attentively hearing their master's precepts, they should comply with them forthwith and altogether without dispute. For otherwise order will be upset, and ugly deformity will show itself.[1]

As the quotation suggests, Colet's ministerial practice was built upon notions of order and hierarchy.[2] As teacher and dean, he expected his inferiors to obey his precepts promptly and without question. In 1506, Colet proposed some precepts for the inferior clergy at St. Paul's.[3] This chapter examines the consequences of his proposals and argues that he was unsuccessful in his attempt to apply his ecclesiology, developed at Oxford, to his ministerial practice at the cathedral. Dean Hook's late nineteenth-century assessment of the effect of Colet's manner serves as a useful starting point for this examination of his approach to reform:

> It is not precisely what you do that gives offence, but an unhappy manner of doing it. Colet so conducted his reform as to excite against himself the animosity of all the underlings of his church. The dean found it more difficult to contend with the cretan bellies of his petty canons than to struggle against the Boeotian intellects of his opponents at Oxford.[4]

This passage may not be fair in its description of the minor clergy, nor of Oxford intellectuals, but it is correct in three important respects: firstly, that Colet approached his reform in an inappropriate way; secondly, that this gave rise to opposition; and thirdly, that the situation was totally different to the one he had known at Oxford. In consequence, he had little influence over the minor clergy at St. Paul's Cathedral during his time as dean, despite his attempted reform of their behaviour. In order to identify the historical basis for this chapter, I propose to begin by outlining the relevant events.

In the summer of 1506, after he had been dean for a year, Colet formally visited St. Paul's.[5] As a result, he produced a manuscript, now lost;[6] part one contains extracts from the existing cathedral statutes, while part two contains Colet's proposed injunctions for the government of the institution's minor clergy. The 1506 document constitutes important evidence of Colet's motivations and his methods of administering the cathedral. Although we have Simpson's purportedly full Latin transcription of the manuscript,[7] the issue of whether or not these injunctions were ever accepted and implemented by chapter remains a mystery.

Judging by Simpson's printed transcription, the text is in two sections. The first four paragraphs constitute the first section and comprise extracts from the pre-Colet cathedral statutes concerning the chantry priests and minor clergy.[8] In the introductory paragraph, Colet explains that he does not wish to see the *capellanos*, or chantry priests, err due to ignorance of the rules, and has therefore compiled the relevant ones for them.[9] Then follow some excerpts from the statutes concerning admission to the choir, and the necessary testimonials, high moral life and learning. The succentor was to test a candidate's musical knowledge, while the dean was to order those intending to be chantry priests to learn the obligations of their chosen chantry. The oath sworn by minor clergy on admission to the cathedral community is set out in full. A large part of this oath emphasizes obedience to the dean. The second section comprises Colet's injunctions for minor clergy; they relate to the minutiae of religious observance. The injunctions demonstrate Colet's personal designs, his meticulous, ascetic nature, and his high ideals. They concern such details as the choir's entrance to, and exit from, the choir-stalls ('*ingressus chori, egressus chori*'); their behaviour during services ('*decorum servandum*'); their conduct during processions ('*De Processione*'); and their accountability to their superior clergy for extra-curricular activities. The final paragraph deals with the rules for Saturday chapter meetings: all who wore the habit were to attend and hear the dean's decrees; all offenders were to be corrected and do-gooders were to be praised and rewarded. These injunctions are a detailed account of the expectations, procedural and other, that the dean had for the Saturday morning appraisals. Priests were to bow to, and prostrate themselves before, the dean; carry no weapons; visit no taverns; nor talk openly with women;

nor have a proud look. They should not make impertinent replies, but meekly bear the dean's discipline and hear him on good manners and spiritual edification.[10]

As Colet's first documented administrative act as dean, the work embodied his hopes and ideals for the Church, which had been nurtured and expressed during his time at Oxford. In his edition of the document, Simpson interpreted the 1506 work as Colet's continuation of statute reform carried out by his predecessors[11] and the beginning of his own inexorable journey towards Church reform, which would blossom into the Protestant Reformation itself.[12] Since Simpson's time, relevant scholarship on this issue has been limited: Carpenter baselessly asserted that Colet's reforms (in general) failed because of the 'slackness of the chapter and its unwillingness to allow any drastic change in its pattern of life'; while Trapp simply acknowledges the sometime existence of the manuscript that has 'disappeared from view'.[13] From Simpson's description of the document, Trapp suggests that it '... was most likely written out by Peter Meghen'. If correct, this fact implies that Colet imbued the text with enough significance to warrant the production of a fair-written version. However, until the manuscript is rediscovered, this must remain conjecture. Trapp goes on mistakenly to suggest that '... it was intended to be placed in the choir so that no one henceforth could plead ignorance of his obligations'.[14] As we shall see, it was not the manuscript itself that was to be placed in the choir, but little books containing copies of the statutes and injunctions.[15] The most recent scholarship on the matter of Colet's relationship with the minor clergy unfortunately confuses his 1506 attempts at reform with his efforts of 1518. Thus, Davis suggests that

> ... in an attempt to tackle the abuses, in particular of the lesser clergy, he drew up new statutes to regulate each group of the cathedral clergy. As part of his reforming programme, Colet also produced a corpus of extracts from the collected statutes to provide an easily accessible code of statutes so that chantry chaplains could not plead ignorance of what was expected of them.[16]

Davis, like Trapp, misleadingly conflates Colet's 1506 and 1518 reform efforts by citing Simpson's editions of both texts, but without distinguishing between them.[17] As we shall see later in this study, Colet's 1518 proposals are entirely different to those discussed here.[18] This chapter seeks to clarify which of his proposals belong to 1506, just as I later aim to identify those reform proposals composed in 1518.

Thus, in order to understand Colet's motivation in 1506, it is necessary to set his work within the context of other English secular cathedrals, whose records relating to the minor clergy are more substantial than those for St. Paul's, and to give a fuller picture of early sixteenth-century ecclesiastical history. Section one of this chapter will therefore examine the lives and duties of minor clergy in some of these other institutions, comparing them to the St. Paul's minor clergy. Aspects to be investigated include the respective numbers, wealth and duties of the vicars-choral, the chantry priests and the minor canons. For the purposes of this exercise, these three groups will be referred to, collectively, as 'minor clergy'. In section two, Colet's motivation for compiling these statutes, and for writing new injunctions for the minor clergy, is analysed. Three reasons are suggested: firstly, in order to improve standards; secondly, in order to control finances; and thirdly, in order to comply with norms of statute reform within English secular cathedrals. Part three of this chapter explores Colet's ecclesiological concerns and how he attempted to apply them in 1506. It is suggested that he possessed five chief ecclesiological concerns in 1506, which I propose to discuss in turn: firstly, the furtherance of clerical learning; secondly, the avoidance of error; thirdly, the promotion of Godly conversation; fourthly, the practice of Christian morality; and lastly, the observance of good clerical behaviour during the offices. The fourth section of the chapter examines how the dean's statute proposals were received. I argue that his ascetic ecclesiological ideals were expressed antagonistically in his withdrawal of traditional decanal hospitality.

Minor Clergy

Early sixteenth-century English secular cathedrals[19] were mostly healthy, stable, well-organized communities with a single purpose: the continual cycle of prayer and praise known as the *Opus Dei*, the work of God.[20] The canonical hours of matins, lauds, lady mass, prime, tierce, high mass, sext, nones, vespers and compline formed the cycle of worship which it was the responsibility of every cathedral, whether monastic or secular, to perform.[21] The lower clergy in secular cathedrals were essential to this primary duty and most immediately involved in it.[22] As Edwards explains, every

> ... cathedral gained a permanent body of inferior clergy, specially trained in singing. Under the direction of the precentor and residentiary canons the vicars-choral were able to celebrate the *Opus Dei* with probably greater skill than the absent canons, who, for the most part, had no special qualifications in singing.[23]

At secular cathedrals, the lower clergy were divided into three groups: vicars-choral, poor clerks and chantry priests.[24] In theory, the work of these three groups was distinct: the vicars-choral deputized for the non-resident canons in singing the offices; the poor clerks prepared the altars and assisted at mass; and the chantry priests were responsible for saying masses for the deceased who had left endowments to pay for prayer for their own souls and those of their families.[25] In practice, there was often an overlap between vicars-choral and chantry priests, as vicars-choral could sometimes obtain a chantry after ten years of service, or five years after ordination to the priesthood.[26] In 1514, a quarter of all Lincoln's vicars-choral had been promoted from being poor clerks and two-thirds were in priestly orders,[27] signifying the tendency for the lower orders to aspire to promotion. As Colet's work related to all three groups of clergy, a description of the lives and duties of each group follows, beginning with the vicars-choral.

The term 'vicar' (or *vicarius*) means substitute; substitution was their main duty. At St. Paul's, the original number of vicars-choral was the same as the number of canons, which was thirty, so that each canon had a deputy to sing the offices for him, should he be non-resident or incapable of singing.[28] In practice, the canons probably left all singing duties to the minor ranks. The vicars-choral, as well as singing the offices instead of the canons, assisted at the altar during mass.[29] Although all minor clergy had singing duties, the vicars-choral bore the brunt of the daily choral routine and were answerable, in the first instance, to the minor canons for their standards of behaviour.[30] On special occasions, such as large services, the vicars-choral would join forces with the chantry priests and minor canons to form the full choir, along with twelve boy trebles.[31] This amalgamation could be said to have formed *the* St. Paul's Cathedral choir. However, due to the varying duties of each minor cleric, the choir expanded and contracted according to the office or service. In this sense, it differed from the large group of full-time professional musicians employed in the Chapel Royal. Being the lowest in status of the three main groups of minor clergy, the vicars-choral at St. Paul's were not ordained priests, but were deacons or sub-deacons only and, therefore, could not celebrate the Eucharist. Appointed by the dean and chapter, vicars-choral had to be free men of good character possessed of a good voice. Their dress was a plain almuce of black cloth,[32] as opposed to the minor canons, who wore fur collars like the canons. The vicars-choral lived together in a common hall from 1273 onwards.[33] Similar in status to the poor clerks of Lincoln, they were sometimes referred to as '*Pauperes clerici*'.[34] The vicars-choral were not an independent body; rather, they were closely involved in the canons' lives, as at other secular cathedrals. At York, the vicars-choral had rights to receive hospitality in the canons' houses.[35] The vicars-choral of Lichfield gave up similar rights in 1374 in exchange for increased incomes.[36] At Salisbury, most vicars-choral lived with the residentiary canons and were treated as household members. Canons sometimes referred to their personal vicar-choral. For example, in 1498, canon John Anstell of Wells bequeathed a silver saltcellar to 'his' vicar-choral, John Fox. Certain canons, likewise, had responsibility for the vicars-choral. At York, for example, the precentor was chief cantor, or singer, whilst the chancellor instructed choristers and vicars-choral on divinity and Church history and examined the vicars-choral in psalms and histories at the end of their first year.[37] One Richard Smith failed to achieve the required standard in his one-year's probation at Salisbury:

> [Smith] Hath no fitt voyce to singe the tenor for that it is to small, neither the countertenor for that it is not tunable therunto, neither the bass for that itt is utterly unfitt for that parte.[38]

Due to a fall in endowments, increased poverty amongst the lower clergy became problematic in all secular cathedrals towards the end of the fifteenth century and into the sixteenth.[39] At York, in 1484, the dean and chapter enlisted Richard III's support in acquiring Cottingham church for their vicars-choral.[40] Nevertheless, the incomes of York vicars-choral declined due to the poverty of their rents and possessions through the early sixteenth century. By the 1540s, eighteen out of the twenty vicars-choral supplemented their income with a chantry, 'The occasion whereof is by reason of decaye of landes and revenues of the cytie of York, beyng sore in ruyne and decaye.'[41] In 1432, the vicars-choral of Lincoln received no income for seventeen weeks and consequently were forced to sell their vicarage.[42] By the end of the fifteenth century, the number of vicars-choral at St. Paul's numbered only six.[43]

The second group of minor clerics were the chantry priests, who were employed, by endowment, to sing mass for the dead according to the conditions of the founder's will.[44] These offices took place in the many chantry chapels inside St. Paul's, and could be served by an individual or a small group of chantry priests.[45] When Bishop Braybroke visited the cathedral in 1391, the chantries were so poor that they were being given to beneficed clergy, who thereby became pluralist.[46] As a last resort, he therefore ruled that no beneficed cleric should hold a chantry, except for the minor canons. In June 1391, Braybroke obtained a royal licence to rationalize the fifty-seven chantries into thirty-one groups in order to cut costs.[47] At St. Paul's, the chantry priests lived in the 'prestshous'; those who were also minor canons lived in St. Peter's College, situated in the cathedral precincts, on the north side.[48] Those priests who were attached to the chantry of the Duke of Lancaster lived in Lancaster College, situated by the cathedral's south gate.

However, in general, the number of chantry foundations increased annually through the fifteenth and early sixteenth centuries. In Wells alone, there were twenty-eight chantry foundations in 1372-3, thirty-two in 1480-1 and forty-three in 1524-5.[49] This rise reflected a growing belief in the doctrine of purgatory.[50] Good works, including prayers, were believed to diminish the soul's suffering in purgatory and assist its journey to heaven. Chantries were also a way of giving to the Church in an affordable and convenient way, with the founder allowed to dictate the details. The more one could afford to bequeath for the purpose, therefore, the more frequent and elaborate the prayers and masses could be.[51] This meant that chantry chapels were often magnificent additions to cathedrals and that chaplains received reasonable payment for their duties.[52] The bequests for the performance of these prayers and masses served to strengthen the Church's practice of daily devotion and people's commitment to it. St. Paul's had the largest group of chantry priests of any secular cathedral, numbering over fifty.[53] This fact suggests that, when Colet arrived in 1505, there may have been a decline in the wealth of the minor clergy in general, but not of their enthusiasm to serve chantries.

The third, and most senior, group of minor clergy at St. Paul's comprised the minor canons.[54] The minor canons were financially independent of the canons they served. They were higher in status than the chantry priests – each had a stall in the choir – and their clerical dress was the same as the canons.[55] They were allowed to celebrate mass at the high altar in the cathedral and were responsible for the day-to-day liturgy. As such, they were in charge of the choral services and the singers; some also served a chantry.[56] Originally, the minor canons' income consisted of a weekly prebend from the general cathedral income; food allowances; and a share of payments for obits, the annual commemoration of a person's death.[57] Gradually, each of the twelve minor canons' cathedral stalls acquired its own benefice for the maintenance of the stallholder.[58] Additional revenues, such as the tithes of the adjacent parish of St. Gregory, were collected as income in common for the minor canons.[59] The hierarchy amongst the twelve minor canon stallholders consisted of the sub-dean; two so-called 'cardinals'[60] of the college, one senior and one junior; the warden; the divinity lecturer; the sacrist; and six others.[61] The organization of the minor canons survived the Reformation unchanged, although they were reduced to six in 1875 and now number three.[62] According to the existing statutes, Colet held certain powers over the minor canons: he could correct them, temporarily forbid their entry into the choir[63] and grant them leave of absence for up to eight days, but not for longer without the chapter's consent.[64]

Colet's injunctions related to all three of these groups of minor clergy, who were collectively responsible for singing in the cathedral.[65] One of Colet's particular concerns was that the *capellanos* were especially ignorant of the required standards of behaviour, but the rules applied to all those involved in choral duties. The problems that Colet's injunctions addressed were those of status, attendance and behaviour during the offices. The dean was attempting to guard against potential problems, 'lest they [i.e. the minor clergy] should fall into error'.[66] Let us now consider his method of guarding against error, and his level of success.

It was normal procedure for ordinaries to undertake visitations of their jurisdictions soon after taking office.[67] In this respect, Colet was following common practice for a new dean. It was also normal for a visitation to end with the promulgation of a set of corrective injunctions.[68] There is no direct evidence to indicate that Colet wished his injunctions to be incorporated into the cathedral statutes. However, the manuscript printed by Simpson suggests that the dean wished to make the minor clergy aware of the existing statutes and to enable those clergy to have access to them in the form of *libelli* (little books),[69] placed in convenient locations. None of these books is apparently extant. Moreover, Colet's 1506 visitation expenses include no entry relating to the copying of the injunctions into the prescribed little books, or even into one book.[70] This omission may indicate that he lost interest in the project before the expenses were drawn up, and decided not to go ahead with the copying of little books, or that the books were manufactured after the visitation expenses had been compiled. Alternatively, it may point to some obstacle or opposition to the project. However, a document of 1559 hints that these *libelli* may have been produced,[71] a possibility wholly unnoticed by previous Colet scholars. The document, a small vellum roll, contains a list of

> Bookes and other Writings appertayninge to the Cathedrall Church of Saint Paule in London and to the Deane only and the Deane and Chapitor of the sayd cathedral church. Delivered by Mr. Henry Cole late Deane of the same Church to Doctor May now deane this the xxth Daie of September A[nno] 1559.[72]

Amongst the items listed are the following:

> ... Item, a booke entitled statutes used in Deane Collette's Dayes
> Item, a booke entitled *Liber visita[ti]o[n]es Joa[nn]is Collett, Decani ecc[les]ia Sancti Pauli London sub A[nno] D[o]m[in]i 1506*
> Item, a booke written in parchment of certayne statute[s] collected by Deane Collet, Beinge bound in boards and covered with black leather ...[73]

The description of these three items is evidence firstly, that there was a book of statutes recognized as being used particularly during Colet's tenure as dean; secondly, that there was a book containing information concerning his visitation of 1506;[74] and thirdly, that there existed at least one book of statutes, compiled by Colet, and bound in black leather. The second of these three items links the dean's name with a compilation of statutes and the visitation of 1506. The question also arises of whether or not the black leather-bound book was one of the *libelli* mentioned in the lost 1506 manuscript.[75] Whilst it cannot be proved that this item was an example of Colet's 'little books', the evidence suggests the possibility that he successfully commissioned the manufacture of at least one of the *libelli*. However, this conclusion must remain conjectural, unless further evidence is found to suggest that his proposals made a larger impact than the production of one small book. I now turn to examine the reasons for Colet's attempted reforms of 1506.

Colet's Attempted Reform

As Colet's 1506 reform efforts have been almost entirely ignored by scholars until now, naturally no reasons for his actions have been offered. I argue that there are three explanations for the dean's compilation of statutes and fresh injunctions concerning the minor clergy at St. Paul's: firstly, his desire to improve standards; secondly, his desire to control finances; and thirdly, his desire to act in accordance with secular cathedral practice. Each of these reasons will be examined in turn.

Erasmus tells us that Colet could not endure 'slovenliness'.[76] The dean's worry that the chantry priests might fall into sin, were it not for his intervention, was his given reason for drafting the injunctions.[77] In order to determine how justified these anxieties were, it is necessary to contextualize them by examining late-medieval clerical standards. Statutes and disciplinary records for St. Paul's, and for other English secular cathedrals, suggest that, although entry procedures were rigorous, there were lapses in devotion to duty. The 1506 manuscript implies that Colet found it personally necessary to instil discipline in the minor clergy from early on in his career as dean, although in any case it was not unusual for rules to be provided for chantry priests, and other secular cathedral clergy, in the fifteenth century.[78] Colet's efforts, therefore, were partly a personal wish, and partly a continuation of, ecclesiastical norms. Payments for the performance of chantry duties were relatively high compared to the ordinary income that a minor cleric could expect to receive as a share of his college's revenue, making competition for cantarist (chantry priest) positions fierce.[79] As Davis rightly observes,

> Bishop Braybroke amalgamated the chantries in twos and threes to provide an income which was often substantially above the recommended stipend of seven marks (£4 13s. 4d.) p. a. ... This meant that the men serving the chantries were often well rewarded and might have been expected to have been committed to their posts.[80]

St. Paul's and its precincts were a meeting ground for chaplains offering themselves for hire.[81] Once a chantry had been obtained, it would not have been in their interests for cantarists to misbehave and risk losing the income.

Standards of behaviour were also expected to be high for the vicars-choral serving in other English secular cathedrals. According to their adopted Norman rule of Chrodegang, Minster officials at York were expected to show humility, moderation, diligence, piety, dignity, seriousness of purpose, charity, chastity and urbanity. More specifically, they were required to obey the capitular statutes of 1396.[82] Injunctions were added from the mid-sixteenth century. Moreover, the vicars-choral had formulated rules to govern their own community. The succentor drew up a 'single-table', or rota, for their canting duties: there were to be the correct number of vicars-choral on each side of the choir; if a vicar-choral was to be paid, then he had to be in place by the *Gloria Patri* at the end of the first psalm. In addition, the 1252 statutes, which required all vicars-choral to be present at all the offices or incur a fine, were still in force in the fifteenth century.[83] Some of the rules at York, such as those concerning fines and the holding of Saturday morning chapter meetings for instruction and the imposition of discipline, also appear in Colet's 1506 proposals.[84] As Colet held the York prebend of Botevant, it is possible that he was influenced by York administration.[85] More importantly, however, it demonstrates that Colet's proposed injunctions were not particularly radical in substance compared with those of other institutions.

Recent scholarship suggests that the minor clergy of English secular cathedrals were badly in need of behavioural discipline on the eve of the Reformation:

> Drastic reform was certainly necessary at this [junior] level of the clergy, whose idleness and immorality provoked much of the satirical and sermonising literature against clerical misconduct ...[86]

Whilst this assertion rather overstates the case – good behaviour was naturally not documented – there is evidence of occasional misbehaviour amongst minor clergy. For instance, at York, John Middleton was fined 6s. 8d. for striking Joanna Cawood in 1419; in 1421, John Hedon was fined 12d. for disorderly and opprobrious words and Thomas Burdett was fined 20d. for spending £3 too much in 1446, perhaps acquired from a well-paid obit. However, this evidence is drawn from over twenty-five years and cannot be accepted as the norm. Of far more importance was the daily devotion to the *Opus Dei*. A 1507 York statute and minute book placed an emphasis on musical and vocal rules. For instance, vicars-choral were to learn the psalms by heart and become 'perfect in their singing'. They were also to swear an oath that, until a vicar-choral was competent in music and singing, he would not claim, receive or sell his share of the receipts from the benefices appropriated for their maintenance. If anyone had a tenor voice, he was to learn pricksong (polyphonic music) and fauxbourden (alternately plainsong and polyphonic music). If he was not a tenor, then he had to learn the descant as well.[87] At Lincoln, however, there was an attendance problem concerning vicars-choral and poor clerks at the daily offices. In 1503, four poor clerks were brought before chapter for non-attendance.[88] In 1505, the vicars-choral were once accused of not attending matins (at two a.m.) and once again, in 1508, when they were discovered in an alehouse instead. However, things improved that year, when Henry Alcock was appointed teacher of grammar to the choristers and, in 1511, to teach 'plainsong, pricksong, discaunt, counterpynt' to all singers.[89] In 1509, new rules were drawn up, ordering vicars-choral to be present in the choir for services, and not just in the nave. Absence from mass, vespers, or their processions, incurred a fine of 1*d.* This new regime had the effect of improving the quality of music and worship. The singing was proficient enough by 1511 for none of the singers to be removed from the cathedral, unless requested to sing for the prestigious Chapel Royal.[90] Cases of expulsion were rare, the only case being that of Robert Craggs, expelled on 14 June 1538, but later readmitted.[91] The worst offender of all was William Burdcleuer, a vicar-choral from 1459 to 1506; all his documented offences involved fornication. In 1461, Burdcleuer was fined and ordered on an eight-day pilgrimage for harbouring Margaret Shilton and two children; in 1466, he was found guilty of adultery with Joan Taylor, his punishment being to carry the Psalter in procession at high mass for three consecutive days. The significance of this punishment is that it was a public acknowledgement of guilt and, therefore, a humiliation. In 1470 and 1472, he was given the same punishment for committing the same crime with Margaret Middleton and Joan Wilson respectively. But, for all this, he was not expelled; in fact, he became succentor from 1483 to 1489, and canon of the chapel of St. Mary and Holy Angels.[92] Although lower clergy were sometimes guilty of minor offences, it was not unknown for senior clergy to misuse their authority in a much more serious way. At the Nottinghamshire collegiate Church of Newark, which lay in the diocese of Lincoln, Dean George Gray attempted to gain rights of patronage over all benefices belonging to the whole chapter and tried to keep custody of the chapter seal, even if he was away.[93] Naturally, the canons resisted, whereas cathedral clergy generally met well-exercised decanal authority with a positive response. For instance, during Thomas Heywood's time as dean of Lichfield (1457-92), there was no recorded hostility between the dean and other clergy, or between the chapter and the vicars-choral; so popular was he that Heywood was admitted to the vicars' confraternity.[94] In 1461, nine Lichfield clergy were accused of fornication, four of fathering illegitimate children. Heywood reacted positively, and pragmatically, by ordering couples to marry that could possibly do so.[95] Heywood's interest was in upholding marital values above clerical vocation. Unlike Colet,[96] he was a generous benefactor to the vicars-choral, repaired their communal house and built an infirmary and a chapel for them.[97] He also improved the 'New College' of the chantry chaplains by adding a bakehouse and a brewhouse. As Kettle explains,

> Heywood was, above all, devoted to the church which the close and its inhabitants existed to serve and he did much to improve its appearance.[98]

Some years later, in 1522, one of Heywood's successors at Lichfield, Dean James Denton, took a similarly gentle approach and became a prominent benefactor of music and of the choir.[99]

Thus, training and discipline were imposed on the minor clergy at all secular cathedrals during the fifteenth and sixteenth centuries.[100] Clerical behaviour at St. Paul's does not appear to have been any worse than at other English secular cathedrals. As for the St. Paul's minor clergy, recorded complaints were relatively trivial. One grievance was that the minor canons were rarely all present at the same time; another was that there was disagreement between chaplains and vicars-choral as to precedence.[101] The negligence of the minor canons in making confession to the penitentiary, and negligence in performing the divine office, are also mentioned.[102] In his Convocation sermon, Colet asked for 'the reformation of ecclesiastical affairs, for never was it more necessary and never did the state of the Church more need your endeavours'.[103] But this was more of a rhetorical device than an objective truth. Haigh has suggested that the dean was part of a long tradition of protestors against earthly ambitions corrupting priests' Godly work.[104] For instance, Bernard of Clairvaux in the twelfth century, Bishop Grosseteste in the thirteenth, William Langland in the fourteenth, and Thomas Gascoigne in the fifteenth century, were all critics of worldliness and neglect in the Church. But Colet was not concerned with that tradition or with his place within it; he was concerned with the Church only in his own time. Even though he desired improvement in clerical standards, it would be misleading to conclude from the available evidence that cathedral minor clergy were worse offenders than parochial clergy – and for the following reasons: firstly, because extant cathedral records are often more detailed than parish ones, cathedral clergy's sins are naturally better documented, but this does not necessarily indicate their greater culpability; and secondly, because parish clergy were only inspected during visitations,[105] whereas cathedral clergy were held to account every week at documented meetings.[106] Reforming action was, in fact, more appropriate at the end of the fourteenth century, when energetic deans, such as William Mancetter of Lichfield and John Godeley of Wells, led it.[107] For instance, Deans Thomas Montagu of Salisbury and John Maidenhith of Chichester did much to reform and reinvigorate their respective cathedrals in the 1390s. The sixteenth century was not unique in having a figure like Colet to take the moral high ground.[108] The reasons for Colet's attempted reforms lay not in a Church crisis, but, as we have seen, within his own particular ecclesiology.

While concern about clerical standards was Colet's primary motivation for producing his injunctions, the second reason was money. Although the minor canons were a financially independent body at St. Paul's, during the dean's time chantry priests were paid *via* the dean and chapter, who held endowments in trust for the deceased founders.[109] Therefore, the dean and chapter could withhold payment if behaviour was bad or rules were broken. This was one way in which the cathedral authorities exercised control. Following Bishop Braybroke's rationalisation of the St. Paul's chantries, the number of chantries per priest at St. Paul's, and therefore of chantry income per priest, had risen. The total stipend, at around £8 a year, compared favourably to the ordinary income a minor cleric could expect to receive from a share of his college's revenue, at around 5*d.* a week plus food.[110] Due to this financial attraction, chantry foundations were outnumbered by minor clerics seeking to serve them,[111] with the result that a priest could wait years to gain a chantry.[112] Only nine chantries were founded in London and Middlesex between 1500 and 1534.[113] Therefore, Colet wished to keep a tight rein on the finances of chantries as a means of controlling behaviour.

The third reason for Colet's attempted reforms was his desire to effect statute reform like his predecessors: an unfashionable enterprise in the early sixteenth century. Attempts at statute reform in secular cathedrals were increasingly unusual as the pace of statute making in general declined during the fifteenth century and became rare in the sixteenth.[114] Only at Exeter (in 1511 and 1519) and Lichfield (in 1526) were new ones issued. Colet's attempts were based on those of his, more successful, predecessors: Ralph Baldock (dean 1294-1305)[115] and Thomas Lisieux (d.1456).[116] Contemporaneous deans had also achieved greater success than Colet at statute reform: Thomas Heywood renewed the 1441 charter of judicial independence of the Lichfield cathedral close in 1465;[117] he ordered the canons to treat the close as a sacred place and punished vicars-choral and chantry priests who left the close without permission, or who misbehaved. Other deans, therefore, tended to lead by example and gentle persuasion, within the boundaries of their position. Thus, Colet was not unique in attempting statute reform, but his ecclesiological motivation for wishing to attempt it was his own and he felt compelled to exceed the burden of his office.[118] The origins for this urge are to be found in his intellectual past, when his ecclesiological vision was formed. It is therefore appropriate to consider Colet's idealism, particularly as it relates to his work in 1506.

Colet's Concerns

In his 1506 manuscript, Colet made clear his concerns regarding the minor clergy: that they should not be ignorant, but learned; that they should not fall into error; that they should be of good conversation; that they should be honest and live according to high moral standards; and that they should behave well during services.[119] I argue that these concerns were rooted in the dean's ecclesiology. In order to illustrate this point, each of the ideals expressed in 1506 will be examined in turn, in the context of his ecclesiological works.

Firstly, Colet was concerned with learning, in which sphere his achievements were exemplary: Erasmus explained to Jodocus Jonas in 1521 that he 'never saw a more highly gifted intellect'.[120] He also called Colet 'a most farsighted man',[121] who 'diligently mastered all the philosophy of the schools and gained the title expressive of a knowledge of the seven liberal arts'.[122] However, we must not wholly rely upon Erasmus – a man given to flattery.[123] Nevertheless, Colet's manuscripts themselves contain evidence of the high quality of his theological knowledge, especially concerning St. Paul and Pseudo-Dionysius. In 1506, therefore, Colet wrote from a position of authority. In the case of the minor clergy, he specifically required that they should have adequate learning in literature and doctrine ('*sufficientiam litteratum et doctrinam*') and sufficient art to be able to sing the offices in the choir ('*arte sufficiens ad necessaries chori labores extiterit*').[124] The latter requirement was naturally to be expected of anyone wishing to perform the choral duties of the *Opus Dei*. The former requirements, however, were a personal request from the dean ('*tum exquirat Decanus*')[125] As to literature, Erasmus relates that Colet was familiar with a wide variety of writers:[126]

> He had previously, however, roamed with great zest through literature of every kind, finding most pleasure in the early writers, Dionysius, Origen, Cyprian, Ambrose, and Jerome.[127]

One would therefore expect Colet to have encouraged his inferiors to read widely in many different authors; this, however, was not the case. He recommended only one source of learning – the scriptures:

> Whatever it be that a man partakes of, he becomes that sort of thing. From this part we can also infer that those who are consecrated to God in Christ, so that they may banquet on Christ, ought not to betake themselves to any table except that where Christ is set forth. Now this table, made up of Christ's many foods and courses, is Holy Scripture, in all the parts of which there is the savour and the solid nourishment of Christ the life-giver ... Only with Christ,

then, should we be banqueters, at the splendid table of the Scriptures; and in the New Testament we should feast the more abundantly, since there the water of Moses has been changed by Christ himself into wine.[128]

In contrast to the goodness of scripture, which he believed should be interpreted with the aid of the Holy Spirit rather than merely by human intellect, Colet emphasized the evil of secular literature, even though he read works by non-Christian authors himself:[129]

At other tables, in other books – those of the pagans – where there is nothing with the savour of Christ and nothing without the savour of the Demon – in those places, surely, no Christian man ought to seat himself, unless he should wish to appear a guest of the Demon rather than of the Lord.[130]

This prohibition was not the only occasion on which the dean did not practice what he preached. For instance, in his Convocation sermon, he preached against pluralism, even though he held several benefices himself.[131] However, the denunciation of plurality whilst being a pluralist oneself was a 'fact of life', according to Gleason.[132] Therefore, Colet was not unique in his apparent hypocrisy on this issue. Nevertheless, he clarified his wish for fellow Christians to be absorbed in the scriptures: by so doing, one could enable divine grace to operate; by reading heathen authors, one impeded the operation of grace:

When you act thus, you show distrust of your ability to understand Holy Writ through grace alone and prayer, through the help of Christ and of faith. Instead you put your trust in the principles and the assistance of pagans.[133]

For Colet, therefore, literature and doctrine were inextricably linked. In 1506, when compiling his manuscript, he would have had these thoughts in mind: 'We must read only those books in which there is a saving taste of Christ; in which Christ is set forth for our feasting.'[134] If the minor clergy read such books, then, in the dean's view, they would have had *sufficientiam litteratum et doctrinam*.

The second of Colet's concerns in 1506 was that the minor clergy should not fall into doctrinal error. The avoidance of error was a key feature of his ecclesiology of perfection. For Colet, the question of how to avoid sin, within the lower clerical orders, was answered by the enforcement of obedience and by encouragement to agreement. On the dangers of disobedience, Colet wrote thus:

> ... if any human principle, any human anger or cupidity, should break forth and too presumptuously transgress the bounds set by God's Spirit, then everything in God's Church is wretchedly thrown into confusion and foully beset by disorders.[135]

Colet insisted upon agreement:

> And we must ever strive after agreement, which is the soundness of the Lord's body, and the health of the Church; that so, by souls conspiring together, God may be worshipped and adored; for this is the object of the Church's assembly and congregation, and of the Christian society.[136]

In this passage, he described the purpose of gathering to celebrate the daily offices as the worship of God. This worship required the union of Christian souls in the fulfilment of their duties. High standards and an avoidance of error were therefore of paramount importance in his ecclesiology. In this ambition for agreement, Colet remarked that the strong should help the weak:[137] 'We must therefore take a kindly account of the weak, and beware of laying any burden upon them.'[138] Moreover, each person should love one another, in order to assist the performance of worship in the Church:

> In this mutual love consists all order, duty and office in the Church; and the whole Ecclesiastical Hierarchy in it rests on the love of God and of our neighbour.[139]

Colet's insistence upon perfection, therefore, was not the unfeeling dictatorship of a military regime. It was a compassionate desire to see the people of the Church achieve their potential of mutual love and unity with God.

Colet's third concern was the promotion of Godly conversation. The dean was very particular about his conversation: the nature of the subject, the length of the conversation, and the identity of his interlocutor, as Erasmus related when describing dining with Colet:

> He would then usually repeat some passage selected from the part read [at dinner] and draw a topic of conversation from it, inquiring of any scholars present, or even of intelligent laymen, what this or that expression meant. And he would so season the discourse that, though both serious and religious, it had nothing tedious or affected about it ... The pleasure he took in conversing

with friends was extreme, and he would often prolong the talk till late at night. But still it was all either about [sacred] literature or about Christ.[140]

The dean was a conditionally enthusiastic conversationalist – the condition being an insistence that the subject matter was to be either Christ, or the Scriptures, or both: Erasmus related that he rarely ventured into company, but that when he did 'his talk was always of Christ'.[141] By the term *literis*, Erasmus must have meant sacred literature, rather than secular literature, given Colet's opinions concerning classical and pagan authors.[142] His conversation therefore seems to have lacked variety. Yet his written work demonstrates the reason for his views on the subjects acceptable for Christian conversation. If one conversed only of Christ, then one could avoid the pitfalls of heresy and falsehood, for 'What is so deadly as sects and heresy?'[143] The Christian's duty was to concentrate on the spiritual life; therefore, one's talk should be of spiritual, rather than earthly, things: 'For in Christ a man must cease to be whatever he is, and must yield to the Spirit of God, and must live, not according to the flesh i.e., in man's way, but according to the Spirit.'[144] Just as Colet ordered his own life so as to avoid evil conversation, so he encouraged the minor clergy, in his 1506 proposals, to be of good conversation.

Colet's fourth concern was the upholding of Christian moral values. When he spoke of morality, he did not mean the morality of human law and reason; he meant God's law. For Colet, there was a huge chasm between the two:

> But as for the Civil Laws of the old, corrupt man, they have nothing to do with the healthy state of Christians. Human reason is the enemy and opponent of grace. If men establish a law of their own, they are not subject to the law of God.[145]

Thus, Colet expressed his distaste for the scholastic use of reason.[146] Just as he believed that reading the wrong books could inhibit the working of divine grace in a Christian soul, so he believed that human intellect could be a barrier to grace.[147] Therefore, he was doctrinally motivated to facilitate the work of God's grace in the Church, by advocating God's law over human law. In fact, for Colet, 'All laws may be reduced to these three – the law of corrupt nature; the law of God which recalls us to Christ; and the law of God which makes perfect in Christ.'[148] Colet urged his clergy to follow the latter path and obey God's moral code, as embodied in canon law. Because Canon law was inspired directly by God, it was superior to those laws created solely by human reason.[149] In his Convocation sermon, he advocated a return to the 'old laws';[150] likewise in 1506, he advised adherence to a higher moral code than human reason would allow.

On a practical level, Colet's fifth concern was correct behaviour during services. On the basis of his ecclesiological understanding of his role at St. Paul's, and that of his junior colleagues, it is not surprising that he expected the highest standards during the offices. The disciplines of learning, of avoiding error, of engaging in holy conversation, and of leading an honest and Godly life were the grounding for the clergy's performance of the *Opus Dei* at St. Paul's, for there was nothing more sacred, except for priesthood itself, than the unifying sacrament of the Mass:

> In the blessed cup and the broken bread is saving communication of the true body and blood itself of Jesus Christ, shared by many that in it they may be one.[151]

Whatever role each played in the office, perfection was required in this awesome task, which could bring unity with each other and with God. Colet attempted to impress upon his clergy the greatness of the trust that had been committed to them.

In examining Colet's five concerns of 1506, it has been possible to link each one with his ecclesiology. On the subjects of learning, correctness, conversation, morality and diligence during services, Colet led by example. His strict behavioural codes were also projected onto his cathedral colleagues. As we shall see in the next section, this was not a welcome approach.

Colet's Unpopularity

At the beginning of his 1506 manuscript, Colet expressed a concern that the minor clergy were ignorant of their statutes. The question of why this might have been has several possible answers: either they couldn't care less about them; couldn't find them; didn't know about them; or did care and know about them, but were unable to get their hands on them due to difficulty of access, or perhaps lack of sufficient copies. Whatever the case, I argue that it was Colet's prime objective in 1506 to remedy this ignorance by making the existing statutes, and his new injunctions, known to the minor clergy. If at least one of the dean's *libelli* was manufactured, then it can be conjectured that his proposals achieved at least partial success. However, the production of little books would not imply success in the restoration of the allegedly decayed discipline. In allowing Erasmus's statements concerning Colet's success in reviving the decayed discipline of the cathedral clergy to be included as evidence, we must take account of his tendency towards exaggeration.[152] Furthermore, it should be noticed that Erasmus was casting his mind back sixteen years to Colet's arrival as dean, and his memory may not have been entirely reliable. I suggest, in this section, that Colet *attempted* to impose discipline upon the cathedral body. It can reasonably be conjectured that his reform efforts were thwarted due to his unpopularity. In order to assess this conjecture, it will be helpful to analyse Colet's reputation, and to explain the reason for his unpopularity. I argue, in this section, that he was not highly respected due to his withdrawal of decanal hospitality.

Colet's antagonistic and unusual withdrawal of traditional decanal hospitality resulted in a tangible loss for the minor clergy. As Kleineke and Hovland explain:

> By the end of the fifteenth century, the splendid hospitality on offer at the dean's table was widely renowned, but within a few years the tradition was discontinued by the more austere John Colet.[153]

In the economic circumstances of the early sixteenth century, the minor clergy were not rich and would have been much affected by this withdrawal of their traditional rights. There was an inequality in the Church between those who were very wealthy and those with almost nothing.[154] Although the Church owned a huge amount of land, a small minority of clergy owned the bulk of the wealth; inequality of distribution was more pronounced in the Church than in the secular world.[155] Not only was Colet one of the minority of wealthy, he was very rich indeed.[156] His inherited fortune was large enough to found a school, in contrast to those with less than £5 in assets, who made up eighty per cent of London's clergy. Only the top five per cent of all English testators had over £100, and only forty-five London testators had over a thousand.[157] Those minor clergy with reasonable incomes spent about half their money on food. For instance, two chantry priests at Bridport, Dorset, had a yearly income of below £20 in the 1450s; more than £10 of this was spent on food.[158] Smaller households and colleges spent most on ale, wheat (for bread) and oats (for pottage).[159] However, urban living brought an extra cost due to a lack of self-sufficiency. They could not produce any crops and therefore had to buy them. Due to the decline of land revenues towards the end of the fifteenth century, the income of the minor clergy was limited to stipends alone.[160] Although funding for new chantry foundations and the payments of small sums in oblations increased chaplains' incomes, these payments were controlled by the dean and chapter and often were of little help to a minor canon or vicar-choral.[161] It was, therefore, essential for survival that minor clergy were offered hospitality on a regular basis. For instance, at Exeter, in 1508-9, Bishop Hugh Oldham allowed provision of regular common meals in college. Moreover, each canon was assigned a secondary (poor clerk) and chorister and gave them meals and hospitality. Furthermore, in 1511, Oldham officially recognized the rights of secondaries to engage in study. He ordered that they should be excused choral duties in order to attend the song school or the city high school.[162] Consequently, many minor clergy rose to higher positions. Hospitality provided financial support for the poorer members of the Church and was a basic function of all medieval households, however humble.[163] For instance, the two priests of Munden's chantry in Bridport, Dorset, who had only one servant, gave hospitality to between two and six guests a week from 1454 to 1457.[164] Hospitality followed an Old Testament and apostolic tradition and was, therefore, a mandatory duty for the clergy.[165] At Exeter, in 1448, the residentiary canons provided 'good cheer and right welcome, good welfare, and great feasts.'[166] At Salisbury, choristers dined at the canons' tables throughout Christmas. Hospitality was well regulated and the failure of a residentiary canon or dean to keep hospitality would be exposed through episcopal visitations and chapter meetings.[167] Hospitality amongst secular clergy was different to that of regular, or monastic, communities, which generally gave food and shelter to strangers and the local poor. Within secular cathedrals, it was traditional to offer hospitality to one's own staff or flock, like in a great lay household.[168] At the head of these ecclesiastical households were the deans and bishops. In the 1480s, Dean Worsley of St. Paul's often spent £40 a year on food for his household; sometimes the figure was £60.[169] This was a large sum compared to late fifteenth-century lay households, where an esquire was expected to spend around £24 a year on food and fuel.[170] Colet seems to have been motivated by principle instead of perceiving the reality around him and acting upon it. Erasmus tells us that Colet ate parsimoniously himself:

> ... he would partake sparingly of one dish only and be satisfied with a single draught or two of ale. He was abstemious in respect of wine, appreciating it if choice, but most temperate in the use of it.[171]

Colet's changes began from his own table, as he 'brought the traditional hospitality of the deanery within more decorous limits'.[172] Erasmus was, on the one hand, proud of Colet's asceticism, relating that 'The dean's table, which in former days had ministered to luxury under the guise of hospitality, he brought within the bonds of moderation'.[173] On the other hand, Erasmus was not always an admirer of Colet's ways. For instance, when he had been a guest himself, he found the hospitality wanting:

> Again, towards the end of the meal, when the requirements of nature, at any rate, if not pleasure had been satisfied, he started some other topic; and thus bade farewell to his guests, refreshed in mind as well as in body and better men at leaving than they came, though with no overloaded stomachs.[174]

Although it is not known exactly when Colet began to withdraw these privileges, it appears that he was consistent in his austerity, even though the St. Paul's cathedral chapter, and minor clergy, were used to being offered hospitality as a Christian duty. Dean Worsley's accounts from 1479/80-1496/7 show an annual income of £300-£800.[175] Wealth was not unknown in the deanery, but it was expected that those with the means to do so should offer hospitality, as Worsley did.[176] In contrast, Erasmus tells us that Colet's fortune was spent on charity: 'His private fortune, a very large one, he would himself dispose of for charitable purposes.'[177] His attitude to the company of society was to reject it. According to Erasmus,

> ... he kept away, as a rule, from laymen's society, and especially from banquets. If forced at times to attend them, he would take me or some similar companion with him in order, by talking Latin, to avoid worldly conversation.[178]

This attitude contrasted with that of contemporaneous deans and canons. The households of other cathedral canons were run on a huge scale seemingly inconceivable to his ideal of Christian living. At Lincoln, canon William Skelton (d.1501) had nine servants; Archdeacon Smith (d.1528) had twenty-two; and Martin Collins, treasurer of York in 1509, had twenty-six.[179] At Exeter in 1522, the ten residentiary canons had between four and ten servants each, a total of sixty-six. Like secular lords, canons issued liveries to their servants according to their rank. Dean Worsley provided robes of russet and mixed colours of 'fyne scarlet', with violet robes distributed for the Christmas of 1480. He clothed his St. Paul's retinue in black for the funeral of Edward IV in 1483.[180] In contrast, Erasmus tells us that Colet wore only black; moreover, the 1506 document states that Colet ordered the minor clergy to wear only black.[181]

Colet's failure to offer hospitality could not have gone unnoticed at chapter meetings and was certainly noticed by Bishop Fitzjames, who accused the dean of not fulfilling his duties of hospitality:[182] Fitzjames alleged that Colet's interpretation of the scriptural passage concerning Jesus's command to 'feed my sheep' was incorrect.[183] The traditional medieval interpretation was that it was a command to give food and drink to the poor, travellers and fellow men. Colet's interpretation, however, was that it referred to spiritual food, which he delivered in the form of sermons. Erasmus tells us that Fitzjames concluded

> ... that he [Colet] had done away with the hospitality commended by St. Paul, seeing that in expounding the passage from the Gospel with its thrice repeated 'feed my sheep', while he was in accordance with other expositors on the first two heads (feed by example of life; feed by the word of doctrine), he had disagreed with them on the third, saying that it was not meet that the Apostles,

poor as they then were, should be bidden to feed their sheep in the way of any temporal support; and he had substituted some other interpretation in lieu of it.[184]

The bishop believed this to be an invalid interpretation and implied that it was an excuse for Colet's meanness. Erasmus relates that the chapter lost patience with Colet's ascetic views:

> Colet was no great favourite either with many of his own college, being too strict about canonical discipline; and these were every now and then complaining of being treated as monks ...[185]

Colet's frugality, which he impressed upon the cathedral clergy, was, no doubt, an unpopular move by the dean.

Circumstantial evidence suggests that Colet's attempted reforms of 1506 may have resulted in the production of one small book of statutes and injunctions for the minor clergy's use. It would not be surprising, however, if this was the limit of his success at this stage. Given his lack of administrative experience, and his ungenerous withdrawal of decanal hospitality, it is hard to imagine that the cathedral clergy were enthusiastic to implement Colet's ascetical and purist ecclesiological ideals.

Conclusion

The events of 1506 show how little Colet understood ecclesiastical life in practice. His proposed statutes and injunctions would have made little sense to the clergy, not because they were radical, but because he did not understand the Church he was trying to improve. His ideal of unity moving towards perfection was to disappoint him. The early sixteenth-century Church was a healthy, vibrant, exciting and expanding organization devoted to performing the *Opus Dei*. As long as the dean's attempts were based purely on an ideal, however laudable, they could never have been understood, and probably never were.

Colet's idealism, as has been argued, was the primary motivation for his attempted reforms and, along with his attitude towards hospitality and manner of appointment, would have been reason for the St. Paul's minor clergy to suspect his reforms. He possessed a fervently idealistic vision, but had little experience of how to implement it. He was unfamiliar with ecclesiastical affairs and had, therefore, a misguided sense of how to practise reform. He had been presented with a succession of benefices from an early age, but in reality was resident at none of them, except St. Paul's.[186] Therefore, with little practical knowledge of the Church, Colet came to a busy cathedral, at the heart of a busy city, with the largest group of minor clergy of any cathedral, possessing virtually no relevant experience. As Lupton put it:

> He came, obviously against the goodwill of the bishop, simply as the nominee of Henry VII. To the Chapter he would be known as an Oxford theologian imbued with the new learning [sic].[187]

Colet's attitude is typical of his hierarchical ecclesiology. By rigid discipline, withdrawal of hospitality and the assertion of his own authority, he attempted to bring the cathedral to order, and therefore beautiful perfection, by means of obedience and unity.

I have argued that cathedral clergy were scrutinized more frequently than parish clergy and that statute reform had been widespread in the late fourteenth century: at St. Paul's, Baldock, Braybroke and Lisieux were key figures.[188] In the mid-fifteenth century, clerical numbers boomed and there was an increase in lay endowments and masses for the dead.[189] Bishops were well educated: ninety-one per cent went to either Oxford or Cambridge, and many had doctorates, though not necessarily in theology.[190] Furthermore, bishops founded nine Oxbridge colleges between 1350 and 1525.[191] Minor clergy, however, did not have the financial and educational advantages of Colet and the bishops. On the whole, they had low incomes and simple educations as choristers and vicars-choral, some becoming chantry priests or minor canons. Their existence involved the execution of cathedral duties, the struggle for income, and the competition for promotion, which resulted in high musical and liturgical standards.

As the quotation at the beginning of this chapter suggested, Colet arrived at St. Paul's with the ecclesiological assumption that 'disciples should obey their teachers' and 'should comply with them forthwith and altogether without dispute'.[192] If he considered himself to be the teacher, and the minor clergy to be the disciples, then his assumption appears to have been misplaced: his first attempt to implement his hierarchical ecclesiology had failed. Had Colet been more aware of minor clerical poverty and diligence, his attitude may have been more like that of Thomas Heywood, the generous, encouraging Dean of Lichfield. Under such leaders, the secular cathedral choirs flourished throughout the fifteenth century. Perhaps if he had lived longer, or nurtured skills of a different nature, he may have been as successful within the Church as he was outside it.

Having considered how Colet's reformist activity related to the relatively small group of minor clergy at St. Paul's, the next chapter explores Colet's influence upon wider London society.

4

LONDON LIFE: THE MERCERS AND ST. PAUL'S SCHOOL

Thus far I have limited my study to Colet's ecclesiastical connections and activities. However, Colet and his family were intimately connected with the heart of London's secular and mercantile life. His greatest contribution to city life was, of course his school. But the dean, as a prominent member of the Mercers' Company, was responsible for reforming other institutions not strictly related to cathedral business, namely, the hospital of St. Thomas of Acre and the Guild of the Holy Name of Jesus, both of which became the object of Colet's attention before the foundation of his school.

This chapter examines Colet's reforming activities outside the confines of the cathedral and ecclesiastical politics and discovers a likeable and dynamic London citizen who was adept at organizing the great and the good in order to achieve precisely the result he wanted. In short, he made things happen, which is perhaps in contrast to his decanal dealings. I shall first discuss Colet's credentials as a mercer and Londoner of note followed by an assessment of his re-foundation of the Guild of Jesus, which was substantially the preserve of the mercers. This will be followed by an examination of Colet's involvement in reforming St. Thomas's Hospital, situated adjacent to the company buildings, which activity was the forerunner of his re-foundation of St. Paul's School. An investigation into the state of the pre-existent school will lead to a description of Colet's new school foundation, its curriculum, statutes and significance.

Colet the Mercer

Colet's roots in the Mercers' Company were established by his father, Henry, and much data concerning his family's mercantile history is found in the *Acts of Court* of the Mercers' Company and in Anne Sutton's excellent history of the mercery from the twelfth to the sixteenth centuries.[1] Henry's significant activity at the mercery included licensing, in 1480, the wardens of the company (and their wives) to have private altars erected where they and their families may receive the holy sacrament. Henry was master at the time (1479-80).[2] As I have mentioned, Henry was twice mayor, from 1486-7 and 1495-96, and his son John was lucky to have been the only child of Henry and Christian to survive from their twenty or so progeny.[3] As master, alderman and mayor, Henry kept a tight rein on the mercers' business dealings, in 1479 making decrees concerning the late payment of bills;[4] in 1485 being involved in the discipline of a mercer for buying goods contrary to the company's ordinances; and, in 1487, forbidding freemen of London to send goods to provincial markets and fairs for seven years.[5] He expanded his business connections in Buckinghamshire, his place of origin, and Essex, buying stalls and other property in Colchester in 1485.[6] Nevertheless, Henry's wealth was founded upon and enhanced by overseas trade, which has been well established in the company in the 1430s.[7] Henry's most famous and significant contribution as Mayor was his personal guarantee in the *Magnus Intercursus* treaty of 1495, allowing dealings with the low countries to continue, which marked an important moment in his relationship with King Henry VII and, as has been mentioned elsewhere in this book, eventually had significance for John Colet's career.[8]

The Mercers' Company had been dominated by the Colet family for the last two decades of the fifteenth century and it is not surprising therefore that the return of Henry Colet's only surviving son to London was a significant one for the company and an event that was to deeply effect them for the first two decades of the sixteenth century. John was admitted into the company in 1508 and from 1510 was looking forward to the possibility of a new school.[9] However, before he was even formally admitted to the company, the dean was forging links between the mercers and the cathedral by means of the re-foundation of the Guild of Jesus, which I shall consider now.

The Guild of Jesus

The Guild of the Holy Name of Jesus, of Colet's time, met in the crypt of St. Paul's Cathedral, although it is not certain that it originally met there. Membership not only provided regular private liturgy and annual ceremonies but also guaranteed that one's soul would be prayed for after death, which was in fact its main *raison d'etre*.[10] As the name suggests, there was a heavy stress placed upon the name and character of Jesus, which was celebrated as a particular feast on 7 August annually from 1488-9 onwards. In fact it was not uncommon for confraternities to devote themselves in this way: another example is the Jesus chantry established in Manchester's collegiate church in the early sixteenth-century.[11] The Brigittine monastery at Syon, and the highly influential benefactor, Lady Margaret Beaufort, were supporters of the London fraternity.[12]

That the Mercers' Company were a significant element in the guild is beyond doubt. The fraternity was wealthy from those who left bequests. Naturally, the more one bequeathed the more prayers one bought for the departed soul. Records show at least twenty bequests from the Company between 1513 and 1535, although evidence of mercer bequests goes back as early as 1455.[13] As Sutton relates, the two earliest known bequests made to the guild were from Thomas Batail, and his widow Joan, of forty shillings and twenty shillings respectively for the years 1455 and 1457.[14] Indeed, it appears that the fraternity was in good shape at the middle of the fifteenth century, receiving letters patent from Henry VI in 1459 and a grant of land in 1471. Mercer officials, such as Nicholas Lathell, Clerk of the Pipe and later a Baron of the Exchequer, were involved in these transactions, thus demonstrating further connections between the guild and the Mercers' Company from an early date.[15]

Why the guild needed to be re-founded, and what had happened to it by the beginning of the sixteenth century is not clear. There is some evidence of accounting irregularities and a drop in liturgical standards.[16] Whatever the reason, it was in 1507 that Colet put new life into the organization by re-founding and re-energizing it, automatically becoming its rector. It was his first successful reforming act as dean, his attempted discipline of the cathedral's minor clergy, in 1506, having been a failure. William Brownwell (mercer – of course) was one of the first two wardens in Colet's revived fraternity. Other mercer wardens were to follow: Thomas Hynd (1520-22) and William Botry (1520-30).[17] In the very year of Colet's re-foundation two members of the guild were also wardens of the Mercers' Company: Richard Haddon and Benjamin Digby. It is most likely that they too were involved in supporting Colet's reforms. Indeed, Digby was a personal friend to Colet, receiving a silver ewer from the dean in his will.[18] Other connections between mercer recruits to the guild and Colet's family can also be made: Thomas Wyndout (d.1500), for instance, had been Henry Colet's apprentice. Other members included Wyndout's own apprentice, Thomas Baldry, and Richard Haddon, who married Wyndout's widow. These very intimate connections and the seriousness with which the guild was taken within the mercery is demonstrated by the fact that, in 1507, Colet agreed with the mercer wardens (including Baldry) that prayers and masses should be said for the recently deceased mercers Thomas Wyndout and John Stile (d.1507) for a hundred years.[19] The magnitude of the decree reflects not only the size of the two dead men's bequests, but also the prominence of the guild within the life of the Mercers' Company and, perhaps most important of all, the traditional Catholic nature of the religion observed at the beginning of the sixteenth century.[20] The indication is, therefore, that Colet was not alone in his conservative Catholicism.

Sutton suggests that these conservative mercers were not looking for religious change, nor would they recognize it when it came:

> The most difficult to identify in these years are those mercers who quietly endured changes, which they did not comprehend or feared to oppose. The changes were slow, their effect could often not be foreseen, nor how one thing could lead to another: those who rejoiced at the defeat of the clergy over mortuaries or tithes, did not necessarily want the demise of the religious house or the Bible in English.[21]

This passage could be speaking of Colet alone. It was he who led the way in traditional Catholic reform, which required the traditions of medieval religion to be observed in abundance, yet without perceiving what religious change would ultimately mean. Colet did not live long enough to see where his Church was heading; other mercers did.

The guild, like St. Thomas of Acre and St. Paul's School to come, was in the firm grip of the mercery and was controlled by a nucleus of wardens and their assistants. It attracted a 'pious minority' who, though already belonging to other fraternities, were often invited to join.[22] Thus, the membership, the quality of the liturgy and the income were elite. The large income from alms giving, in return of course for prayers and indulgence, was over £200 in 1524-3 and over £400 in 1534-5. The Mercers' Company, successively thirteen wardens and seven masters to be precise, naturally managed this money.[23]

After Colet's time there remained a strong element of religious conservatism within the guild, demonstrated by the reaction of one William Pavier to the Church's potential break with Rome and use of the English Bible. In May of 1533, according to Hall's *Chronicle*, he hanged himself.[24] However, the guild also possessed men of more moderate conservatism, such as Sir John Alen, a favoured mayor of Cromwell, who rode the waves of change until his death in 1545. Orthodox and traditional though most of these mercers and guildsmen were, it is worth noting, as Sutton does, that none of them suffered persecution or death during Thomas More's campaign of 1529-32. Whether they were protected or chameleon-like in their allegiances is not certain. What is clear is that well after Colet's death and into the mid-sixteenth century, the guild that the dean had re-founded was greatly loved, performed a service that wealthy Catholic conservative Londoners required, and was a haven of quality liturgy, including regular prayers, indulgences and masses for the dead.

More importantly, for Colet scholarship, the revival of the guild provides further evidence for the justifiable generalization, made throughout this book, that Colet's reforming activities were more successful when touched by the secular world of the mercers – the guild, St. Thomas's and the school – than when he attempted to restore clerical discipline and high liturgical standards at the cathedral in a purely ecclesiastical environment. Although the first two of these enterprises have now dissolved, the third – St. Paul's School – will shortly be celebrating its 500th anniversary: a fitting tribute to the dean's creativity and idealism.

St. Thomas of Acre

St. Thomas's Hospital was situated adjacent to the Mercers' Hall and, upon Colet's return to London, was in a poor state. The bad running of the hospital may have been the fault of Richard Adams, who was master by 1505 and was dismissed in 1510, by which time the mercers decided that they needed a new hall and chapel. St. Thomas's being down at heal, the mercers sought to take over the establishment, become its patrons, and profit their own company into the bargain. It was John Young, Rector of All Hallows, Honey Lane, who was made Master of St. Thomas's on 15 September 1510. With reformist ideals he disciplined the chaplains of the company and made plans to expel the laity from his church and construct an enclosure for his own brethren. As Sutton puts it: 'There seems little doubt that Young was a man after Colet's own heart.'[25] Only one week after his appointment as master, Young was called to conference with the dean, who had been informed of the inadequacies of the company's existing banqueting hall and chapel. It was agreed that, by levying each man according to his wealth, the chapel could be expanded and further rooms built above.

The purchase of the land was completed in February 1512. Various monetary gifts from merchants contributed to the cost of the new building. Young continued to prosper as Master of St. Thomas's, becoming a Prebendary of St. Paul's in 1511, Suffragan to Bishop Fitzjames in 1513, and Bishop of Gallipoli, in Trace, as well as Archdeacon of London in 1514.

Thus, Young set in motion plans for a new hall and the reform of the hospital by making the Mercers' Company its patrons. In 1510 the hospital had debts amounting to over £718, with its properties in poor repair, and only eight brothers remaining. Young paid off the debt and found over £1400 for repairs over the next eight years. The house was just about solvent when Young presented the accounts to Wolsey and the papal legate, Cardinal Campeggio, on 1 March 1519, the year of Colet's death. By negotiating agreements with the company concerning chantries, loans, and the sale and exchange of land, the mercers were able to build themselves a new hall and chapel on and near their existing site.

It was not until 1524, however, that the plans finally came to fruition and on 26 May 1525 the new chapel was consecrated. The total cost had now amounted to over £2700 and the building reflected the grand price tag: the hall had a battlemented frontage on Cheapside of around one hundred feet, with a central porch, underneath a statue of St. Thomas Becket. Behind this frontage was the vaulted chapel with the hall above, which measured about fifty-four feet by thirty feet. There were other rooms to the west.[26]

As Sutton summarizes, the whole exercise of making the mercers patrons of the Hospital of St. Thomas of Acre foreshadowed Colet's entrusting of his school into the hands of the lay mercers. Both arrangements had the effect of emphasizing the mercers' exceptionally powerful position within London society. Although Colet was not the main protagonist in this episode, he was involved at the inception of the idea and would have watched the progress of reform and rebuilding with interest. This episode no doubt played an important role in shaping his own plans for the governance of his school. Moreover, his presence as dean and mercer no doubt shaped the plans of the Mercer's Company and the dynamic John Young in return.

The Old School

Apart from the choir school, it is certain that a St. Paul's school existed next to the cathedral for many centuries before Colet arrived to be dean. Papal injunctions of the eighth century required every conventual church to have a school adjoining it, and to be under the cathedral's immediate supervision. Furthermore, the eleventh Lateran Council, of 1179, decreed that, 'in every Cathedral Church a master ought to teach poor scholars as has been accustomed'.[27] Thus, there had been two cathedral schools at St. Paul's in existence for centuries. Not only the choir school, or singing school, located in the church of St. Gregory adjacent to the cathedral, but also the Grammar School, apparently located near the cathedral in Sharmovres Lane.[28]

The earliest extant reference to St. Paul's School is found in a charter by which Richard de Belmais or Baumes, Bishop of London c.1112, granted to Canon Hugh the schoolmaster, a habitation in a bell-tower, where he was also to look after the cathedral library. Around 1120, the schoolmasters' job passed on to a Canon Henry, with the additional grant of a meadow in Fulham, along with tithes of Ealing and Madeley. The status of St. Paul's School was high at this time, judging by the mandate issued by Henry of Blois, Bishop of Winchester acting as ordinary of London in 1137, that no one be allowed to teach in London without a licence from Canon Henry, Master of St. Paul's School.[29] Thus, the St. Paul's schoolmaster gained the title; '*Magister scholarum in tota civitate London*', whereas in other cathedrals the *Magister scholarum* was invariably the Chancellor of the cathedral. The first Chancellor of St. Paul's to be the *Magister scholarum* was Johanne de Cantuar in the early thirteenth century. Dugdale's edition of the cathedral statutes states:

> The Chancellor is head over the learning, not only of the Church, but also of the whole city. All grammar masters are under his authority. He sets over Paul's School a suitable master, after first presenting him to the Dean and Chapter, and he repairs the buildings of that school at his own expense.[30]

In 1308, Dean Ralph de Baldock confirmed the tithes of Ealing, granted nearly two hundred years earlier, on condition that the chancellor should himself, or a deputy, provide lectures in divinity. The school is mentioned again in records of 1393, when the Archbishop of Canterbury, the Bishop of London, the Dean of St. Martin le Grand and the Chancellor of St. Paul's made a petition to the king in parliament to stop the spread of fraudulent grammar schools. Other schools sprang up, however: there was a grammar master at St. Michael's Cornhill around 1420; Eton was established by Henry VI in 1440; and St. Anthony's School, in Threadneedle Street, was founded under royal auspices in 1442. It was possibly attended by Colet himself.[31] Nevertheless, in 1447, the Archbishop of Canturbury and Bishop of London again found it necessary to complain that 'many and divers persons not adequately learned in the art of grammar have presumed to keep common grammar schools in the city, thereby wickedly defrauding some boys and their friends who maintain them at school.' Thus they decreed:

> There shall be five grammar schools and no more in the said city, namely on in St. Paul's Churchyard, another in the Church of St. Mary le Grand, a third in the Church of Blessed Mary in the Arches, a fourth in the Church of St. Dunstan's in the East, and a fifth in St. Anthony's Hospital.[32]

Nevertheless, four more grammar schools appeared, namely, in the parishes of All Hallows the Greater, St. Andrew's Holborn, St. Peter's Cornhill, and St. Mary Colechurch.

In the fifteenth century, a *Magister scholarum* of St. Paul's grammar school, James Garnon, obtained a licence to become Master in Grammar at Oxford in 1449. Another mention of St. Paul's school occurs in Hall's *Chronicle* that a schoolmaster of St. Paul's was present at the proclamation of Richard III concerning the death of Lord Hastings in 1483.[33]

Thus, the existence of St. Paul's school's at the end of the fifteenth century is beyond reasonable doubt. Yet the question of what state the school was in upon Colet's arrival at St. Paul's as dean, and why he found it necessary to reconstitute the establishment, is one that has vexed scholars over the years. This can be demonstrated by this passage from McDonnell's 1954 *Annals of St. Paul's School*:

... it should be noted here that the very limited amount of information which has survived respecting the Cathedral Grammar School in the last three-quarters of a century preceding Dean Colet's re-foundation of the School in 1509, clearly shows that the Dean was fully justified, in his petition to the Pope in 1512 ... in referring to the fact that the old Cathedral Grammar School was '*Scola nullius plane momenti*', a school manifestly of no importance, and that Leach's attempt to convict Colet of denigrating the old school in order to gain greater credit for his new foundation is based on no substance whatsoever.[34]

It is to this question of what Colet was trying to achieve and why that we now turn.

Colet's Motivation

Lupton implied that Colet's school was new in every respect, although acknowledging that a school had been attached to St. Paul's cathedral before Colet came along.[35] However, Arthur Leach and Sir Michael McDonnell both argued that Colet's school superseded the existing grammar school on a larger scale, Leach arguing that the pre-Colet school was a good one, but McDonnell claiming that it was not so. Gleason asserts that the upshot of this debate is that Colet was correct in his 1512 assertion to Pope Julius II that 'the previously existing cathedral grammar school was 'manifestly of no importance' (*nullius plane momenti*)'.[36] However, one would expect Colet to argue such as case, as he was petitioning the Pope for permission that the school could be administered by the Mercer's Company, whilst the cathedral chancellor retain legal authority. Thus, the old school was re-founded by Colet, or rather, it was absorbed into the new one. The song school for the education of the choristers continued to operate as a separate institution, as it does today.[37]

Colet was not known for being over-generous with money. He lived a frugal life and encouraged others, even his close friends, to do so too, as Erasmus attested. However, Colet was the only surviving child of a very wealthy man and was to inherit a great fortune. John's brother, Richard, had died around 1503-5, when their father, Henry was in his seventies.[38] The Dean was therefore left with a moral dilemma: he despised worldly things and yet, at some point during his tenure as dean, would become the possessor of much money, gained from the all-too worldly trading activities of his father, whose social position and manoeuvring with King Henry VII had facilitated Colet's move to the deanery of St. Paul's. Perhaps aware of this debt to his father and the advantages of his London background, Colet decided to re-found the school next to St. Paul's in London.

However, the idea did not come out of the blue, for Colet was not the first humanist cleric, or guild person, to attempt such a foundation: others had done so in other cities, such as Stockport Grammar School, founded by Sir Edmund Shaw in 1487-8 and the Cromer Grammar School founded by Sir Bartholomew Read in 1503.[39] Indeed, Manchester Grammar School was founded by Colet's own Bishop (of London), Richard Fitzjames.

Neither was it uncommon for new grammar schools, established in the early sixteenth century, to be placed into the hands of livery companies or laity: Stephen Jenyngs foundation at Wolverhampton (c.1512) was under the control of the Merchant Taylor's Company, and the school at Bridgenorth (Salop), founded in 1503, was put into the hands of the local court of Burgesses. 'Such activity', remarks Kenneth Charlton, 'untouched by the chantry legislation, was continued after the Reformation.'[40] For instance, Andrew Judd, Skinner, founded a school at Tonbridge in 1553; Lawrence Sherrif, Grocer, established one at Rugby in 1567 and Peter Blundell, wool merchant, one at Tiveton in 1599. The age of entry for these schools was usually six or seven.[41]

However, Colet was not simply jumping on a bandwagon. He had genuine experience with young people as a teacher, such as his work on Romans for a boy named Edmund, and the 'poore studentes and especially to suche as hath bene scholars with me', to whom he left books in his will.[42] One such pupil was almost certainly Thomas Lupset, who can be identified as the 'Gaspar' of Erasmus's colloquy '*Pia confabulatio*'.[43] Gaspar was apparently grateful to his old religious teacher (Colet). Lupset was trained by Colet not to show too much affection for his pupils, but in a treatise written late in his life, Lupset revealed to one of his own pupils, Edmond Withipole, what he thought of Colet as a teacher: 'Longe I haue ben taught, that the mayster neuer hurtethe his scholar more, than whan he uttereth and shewethe by cheryshyng and cokerynge, the loue that he bearethe to his scholars.'[44] Too much affection would, in the eyes of the teacher, spoil the pupil, a sentiment consistent with Colet's character.

For Colet, moral education was paramount; he preached it to his congregations, he used it as the basis for his administration of the cathedral, and he built his school upon the ideal that he could create generations of morally upright pupils from his London base. What Colet had learned in Italy and Oxford concerning the need for humanity's purity and struggle towards perfection was to drive Colet on to an evangelical effort to encourage as much moral and religious piety in young people as he could. He would do so by the same ascetic and rigorous method as he attempted to employ at the cathedral, emphasizing discipline, routine, and very hard work, being careful to avoid all worldly things. Colet's hierarchical view of the universe applied to both ecclesiastical and educational institutions. As the pupils were more subservient, impressionable and malleable than the obstinate clergy, Colet was to achieve much more success at the school than he did within the Church. It is to Colet's new establishment that we now turn.

The New School

Henry Colet died on 1 October 1505, leaving John to consider how best to begin his school-building project. Colet's immediate instinct was to involve the Mercers' Company in the preliminary work, rightly supposing that their support for the school would mean significant financial gain for the project. By 1508, a large schoolhouse of stone had been erected in St. Paul's Churchyard, to the east of the old cathedral building. In 1509, the Mercers' Company, by way of a real estate endowment, offered financial support.[45] The pre-existing grammar school was still evident in 1509, attested to by an indenture, dated 1 July (I Henry VIII) 1509, in which Colet and mercers agreed to grant one William Gerge, his heirs and assigns, a manor in Hertfordshire on condition that Gerge and his heirs should pay the company £8 a year for the use of the school.[46]

The paperwork for the official foundation of the school was sorted out speedily in 1510: on 9 April 1510, Colet formally notified the company of his intention to found the school. This date marks the first mention of the school in the *Acts of Court* of the Mercers' Company and it is interesting to note that Colet's reforms were again being supported by his mercer friends who belonged to the Guild of the Holy Name of Jesus, in this case Master Thomas Baldry. The account reads:

> ... it was shewed by Maister Thomas Baldry, mercer, that Maister Doctour Colet, Dean of Poules, had desired hym to shewe unto the Compeny that he is disposed for the foundacion of his scole to mortise certen londes whiche he wold that this Compeny shulde have if they wolde be bounde to maynteyn the said scole accordyng to the foundacion aforesaid, and after longe Communicacion had amonge theym, it was agreed that Maister Thomas Saymer, oon of the Wardens and the saide Maister Thomas Baldry shall have Communicacion with the said Maister Deanein the said mater. And as thei shall se theryn to bring reporte again to the Co[m[peny of assistens.[47]

Only three days later the *Acts of Court* attest that communication had indeed taken place:

> Maister Thomas Saymer, oon of the Wardens, shewed that he and Thomas Baldry had ben with Maister Dean of Poules, according as it was agreed at the last Courte of Assistens, and had felde parte of his mynde for the foundacion

of his scole in Poules Church Yarde, whereof he purposeth to make oure Compeny conseruatours and Rulers ...[48]

On the 16 April, Colet submitted a list of lands in three counties whose revenues were to be allocated for the support of the school, compensating the company by donating some London land to them. The company accepted this proposal the following day, becoming trustees.[49]

The master's house, a timber-framed structure, was built sometime between 17 August 1510 and before 28 March 1511.[50] On 21 July 1511, Colet conveyed some 2000 acres of land in Buckinghamshire to the Mercers' Company for the support of the School:

... the said Maister Wardens shewde unto the Compeny that Maister deane of Poules wolde gyfe us possession in suche londes as he hath mortised in Buckynghamshire for the foundacion of the scole in Poules Churche yerde ...[51]

On 6 September 1511, the Dean and Chapter of St. Paul's Cathedral conveyed a small piece of land on the east side of the cathedral so that the boys could relieve themselves. The rent was one red rose every ninety years![52] On 4 November of the same year, further London lands and tenements were transferred to the mercers.[53]

Thus, the school began to function as such towards the end of 1511. The mercers described the school as being 'new' on 30 March 1512, so it could not have been in use for long at this point.[54] Furthermore, Colet proposed the articles of governance on 15 June 1512.[55] On 16 April 1513, Colet obtained a licence 'to found a perpetual chantry for one chaplain in the chapel of St. Mary and St. John on the south side of the school in the cemetery of the church of St. Paul, to be called the chantry of St. Mary.'[56] In June 1514 Colet executed a second will in which he left to the mercers, in addition to lands and houses already granted, some tenements in Old Change, London, and the whole school, 'and in which', wrote the dean 'at present I am solely seized in my demesne as of fee.'[57] The full list of London property bequeathed by Colet was as follows:

1. A messuage, with shops, cellars, and appurtenances, in Sopar-lane; and two tenements appertaining to the parish churches of St. Mary Colechurch and St. Mary-le-Bow. 2. Two messuages in the parish of St. Magnus, London-bridge. 3. His grammar-school and chapel founded with the same, and the master's house in St. Paul's church-yard. 4. His grammar-house, lately called *Paules School*, and four shops under it. 5. Two messuages in the Old Change, London.

6. And six tenements in the parish of St. George, Pudding-lane, Billingsgate: all for continuing the same school.[58]

On 8 August 1516, Colet executed a deed by which he granted to the Mercers' Company property in the eastern counties

> ... for the sustenation of one perpetual chantry, of one chaplain to celebrate divine worship in a certain chapel of the blessed Virgin Mary and of St. John the Evangelist, near the school at the southern part of the said school in the churchyard of the said cathedral, by the said John Colet then newly founded and built.[59]

Colet showed no intention of trusting the administration of his school to anyone other than the laity of the Mercers' Company. As we have seen, there was precedent for lay trustees at other schools, going back at least to the beginning of the fifteenth century.[60] The mercers themselves had run the college of Robert Whittington, former master of the company, since 1421, as well as the school at Faryngho (or Farthingoe) since 1443.[61]

There are several reasons why Colet may have preferred laity, rather than clergy, to take charge of his school. Firstly, Colet apparently found less corruption in 'married men of established reputation' than in clerics.[62] This fact must have caused Colet a great deal of sadness considering his lifelong ambition for clerical perfection. Secondly, Colet was himself a long-standing mercer who would have felt comfortable entrusting the precious pupils and financial matters to those whom he knew personally to be of good moral standing. He would have had ample opportunity to evaluate the trustworthiness of the mercers in dealing with statutes, for instance.[63] Thirdly, Gleason argues that Colet foresaw the coming ecclesiastical, economical and political changes of the Reformation, such as the suppressing of monasteries and chantries, and that a school controlled by laity would give no pretext for a takeover by Wolsey and the king, or the sequestering of its funds.[64] This argument flatters Colet as being gifted with the most amazing foresight and political insight. I would prefer to argue that, at this stage, Colet was rather politically naïve, making it hard to go along with Gleason. The fact that Colet's school survived the Chantries Act of 1547, when other ecclesiastically controlled schools did not, is probably more a matter of good fortune than fortune telling.

Although the mercers were officially responsible for the school, Colet held a tight grip on its affairs. He personally selected the first highmaster, William Lily, who was already known to Colet as the Godson of the Oxford scholar William Grocyn. Lily was educated at Magdalen College, Oxford from 1486. After graduation, he went on pilgrimage to Jerusalem, returning via Rhodes and Italy, where he perfected his knowledge of classical languages and authors.[65] Lily's pay at St. Paul's School was extremely high for the time, at over £20 per annum.[66] Lily appointed his son-in-law, John Ritwise, as surmaster, thus qualifying him, under the terms of Colet's own school statutes, to succeed Lily as highmaster in due course. According to McDonnell, Colet apparently selected and paid for the chaplain.[67] Colet also kept a close eye on the administration of the trust, insisting upon a separate account for the trust from all the other Mercers' Company business.[68] The dean presented his school statutes to the company on 15 June 1512 and sneakily, on the same day, introduced his agent, William Newbold, who was to oversee the proper administration of the trust.[69] The master and four other wardens of the company ran the trust from then on, with Newbold becoming an accepted member of the company and secretary from 1 February 1521/2, after Colet's death.[70]

According to Lupton's research, the Mercers' Company found themselves in debt to the school in the latter part of the eighteenth century. Beginning around 1713 the mercers had borrowed money from the school in order to meet the costs of rebuilding the Royal Exchange, amongst other projects. A report of 1820 demonstrates that, in 1713-4, the company owed the school £13, 571, 7s. 4 ½ d. Furthermore, in 1745, there was a debt to the school estate of £34, 637, 15s. The situation was remedied by an investment of £5000 in 1808 and annual payments of £1000 from 1814 onwards until the entire some was repaid.[71] Before Lupton's time as surmaster of the school, not only had the debt been repaid but lavish new buildings had been erected in Hammersmith, West London.

Curriculum

In 1518 Colet wrote:

> ... I will the Chyldren lerne ffirst aboue all the Catechyzon in Englysh and after the accidence which I made to sum other yf eny be better to the purpose to induce children more spedely to beten speech And thanne Institutum Christini hominess which that lernyd Erasmus made at my request and the boke called Copia of the same Erasmus And thenne other auctours Christian as lactantius prudencius & proba and sedulis and Juuencus and Baptista Mantuanus and suche other as shalbe tought conveyent and moste to purpose vnto the true letan spech, all barbary all corupcion all laten adulterate which ignorant blynde folis brought into this worlde and with the same hath distayned and poysenyd the old laten speech and the varay Romayne tong which in the tyme of Tully and Salust and Virgil and Terence was vsid which also seint Jerome and seint Ambrose and seint Austen and many hooly doctors

lernyd in thyr tymes, I say that fylthynesse and all such abusyon which later blynde worlde brought in which more ratyr may be called blotterature thenne literature I vtterly abbanysh and Exclude oute of this scole.[72]

This extended quotation from Colet's school statutes highlights not only the vehemence of his passion for the learning of good Christian and classical literature, but also the contradictory nature of his ordinance. As McDonnell observed, of the six authors mentioned, not one belonged to the period of classical Latin.[73] Nevertheless, the fact that Colet placed the running of his school into secular hands did not indicate that the education was to be secular as well. The inscription on the façade of the building read '*Schola Catechizationis Puerorum in Christi Opt. Max. Fide et Bonis Literis*' ('School for the Instruction of Boys in the Faith of Christ Best and Greatest, and in Good Literature').[74] Although the 'good literature' was not confined to Christian writers, the Christian basis for the school was symbolized by the number of boys to be educated there at any one time: exactly 153, taken from the number of fish caught by Simon Peter on the sea of Tiberius after Jesus's resurrection (John 21:11). Colet also arranged the statutes so that the pupils received exactly 153 days of holiday each year.[75] Colet no doubt saw his pupils as being drawn out of the murky darkness into the light of Christ by the Gospel, thus there was an evangelical nature to the foundation of the school. There is also a more mystical significance to the number 153, which is explained by Gleason, following Grant:[76] as Augustine pointed out, the number is the sum of every number from one to seventeen added together. If, therefore, one considers seventeen to be the base number of a numerical triangle with the smaller numbers rising above until it reaches the apex of the number one, then this can be taken as a numerical representation of the Trinity, comprising of three sides with the unified 'One' (of Platonic and Neoplatonic philosophy as well as Christianity) at the top.[77]

Whatever the reason for the precise number of boys to educated at any one time, it was a notably larger number of pupils than other schools at the time. For instance, Winchester and Eton possessed seventy scholars each, excluding choristers.[78] It was also decreed in Colet's statutes that the boys should come from every nation, giving the city-centre school a distinctively cosmopolitan outlook.[79] In this respect, Colet's idealism was to the fore, as he put his hope for the future of Church and society in the young. As Erasmus explained, Colet 'finding his own age deplorable in the last degree, fixed on tender youth as the new bottles to which he would entrust the new wine of Christ.'[80] However, Colet was a humanist as well as a pious Christian and, as Gleason rightly points out, a humanist curriculum, which emphasized humanity's greatness in literature, law, music, art and in the very buildings themselves, would have undermined Colet's otherworldly agenda.[81] Thus, Colet moderated the secular aspects of the curriculum, making St. Paul's more Christian in emphasis than the humanist schools at Winchester, Eton and Ipswich (the latter founded by Wolsey).

It was upon the issue of Latin and Greek that Colet's school would differ from its contemporaries.[82] The question, for Colet, was whether the wisdom of classical antiquity was one that could supplement the essential truths of Christian teaching, or whether they were to be ignored in favour of a purely scriptural curriculum. As the inscription on the school's façade indicated, Colet wished to emphasize education in the faith first, with knowledge of good literature second place: 'for my entent is by thys scole specially to incresse knowledge and worshipping of god and oure lorde Crist Jesu and good Cristen lyff and maners in the Children'.[83]

Colet achieved his aim by clearly specifying, in his school statutes, what he meant by good literature: firstly, those works especially commissioned for the school; and secondly, good Christian authors such as Lactantius Prudentius, Proba, Sedulius, Juvencus and Baptista Mantuanus (1448-1516) – the only contemporaneous writer to be included in the list.[84] He commends the Latin of Tully, Salust, Virgil and Terence, as well as the language of Jerome, Augustine and Ambrose. Although the latter authors cannot be considered as classical, being from the fourth century, they were included in Colet's classical list because of their improving Christian content.[85] As Gleason correctly acknowledges, Colet's extreme position made him one of the least adventurous educators of his age, but Colet saw no conflict in his ideals, for ultimately he perceived no equality between the scriptures and any other writings, most of which he considered not to be literature but, as he called them, 'blotterature'.[86]

Colet did not keep control of the school's curriculum for long, however. The dean had only about ten years to live at the time of the school's foundation, and it was not long after his death that modernization took place.[87] With Lily's death in 1522 the remnant of Colet's control was gone. Within fifty years after Colet's death, only one of Colet's recommended Latin authors, Baptista Mantuanus, remained on the curriculum.[88]

Greek appears to have been largely neglected also in this period. Only Erasmus's friend Herman Hamelman is known to have taught Greek at the school, around 1516,[89] and Lily is supposed to have had some knowledge of Greek, although, as Charlton points out:

> ... it is unlikely that anything more than lip service was paid to Greek and Hebrew in the general run of grammar schools ... Lily, the first highmaster, must have been one of the very few Englishmen of his day to have been so qualified.[90]

Even by 1530 Greek was not in the curriculum at Eton, although it was by 1560.[91]

Colet managed to commission some impressive textbooks for the school, especially from Erasmus, who contributed several '*Carmina scholaria*'[92] and 'A Sermon on the Child Jesus', which was to be read out by a boy in the school each year.[93] A larger work offered by Erasmus was his *De duplici copia verborum ac rerum*, completed in 1508, but only published and given to the school in 1512. The book, known simply as *De Copia*, was reprinted in many editions well into the eighteenth century. In it, the pupil is encouraged to undertake to gain an 'abundance of words' ('*copia verborum*'), by means of finding many different ways of expressing the same idea without changing the meaning of the original concept.[94] Once this skill has been mastered, the pupil is then urged to increase the number of ideas he has to express ('*copia rerum*'), as Gleason translated it, an 'abundance of material'.[95] Erasmus shared Colet's ideal of educating impressionable young minds and, in *De Copia*, Erasmus demonstrated his grasp of both classical and Christian literature as well as a more balance approach to both sources than the conservative dean.

As for Latin grammars, Colet commissioned Thomas Linacre to write a simplified version of his existing grammar, entitled *De Emendata Structura Latini Sermonis*, to which Erasmus also contributed by providing illustrations of the grammatical principles, taken from classical writings.[96] Colet's own offering was his '*Catecyzon*'.[97] Colet's catechism included the first twelve tenets of the Apostles Creed, and then an 'Act of Faith' in 'seuen sacraments of the chirche'; then follows paragraphs on 'Acts of Charity' which consist of 'The loue of God, the loue of thyne owne selfe, and the loue of thy neighbour'. The following are also added:

Penaunce: If I fall to synne I shal anon ryse agayne by penaunce and pure confessyon.

Howelinge: As often as I shal receyue my lord insacrament, I shall with al study dispose me to pure clennes & deuocyon.

In Sekenes: When I shal dye I shal call for the sacraments & ryghtes of Christes chirche by tymes, and be confessed & receyue my lorde and redeemer Jesu Chryst.

In Deth: And in peril of deth I shal gladly call to be enealed, and so armed in God I shal departe to hym in truste of his mercy in our lorde Chryst Jesu.[98]

After this come fifty-one 'preceptes of lyuynge', such as 'Beleue & trust in chryst Jesu, Worship hym and his moder Mary'; 'Be alwaye wel occupied' and 'Lerne dylygently'. The '*Simbolum Apostolorum*', '*Oratio Dominica*' and '*Salutatio Angelica*' in Latin follow the preceptes. Erasmus's Latin version of Colet's catechism ('*Institutum Christiani hominis*') became a popular educational tool throughout Europe.[99]

Amongst the other works written for the school Colet's *Aeditio* was an explanation of the eight parts of speech for beginners. This also became a standard text for schools.[100] The dedication of his *Aeditio* to Lily is dated 1 August 1509.[101] The title page reads: '*Ioannis Coleti Theologi, olim Decani diui Pauli, aeditio, una cum quibusdam G. Lilii Grammatices Rudimenta*'.[102] It contains Colet's catechism, a short Latin syntax by Lily, in English, followed by Colet's *Accidence* and finally, Lily's *Carmen de Moribus*.[103] Lily's Latin grammar became the 'Royal Grammar' in 1540-2, entitled 'A Shorte Introduction of Grammar' and was prescribed in royal injunctions by Edward VI (1547) and Elizabeth I (1559), as well as in Ecclesiastical Canons of 1571 and 1604. It remained the standard text until the Eton Grammar of 1758.[104]

In order to gain a picture of what life was like for the 153 boys who attended the school we must, once again, turn to Erasmus, who gave an account of the school buildings and workings in his letter Justus Jonas:

> Upon the death of the father of Colet, when by right of inheritance he was possessed of a considerable sum of money, lest the keeping of it should corrupt his mind and turn it too much to the world, he laid out a great part of it in building a new school in the churchyard of St. Paul dedicated to the Child Jesus, a magnificent fabric; to which he added two handsome dwelling-houses for the two several masters, to whom he assigned ample salaries, that they might teach a certain number of boys gratuitously. He divided the school into four apartments. The first is the porch or entrance for catechumens (or children to be instructed in the principles of religion); and no child is admitted there unless he can already read and write. The second apartment is for the *Hypodidascalus* (or usher). The third is for those who are more learned (under the highmaster). Which former parts of the school are divided from the other by a curtain, which can be drawn or undrawn at pleasure. Over the master's chair is seated a figure of the Child Jesus, of excellent work, in the act of teaching; whom all the assembly both at coming in and going out of the school salute with a short hymn. There is also a representation of God the Father, saying 'Hear ye him': but these words were written there at my recommendation. The last apartment is a little chapel adapted to divine service. Throughout the school there are neither corners nor hiding-places; nor anything like a cell or a closet. The boys have each their distinct forms or benches rising in regular gradations and spaces one over another. Of these every class contains sixteen, and he who is most excellent in his class has a kind of small desk by way of eminence. All children are not to be admitted as a matter of course, but are to be selected according to their parts and capacities.[105]

Thus, unlike Eton, boys were required to be able to read and write on entry to the school. They would first be taught the Catechism in Latin and the elements of Latin grammar in the catechumen's room, which apparently bore the inscription '*Hoc Vestibulo catechizentur pueri in fide moribusque Christianis neque non prius grammatices rudimentes instituantur, priusquam ad proximam hujus scholae classem admittantur*'.[106] We now move on to examine the school statutes.

The Statutes

The Statutes for Colet's School were finally drawn up in June 1518 and, according to McDonnell, appear to be based on those of Stanbridge Grammar School at Banbury, in Oxfordshire, although the latter are no longer extant.[107] Copies of the St. Paul's originals can be found at the Mercers' Company and in the British Library.[108] In the prologue to the statutes Colet states the facts of his school's foundation in 1512 and the motivation behind it: to bring up children in good manners and good literature. Having appointed the highmaster, surmaster, chaplain and mercer governors, it was now Colet's intention to give them rules to work by.[109]

In the first section, Colet sets out the aims, responsibilities and accountability of the highmaster (*De magistro primario*). Accordng to the ancient statute of the old grammar school, taken from the cathedral ordinance,

> The Master of the Grammar School should be a good & honest man of much & approved learning. He shall imbue them [the children] at the same time with both chaste learning and holy morals ... he shall beto them a Master not only of Grammar but of Virtue.

Likewise, Colet's own statutes declare that the highmaster shall be '...honeste & vertuose & learnyd ... [and teach] suych auctours that hath with wisdome Joyned the pure chaste eloquence.' The mercers shall then be able to say to the highmaster: 'Sir, we haue chosyn you ... to teche ... not allonly good literature but also good Maners.'[110]

Unlike the statutes of Eton, which required the master and he undermaster to be unmarried, the highmaser of St. Paul's should be

> ... a man hole in body honeste and vertuose and learnyd in good and clene laten literature and also in greke yf suyche may be gotten a weddid man a single manne or a preste that hath noo benefice with cure nor seruice that may lett his due besynes in the scole.[111]

In the second section the obligations of the surmaster (*De submagistro*) are laid out. The qualifications for this job are identical to the highmaster's role with the exception of the knowledge of Greek.

Thirdly, Colet sets down rules that apply to both officers, concerning sick pay, limitations on their other business affairs, and the running of the school. The fourth section considers the role of the chaplain, who was to sing Mass daily and is to have no other benefice or occupation:[112]

> There shalbe also in the Scole a preist that dayly as he can be disposed shall sing masse in the chapel of the Scole and pray for the Chilldren to prosper in good lyff and in goode literature to the honour of god and our lorde Christ Jesu. At his masse whenne the bell in the scole shall knyll to sacring thenne all the Children in the scole knelyng in theyr Settes shall with lyft up handis pray in the tyme of sacryng. After the sacring whenne the bell knyllith ageyn, they shall sitt downe ageyn to theyr lernyng.[113]

The chaplain was nominated by the mercers and was to 'teche the chikdren the catechyzon and Instruction of the articles of faith, and the x commandments in Inglish.'[114]

The fifth section regards the children themselves, giving specific prohibitions, such as 'I wll they vse noo kokfighting nor rydyng aboute of victory nor disputing at sent Bartilmews whiche is but foolish babeling and losse of tyme'.[115] The sixth section concerns the curriculum and is entitled plainly 'What Shall be Taught'. Much of the content of this part has been discussed already in this chapter. It is here that Colet states clearly his educational philosophy regarding 'the veray Romayne eliquence joined with wisdome specially Cristyn auctours that wrote theyre wysdome with clene and chast laten other in verse or prose.' Therefore, he declares, children are first to learn 'aboue all the Cathechyzn in Englysh', then Erasmus's Latin version followed by *De Copia*. Only then can the children proceed to study Colet's select list of 'classical' Latin and Christian wirters.[116] The seventh section is a charge to the Mercers' Company to diligently oversee the running of the school. The eighth part declares Colet's liberty to add to the statutes as he sees fit. The ninth section lists those lands belonging to the school, of which there are many. Finally, a list of annual wages paid to school employees demonstrates, as has already been noted above, that serving at St. Paul's School was a comparatively lucrative pastime.

The School's Significance

Colet's place in history, had he attempted nothing remarkable as Dean of St. Paul's, nor been an exegete and theologian of note, would have been secure through the foundation of his school alone. Not only was it financially so well endowed that it was assured a long history, but the manner of its establishment was significant. Like contemporaneous grammar schools, St. Paul's was one of a wave of fresh enthusiasm for humanist learning. These schools, in contrast to the older ones of Winchester and Eton, were to be run by laity and married men, to teach Greek as well as Latin to any who had the wit to pass the selection criteria and the desire to learn. But Colet's foundation was also one upon which he fixed his own brand of Christian evangelism. It was not just a place where children learned for its own sake, but 'Good literature' was taught in order that a purer, wiser and more pious generation might prosper, for the sake of their souls and for the good of the holy Church. Colet's aim in founding St. Paul's School was precisely the same as every activity he undertook: to increase Godly purity in his own time and for the future; to shut out worldly sins, deceits and devilry; and to increase holiness within the Church in order that it may climb the ladder to perfection and be united with the divine.

Perhaps Colet was not as adventurous a humanist as some of his contemporaries, such as his successor at St. Paul's, Richard Pace, who spent twenty of his twenty-seven adult years in Italy and produced the treatise *De Fructu qui ex Doctrina Percipitur* (On the Profits of Learning); and perhaps Colet's school was not ultimately more influential than Richard Fox's (1448-1528) humanist Corpus Christi College at Oxford (1516), which provided the first permanent Reader in Greek at Oxford.[117] Nevertheless, Colet cannot be matched for pious enthusiasm and determination, which, aided by the significant talents of Erasmus, Linacre, Grocyn, Lily and others, has provided, for nearly five hundred years, a superior education for many thousands of children.

5

PREACHING TO THE CONVERTED: COLET'S CONVOCATION SERMON OF 1511/12

This chapter examines the second documented event in which Colet's perfectionist vision for the Church was expressed at St. Paul's: his Convocation sermon. I argue that, contrary to recent scholarship,[1] Colet's sermon was not only a re-statement of conservative Catholic reform rhetoric, belonging to a tradition of late-medieval preaching,[2] but also an articulation of conciliarism.[3] Furthermore, although the sermon contains many similarities with contemporaneous English and continental sermons, it is distinctive by virtue of its characteristic ecclesiology, which emphasized obedience to canon law and the ecclesiastical hierarchy, rather than to the penitential system.

Colet's first attempt at clerical reform, in 1506, had achieved limited success, if any. His desire for reform, however, had continued undiminished, as several documented events indicate: in 1507, Colet reorganized the Jesus Guild, which used the crypt of St. Paul's for services;[4] in 1508, construction commenced on his new St. Paul's School.[5] The latter was completed and opened around 1511, in which year the dean appointed married lay mercers, rather than clergy, as school governors.[6] In 1511/12, Colet was invited to preach at the opening service of the Convocation of the Province of Canterbury, held at St. Paul's Cathedral.[7] The invitation came from none other than the Archbishop of Canterbury, and Colet confessed that he could not refuse.[8] Choosing a text from St. Paul, and enthused by his own writings concerning alleged administrative abuses within the Church, the dean again voiced his dissatisfaction with clerical behaviour, as he had done in 1506.[9] Thus, in this middle period of Colet's career as dean, he sought to exert influence by two means:

firstly, by moulding the intellects of children; and secondly, by appealing to the educated minds of senior clerics through his preaching. Thus, renewal of the mind, and consequently the transformation of the Church, was his aim.

Earlier scholarship has failed to locate the sermon's key features within their correct historical and theological context. For instance, Carpenter, following Lupton's portrayal of the sermon as being proto-Protestant, claimed that Colet expressed a desire for a

> ... purified Catholic Church the vision of which equally inspired Erasmus and Thomas More. He believed that a renewed and conscientious episcopate could lead to a revivified clergy and such clergy to a more godly laity.[10]

This analysis is fair in the sense that Colet wished for a purified Church, but wrong in two other respects: firstly, because his vision, as we have seen, differed from that of his humanist colleagues; and secondly, because he was not principally concerned with a Godly laity, but with a Godly clergy. Porter, who narrowly identified Colet's sermon as an attempt to liberate the Church from 'vile' secular things and people, such as Richard Hunne, similarly misunderstood the sermon as being primarily concerned with the laity.[11] Furthermore, Swanson and Sheils have the same misconception: 'Colet would argue ... that clerical reform would lead naturally and straightforwardly to reformation of the laity', a point also made by Dickens and Jones.[12] As I shall argue, this was not Colet's chief aim or concern. However, Swanson does offer the pertinent insight that, for Colet, the Church had to be unworldly: 'Essentially the call was for effective ministry, avoiding the distractions which the Church's integration into the surrounding society imposed.'[13] As we have seen, Colet's ecclesiology required the Church not only to be unworldly, but also to be positively otherworldly. Kaufman considered that the 'criticisms and ideals' of the sermon 'resembled Wyclif's' own, implying that Colet adhered to the Lollard heresy.[14] This misconception has been handed on to the most recent generation of Tudor scholars. Thus, Guy wrongly considers Colet's sermon to be anticlerical, and so 'pungent that he narrowly escaped a charge of heresy himself!'[15]

Haigh, Rex, Harper-Bill and Gleason have successfully dismissed depictions of Colet's sermon as a proto-Protestant tract, as claimed by Brown, Clebsch and, more recently, Alden,[16] although the erroneous notion that the sermon as 'reforming' lingers in some scholarship today.[17] Thus, Haigh rightly suggests that Colet continued a rhetoric of Christian protest against the contamination of God's priests by human ambition, a rhetoric seen in the works of various late medieval writers, such as Robert Grosseteste, Bishop of Lincoln (1235-53); William Langland (c.1330-

c.1390), author of *Piers Plowman*; and the fifteenth-century Church critic, Thomas Gascoigne (1403-58). In Haigh's words,

> Colet was not a proto-Protestant, disgusted with the ecclesiastical structure and the sacramental system; he was a high clericalist, anxious to maintain the privileges of priests by raising their prestige.[18]

Moreover, Rex has suggested that

> Sermons such as that of John Colet, castigating the moral shortcomings of the clergy, were in general delivered to clerical audiences and employ an obviously exaggerated rhetoric in order to achieve the desired end of moral reform.[19]

However, Rex's emphasis upon moral reform neglects to put Colet's words within the context of his overall soteriology, which concerned obedience to the ecclesiastical hierarchy for the purpose of achieving order, the precondition to attaining beauty in an ascent to union with God.

Harper-Bill demonstrates that, in the late fifteenth century, Archbishop Morton had wrestled with the same problems with which Colet struggled in the sixteenth, and had similarly addressed them in Convocation.[20] This evidence indicates that the dean's clerical concerns were not wholly new within English late-medieval Catholicism – an observation also made by Sheils.[21] Yet, as we shall see, those concerns were unique in ecclesiological terms. However, Harper-Bill also argues, rather extremely, that 'The medieval Church was betrayed from the inside', like a wolf attacking sheep, for 'very few wolves were needed to destroy a healthy flock'.[22] But betrayal was the exact opposite of what Colet was trying to achieve, which was the reinforcement of the Church's hierarchical structure. Other scholars have considered the sermon within the context of his thought as a whole.[23] For instance, Gleason believes the sermon to be no more than part of Colet's exegesis:

> Once the canard that Colet's Convocation Sermon was revolutionary has been disposed of, the sermon finds its natural place in this chapter on his exegesis. While not the unique document that Victorian scholars wished to think it, the sermon was thoroughly characteristic of Colet's thought.[24]

Although Colet's sermon is indeed characteristic of his thought, it cannot be related solely to his exegesis, which forms a relatively small part of his extant work, but should also be linked to his ecclesiology: the sermon does, after all, address issues of Church.

Wabuda, MacCulloch, Marshall, Barron, Rousseau and Davis are the most recent historians to discuss Colet's Convocation sermon.[25] Contrary to the reasoning of Haigh, Duffy and Harper-Bill, Wabuda claims that 'Catholicism in England ... was undermined not so much by the wolves within, but by aspects of its own success', including preaching.[26] Whilst this must remain conjecture in terms of Colet's case because of his early death, Wabuda rightly acknowledges that, for Colet, 'we priests ... 'are the mediatours and meanes vnto God for men". However, Wabuda limits her discussion of Colet's vision – of the priestly mediation of God's love to humanity – to the issue of priestly explanation of obscure scripture.[27] Thus, Wabuda fails to recognize Colet's full ecclesiological meaning: priests do not just transmit scriptural truth by means of their superior knowledge (a faculty not wholly admired by Colet), but by their superior conformity to the loving will of God. Therefore, when Colet advocates nonconformity to this world, he is espousing a Platonic and Pseudo-Dionysian conformity to God's love as emanated through the celestial hierarchy to the ecclesiastical one. Nevertheless, Wabuda rightly realizes that Colet wished to raise the dignity of the priesthood by his preaching, even if she falls short of realizing the full perfectionist implications of his ecclesiology:

> John Colet brought about an extraordinary transformation in the ideal of the preacher, by expanding the preacher's role inside the larger frame of the sacerdotal office, in accordance with the example established by the apostles and fathers of the Church, in emulation of the preaching ministry of Christ, the first priest.[28]

Although I believe Wabuda's claim that the dean brought about an 'extraordinary transformation' to be an exaggeration,[29] her summary of Colet's challenge to the priesthood is a useful assessment of one aspect of his Convocation sermon:

> He succinctly challenged priests to aspire anew to live up to the lofty ideals of their calling and seize the full implications of the 'brightnes of this great dignitie'. Once they were reached, the clergy would be prepared to lead a movement of 'reformation', whose goal was the moral and spiritual refreshment of the entire Church, in which preaching played a leading part.[30]

This chapter argues that there is more to the 'full implications' of the dean's vision than Wabuda indicates.

More recently, MacCulloch has rightly placed Colet's sermon within the context of Europe-wide clerical excitement over the Fifth Lateran Council (Rome, 1511/12);

the early sixteenth century was a time when many conciliarists held positions of responsibility:

> Two days after King Henry VIII had formally commissioned English delegates to set off for Rome, Archbishop Warham and his colleagues sat back in their meeting of Convocation to listen in gloomy satisfaction as Dean Colet used his considerable eloquence to lambaste the assembled English clergy for their faults.[31]

MacCulloch goes on to argue that the sermon was a 'penitential version of a school speech day' and was part of a 'year-long initiative by the English bishops to search out, discipline and re-educate Lollard heretics'.[32] MacCulloch's latter assessment, therefore, implies that Colet's clerical criticisms were a formality at such an event and that the real reformist aim of the Convocation was to oust heretics from the Church. Indeed, the dean had sat on heresy trials in the previous year.[33] However, it is worth mentioning three further points. Firstly, Colet was clear that his sermon did not address issues of heresy, but rather the 'wicked lyfe of pristes'.[34] Therefore, although the Convocation as a whole may have addressed the problem of Lollardy, his chief concern was clerical. Secondly, he was not asking for Lollards to recant their heresy with penitent hearts; he was asking the clergy to transform their attitude to their vocation by means of conformity to the loving will of God.[35] Thirdly, I argue that the emphases found in Colet's sermon derived from his peculiar ecclesiology. Written from the perspective of his passionate vision, therefore, the text does not read as a formal speech, but rather as an earnest plea for a reformed clergy.

Marshall's brief assessment of the sermon exemplifies how very recent scholarship continues to emphasize the dean's reforming zeal:

> In around 1511, John Colet ... delivered a thunderous sermon to convocation ... blaming all the ills of the Church on the secular lifestyles and 'covetousness' of the clergy. He castigated their greed for tithes and promotions, and urged 'reformation of the Church's estate'.[36]

Likewise, Barron and Rousseau assert that 'In his famous Convocation sermon, Colet called for the wider Church to reform'.[37] Similarly, Davis notes that '... in 1512 [*sic*], Colet complained that priests were more attracted to greed and gain rather than to religious devotion'.[38] Whilst these observations are valid, scholars have missed the chief ecclesiological characteristics of the dean's sermon: hierarchy, order and conciliarism. This chapter seeks to rectify those omissions.

In order to identify its constituent elements, part one of the chapter summarizes the sermon's contents. Part two examines the sermon in the light of the late-medieval homiletic tradition, arguing that Colet's preaching was part of a well-established tradition, yet individual within that tradition. The sermon's distinctiveness is evident in the light of medieval homiletic forms, styles and themes. Part three argues that Colet was different from contemporaneous preachers: the sermon is compared to those written by another prominent English humanist preacher of the period: John Fisher. I argue that there is a significant difference between the two men's homiletic material, particularly with regard to the subjects of sin, repentance, penitence and purgatory. In the fourth section, a similar comparison will be made with contemporaneous continental preaching and thought, including that of Girolamo Savonarola (1452-98), Johann Geiler von Kaysersberg (1478-1510) and Lefèvre d'Etaples, whose Catholic reform ideals, albeit ultimately distinct, bore some similarities to Colet's own. In section five, the dean's call for more general and provincial councils is assessed in the light of continental Catholic conciliar radicalism of the fifteenth century. I argue that he possessed conciliarist tendencies, which were significant for the application of his ecclesiology, but that he was not ultimately a radical conciliarist.[39] In conclusion, a reassessment of the sermon identifies the similarities between that text and the work of contemporaneous English and European theologians. I contend that the sermon belongs within its own ecclesiological category as an expression of Colet's intense vision of, and desire for, a perfect Church searching for communion with God.

The Sermon

Colet's sermon was written and preached in Latin. It is about 4500 words long and would have taken over half-an-hour to deliver. It follows a simple structure of a brief introduction, followed by two main admonitions: firstly, resist conforming to this world; and secondly, be reformed.[40] Both points are expounded in detail. He began his argument by setting out the benefits of reform, by means of obedience to canon law, and concluded by asking, politely, that his message be received with generosity.

In his introduction, Colet articulates his main argument: the Church needed reform, he said, 'For hit was neuer more nede, and the state of the churche dyd neuer desyre more your endeuors.'[41] The dean demurely admits to his own inadequacy as a preacher: 'But for sothe I came nat wyllyngly, for I knewe myne unworthynes ... that I, a sonne, shulde teache you, my fathers.'[42] He wrote that any of the bishops and other senior clerics would be better qualified than he to preach, but Archbishop Warham had to be obeyed, for the primate was

> ... presydent of this councell, whiche layde vpon me this bourden, truly to [*sic*] heuy for me. We rede that the prophette Samuel sayde: *Obedience is better than sacrifice.*[43]

The introduction ends with Colet's invitation to the congregation to pray for 'our most holy father the Pope', for Christians and clergy, and to say the *Pater Noster*.[44] From the beginning, therefore, Colet's ecclesiological emphasis upon clerical hierarchy is apparent: the Pope and bishops have superiority.

The first part of Colet's argument then ensues. Citing St. Paul as his authority, he exhorts the congregation not to be conformed to this world, indicating how the earthly hierarchy should mirror the celestial hierarchy. Conformity consists of four evils: pride, concupiscence, covetousness and secularism.[45] He explains that pride, within the clerical context, means holding more than one benefice, even though, perhaps hypocritically, he held several himself;[46] concupiscence comprises feasting, sporting, hunting and hawking; covetousness refers to the coveting of other people's benefices, the greedy and overzealous collection of tithes and the immoral activity evident from proceedings in the ecclesiastical courts; and secularism, for the clergy, was a matter of insufficient prayer, preaching and performance of the sacraments.[47] His concerns, therefore, are clearly presented: perfection requires abstinence from four evils. The result of indulgence in any of these four evils is simple: dishonour for, and lay hatred of, the priesthood; the confusion of order in the Church; and the fall of the laity into further sin due to the hypocrisy of the clergy, with the result that all are left spiritually and morally blind.[48] Colet perceived the existence of heretics as both a benefit and a curse to the Church: a benefit because they made the Church wiser, as heretics highlighted evil and good in the Church; but a curse, in that some were seduced by heresy and brought secular living into the Body.[49] He condemned heretics, just as St. Bernard of Clairvaux had condemned them when speaking to Convocation.[50] The dean reminded his listeners that St. Bernard had identified two heresies: wicked teaching and a wicked life:

> For that same holy father, in a certayne conuocation, preachynge vnto the pristes of his tyme ... sayde ... 'There be many catholyke and faithfull men in speakynge and preachynge, the whiche same men are heretykes in workyng ...' By whiche wordes he shewethe playnly to be two maner of heresies; the one to be of peruerse teachynge, and the tother of naughty life: of whiche this later is worse and more peryllous.[51]

Thus, Colet associated himself with St. Bernard as a holy father. The foregoing reference was his attempt, therefore, to maximize his own authoritative status in the eyes of the congregation and to imbue his own ecclesiology, which advocated clerical learning and piety, with great authority.

The second part of the text suggests an alternative to worldly conformity: reform. Being reformed, Colet preached, consists of being meek, sober and charitable. One must also occupy oneself spiritually, that is to say, shun worldly desires.[52] Reformation, thus conceived, must begin with bishops.[53] No new laws need be made, but the old ones should be obeyed. Thus, his ecclesiology promoted obedience within the existing hierarchy, which, if achieved, would create order and beauty:

> But when the spirit keeps all things within Himself and each in its own proper order ... then the Church displays in God a beautiful form and countenance, and is entirely sound, and pure, and alive, and vigorous, and radiant with a Godly complexion.[54]

Colet's conception of order required ordinands to possess priestly qualities;[55] clergy to be promoted on the basis of merit alone; simony to be abandoned; curates to be resident in their parishes; clerks to be virtuous; monks and canons to be ascetic; and bishops, appointed by grace, to be resident in their dioceses.[56] He suggested a fourfold spending plan, dividing expenditure between a bishop's household; clerks, presumably meaning minor clerics serving that bishop, such as his personal chaplain; building maintenance; and the poor.[57] The bishops, Colet preached, should execute the law and so bring light to the laity:[58] senior members of the hierarchy, therefore, were responsible for Church order.

The main part of the sermon complete, Colet encouraged his hearers by predicting the result of such obedience. Firstly, the laity would become submissive to ecclesiastical law and teaching; secondly, the clergy would receive honour; thirdly, wealth would accrue easily to the clergy, as tithes would willingly be given; fourthly, clerics would be immune from lay criticism and legal action; and fifthly, there would be peace within the Church.[59] It was important for his ecclesiological scheme, therefore, that clergy should not dishonour the Church system. A proper ordering of the Church kept the laity in their inferior position and the clergy in their rightful superior position. The dean concluded by asking that his words be accepted gently in order to further the reform of an allegedly decayed Church.[60]

Colet sought to uphold all that was dear to him in the Church: canon law, ecclesiastical hierarchy, lay submission, clerical immunity, order and beauty, ecclesiastical councils and the spiritual supremacy of the Church over the world.[61] By obedience to canon law, the spiritual classes (bishops, priests and deacons) would inherit their rightful place over the earthly classes:

> Wherefore, if ye wyll haue the lay people to lyue after your wysshe and wyll, fyrst lyue you your selfe after the wyl of God; and so, trust me, ye shall gette in them what so euer ye wyll.
>
> Ye wyll be obeyed of them: and right it is … You wyll be honoured of the people. It is reason … You wyll repe theyr carnall thinges, and gather tithes and offrynges without stryuynge. Right it is … Ye wyll haue the churches liberte, and nat to be drawen afore secular iuges: and that also is ryght … Ye wolde be out of busines in rest and peace: and that is conuenient.[62]

A major characteristic of the sermon, therefore, is its hierarchical emphasis. From the introduction to the conclusion, Colet was at pains to express his inferiority and obedience to the bishops because of his ecclesiological outlook:

> These are they, reuerent fathers and ryghte famous men, that I thought to be said for the reformation of the churches estate. I trust ye wyll take them of your gentylnes to the best. And if parauenture it be thought that I haue past my boundes in this sermon, or haue sayd any thynge out of tempre, forgyue it me.[63]

The sermon is thus saturated with his ecclesiology: only the superior, exemplary clergy of his vision could create the order and beauty necessary for unity in the Church, which could lead to the ascent towards perfection and union with God. In order to assess the sermon within its proper context, it is necessary to study its content in comparison with late-medieval homiletic ideas.

Late Medieval Sermons

The distinctive qualities of the Convocation sermon can only be identified against the background of pre-Reformation preaching in general. In this section, therefore, I shall investigate the forms, styles and common themes employed in late-medieval sermons, in contrast to Colet's own sermon, in order to argue that it deserves to occupy a distinctive place within the homiletic tradition.

As far back as 1215, the Fourth Lateran Council had imposed upon the laity the minimum obligation of annual confession, giving clergy an opportunity to assess their parishioners' knowledge of the Catholic faith.[64] However, in order for a parishioner to know his faith, and the value of confession, he had to be educated in that faith by a priest. However, a priest's ability thus to teach and assess was not necessarily assured.[65] Instruction manuals for the benefit of priests therefore began to appear. One famous manual was William of Pagula's *Oculus Sacerdotis*, produced in the fourteenth century.[66] Other manuals for clergy followed, such as John Mirk's late fifteenth-century *Instructions for Parish Priests*, which included instruction on preaching, confession and the giving of the last rites.[67] His *Festial* for the benefit of ignorant priests provided material for Sunday homilies.[68] The earlier homilies on scriptural extracts, prepared in the *Festial*, contrast with Colet's systematic approach to scripture, evident through his reputation for preaching not only on a single text, but often also a series of sermons on a whole biblical book.[69] The idea of ignorant priests using pre-written sermons was one that he rejected; he condemned the practice.[70] However, sophisticated forms of preaching also existed, to which we now turn.

There were two main forms of sermon construction in the medieval period: the 'ancient' and the 'modern'.[71] The ancient form was based on patristic homilies and consisted of the application of a passage of scripture, for instance the epistle of the day, to a topical subject. The modern form was much more complicated and consisted of the following scheme: the *Exordium*, which was the introductory part of the discourse; the Protheme or Antetheme, which was the preamble to the main theme; the Theme; a Prayer; the Division (with or without Sub-Division); and, lastly, the Discussion. The Theme, consisting of a scriptural text from which three main ideas were extracted, formed the basis for the sermon. Thus, the Theme was divided into its three parts, with optional sub-divisions supported by other scriptural passages as necessary. The *Exordium* was based on part of the principal theme, or on another biblical passage not dealt with in the main body of the sermon. After the bidding prayer, the Theme was reiterated for the benefit of latecomers. The Discussion could involve various rhetorical techniques in order to amplify or digress from the core argument.

Colet did not employ the rigid modern form in his sermon, preferring a more direct and topical application of scripture, more akin to the ancient form, as did his contemporary John Longland (1473-1547), Bishop of Lincoln.[72] Although Longland's sermons on the Penitential Psalms are of the ancient form, he nevertheless explored the literal meaning of each psalm, verse-by-verse, and added spiritual interpretations with reference to topical matters of evil, as he saw fit. Similarly, Colet expounded the scriptural text and applied it to a contemporary situation, but he also expanded the form in order to express his ecclesiological interpretation of both text and topical situation. For instance, when he interpreted Christ's words 'You are the light of the world' as being addressed directly to bishops and priests, he eschewed every other interpretation except the ecclesiological:

> That is to say, if prestes and bysshops, that shulde be as lyghtes, ronne in the darke way of the worlde, howe darke than shall the secular people be?[73]

Colet's sermon form – part way between the ancient and modern – was therefore chosen in order to make the maximum possible impact upon his listeners, but without being aggressive. As Gleason rightly observes, 'the highly visible structure' demonstrated to his hearers that the dean 'was not being carried away by the spirit of criticism'.[74] Colet used the same criterion in his choice of style.

Style was an important element in Colet's preaching, as it was for all contemporaneous preachers. Blench identified three homiletic styles used in the period 1450-1547: firstly, the plain, uncolloquial style; secondly, the colloquial style; and thirdly, the ornate style.[75] The plain style used few *exempla* (examples by allegory) and rhetorical *schemata* (artificial word patterns). The colloquial style used *exempla* and stories. The ornate style employed word patterns (*schemata*) purely for rhetorical display and included many *exempla* from literary sources. Colet seems to have used a plain style in his one surviving sermon. He made no use of *exempla*, or anecdotal examples, and had little formal scheme. The plainness of his speech, and of his Latin, enabled him to communicate his theme with clarity. In order to achieve perfection, it was essential that his listeners understood his message of unity and obedience within the ecclesiastical hierarchy.

Another aspect of pre-Reformation preaching was the variety of themes employed. Colet was at one with other late-medieval preachers in condemning worldliness and vanity. During the late fifteenth century and the Henrician period, lament over the transience of worldly things was a frequent theme among preachers.[76] For instance, Fisher's sermons often included a condemnation of earthly vanities:

> Where be now the kynges and prynces that somtyme regned ouer all the worlde, whose glory & tryumphe was lyfte vp aboue the erth. Where is now the inumerable company & puysaunce of Xerxes & Cesar, where is now the grete rychesse of Creses & Crassus ... they had all thyr pleasures at the full bothe of delycyous and good welfare, of hawkynge, huntynge, also of goodly horses goodly coursers, greyhoundes and houndes for thyr dysportes ... But where be they now, be they not gone and wasted lyke vnto smoke of whome it is wryten in an other place. *Mox ut honorificati fuerint et exaltati, quemadmodum fumus defifient* [Ps. xxxvi. 20] 'presently after they shall be honoured and exalted. They shall come to nothing and vanish like smoke'.[77]

Pessimism, in contrast to an ideal of the perfect life, was also prevalent on the continent. As Huizinga put it:

> At the close of the Middle Ages, a sombre melancholy weighs on people's souls. Whether we read a chronicle, a poem, a sermon, a legal document even, the same impression of immense sadness is produced by them all. It would sometimes seem as if this period had been particularly unhappy, as if it had left behind only the memory of violence, of covetousness and mortal hatred, as if it had known no other enjoyment but that of intemperance, of pride and of cruelty.[78]

Colet's vision of an ideal life was similar to continental ideas of forsaking the world, raising the question of how much he knew of continental thinking, an issue that I shall consider below.[79]

However, the sermon did not accord with all pre-Reformation homiletic concerns, such as the condemnation of the vanity of men's dress, including brightly jewelled or coloured garments, or even shoes chained to the waist which prevented the wearer from kneeling to say prayers;[80] apprentices' lack of obedience to their masters; the misuse of holy days; swearing and blasphemy; the greed and dishonesty of merchants; the decay of grammar schools and universities; and the decline of hospitality.[81] With so much complaint, generally against the physical in favour of the spiritual, some preachers chose penance as their subject. Fisher and Longland, for example, selected texts such as the Penitential Psalms on which to preach.[82] Moreover, penitence was a key feature in European printed model sermons of the late fifteenth and early sixteenth centuries.[83] Preachers taught their congregations to confess their sins to a priest acting as both judge and doctor. Prior to the acceptance of Lutheran doctrine on the subject during the Reformation, Christians were called to confession and the sacramental power of the priest to absolve sin. The priest was considered absolutely necessary in the penitential process. In 1511/12, Colet neither preached in this vein nor requested that his listeners repent to him as judge and doctor in personal penitence. Thus, his ecclesiological logic for the redemption of the Church emphasized a glorious ascendancy above the world by means of the laws of hierarchical discipline.[84] Whilst Colet was well aware of the need for individuals to repent, and the consequent necessity of the sacrament of penance, he had little time for either:

> ... it is obvious that no wicked Christians can be in the Church, but that they must be cleansed while still without ... But when the sacraments are being

administered they must be driven off, for the base and unclean cannot receive the illumination needed to perceive the mysteries.[85]

In this passage, the dean's reference to 'the sacraments' refers only to the administration of the Eucharist. For him, the wicked could be reconciled through the sacrament of penance, but they shall not be admitted to receive consecrated bread and wine until reconciliation had been accomplished. However, for Colet, something more than penitence was required for the Church to achieve the perfection that he desired:

> When one is sorry for the sins he has confessed, there is still no forgiveness unless one makes good use of his time by making amends and offering satisfaction, rising up again to win the victory even after being vanquished.[86]

Colet could have been referring to the practice whereby the priest granted absolution on condition that the sinner perform the prescribed penance(s). Thus, the absolution only became operative once the penance(s) had been performed. Perhaps he was suggesting that people had been receiving absolution, but then not performing the penances, possibly because they were buying indulgences. Whatever the case, Colet's rather Pelagian outlook, with its emphasis upon good works, relegates the sacrament of penance to a relatively small place in his ecclesiology; his chief subject was the sacrament of ordination.[87] For Colet, the priesthood was the Church's main hope:

> Thus the first effect of priesthood upon the lower part of the Church is hope in God, which results from cleansing. This same hope is also humility, obedience, and subjection to God, so that by Him man may be exalted to a divine form.[88]

Thus, for the dean, repentance was not the key to the Church's problems. In contrast to Fisher's and Longland's homiletic admonitions against the fleshly concupiscence of this world,[89] he insisted upon a return to canon laws more concerned with institutional obedience to the ecclesiastical hierarchy than with individual renewal.

To conclude this section: for Colet, obedience to the law, including canon law, statutes and scripture, was order – and in his ecclesiological scheme, order equalled beauty.[90] Therefore, those laws concerned with virtue were especially important to him. Obedience to all the laws brought unity to the Church, which enabled it to accept God's spirit, emanated *via* the angels to humanity by grace, and thus make the ascent to God through a process of illumination and purification towards a state of perfection and deification, that is to say spiritual union with God. In this sense, the sermon was unusual amongst late fifteenth and early sixteenth-century sermons as it combined Colet's peculiar ecclesiology and clerical criticism, aimed at achieving perfection in the Church, with a notable absence of penitential doctrine. The dean shared some characteristics with other preachers of his time (he was not alone in advocating the revival of clerical excellence), but his ecclesiology took him further than other preachers in his desire for a perfected Church.[91] He was uncompromising in his belief that the existing structures and hierarchies of the Church contained the key to its regeneration. He wrote in Latin; he prayed for the Pope; he respected bishops and all forms of order; he spoke against all things secular. He preached not of repentance, faith or purgatory, but of law, discipline and obedience. He believed, perhaps unrealistically compared to his contemporaries, that if the Church could order itself, it would have obedience, honour, riches, liberty and peace.[92] Colet's ecclesiological distinctiveness is especially apparent when we compare him to his humanist contemporary, John Fisher.

John Fisher's Sermons

Bishop John Fisher of Rochester took a high view of the priesthood and its privileges, believing that only the ministrations of a virtuous clergy could bring the laity to Christ and, through Him, to salvation; he feared that worldly priests would not proclaim Christ's call.[93] Fisher stressed sin and repentance because human defects threatened the salvation of the Church. Therefore, he attempted to set an example. An outline of the bishop's clerical career will serve as a basis for comparing Colet's and Fisher's ecclesiological visions.

At first sight, Fisher appears to have lived out Colet's ecclesiological and educational ideals. Born in 1469 into a mercantile family, he went to Cambridge University in 1483, serving it as chancellor from 1504 to 1535. There, he worked on behalf of Lady Margaret Beaufort (1443-1509), re-founding God's House (1439) as Christ's College (1505/6).[94] He also drew Lady Margaret's attention to the dilapidated hospital of St. John the Evangelist, which was re-founded as St. John's College shortly after her death in 1509. Within this university context, both Colet and Fisher owed an intellectual debt to English humanism. As Rex notes:

> Through the contacts of English scholars such as William Grocyn, John Colet and Thomas Linacre with Italian culture, and partly through the friendship of Desiderius Erasmus with such key figures of English culture as John Colet, Thomas More and John Fisher, the influence of what everyone knew as 'good letters' or 'good arts' (*bonae literae* or *bonae artes*) was felt in England from the

reign of Henry VII, especially at the royal court and in the universities of Oxford and Cambridge.[95]

Colet and Fisher, therefore, had much in common. A humanist scholar who knew Greek,[96] and then learned Hebrew at a late age, Fisher was a friend of the German Hebraist Johannes Reuchlin (1454-1522), Erasmus and More.[97] He has sometimes been thought of as a traditionalist, as well as a humanist, because he was a defender of orthodoxy.[98] Both Fisher and Colet took an interest in Erasmus's work and both men regularly corresponded with him and exchanged ideas. For instance, in October 1513, Erasmus wrote to Colet that 'If my Matthew is not in your possession, it must be in the Bishop of Rochester's'.[99] Fisher's interest in Hebrew had derived from reading the work of Pico della Mirandola, who had rediscovered the cabbala, the ancient Hebrew oral tradition of divine wisdom.[100] It was Erasmus who was keen to nurture the relationship between Reuchlin, Fisher and Colet; to Reuchlin he wrote, 'The Bishop of Rochester has an almost religious veneration for you. To John Colet your name is sacred.'[101] However, a divergence emerged between Colet's and Fisher's thought when the dean began to question Reuchlin's *De Arte Cabbalistica* of 1517, rejecting 'Reuchlin's pythagorical and cabbalistic philosophy' and preferring 'the short road to the truth', which was 'the fervent love and imitation of Jesus'.[102] Nevertheless, Fisher was everything Colet would have had a good bishop be: he had one See, admittedly a very small one, in which he was resident for ninety per-cent of his time; he was well educated and a prolific preacher; he was conscientious about ordinations; he co-operated closely with the Cathedral Prior on ordination examinations, elections and heresy trials; he collated many graduate clergy to benefices in his diocese; and he disapproved of pluralism, although in practice bishops could do little to stop pluralism in their dioceses if a cleric had a papal dispensation or a letter from the king.[103] Fisher also preached on many state occasions: he preached to Lady Margaret Beaufort (1508); at the funeral of Henry VII (1509); and at the court of Queen Katherine of Aragon (1513) – he is even said to have preached at the Field of the Cloth of Gold in 1520.[104] He preached against Luther at St. Paul's in 1521, and again in 1526, at the formal abjuration of Robert Barnes and other 'heretics'.[105] This was the last official occasion on which he preached because his support for Katherine of Aragon put him out of favour with the king, a position Colet also experienced in 1513.[106] It is unsurprising, therefore, that much of Fisher's sermon material bears a resemblance to Colet's own. Fisher's themes, like Colet's, contrasted with Luther's. As Dowling explains:

In his stress on the role of free will in repentance Fisher stands in stark contrast to Luther, who sees man as helpless to avoid sin and reliant on faith alone to save him.[107]

Like Colet's, Fisher's sources were generally scriptural. In his extant sermons, one can find only a single quotation from St. Thomas Aquinas (1225-74), one allusion to St. Francis of Assisi (1181/2-1226) and four references to St. Bernard of Clairvaux. Moreover, Colet was not the only Englishman to warn against conformity to this world; Fisher also rebuked the Renaissance Church for its wealth, which contrasted with the early Church's asceticism:

> Truly it was a more glorious sight to se saynt Poule whiche gate his lyuynge by his owne grete labour in hungre, thurst, watchynge, in colde, goynge wolward, & berynge aboute the gospell & lawe of cryst bothe vpon the see & on the londe than to beholde nowe tharchebysshoppes & bysshoppes in theyr apparayle be it neuer so riche. In that tyme were no chalyses of golde, but than was many golden prestes, now be many chalyses of gold, & almoost no golden prestes ...[108]

Similarly, as we have already seen, the dean's ascetical character was manifested in his penchant for plain black attire – and he encouraged his clergy to follow suit.

However, Colet's Convocation sermon can also clearly be distinguished from Fisher's own preaching: Fisher built upon medieval tradition in his preaching by incorporating spiritual allegory and Latin quotations with translations, whereas Colet preached entirely in Latin to the educated Convocation congregation.[109] Fisher's homiletic themes were centred on the urgent need for repentance. He therefore spoke of the loathsome nature of sin, the pains of purgatory and hell, the inferiority of earthly pleasures, and the love and mercy of God.[110] Sin was 'the filthy voluptuousness of the body, wherein the sinner watereth and wrappeth himself as a sow walloweth in the stinking gore pit'.[111] Although Colet condemned carnal concupiscence, which can be equated with Fisher's condemnation of earthly pleasures,[112] the themes of individual sin and repentance, purgatory and hell, and the mercy of God form a small part of Colet's written works, and are absent from his Convocation sermon altogether, indicating a contrasting ecclesiological emphasis. Fisher preached to the individual, condemning unrepentant sinners and taking compassion on repentant ones:

> The Persone which hath all thre partes of penaunce: contricyon, confession, and satysfaccyon is never begyled but doubtless he gooth in the right path that ledeth the waye vnto euerlastynge blysse.[113]

Colet and Fisher both condemned worldliness, clerical abuse and heresy.[114] However, where Fisher stressed fear of purgatory and amendment of life, Colet emphasized laws requiring institutional obedience. Both men perceived that orthodoxy had to be upheld in order to defend the Church from criticism. For Fisher, but not so much for Colet, Church purity was to be effected through the sacrament of penance; as Dowling suggests:

> For Fisher ... the Church was not a static, pristine institution free from blemish and threatened only by the onslaughts of vicious heretics beyond the pale. He was no complacent defender of orthodoxy; rather, he recognized that if doctrinal deviation was to be resisted the Church itself must be regenerated.[115]

For Colet, the Church had the potential to be unblemished and free of the taint of the world if it could be obedient to canon law and thereby regain its order and beauty. In this sense, he was more idealistic than Fisher; his vision for the Church involved a glorious rising above the world to God. Where Fisher preached in English, Colet's Convocation sermon was delivered in Latin; where Fisher talked of vanity, Colet denounced multiplicity and advocated unity; where Fisher expatiated on purgatory and hell, Colet spoke of the Church's potential in the present; and where Fisher preached of love, Colet wrote of perfection. Above all, Fisher's emphasis on penance contrasted with Colet's emphasis on obedience. As such, Colet reflected Erasmus's humanist pattern for living, as proclaimed in his *Enchiridion* – 'Free yourself from the errors of this world; find your way into the light of spiritual living' – and sought to apply it to the whole Church.[116]

To summarize this section: the dean's homiletic ideas contrasted with the bishop's in several ways. The evidence suggests that Colet preached frequently, enthusiastically and plainly, with a degree of scriptural interpretation which departed from scholastic models in some respects, but which accorded with Fisher's views. However, the content of Colet's sermon indicates that, although he was broadly addressing the same ecclesiastical issues as Fisher, his proposals for reform were different. Worldliness and decay were of desperate importance to Colet in his sermon, as they were to Fisher, but instead of emphasising the sacrament of penance, Colet endorsed existing canon laws relating to ordination, election, residence, Church courts, ecclesiastical councils, expenditure, and secular dealings.[117]

The dean did not preach a sermon asking for a penitent heart, but advocated outward, formal discipline to be achieved through the renewal of the mind.[118] The clergy had not only to be good; they had to be seen to be good, for the benefit of the whole body, not just the individual.

Having compared Colet's sermon to those sermons given by another pre-Reformation English preacher, I shall now consider his thought, as evident in the Convocation sermon, in relation to that of continental theologians.

Continental Preachers

In a general overview of late-medieval piety, Huizinga suggested that pessimism, combined with an ideal of life, became well-worn themes.[119] The pessimism concerned humanity's depravity. The ideal was, therefore, to banish worldliness, to promote institutional change and, as the second of these *desiderata* was considered impossible, to change oneself. This otherworldly piety was expressed in devotional writings, such as those deriving from the fourteenth-century Dutch movement, the *Devotio Moderna*. The *Devotio* promoted personal purity, with an emphasis upon meditation and prayer. It was founded by Gerard Groote of Deventer (1340-1384) and inspired two religious societies: the Brethren of the Common Life and the Canons Regular of Windesheim.[120] Thomas à Kempis (c.1380-1471), a canon in the monastery of Mount St. Agnes near Zwolle, was a follower of the *Devotio Moderna*, which influenced his most famous work, *The Imitation of Christ* (c.1401).[121] The Brethren influenced Erasmus, Lefèvre d'Etaples and Gabriel Biel (c.1420-95), who, until his death, was prior of an experimental house of the Brethren at St. Peter's at the Hermitage, near Tübingen.[122] The Brethren taught that improvement of political, social and moral conditions was an unobtainable ideal because institutions such as the Church, although good in terms of their divine ordination, were bad inasmuch as humans corrupted them. Remedy of the individual soul became the only answer, and therefore confession, penance and personal devotion were paramount.[123]

Thus, continental preachers and reformers, such as Johann Geiler von Kaysersberg and Girolamo Savonarola, preached individual repentance and salvation. Colet, by contrast, believed in an institutional soul capable of communal moral improvement and salvation. Colet had a vision of a beautiful world, not based on individualism, but on joint awareness of past wisdom and law.[124] However, Colet's ecclesiology, in relation to continental ideas, has been fundamentally misunderstood in modern scholarship. Kaufman, for instance, writes that

> Laurentius Valla ... noted that *religiosi* sealed their promises to be chaste and obedient with elaborate consecrations, yet he pronounced that the piety behind the promises meant far more than the profession that confirmed them.

> John Colet implied that those same promises transformed virtuous laypeople into a spiritual **priesthood** [*sic*] that might do far more for the spread of righteousness than the ordained clergy.[125]

Kaufman here makes two errors in portraying Colet's aim: firstly, he argues that Colet made the same contrast as Valla between the *religiosi* (pious layfolk) and the ordained priesthood. However, Kaufman clumsily uses the word 'priesthood' to describe virtuous lay people. A better definition might be 'spiritual caste'. Thus, Kaufman's second error is to suggest that Colet wished the laity to supplant the clergy as the chief distributors of God's righteousness.[126] This is not true of Colet's ecclesiology. Nor is Harper-Bill's suggestion that the dean proposed nothing radically new in his Convocation sermon, but was simply echoing preachers such as St. Bernard of Clairvaux.[127] Colet differed from past continental preachers, and from contemporaneous ones, because he believed in the possibility of an institutional perfection and was not merely advocating individual repentance.

In the following study, no attempt is made to prove that Colet came into personal contact with the continental theologians mentioned, although their works were available in England during Colet's lifetime.[128] I argue that, while there are similarities between the ideas evident in Colet's sermon and aspects of continental thought, he was not necessarily reliant upon the ideas of others.

Between 1492 and 1496, Colet travelled to Italy.[129] Possibly encouraged by his humanist friend William Grocyn (1449?-1519), in encountering Europe, he saw it through humanist eyes. Colet reached Rome by September 1492, staying there for a year at the English Hospice, where he became an official *confrater* on 3 May 1493.[130] As a consequence of his Italian experience, many new humanist works would have become accessible to him, such as Pico della Mirandola's commentary on Genesis (the *Heptaplus* of 1489), which Colet quoted in his treatises.[131] It is evident that he became infatuated with the works of Marsilio Ficino and, at some point, entered into correspondence with him.[132] Given Colet's passion for preaching, it would be extraordinary if he had not heard many sermons on his Italian travels; as Jones plausibly suggests, Colet was considerably affected by Italian humanism: 'It is clear that Colet left Italy imbued with the reforming zeal of men like Pico and Savonarola.'[133] Thus, the Florentine Savonarola's preaching – particularly popular in the 1490s – would possibly have come to Colet's attention.[134]

When Savonarola preached *On the Renovation of the Church* in the Duomo on 13 January 1494/5, shortly after the fall of the Medici regime,[135] Colet had been in Italy for three years. In his sermon, Savonarola called for reform of a morally corrupt Church and pronounced judgement on a sinful world. His specific indictments were against the pollution of prelates; the death of the good; the exclusion of the just; the multitude and stubbornness of sinners; the lack of charity and faith; and the ruin of sacred worship.[136] In some ways, Savonarola's rhetorical style anticipated that of Colet's own Convocation sermon. For instance, Savonarola concluded by scolding both world and Church:

> O Italy, O princes of Italy, O prelates of the Church, the wrath of God is over you, and you will not have any cure unless you mend your ways! And I will begin at my Sanctuary. O Italy, O Florence, misfortune befalls you because of sins! O noblemen, O powerful ones, O common people, the hand of the lord is upon you and neither the power of wisdom nor flight may withstand it! ... O princes of Italy, flee from the land of the North! Do penance while the sword is out of its sheath and while it is not stained with blood!'[137]

This tendency to apostrophize his hearers is also found in Colet: 'O Fathers, O pristes, by whiche we are conformable to this wordle' and 'O Couetousnes! Of the cometh these chargefull visitations of bysshops.'[138] However, Savonarola's words also highlight a fundamental difference between the two preachers: Savonarola urged penance in his fire and brimstone sermon; Colet, on the other hand, neither warned of the flames of hell nor advocated penance. Moreover, unlike Colet, Savonarola preached in parables and visions, also reminding the Florentines of what he had told them over the past four years,[139] which Colet could not do as he had probably not preached at Convocation before.[140] Therefore, there is a clear distinction between Savonarola's preaching and Colet's Convocation sermon in both form and content.

Another European figure whose preaching can usefully be compared to Colet's is Johann Geiler von Kaysersberg. Geiler was a preacher at Strasbourg Cathedral from 1478 until his death in 1510 – a significant location because Strasbourg was to become immensely important in the European Reformation.[141] Due to the development of Strasbourg's printing industry in the late-medieval period, Geiler's work had increasing potential to be read widely – a compilation of his sermons was duly published in 1508.[142] Indeed, during the period 1480 to 1499 – for part of which Colet was travelling in Italy – most works published in Strasbourg were sermons; individual repentance was a common theme. In fact, Colet's European travels took place at the very height of this boom in Strasbourg sermon publication: 106 collections of Latin sermons were printed there between 1480 and 1500, whereas only thirty-five such collections were to appear there in the next twenty years.[143]

Thus, Geiler is extolled by Douglass as the most significant preacher of his time. Although one of the most famous preachers north of the Alps, he cannot be called radical, as he maintained a conservative doctrinal position and upheld the teaching and authority of the Church.[144] Rather like Colet, Geiler was asked to give the opening address at a provincial council, in this case the 1482 Strasbourg synod, and took the opportunity to call for reform. He contrasted the corrupt clergy of his day with the lives of Jesus and the Apostles. Like Colet, his attempts yielded no tangible results, but were rather part of a prophetic ministry.[145] Both Colet's preaching in England, and Geiler's in Strasbourg, may have been 'preparing the future, but it was not much altering the present'.[146] Indeed, Geiler was interested in re-establishing Christian discipline by means of simple obedience to set rules:

> Geiler's concern for the instruction of the people led him to preach again and again on the meaning of the commandments and the Lord's Prayer. Many laymen did not understand even these basic elements of the Christian faith.

Colet would have approved of his simplicity and comprehensibility; Geiler warned of the depravity of sin against the background of late medieval theology:

> Geiler has proved to be familiar with the position of Thomas [Aquinas] as well as that of Scotus and the nominalists. But his pastoral concern that men accept full responsibility for their status in relation to God draws him to the nominalist position ... Though the mercy of God is an important element in his preaching, he is convinced that in his day Christians are all too much aware of this aspect of the Gospel and need far more to be warned against presumption on grace.[147]

Colet would also have approved of Geiler's 1500 condemnation of magistrates' efforts to restrict clerical privileges and incomes. Although Geiler admitted that canon law had become so elaborate as to mask the simplicity of the Ten Commandments, like Colet, he nevertheless proposed no change in Church law or doctrine.[148]

The similarity between Geiler's and Colet's idealism is exemplified by Geiler's condemnation of the circulation of German Bibles; he objected to the notion that the laity could understand Scripture by themselves. This belief in lay theological and linguistic inadequacy is reflected in Colet's ecclesiological conception of an exalted priesthood and an inferior laity.[149]

Although there is no evidence that Colet was familiar with Geiler's preaching, there is much in common between the two men: both were doctrinally conservative; both advocated provincial councils; both condemned corrupt clergy; both wished to preserve clerical privileges; both considered the laity inferior to the clergy; and neither achieved change. However, Geiler's call for individual repentance contrasts with Colet's call for institutional discipline, indicating the different soteriological emphases of the two men's ecclesiologies. Like Colet, Geiler had little to show for his lifelong attempts, except perhaps the knowledge that he had encouraged individuals to repent and be saved. As Colet was not primarily concerned with the individual, however, he would not even have had that consolation.

The third continental theologian to have had some ideas in common with Colet was Lefèvre d'Etaples.[150] Although no examples of Lefèvre's preaching survive, his expository fervour is evident in texts such as the 1521/22 preface to his *Commentaries on the Four Gospels*. In explaining that the Gospel should be proclaimed, he wrote that

> Bishops should have the first and highest roles in this, and above all he who is declared the first, highest, and greatest of those in visibly carrying out the sacred offices. For a person can only be designated such by virtue of that immortal, incorrupt, and spiritual love of Christ and the Gospel. Then may kings, princes, and all important personages, and thereupon the peoples of all nations, reflect on nothing else, embrace nothing so much, manifest nothing to the same extent as Christ, the vivifying Word of God, and His holy Gospel.[151]

This passage echoes Colet's sermon in several respects: the stress on episcopal duty; the placing of bishops at the top of the Church hierarchy; the emphasis on the clergy's spiritual status, as opposed to the laity's secular preoccupations; the inferiority of the secular hierarchy; and the belief that Christian knowledge is handed down through the ecclesiastical hierarchy to the secular one. The overall result was the propagation of the gospel from the highest to the lowest, which was to the benefit of all, but which could not take place unless those at the top of the ecclesiastical ladder performed their duties correctly. Perhaps unknowingly, Lefèvre echoed Colet's sermon again when he likened the ecclesiastical hierarchy to that of the celestial:

> And certainly every bishop ought to be like that angel whom John in the sacred Apocalypse saw flying in mid-heaven, having an everlasting Gospel, crying out above every nation and tribe and tongue and people: Fear the Lord, and give Him honour.[152]

Lefèvre's remedy for any shortcomings in society or Church was, once again, repentance: 'Believe in the Gospel, He says. But first He commanded that we have a change of heart, when he said: Repent.' Although Colet preferred not to proclaim repentance as a cure for the Church's ills, he and Lefèvre had the same end in mind: a revitalized institution:

> And why may we not desire that our age be restored to the likeness of that primitive Church? Then Christ was worshipped more purely, and His name shone forth more widely.

Lefèvre's linguistic usage reflected his interest in the work of Pseudo-Dionysius.[153] Advocating more than just an imitation of Christ, Lefèvre endorsed the Pseudo-Dionysian concept of conforming to Christ by activity: the term 'Christoformity', used by Lefèvre, derives from Galatians, 4:19.[154] Colet's ecclesiological thought was very similar to that expressed by Lefèvre in the following passage:

> For there are three things which our forefathers have set down: purgation, illumination, and perfection, whereby what is lower leads to what is higher. Among these perfection holds the highest place, illumination the middle, purgation the lowest ... May God grant that there be those who will add commentaries of illumination and (as He wills) perfection, for it is He alone to bestow every divine gift and especially what achieves perfection.[155]

The scheme is Pseudo-Dionysian, to which Lefèvre later added Pauline quotations for enhanced authority. Lefèvre believed Pseudo-Dionysius's work to be pre-eminent amongst the Fathers:

> [These Works] which have come down to us from apostolic times, seem to differ from others as living things differ from the dead, heavenly from earthly, mortal from immortal; for they are works which preserve in themselves a living force and a marvellous light beyond all others.[156]

Similarly, there is no evidence that Colet believed Pseudo-Dionysius to be anyone other than the Areopagite. At the time when Colet's sermon was preached, in 1511/12, his other writings suggest that he would also have regarded this Pseudo-Dionysian scheme as apostolically authoritative. No conclusion can be drawn concerning the mutual interdependence of Colet and Lefèvre. Although there is evidence that Colet was aware of Lefèvre's work, there is no evidence that Lefèvre was familiar with that of Colet.[157] Nevertheless, Lefèvre's thought is the closest match to Colet's own outside England. Like Colet, Lefèvre wrote commentaries on scripture, but seems to have had no coherent programme of reform.[158] The constant elements of his thought were the Apostolic Fathers, Pseudo-Dionysius, the Christian Cabbala, the Mystics, and the conciliarism of Nicholas of Cusa (1401-64).[159]

Thus, there are similarities and differences between Colet's work and all the authors discussed above. One major contrast was over the issues of repentance and purgatory, subjects not addressed in his sermon, but of apparent centrality to other preachers. Instead, Colet shifted the balance from fear of the unknown fires of the afterlife to fear of what might happen to the Church in the present. He remained optimistic that an institutional change could be achieved by means of legal obedience. Other late-medieval preachers were concerned with an individual's journey through purgatory to heaven; Colet was concerned with the Church: its order, power, rights, privileges on earth – and its perfection. However, with only one extant sermon text as evidence, we cannot assess how he may have preached concerning penance and purgatory in his other sermons, now lost. It is possible, nevertheless, to establish a connection between his ecclesiological preaching and a significant continental movement: conciliarism.

Conciliarism

In his sermon, Colet called for more councils, which were

> ... to be oftener used for the reformation of the churche. For there never hapneth nothyng more hurtefull to the churche of Christe, than the lacke both of councell generall and provinciall.[160]

The context of the word 'councell' here indicates that he did not mean merely the giving of counsel, or advice, in any loose sense, but was speaking rather of council – a body of people, possibly convened for the purposes of giving counsel. Thus, Colet's demand for more councils raises the question of whether or not he possessed conciliarist tendencies, and, therefore, of whether or not the sermon has, in part at least, a conciliarist agenda.

Conciliar theory held that the Pope was not an absolute ruler, but rather a constitutional monarch and that final authority lay with the whole body of the Church, or, in practice, with their representatives gathered in a general council.[161] Conciliarism had its roots in the early fifteenth century. The Councils of Pisa (1409) and Constance (1414-7) had assembled in order to put an end to the great schism of 1378 between the Roman and Avignonese papacies, giving rise to the conciliarist movement.[162] At the next general council, convened at Basel (1431-7), radical conciliarists, led by a Paris University delegation, defied the authority of the pontiff, but failed to gain support from their hearers for a transfer of authority away from the Pope and towards a council.[163] Colet's call for more frequent councils echoed the conciliarist decree of *Frequens* resulting from the Council of Constance. As Mullett explains:

The decree of Constance, *Frequens* (1417), made provision for regular meetings of councils. The aftermath was a period of frequent council sessions, at Basel between 1431 and 1437 and at Florence and Rome between 1438 and 1445. Claims that the authority of the council was equal or even superior to that of the pope – 'conciliarism' ... was a recipe for a running conflict between popes and councils.[164]

The *Frequens* decree was still in force at the end of the fifteenth century.[165] Thus, it may be conjectured that Colet was advocating the implementation of *Frequens* itself.[166]

The last council to meet without papal convocation was held at Pisa (1511-12), although a papal council, Lateran V, was convened soon after (1512-17). In Pisa, Jacques Almain (1480-1515), the Parisian Theologian, and John Major or Mair (1467-1550), the Scottish scholastic, were conciliarism's chief apologists.[167] Almain believed that the ecclesiastical power residing within the Church was not only more direct than that residing in the Pope, and 'greater in extension' to it, but also that it was 'greater in perfection', a phrase reminiscent of Colet's ecclesiology.[168] For Almain, the Church represented in a general council could not err in decisions because the Holy Spirit aided it. On this point, Almain was engaged in an ongoing debate with his Paris University colleague, Thomas de Vio Cajetan (1469-1534).[169]

Three common characteristics of conciliarism to emerge from the debates at Pisa were the demand for reform of the Church by the periodic assembly of general councils; a vision of an oligarchic government consisting of bishops and cardinals; and the assertion of the superiority of the general council to the Pope.[170] Thus, through his continental travels, Colet may well have been familiar with conciliarist arguments. As MacCulloch rightly observes, Colet's sermon was delivered at a time when 'there were still plenty of conciliarists in positions of authority ... who might have exploited the mood of reform if an effective General Council had been called'.[171] However, as Oakley notes, 'the lack of English participation in that ill-attended assembly [Pisa] provides no grounds for speculation about the ecclesiological proclivities of English Churchmen.'[172] In fact, there is no evidence of widespread conciliarism in early sixteenth-century England.[173]

Furthermore, Colet's sermon is tame in comparison to effusions of radical conciliarists, such as Dionysius Carthusianus (1402-71):

> Where in the Church can one find anything that is not soiled or corrupt? Does there remain a spark of integrity in ecclesiastics, of nobility in the powerful, of loyalty in the common people? Everything is spoiled and overthrown: from

head to foot, all is but one wound. The evil is so great that no private initiative can cure it; it requires the effort of all to extinguish the conflagration that is overwhelming the Church. That is why all the world cries for a council.[174]

Whilst Dionysius the Carthusian's conciliarism far exceeded Colet's own tendencies, Colet's ecclesiology has nevertheless recently been linked with that of Jean Gerson (1363-1429), Chancellor of Paris University and a prominent conciliarist at the Council of Constance:

> Gerson, like Colet, was an enthusiast for Dionysius the Areopagite, and set the highest standards possible for the clerical order; so he was not seeking to destroy Church structure, simply to recall them to purity.[175]

Thus, Colet and Gerson, in some regards at least, shared a common vision for the Church: high standards and a desire for purity.

Although there is no direct evidence to suggest that Colet was familiar with conciliarist thought, his call for more provincial and general councils, aimed at promoting reformation, echoes conciliar idealism.[176] Both Colet and the conciliarists of Pisa emphasized the Church's role as the Mystical Body of Christ.[177] Colet might pray in his sermon for 'our most holy father the Pope', but his main emphasis was upon the supremacy of bishops and clergy within the ecclesiastical hierarchy.[178] Likewise, although conciliarists did not deny the validity of the papacy, and may well have been happy to pray for the Pope, they questioned the limits of papal power, just as Colet emphasized the power and responsibility of all priests and bishops, not just the Bishop of Rome. Hence, there is reason to believe that Colet considered councils to be an effective way of administrating Church business. Moreover, his call for more councils was consistent with conciliarist ideas. Although, Colet retained and expanded the hierarchical ideas of Pseudo-Dionysius, these notions were not antithetical to conciliarist ideals.[179] At the very least, we may conclude that Colet was probably not anti-conciliarist. My conjectural interpretation of Colet's call for more general and provincial councils is that it indicates conciliarist tendencies within his sermon, which were consistent with, and developed as a consequence of, his ecclesiological idealism.

Conclusion

It can rightly be claimed that Colet's Convocation sermon is in tune with several features of traditional late-medieval Catholic practice in terms of style, method and content. The dean was preaching on renewal, as many others had done before him and would continue so to do. But his sermon was new in one important respect: it was, as far as is known, the first occasion on which Colet's unique ecclesiology was expressed in sermon form to the heart of the English Church. Previous scholars have characterized the sermon as traditional, non-radical, and consistent with its author's exegetical thought. However, this chapter has, more precisely, argued that the sermon is characteristic of Colet's ecclesiology in its emphasis upon unity, a unity based upon law and obedience within the ecclesiastical hierarchy, resulting in a rightful superiority of the priesthood over the laity. For Colet, only through such a structure could humanity be reconciled to God – through the reception of God's truth and by the subsequent ascent of the Church towards union with God. The sermon was part of a late-medieval preaching tradition, and yet is clearly distinguishable from that tradition for the following reasons: Colet used a half-ancient, half-modern form, but expanded it to include his ecclesiological emphases on both text and contemporary issues; he used a plain style in order to communicate his message, but used Latin only, in order to retain theological credibility amongst his peers;[180] his theme of non-conformity to the world, yet of reformation, echoed a common theme in late-medieval preaching, but he ignored other common topics, such as individual sin, repentance, purgatory and hell, instead preferring to advocate his own characteristic ecclesiological concept of obedience to canon law as the answer to the Church's alleged inadequacies. Similarly, Colet's text bears some resemblance to English and continental sermons of the period, but is again distinct by virtue of its stress on obedience, rather than repentance. He included a call for more councils, indicating conciliarist tendencies, which are wholly consistent with his ecclesiological ideals.

Colet took the opportunity, at the 1511/12 Convocation, of sharing his very positive vision with those who also, as authorities in the Church, could effect change by enforcing behavioural standards in their jurisdictions. Colet believed that, if the Church was to fulfil its considerable potential, then law, order and beauty must be distributed through it from the top down. If he could persuade the bishops that the Church was capable of Pseudo-Dionysian perfection, not as separate individuals, but as a body, then it had a chance of avoiding internal disunity. With this defence, the Church could heal itself from within and grow towards perfection with God, both in this world and the next.

Colet's potential for success, however, was perhaps limited by two main factors: firstly, those who would have agreed with his ideals, like Fisher and many other senior clergy, such as Richard Fox (Bishop of Winchester) and Robert Sherburne (Bishop of Chichester), were already aware of the need for constant vigilance against worldly influence in the Church. These conscientious bishops had been attempting a revitalisation of the Church through preaching, administrative reform and the foundation of educational institutions.[181] The dean was, therefore, largely preaching to the converted. Secondly, the minority of errant bishops who neglected their dioceses and were guilty of all Colet's charges and more besides – one thinks of the Italian bishops of Bath and Wells and Worcester, as well as James Stanley of Ely[182] – would have shown no interest in Colet's perfectionism.

Colet's emphasis upon the importance of hierarchy led him, in subsequent years, to become critical of those in authority, with the consequence that he was perceived as a threat by senior clergy, and even by the king. His preaching would cause controversy, to the extent that, in 1513, Henry VIII rebuked him and, in 1514, his bishop, Richard Fitzjames, made some critical allegations to do with what Colet had said about images, hospitality and preaching itself.[183] These reactions, and those of others, will be examined in the next chapter.

6

PREACHING AND CONTROVERSY: THE KING, THE BISHOP AND THE CARDINAL, 1512-15

This chapter argues that the perfectionist idealism of Colet's ecclesiological preaching provoked far more extreme reactions, both negative and positive, than have previously been recognized. It also contends that the dean's sermons were more directly responsible for the decline, and subsequent rise, in his clerical and political fortunes between 1512 and 1515 than scholars have so far admitted. For instance, the king forced him to retract some anti-war statements made in a sermon preached at Court on Good Friday 1513; his sermons provoked Bishop Fitzjames to make allegations against him in relation to his views on images, hospitality and preaching;[1] the St. Paul's Cathedral chapter complained about his preaching; and he was even admired by heretical Lollards. Colet's controversial preaching, therefore, was criticized by the highest authorities for undermining both ecclesiastical and secular rulers. Moreover, he attracted the admiration of heretics. More positively, however, Colet's reputation benefited from a sermon, delivered at Wolsey's Westminster Abbey installation as cardinal in November 1515, in which he diplomatically supported Henry VIII's and Wolsey's superior authority, thus winning their approval and a place in the King's Council.[2] On the one hand, therefore, his naïve ecclesiological absolutism was perceived as constituting an attack on the established authority of both the Church and, unusually for Colet, the Crown.[3] On the other hand, the Establishment, as personified by king and cardinal, welcomed the dean's public endorsement of the ecclesiastical hierarchy in 1515.

Evidence concerning Colet's skill and reputation as a preacher, and concerning the impact of his sermons, may be found in contemporaneous sources as well as in documents of the later sixteenth and seventeenth centuries. Besides printed editions of his Convocation sermon, accounts of his preaching on war, and a fragmentary version of his sermon delivered before Wolsey in 1515, are extant.[4] Information about how Colet's preaching was received by the wider Church and society exists in documents written by Erasmus, , Tyndale and Latimer.[5]

Historians interested in this period of Colet's life have understandably tended to focus on the particular issues of his relationships with Fitzjames, or with the king, or with the wider Church, or with Wolsey.[6] For that reason, I shall assess the relevant scholarship within the appropriate sections of this chapter. However, two scholars' viewpoints in particular demonstrate the confusion surrounding the various episodes. Lupton, for instance, argued that the king condoned Colet's sermon on war; that Fitzjames's attack on Colet was spiteful and unjustified; that the cathedral clergy were in desperate need of reform; that Colet welcomed Lollard attention; and that his sermon preached to Wolsey was a continuation of the dean's fearless reform project.[7] As we shall see, all of these assertions are incorrect. Only Gleason has so far given a coherent overview of the period, arguing that Colet's relationship with the king remained unshaken by their confrontation; that the two men had a close working relationship in London; and that the dean was innocent of any allegations that Fitzjames may have made against him.[8] Gleason also suggests that Colet's real conflict was with his own cathedral chapter and that Fitzjames's animosity was not directed at the dean, but rather at Wolsey.[9] However, the evidence suggests, notwithstanding Gleason's interpretation, that Henry VIII, Fitzjames and some elements in the wider Church did harbour genuine concerns about Colet's ecclesiological preaching. Contrary to Gleason's ideas, Colet was ironically both a provocative nuisance and a welcome supporter of established order in both Church and Court.

The King

Between March 1510 and April 1517, Colet preached at Greenwich at least eight times, four of which were on Good Friday.[10] His appearance at Court was thus almost traditional, though there was a gap in 1514. Erasmus reported that, on an unspecified occasion, Colet had advocated Cicero's just war theory to the king. According to Erasmus's chronology, this episode took place whilst Fitzjames was seeking evidence of Colet's alleged heresy:

> Still the old bishop's animosity was not allayed. He tried to excite the court, with the king at its head, against Colet, having now got hold of another weapon against him. This was that he had openly declared in a sermon 'an

unjust peace was to be preferred to the justest war,' a war being at that very time in preparation against the French.[11]

Far from being put off by Colet's radical opinion, the king encouraged Colet to continue preaching on morality and, according to Erasmus, became the dean's protector against criticism:

> At this juncture the noble young king gave a conspicuous token of his kingly disposition, for he privately encouraged Colet to go on without restraint, and improve by his teaching the corrupt morals of his age, and not to withdraw his light from those dark times. He was not unaware, he said, of the motive that incited those bishops against him, nor unconscious of the benefits he had conferred on the English nation by his life and doctrine. He added, that he would put such a check on their attempts that others should clearly see that whoever assailed Colet would not go unpunished.[12]

The exact time of this public expression of apparent support for Colet is not given, but if the foregoing statement is true, allowing for Erasmus's tendency towards hyperbole, then it was a valuable endorsement of Colet's status as a preacher. Henry's toleration of Colet, however, was put to the test when the dean preached again on war, this time at Court, and when war was imminent: having joined Pope Julius II, the Emperor Maximilian and Ferdinand of Aragon in a campaign against Louis XII,[13] by early 1513 the king was preparing to attack France. According to Erasmus, Colet preached at Court on 27 March 1513, denouncing Henry VIII's projected expedition:[14]

> An expedition was being got ready against the French, to start after Easter. On Good Friday, Colet preached a noble sermon before the king and his court on the victory of Christ, exhorting all Christians to war and conquer under the banner of Him their proper King ... Let them follow, he added, the example of Christ as their Prince, not that of a Julius Caesar or an Alexander.[15]

Olin plausibly argued that Colet's reference to Caesar and Alexander referred to the notoriously belligerent Pope Julius II, who had died the month before in February 1513, and to his predecessor, Alexander VI. Whether he was referring to Roman Emperors or Popes, Colet not only condemned all wars except spiritual ones against the temptations of this world, but also exhorted his hearers to eschew temporal rulers in favour of Christ. This notion, as expressed above, arose directly from his ecclesiological notion that conflict should be absent from the Church, the Body of Christ:

> Among the members of Christ's body ... there ought to be humility, toleration, constancy in good at all times and without cessation, a doing good even to those who do us evil and provoke us wrongfully; that every member, so far as it can, may imitate Christ its head.[16]

Thus, his ecclesiology held that, in contrast to conflict and war, everyone should strive for 'the profit of the society, and the preservation of unity and peace'.[17] In March 1513, therefore, Colet spoke from a position of ecclesiological idealism, rather than pragmatic politics. By so doing, he had challenged the king's authority, which was a dangerous business, as Seebohm suggests: 'The king ... coming directly from his fleet full of expectation, was not likely to be in a mood to be thwarted by a preacher.'[18] Even Erasmus's glowing account of Colet's homiletic success admits, at this point, that Henry received this sermon with apprehension, worried that his soldiers might lose their courage for the cause. Erasmus recollected that Colet was summoned to the king:

> By the king's order Colet was sent for. He came and had luncheon in the Franciscan convent adjoining Greenwich Palace.[19]

Erasmus's narrative relates that Henry wished Colet to clarify, in public, what he had said concerning war. In other words, the dean was being ordered to retract his statement:

> ... the king and he [Colet] were at one upon all points, save only that the king wished him to say at some other time, with clearer explanation, what he had already said with perfect truth, namely, that for Christians no war was a just one. And this for the sake of the rough soldiers, who might put a different construction on his words from that which he had intended.[20]

Fearing that support for his campaign would be weakened by such an attack, Henry could not have been pleased with an anti-war sermon at this time. In the private interview, Henry asserted his authority and Colet subsequently retracted his objections to Henry's war: 'Colet, as became his good sense' had to 'set the king's mind at rest' before Henry would let him go.[21] In the exposition of his otherworldly perfectionism, therefore, Colet had exposed himself to Henry's chastising authority and was consequently rebuked.

The episode surrounding Colet's 1513 Good Friday sermon before Henry VIII, and his subsequent audience with the king, allegedly concluded with the latter's exclamation: 'Let every man have his own doctor, and show his favour to him. This is the doctor for me!'[22] Thus, Erasmus's account, which possibly had its source in Colet himself, was designed to show Colet in the best possible light.[23] Accordingly, Gleason, like Lupton and Hunt, interpreted this evidence as an indication of Henry's support for Colet.[24] Yet my foregoing argument suggests that, by denouncing war and advocating Christ as the only 'proper king' at a time when Henry VIII had, as Brigden states, 'launched grandiose campaigns', Colet had given Henry reason to be seriously concerned about his sermon.[25] This concern has rightly been recognized by Dickens and Jones, who state that Colet 'had to avert the royal displeasure in a long if ultimately successful interview'.[26] However, the interview was neither long nor, for Colet, successful.

To conclude: since Henry VII's creation of a 'political theology', the King of England had held a claim of ecclesiastical authority over the English Church.[27] Colet's hierarchical ecclesiology necessitated the honouring of the king's authority, a king who possessed the power to effect considerable change in the Church.[28] Ironically, however, Colet's ideals were hindered by the ecclesiastical situation precisely because he and his Church were subservient to the king and laws of England:

> The Church was both a spiritual and a temporal institution; it existed within the realm; the church building was regarded as a piece of real estate; and prelates held their estates of the king by the same tenure as lay lords. The Church was both subject to and protected by the laws of England.[29]

This 1513 episode indicates Henry's negative reaction to Colet's otherworldly idealism. On the one hand, Henry encouraged the dean to preach and invited him to Court. On the other hand, the king felt it necessary to temper Colet's message for the sake of maintaining a unified purpose to his military campaign against France. The dean's ideal of moral purity was acceptable to the Crown as along as it did not overstep its ecclesiastical boundaries and impinge upon military and foreign policy. After all, Henry VIII's prerogative was to '… reject those elements which ran counter to the customary law of the Kingdom or derogated from [His] own royal dignity.'[30]

The principles of Colet's purist ecclesiological pacifism, therefore, had no application to royal political decisions as far as Henry VIII was concerned. Colet was offered tacit royal support for his work, but only on condition that he did not interfere with the king's affairs: for Henry, the only superior was God alone.[31] Thus, in 1513, Colet had learned the consequences of preaching controversial ideals: a royal rebuke. The fact that he eventually benefited from this lesson in diplomacy is evident in his sermon delivered to Wolsey in 1515, which I shall examine later in this chapter.[32] Following this episode with the king, Colet's contentious sermons and uncompromising ideals received a further negative reaction, this time from Fitzjames.[33]

The Bishop

In 1513/14, Fitzjames accused Colet of preaching against the veneration of images, of misinterpreting the scriptures concerning hospitality and of criticizing episcopal preaching standards. Thus, according to Erasmus,[34] the allegations were threefold:

> His [Fitzjames's] weapons were just what such persons resort to when plotting anyone's destruction, that is to say, he laid an information against him before the archbishop of Canterbury, specifying certain articles taken from his sermons. One was that he had taught that images ought not to be worshiped. Another, that he had done away with the hospitality commended by St. Paul ... A third article was that having said in the pulpit that there were some who preached written sermons – the stiff and formal way of many in England – he had indirectly reflected on his bishop, who, from his old age, was in the habit of so doing.[35]

As well as the accusation concerning images, Fitzjames allegedly claimed that, in his exposition of John 21:15-17, Colet had made a false interpretation of the command 'Feed my sheep'.[36] According to Erasmus, the traditional medieval interpretation of the Vulgate Latin *pasce* was that 'feed' meant to feed by doctrine, by example of life and by hospitality.[37] Whilst Colet agreed with the first two interpretations, he denied the third, arguing that the apostles were too poor to have offered any hospitality, and that therefore the third command to 'feed my sheep' must have referred to the practice of preaching. The problem of interpretation was exacerbated by the Vulgate's use of the single Latin word *pasce* for the word 'feed', unlike the Greek text of the New Testament, where two different words are used.[38] The Greek makes a clear distinction between the word βοσκε, meaning 'feed', and the word ποιμενη, for the second command, meaning 'tend'.[39] The third allegation against Colet was that he had spoken out against those who preached written sermons in a stiff and formal way.[40] Foxe referred to these types of sermons as 'Bosom Sermons':

> The third crime wherewith they charged him [Colet], was for speaking against suche as used to preache onely by bosome sermons, declaring nothing els to the people, but as they bring in theyr prayers with them, which because the Bishop of London used then much to do for his age, he tooke it as spoken against him, and therefore bore him this displeasure.[41]

In considering this episode, some scholars have relied solely upon Colet's 1511/12 Convocation sermon for evidence of his provocative teaching, leading to the misconception that the Convocation sermon itself prompted Fitzjames's allegations.[42] This cannot have been the case, as Fitzjames's specific accusations do not relate to that sermon's content. Indeed, the difficulties arising for students of this episode are evident in the confused scholarship surrounding it.[43] For instance, the nineteenth-century scholar Sir Sidney Lee suggested that Fitzjames's grievance was born out of simple jealousy: 'The aged Bishop Fitzjames, who was jealous of Colet's reputation, took advantage of his popularity.'[44] Consequently, Lee ignored Fitzjames's genuine accusations concerning Colet's views on images, hospitality and preaching. Kaufman mistakenly concludes that the dean's confrontation with Fitzjames arose because of Colet's frustration at Fitzjames's 'unflinching demand for obedience' from the laity.[45] Thus, Kaufman wrongly depicts Colet as the laity's champion and Fitzjames as the clergy's advocate. Kaufman's misrepresentation of Colet's ecclesiology as an attempt to elevate the laity to priestly status must be rejected. In fact, both Colet and Fitzjames desired the continued elevation of the clergy above the laity, the dispute between them arising from other ecclesiological issues. Gwyn suggests another reason for the conflict:

> What makes it [appraisal of Fitzjames's and Colet's relationship] difficult for the historian is that both radicals [like Colet] and conservatives [like Fitzjames] tended to use the language of renovation and renewal to mean different things; and that these differences could and, in the case of Colet and Fitzjames, did lead to conflict ... And whatever difficulties he [i.e. Colet] may have had with Fitzjames, it is clear that the Church hierarchy was by no means opposed to everything he stood for.[46]

Gwyn also argues that the Church authorities were not opposed to Colet, on the basis that Warham invited him to preach at Convocation (1511/12) and that Wolsey invited him to preach at his installation as cardinal (1515). Gwyn's plausible scenario contrasts with Gleason's mysterious denial that any conflict existed between Colet and Fitzjames at all, on the grounds that 'the two men worked together amicably for years'.[47] Thus, Gleason ignores the significance of Fitzjames's accusations against the dean. On the other hand, Dickens and Jones, who are deeply suspicious of Gleason's biography, consider that 'Colet did not hesitate to defy his own diocesan Bishop Fitzjames, who badly wanted to crush him by a charge of heresy'.[48] However, we are given no indication of what this defiance was, or of what the heresy charge consisted. Brigden tantalizingly suggests that Colet 'began to touch upon matters which were politically controversial and seen as doctrinally unsafe'. However, when Colet is supposed to have engaged with such unsafe matters remains unexplained.[49] I aim to demonstrate below that Fitzjames was neither jealous of, nor friendly with, Colet; that the allegations did not amount to heresy charges; but that Fitzjames was sincerely concerned that the dean's preaching, on three ecclesiological issues, could harm the Church.

Personal details of Colet's vexation are revealed in correspondence. In a letter of 11 July 1513, Erasmus expressed his concern that Colet was being harassed:

> I was distressed to read what you wrote at the end of your letter: that the burden of business was oppressing you more vexatiously than usual … Meanwhile, confront the malicious gossip of ill-disposed people with an upright and pure conscience. Immerse yourself in the one and simple Christ and the complexities of the world will disturb you less.[50]

Gleason has suggested that this passage only makes sense if referring to Colet's battles with his chapter rather than with Fitzjames.[51] Although Colet was harassed by his own clergy, it does not follow that he was therefore left untroubled by his bishop, an issue upon which Gleason does not come to a satisfactorily conclusion, offering no explanation for Fitzjames's apparent attack.[52] Nor does Gleason corroborate his argument by providing details of Colet's alleged vexation.

However, further evidence of Colet's unhappiness is revealed in a letter, dated 20 October 1514, from Colet to Erasmus:

> Your friends here are all well: the archbishop of Canterbury is as sweet and good as ever; my lord of Lincoln [Wolsey] now reigns as archbishop of York; he of London still plagues me. I think daily of retiring and taking refuge among the Carthusians. My nest is nearly finished. When you return to us, as far as I can guess, you will find me there dead to worldly things.[53]

This letter reveals much about Colet's situation towards the end of 1514: it demonstrates that he had an ally in Archbishop Warham,[54] and it suggests that Fitzjames's attacks on Colet had continued (*non cessant*) to the point of the dean's weariness. The nature of those attacks will now be assessed.

With regard to the first accusation concerning Colet's views on images, Gleason has convincingly demonstrated that Colet was not averse to the veneration of images.[55] However, as Erasmus explained in 1521, Colet's views on images, derived from Pseudo-Dionysius, were not always clear to others:

> He had a leaning to some opinions derived from Dionysius and other early divines, though not to such a degree as to make him contravene in any points the decisions of the Church. Still, they made him less hard on such as disapproved of the universal adoration of images in churches, whether painted or of wood, or stone, or bronze, or silver.[56]

This quotation implies that, although Colet was not a heretic, he gave his critics evidence that he sympathized with those who rejected the 'adoration' of images, namely Lollards.[57] Regardless of the fact that Colet left sacred images in his will, it was apparently his teaching on the matter that concerned Fitzjames.[58]

With regard to the second charge, Colet's interpretation of John 21:15-17 was not heretical, although he saw the text as permitting him to substitute pious preaching for generous hospitality, thus giving practical expression to his ascetical ecclesiological values.[59] Colet's refusal to offer physical sustenance to his flock set a bad example to parochial clergy:

> Since even the parochial clergy were supposed to bestow a quarter or third of their income in acts of charity, these expectations were large indeed. Most ecclesiastics examined by the late-medieval writers, as well as by their sixteenth-century successors, inevitably failed to do so much.[60]

Colet's abstemious attitude not only undermined the practice of hospitality by his juniors, the parochial clergy, but also his seniors, for it was also a requirement of bishops: 'For, albeit that hospitality is required in all spiritual ministers, yet in bishops chiefly. A bishops' house without hospitality is as a tavern without wine.'[61]

The dean's refusal to offer hospitality contrasted with his personal opinions on the matter, as expressed in his writings. In his Romans lectures, he wrote thus:

> Feed your enemies; and if an adversary thirst, give him drink; and whatever service you can confer, render it cheerfully and willingly to all. For assuredly by this alone will you conquer evil, and win over even the ill disposed to yourselves as friends. By your love and kindness you will warm those that are in the chill of malice and wickedness; and by your tenderness you will soften the hard and unbending.[62]

The hypocritical nature of this behaviour was compounded by his insistence that preachers should practice what they preach:

> But if men's lives do not answer the words they have understood, then they are makers of harangues in an alien tongue; they are men speaking to the air; they are like a cithern whose harping goes unheeded, so that men do not understand the air to which they should dance and beat the ground. They hear something – they know not what – but they see nothing. In action, everything shines forth clearly.[63]

The only excuse Colet gave for this inconsistency of word and deed was contained in his idea that if one could not give willingly, then it was better not to give at all: 'Therefore men are admonished, not so much to give, as to give willingly.'[64] As Bishop of London, Fitzjames would have been well aware of Colet's practices with regard to hospitality. Fitzjames's accusation, therefore, did not only concern scriptural interpretation, but was also an attack upon Colet's mean-spirited and ascetic ecclesiology.

Information about Colet's culpability regarding the third allegation can be found in his ecclesiological works: his commentary on the *Ecclesiastical Hierarchy* of Pseudo-Dionysius explains that bishops should preach extemporaneously and passionately, not from a book of sermons:

> The bishop, exhibiting in himself the form of Christ, and preaching and exhorting and admonishing all men to desire to be fashioned after that form, that being like Christ they may be saved in him, must needs move some, by reason of the power of the word of God.[65]

It is probable, therefore, that he also expressed this view from the pulpit, as Fitzjames claimed. Thus, the bishop's third accusation, as presented by Erasmus, was apparently valid.[66] Moreover, it amounted to a personal criticism of Fitzjames's preaching habits.[67]

Evidence suggests that Fitzjames, and perhaps also friars Bricot and Standish, persistently harassed Colet from 1512 to the end of 1514.[68] His allegations against Colet were probably not official heresy charges: had the 'old bigot'[69] been serious about prosecuting Colet, he would surely have succeeded, just as he had in many other cases. For instance, Foxe recorded many instances of successful prosecutions brought by Fitzjames, including, during the years 1510 and 1511, those of twenty-two Londoners, who abjured heresies concerning image worship in the Church.[70] In

November 1511, Erasmus even joked that all the burnings must have been costing a great deal in fuel.[71] Nevertheless, Fitzjames's accusations demonstrate that the dean's preaching was a serious annoyance to the bishop, because Colet's teaching on images was unclear; because his rejection of the rules of hospitality was an insult to the established order; and because he had implicitly criticized Fitzjames's method of preaching and, therefore, undermined his episcopal authority.

In the years following Erasmus's 1521 biography, more melodramatic accounts of Colet's conflict with Fitzjames emerged: Tyndale opined that Warham had saved the dean from execution, implying that Colet had been prosecuted for translating the *Pater Noster*, the Lord's Prayer, into English:

> William Tyndall in hys booke aunswering ... M. More, addeth moreover, and testifieth that the Byshop of London would have made the said Colet Deane of Paules, an hereticke for translating the Pater noster in Englishe, had not the Bishop of Caunterbury holpen the Deane.[72]

In a sermon of 1552, however, Hugh Latimer mentioned that Colet had been saved by an even higher power. He claimed to remember that, as he was taking his MA at Cambridge, he had attended a divinity lecture given by George Stafford, which occurred

> ... even at that time when Doctor Colet was in trouble, and should have been burnt, if God had not turned the King's heart to the contrary.[73]

Although Tyndale's and Latimer's recollections, written after Colet's death, do not match those of Erasmus, their accounts nevertheless relate the seriousness of Colet's position in 1513/14.

To conclude: it appears, on the evidence of Erasmus, Foxe, Tyndale and Latimer, that, during 1513/14, Fitzjames persecuted Colet. Moreover, it seems that the allegations were based on material taken from sermons preached between 1512 and 1514, the texts of which are now lost, if they ever existed at all. Fitzjames's opposition to the dean is significant as an example of an extreme reaction to Colet's ecclesiology, as presented in his sermons, which Fitzjames considered to be a threat to the hierarchy of the Church and to the authority of bishops. Thus, the practical consequence of Colet's ecclesiology, as developed in his written works and expressed in his sermons, was that he was perceived to be a challenge to some parts of the Establishment. Unfortunately for Colet, this was precisely the opposite of his desire. His ecclesiology aimed to uphold Church structures and hierarchy, not to destroy them.[74] Fitzjames's reaction, therefore, demonstrates that Colet's message, for at least one bishop, had misfired. In his desire to reform clerical morality and spirituality, his bishop perceived him as dangerously critical and anticlerical at a time when the Church was attempting to improve its image.[75] The reactions of that Church to Colet's ecclesiological preaching will now be considered.

Reactions to Colet's Preaching

Colet's uneasy relationship with his clerical colleagues was recorded by Erasmus and has been noted by scholars ever since.[76] Lupton, rather simplistically, explained the antagonism as a clash between Colet's piety and the cathedral clergy's corruption; Porter, following Lupton and Carpenter, re-emphasized Colet's hatred of clerical abuses. Harper-Bill, however, has rightly reassessed his clerical criticism to have been 'unfounded' and 'misconceived'. Thus, Lupton's proto-Protestant Colet has properly been replaced by Harper-Bill's characterization that the dean's criticisms were not always valid. Even so, it must be noted that Brigden remains convinced, wrongly I believe, that upon Colet's arrival in London, 'Reform was needed, and urgently.'[77] Gleason concludes rather that Colet was at fault:

> ... stiff fines imposed for non-performance of clerical duties and a rich man's tactless refusal of hospitality are far more likely than heresy to be the source of Colet's frustrations in 1513.[78]

Gleason's strict and mean-spirited Colet is a more plausible portrait than the Victorian one, repeated by Brigden, but Gleason is too optimistic in suggesting that the cathedral chapter was the dean's only source of frustration in 1513. As for Colet's London preaching, Dickens and Jones have succinctly summarized Erasmus's testimony: 'Colet certainly took routine preaching most seriously, planning not merely individual sermons but also integrated courses for his London congregation.'[79] I argue below not only that Colet antagonized his own cathedral clergy by his preaching, but also that his idealistic ecclesiology was perceived as being so extremely critical of the Church as to attract the unwelcome, and dangerous, attention of heretical Lollards. I begin by examining how Colet's ecclesiology related to his clerical colleagues at St. Paul's.

Colet had a problem with the Church: how to reconcile the wickedness of humankind to the divine perfection of God:

> For this world is so wholly placed in the power of the wicked one, that its countless wickedness cannot be overcome save by infinite good.[80]

The solution to the problem, for Colet, was the light of Christ, which, by divine action and *via* the celestial and ecclesiastical hierarchies, was able to bring unity to the Church. Unity was at once the means and the end of the reconciliation process:

> This Sun [Christ], shining upon the minds of men ... at once unites them in strength, elevates them to light, kindles them into flame.[81]

However, Colet was a member of the clerical elite:[82] born into a wealthy mercantile family and a pluralist.[83] Prior to his tenure of the deanery, his ecclesiastical experience had been minimal. His language of decay and reform was alien to those parishes where pious clerical and lay conscientiousness was the norm, but where humanism was exceptional.[84] His high-minded message was based on a general ignorance of ordinary parishes and their priests, who suffered economic hardship in the early sixteenth century:

> When Dean Colet in his Convocation Sermon accused such men of inordinate greed, he was echoing a long tradition of criticism which may have been valid when first extensively ventilated a century and a half before, but bore no relation to the contemporary condition of a clerical 'proletariat' which was economically depressed but which in general served well the religious needs of the laity.[85]

Thus, Colet's critical ecclesiology would hardly have resonated with parish priests. Although some senior clerics, such as John Taylor and William Melton, concurred with his ideals, not all did so.[86] Regardless of clerical hardship, Colet considered the objective of achieving a harmonious Church to be possible through diligent contributions to the body ecclesiastical. As Colet asserts:

> ... so likewise ought there to be in the Church, and among all faithful people, such a mutual love and interest, as for each to believe that his own powers, whatsoever they be, were given him for no other cause, than that he should always be exerting them for the assistance of others, the profit of the society, and the preservation of unity and peace.[87]

Colet attempted to implement this ecclesiology at the beginning of his decanal career by preaching more often than was strictly required and in a methodical manner. As Erasmus related:

Hereupon our good Colet, feeling his call to be for the work and not for the empty honour, restored the decayed discipline of the cathedral body and – what was a novelty there – commenced preaching at every festival in his cathedral, over and above the special sermons he had to deliver now at Court, now in various other places. In his own cathedral, moreover, he would not take isolated texts from the Gospels or Apostolic Epistles but would start with some connected subject and pursue it right to the end in a course of sermons ... He used to have a crowded congregation, including most of the leading men both of the city and the Court.[88]

This account describes some key characteristics of Colet's preaching at St. Paul's: it was connected with the restoration of discipline in the cathedral; he preached frequently; he preached a series of sermons on specific biblical books; and he preached to courtiers who attended his cathedral sermons. However, Erasmus further noted that the cathedral clergy were less than impressed with the ecclesiological content of the sermons, which criticized them and made unreasonable demands of them:

Colet was no great favourite either with many of his own college, being too strict about canonical discipline; and these were every now and then complaining of being treated as monks ...[89]

Since Colet exaggerated the extent to which the resident canons' discipline had decayed, if it had decayed at all, this antagonism must instead be attributed to his unfortunate ascetical ecclesiology.[90] His idealistic criticisms were to gain him an undesirably exalted reputation amongst a heretical section of the Church: the Lollards.

Based on the ideas of John Wycliffe (c.1330-84), Lollards attacked the papacy and advocated Church reform well into the early sixteenth century.[91] They criticized the Catholic doctrines of transubstantiation, confession to priests, penance, papal authority and the sacrament of marriage, as well as the veneration of images.[92] For these heretical opinions, many were prosecuted: Bishop Longland tried three to four hundred Buckinghamshire Lollards in 1521; only four were executed, and most abjured.[93] Gwyn suggests that Fitzjames's objections to Colet's views were that they 'coincided with those voiced by the Lollards. No wonder they went to hear him preach!' However, as Gwyn admits, 'Colet, of course, was no Lollard.'[94] In fact, their approbation would have been abhorrent to him, for he fundamentally disagreed with their teaching. There is plenty of evidence – in his Convocation sermon, in his exegetical writings, and in his life – that Colet condemned heresy at every opportunity.⁹⁵ As he stated categorically: 'What is so deadly as sects and heresy? Yet at the same time, what declares so well the unity and constancy of the good who are in the truth?'⁹⁶ And yet, Colet stressed that heresies had a purpose in the Church, in that they highlighted those who were constant in the faith and those who were not:

> Heresy makes manifest those who have been proved true. When there is division and falling away, it is shown who is constant and self-consistent in the truth.⁹⁷

Nevertheless, some Lollards found Colet's preaching attractive.⁹⁸ Just as Pseudo-Dionysian influence made the dean appear sympathetic to those who rejected the veneration of images, so Colet's enthusiasm for preaching elicited sympathy from rural Lollards such as Thomas Geoffrey of Amersham:

> Thomas Geoffrey maintained that true pilgrimage was bare foot to go and visit the poor, the meek, and the sick; for they are the true images of God.⁹⁹

Foxe reported that 'Thomas Geffrey caused this John Butler [also of Amersham] divers Sundays to go to London, to hear Dr. Colet'.¹⁰⁰ Perhaps, therefore, some of Colet's criticisms of clerical abuses encouraged certain heretics to believe that the dean shared their ecclesiology. Indeed, Colet came from a background in which Lollardy was evident, namely a mercantile environment where 'heterodoxy infiltrated the livery companies at the highest levels'.¹⁰¹ However, we must be cautious – Foxe's account is the only extant evidence of Lollard interest in Colet during his lifetime.¹⁰² Furthermore, Foxe's obviously polemical account attempted to persuade his readers that Colet grew away from Catholicism:

> And although the blindnesse of that time caryd him away after the common errour of Popery: yet in ripenes of judgeme[n]t he seemed something to incline fro[m] ye vulgar trade of that age.¹⁰³

Just as Colet was critical of clerical pride, so was he also critical of the pride that led to heresy:

> This is the goal that all heretics have reached, and for no other cause than that they trusted too presumptuously to themselves, and their own weakness, and would attempt more by powerless reason than by strong and prevailing faith.¹⁰⁴

The dean's reservations concerning clerical standards, the veneration of images and pilgrimages did not undermine his fundamental faith in the sacraments and doctrines of the Church.[105] Although Fitzjames, his ecclesiastical adversary, was on guard for any threats to the Church's authority, so too was Colet. In 1511, he and Fitzjames had been involved in prosecuting Lollard heretics together.[106] The aim of Colet's search for moral reform was to reinforce the existing Catholic structures against such heretics.[107]

To summarize: the St. Paul's Cathedral clergy allegedly disliked Colet's ecclesiological preaching, while some Lollards were apparently attracted to it. The story indicates that not only did the dean's preaching produce an adverse reaction within his own cathedral, but also that his reputation as a preacher had spread beyond the capital. The allegation that two Lollards had been willing to travel the moderate distance to hear him preach is testament to his homiletic notoriety and demonstrates how his idealistic vision for Catholicism could be mistaken for Lollardy. Yet Colet's ecclesiological expression was to change in 1515.

Wolsey

In 1515, Colet received an invitation to preach at the very grand occasion of Wolsey's installation as cardinal at Westminster Abbey.[108] The sermon is now lost. However, what purport to be extracts from the sermon were copied anonymously, in paraphrased form, into a seventeenth-century manuscript containing, amongst other texts, an account of the installation ceremony, deriving presumably from an earlier source, now lost.[109] From the evidence of this manuscript, I argue below that the sermon's temperate and diplomatic character indicates a change of tone following Colet's exposure to damaging accusations and receipt of a royal rebuke. The main characteristics of the sermon, according to the later source, were: firstly, an endorsement of royal authority over clerical authority; secondly, an endorsement of papal and apostolic authority, including that of the cardinal; and thirdly, an absence of clerical criticism.

Existing scholarship regarding this sermon is limited in quantity, but diverse in substance.[110] Whereas Lupton, followed by Hunt, discerned 'the same fearless singleness of purpose that impelled him to preach against war before the king', and Brigden emphasizes that Colet 'inveighed against the sin of pride before the magnificent Cardinal Wolsey', Gleason is keen to notice 'Colet's adulation for the red hat, which every insider knew was the reward of relentless politicking'.[111] Thus, Lupton, Hunt and Brigden portray Colet as a man preaching reform, while Gleason perceives the dean as flattering Wolsey for his own ends. However, this portrayal of Colet as a political manipulator does not sit easily with his otherworldly nature. Lupton's, Hunt's and Brigden's impression of a fearlessly reforming Colet does not take into account his experience of rebuke, persecution and setback between 1512 and 1514.

Gwyn, more realistically, suggests that Colet was neither voicing anticlerical criticisms nor indulging in sycophantic flattery.[112] More importantly, Gwyn notes the most significant aspects of the 1515 sermon: the fact that 'Colet dwelt not only upon those virtues of Wolsey that had led to his 'high and joyous promotion', but on Henry's as well' and that Colet stressed the 'high and great power of a cardinal,' who 'representeth the order of the seraphim'.[113] These emphases derive directly from the dean's hierarchical ecclesiology.[114] Significantly for Colet's career, not only did his sermon express his reverence for superior authority and the established order, but also his almost supernatural elevation of the status of 'cardinal'. Thus, I argue that, although Colet's ecclesiological ideals had remained unchanged since his arrival at St. Paul's, by 1515 he had learned how to express his vision in a more palatable way for his superiors. In order to defend these assertions, I will now explore the sermon's content, as well as the context of its delivery.

The seventeenth-century account captures the high-profile nature of the event, which took place on 18 November 1515, and indicates the eminence of the people to whom Colet was preaching:

Knights, Barons, Bishops, Earls, Dukes and Archbishops all in due order ... And when his grace was come into it, immediately began the mass of the Holy Ghost, sung by the Archbishop of Canterbury; the Bishop of Lincoln, being gospeller, and the Bishop of Exeter,[115] epistoler.[116]

It could not have been a more important occasion of public ceremonial on which to speak. The paraphrased extracts of the sermon, although perhaps not wholly reliable,[117] give the impression that Colet had not changed his attitude towards clerical standards since delivering his 1511/12 Convocation sermon, or indeed since composing his Oxford lectures and treatises. Colet spoke on the title of 'cardinal', what it meant, and how in this case it had been obtained; on the temporal authority attached to the office, as that of a prince and judge; and on its spiritual character, the holder being in this instance an archbishop.[118] Colet spoke generously of Wolsey, reportedly preaching that he deserved his high office:

By what means he obtained to this high honour, chiefly as by his own merits; there naming many divers and sundry virtues that he hath used, which have been the cause of his high and joyous promotion to all the realm.[119]

As Wolsey was already Archbishop of York, by becoming cardinal he effectively outranked Warham in the southern province and therefore, had overall jurisdiction, hence Colet's use of the term 'all the realm'. Nevertheless, Colet suggests, Wolsey was indebted to the superior authority of Henry VIII, without whose support his appointment would not have been possible.[120] Colet endorsed the Catholic hierarchy by stressing that Wolsey's promotion came about by virtue of the goodwill of both pope and king: 'Through our sovereign lord the king, for the great zeal and favour that our holy father the pope hath to his grace.'[121] The king's power over all English clergy had been made apparent to Colet in 1513. However, Colet's mention of the pope's authority indicates his underlying conservative Catholic hierarchical views – choosing not to express the conciliarist tendencies that had been so evident in his Convocation sermon. In preaching on the cardinal's spiritual oversight, Colet acknowledged Wolsey's superior ecclesiastical authority, but also the higher authority of the king and the pope.[122] Colet allegedly continued, in his sermon, to preach '… touching the dignity of a prince, as having power judicial',[123] the significance of the subject being that Wolsey's elevation as cardinal gave him enhanced temporal authority. This authority was conferred upon Wolsey not only by the pope, but also by the king.[124] Thus, by endorsing Wolsey's temporal authority, Colet also supported Henry's supreme authority over the Church in England.

However, the most significant expression of Colet's ecclesiology in this sermon is his direct connection between the ecclesiastical role of cardinal and the celestial role of the angelic seraphim:

> … the high and great power of a Cardinal; how he betokeneth the free beams of wisdom and charity, which the Apostles received of the Holy Ghost on Whitsunday. And a Cardinal which representeth the order of Seraphim, which continually burneth in the love of the glorious trinity. And for these considerations a Cardinal is metely apparelled with red, which colour only betokeneth nobleness; and how these three estates before named [Seraphim, Cherubim and Thrones] be collected and placed in heaven.[125]

Thus, in accordance with his ecclesiology, Colet affirmed Wolsey's power by emphasizing the cardinal's apostolic authority and also the authority deriving from the angelic hierarchy: this notion had been a feature of Colet's Pseudo-Dionysian commentaries. For the dean, a cardinal was quite simply closer to God than those lower down the ecclesiastical hierarchy: 'The foremost and highest men have plainer visions, and on their minds comes a more untempered effulgence of the Godhead.'[126]

Colet's ecclesiology had not changed since he wrote his Oxford treatises and commentaries. In this particular expression of it, neither bishops nor royalty could begrudge his sentiments, as they had done in the previous three years.

Finally, Colet spoke personally to Wolsey, admonishing him to increase in spiritual and moral strength:

> My Lord Cardinal, be glad, and enforce yourself always to do and execute righteousness to rich and poor, and mercy with truth. And [that he] desired all people to pray for him, that he might the rather observe these points; and [declared] in accomplishing the same, what his reward shall be in the Kingdom of Heaven.[127]

Colet shifted his attention from Wolsey's earthly power, albeit exercised within Henry VIII's realm, to his ultimate place within God's heavenly kingdom. He wished Wolsey the greatest of success in both earthly and celestial hierarchies and added a sense of moral fervour – also a feature of his early annotations to a copy of Ficino's *Epistolae*.[128]

To conclude: these paraphrased extracts from Colet's 1515 sermon suggest that that text had characteristics in common with his previous sermons: an emphasis on moral and spiritual standards; a Pseudo-Dionysian view of hierarchy; and an ecclesiology of perfection. One element apparently missing from this sermon, however, is that of criticism. In 1511/12, the dean had upbraided parish clergy and bishops; he had questioned the king's campaign against France in 1513;[129] and, in 1513/14, Fitzjames had complained that Colet had criticized the veneration of images, the giving of hospitality and the practice of preaching from pre-written texts. But the controversial content that had been integral to Colet's earlier sermons was now lacking. During the debate over benefit of clergy, which came to a climax during November 1515, a sensitive and potentially explosive situation had been resolved with an effective defeat for the Church and a victory for the Crown.[130] Wolsey allied himself with the winning side and Colet was given the opportunity to do so as well. His 1515 sermon is evidence that the dean took the chance, reiterating the ecclesiastical need for perfection. Colet had seemingly learned the art of diplomacy and the dangers of appearing either anticlerical or anti-royal. He preached that the ecclesiastical office of a cardinal was a reflection of the celestial office of the seraphim; that a high office required high standards; and that righteousness, mercy and truth, were better than prosecution and litigation: all aspects of his ecclesiology. However, on this occasion Colet avoided criticizing either Church or state. His change of manner, if not of ecclesiology, soon earned him earthly rewards.[131]

Conclusion

Colet was an idealist. His idealism derived from his vision for the Church and, therefore, for the world. In a letter to Colet of 29 April 1512, Erasmus revealed the extent and manner of the dean's preaching:

> You observed that the richest rewards of charity lie in bringing Christ into the hearts of one's countrymen by means of continual preaching and by holy instruction.[132] Now you have already been engaged in this for a great many years, I will not say with great glory, for glory is a commodity you so little regard as even to refuse it, but at least with great fruitfulness; and it is on tis account that your own Paul, for all his pronounced modesty in other respects, occasionally turns boastful and vaunts himself with a kind of sanctified insolence ... Besides, no one could help loving your generous high-mindedness and, so to call it, your holy arrogance in insisting that both of these services to your country must be unpaid, and your motives above reproach; so much so that the laborious preaching you undertook for so many years has not enriched you by a single penny.[133]

Erasmus portrayed Colet's preaching as glorious – a term he knew that Colet would reject, presumably out of modesty. The significance of Colet's preaching, Erasmus wrote, was its effect on others – its fruitfulness – not what it reflected on Colet himself.[134] Elsewhere, Erasmus suggested that Colet's opinions were perceived as verging on the heretical: he jokingly referred to the dean as 'some Wycliffite, I suppose' in a 1522 colloquy. In answer to his own query, Erasmus decided that he was not: 'I don't think so', he wrote.[135] Thus, although Erasmus endorsed the quality and orthodoxy of his preaching, it was how others reacted to the preaching that caused Colet trouble. The evidence, as presented in this chapter, has suggested that, between 1512 and 1514, Colet was harassed because of his preaching.[136] When he preached against war in 1513, he was swiftly rebuked and persuaded to re-think his public statements against the king's plans.[137] Thus, Colet had overstepped the boundary between moral and spiritual teaching and the realm of national foreign policy.[138] Fitzjames, by his extreme reaction, demonstrated how unpalatable he considered Colet's preaching to be – a concern substantiated by the cathedral chapter's distaste for the dean's ecclesiological preaching, and by the suggestion that Lollards were attracted to it. Nevertheless, Colet was respected enough to be allowed to preach at one of the biggest ecclesiastical events of 1515.[139] In the absence of the majority of Colet's sermon texts, it is impossible to give a comprehensive account of his sermon material, or to let the sermon texts speak for themselves. However, from the extant evidence, it is possible to draw some general conclusions.

Negative reactions to Colet's ideas, from clergy or royalty, had one thing in common: in each case, his preaching was perceived as undermining authority, whether the king's, Fitzjames's, or the canons' of St. Paul's. His intention, ironically, was quite the opposite: he aimed to uphold the existing hierarchy. If Colet's message of moral and spiritual absolutes cut to the heart of an individual's power, then that was a side effect of his preaching, and not the main aim. In this sense, Colet's sermons were brilliantly naïve; by expressing his vision of perfection, he challenged both Church and State. This was unacceptable to Henry VIII because it threatened his authority as leader of the English forces; and it was a nuisance to leaders of the Church, seeking to expel heretics and heresies.

Towards the end of Colet's time as dean, Erasmus described him, in a letter to Paolo Bombace, as 'a select preacher', implying that Colet's homiletic standards were consistently high and that they never waned, even at the end of his life.[140] The dean's sermon preached at Wolsey's installation as cardinal demonstrates the consistency with which he held his ecclesiological beliefs throughout a period of persecution from 1512 to 1515. Neither the king's rebuke, nor Fitzjames's hostility, nor the chapter's hatred, nor Lollard attention had tainted his vision. Colet was not a reformer, but a commentator upon reform – he spoke of the need for improved standards, in a prophetic way, but did not effect clerical reforms. As such, he eventually found an acceptable role within the ecclesiastical hierarchy as a preacher. By speaking more diplomatically, he increased in royal favour and achieved political status as a King's Councillor. Colet's political role, and his final attempts at reform at St. Paul's, will be explored in the next chapter.

7

REFORM II: COLET'S FINAL REFORM EFFORTS OF 1518

Between 1515 and 1518, Colet's political associations gave him unprecedented access to ecclesiastical power superior to his own, which he attempted to use for the purposes of advancing clerical reform.[1] Consequently, Colet compiled extracts from the pre-existing cathedral statutes, adding a commentary of his own, and moreover endeavoured to enlist Cardinal Wolsey's help in proposing fresh statute reform at St. Paul's in 1518.[2] Contrary to the notions of existing scholarship,[3] both Colet's commentary and projected new statutes were based upon his ecclesiology; that neither his commentary nor his 1518 proposals can be called statutes because they were not implemented as such; that his ideas were never submitted to the cathedral body for consideration; that Wolsey's statutes for St. Paul's were not based upon Colet's proposals; that both Warham (in 1502) and Wolsey achieved greater success in the field of St. Paul's Cathedral statute reform than the dean; that Colet's efforts have been wrongly described as 'liberal' and 'moderate',[4] but that his recourse to an archbishop, who was also a legate *a latere*, was entirely consistent with his ecclesiological emphases on hierarchy and episcopal authority.[5]

Increasingly ill during the latter years of his tenure as dean, and also embroiled in politics, Colet compiled two separate sets of disciplinary rules concerning canonical residence and the behaviour of the other cathedral clergy and lay staff.[6] The first set, comprising extracts from the fourteenth and fifteenth-century cathedral statutes produced by Deans Ralph de Baldock (1294-1304) and Thomas Lisieux (1441-56), relate to the duties of the dean, canons, minor canons, vicars and virgers. The extracts are interspersed with some comments written by Colet himself, concerning the subjects with which the extracts deal. These extracts have been described, by Simpson in his 1873 edition, as an *Epitome*[7] of the pre-existing laws. The *Epitome* is undated. However, the second set of rules, dated 1 September 1518, comprise a series of *Exhibita*, that is to say proposals concerning the residentiary canons that were exhibited to Wolsey for his approbation, in the hope that, with his support, they could then be presented to the cathedral chapter for consideration as potential additions to the statutes.[8] The original manuscripts of the *Epitome* and *Exhibita* are now lost, and copies are not apparently extant in any sixteenth-century manuscripts. Both texts were reproduced, faithfully or otherwise, by Dugdale in 1658 and by Simpson in 1873.[9] The *Exhibita* concern only the residentiary canons and are largely freshly composed proposals, but bear some resemblance to the *Epitome*. Colet's purpose in producing the *Epitome* is obscure. It is clear, however, that his *Exhibita* were intended to become statutes, but failed to do so because Wolsey withheld his support.[10] By the end of 1518, Colet's health was declining, thus impeding any further reform attempts during his lifetime.[11] He died, in September 1519, without contributing to the St. Paul's statute books.[12]

The scholarship surrounding this period of Colet's career is confused. However, all historians investigating this episode have rightly concluded that his reform efforts of 1518 were a failure. For instance, Milman stated that the proposals 'were, at the time, and remained ever after, a dead letter'; Lupton declared that 'He failed – if the failure is to be called his, and not theirs [the cathedral chapter's]'; Hunt observed that 'Colet's efforts to reform St. Paul's were unavailing'; and Gleason notes that '... no one was interested in seconding his proposals'.[13] Nevertheless, significant mistakes have been made in assessments of Colet's later years and, as a consequence, false conclusions have been drawn, which have been passed on from one generation of scholars to the next: from Erasmus's exaggeration that the dean 'restored the decayed discipline of the cathedral body' to Gleason's conclusion that 'administrative experience had given him [Colet] a healthy respect for the obstructive capabilities of a cathedral chapter'.[14]

Scholarship

Previous scholarship concerning Colet's projected statute alterations has caused confusion by its failure to acknowledge the differences between the *Epitome* and the *Exhibita*, in terms of their dates of composition, contents and styles.[15] Regarding nomenclature, for instance, Lupton variously labelled Colet's *Epitome* as 'ordinances', 'statutes' and a 'revised code'.[16] These terms cannot properly apply to Colet's work. Lupton also randomly referred to both the *Epitome* and the *Exhibita* as 'statutes', leaving the reader in the dark about the distinctive content of each document and uncertain as to which text he was referring at any one time. Marriott wrongly described Colet's *Exhibita* as 'a revised version of the Statutes and Customs of St. Paul's';[17] in fact, Colet freshly composed most of the *Exhibita*. Hunt decided that Erasmus's reference to the dean's alleged restoration of the 'decayed discipline of the

Cathedral' must have referred to 'Colet's Cathedral Statutes, which embodied 'with many omissions and adaptations, the earlier ones of Baldock and Lisieux".[18] Only the *Epitome* fits the latter part of this description. Thus, Hunt, following Lupton, must have been referring to the *Epitome* rather than to the *Exhibita*. However, Colet never successfully promulgated any cathedral statutes, so Hunt's terminology is inaccurate. Gleason is particularly unhelpful in ignoring the distinction between the two works in question, referring only to 'statutes':

> Colet ... took it upon himself to tighten discipline in the chapter, and for that purpose he drafted statutes for the governance of the cathedral clergy ... Fitzjames never 'commended' his statutes ... Wolsey, equally judiciously, 'witnessed' the statutes but did not sign them.[19]

Thus, Gleason appears to have been unaware of the distinction between the *Epitome* and the *Exhibita*. Moreover, there is no evidence of Fitzjames's involvement with either work.[20]

Similar confusion exists concerning the compositional date of the *Epitome*. Hunt implied that the 'statutes' – meaning in this case the *Epitome*, as is evident by his references to Simpson's edition of the same[21] – were composed relatively early on in Colet's tenure as dean, thus confusing them with Colet's 1506 injunctions. For instance, Hunt declared that, upon his arrival, 'St. Paul's was being desecrated by all kinds of profanation' and that the new dean therefore 'set about putting the house in order', implying that he did so immediately.[22]

Gleason gives no indication of when he considers the 'statutes', meaning either the *Epitome* or the *Exhibita*, to have been composed. Indeed, his chronology of events is very muddled. After stating that Wolsey had failed to sign the 'statutes' (i.e. the 1518 *Exhibita*) that he had witnessed (i.e. read), Gleason declares that:

> Refusing to concede defeat, Colet nevertheless threw himself ... into a fray ... In his frustration he adopted such measures as lay within his power. One of the most resented of these was curtailing almost to the vanishing point [*sic*] what was then called hospitality.[23]

Thus, Gleason mysteriously jumps from Wolsey's rejection of Colet's *Exhibita*, in September 1518 at the earliest, to Colet's withdrawal of decanal hospitality, which arguably began early in his tenure, around 1506, and which was certainly commented upon by Fitzjames, in his accusations of 1513/14, long before the 1518 *Exhibita* were composed. More recent scholarship on the matter also confuses Colet's 1518 reform efforts with those of 1506.[24]

By contrast, Lupton's suggestion that the *Epitome* and the *Exhibita* were composed consecutively, and at a similar time, is the most probable reconstruction:

> It would seem as if Colet had at first endeavoured to get his own revision of the statutes accepted by the bishop and chapter and, failing in that, had tried, as a last resource [*sic*], to invoke the legatine authority of Wolsey.[25]

As Colet's invocation of Wolsey's authority was attempted in September 1518, Lupton plausibly implied that the *Epitome* was composed a short while before hand.

The arguments for the conjectural compositional date of Colet's *Epitome* rely partly upon internal evidence, namely the fact that certain textual passages appear in both the *Epitome* and the *Exhibita*, suggesting that they may have been composed nearly contemporaneously.[26] Moreover, the *Epitome* contains passages that are also found in Colet's statutes for St. Paul's School, dated 18 June 1518, possibly indicating a similar compositional date for the two works.[27] It is unlikely that the *Epitome* was written after September 1518 for reasons of Colet's failing health. Furthermore, the *Epitome* comprises extracts from the existing cathedral statutes, together with Colet's commentary, which consists of angry outbursts rather than a considered set of statute proposals. Thus, it is far from certain that Colet's *Epitome* was intended for anyone's attention except his own. By contrast, the *Exhibita* are a more measured set of proposals, specifically addressed to Cardinal Wolsey. Therefore, as Lupton suggested, the most plausible explanation is that the *Epitome* was composed before the *Exhibita*, but exactly when is indiscernible. Given that the *Epitome*, *Exhibita* and school statutes contain material in common, the compositional dates of all three works were probably close together. Thus, we can conjecture that the *Epitome* was composed sometime around 1518, along with the other two dated works. The significance of this probable dating is that the *Epitome* and the *Exhibita* thus provide evidence of Colet's continuing ecclesiological concern in his later years as dean, expressed roughly in his *Epitome*, but in a more refined style in the *Exhibita*. However, despite his close political association with Wolsey after 1515, his 1518 *Exhibita* remained unsigned by the cardinal and were therefore not presented to the cathedral chapter for consideration as potential statutes. Hence, whatever the compositional date of the *Epitome*, Colet's *Exhibita* of 1518 were a failure.

In addition to the scholarship outlined above, five basic inaccuracies, deriving from several generations of scholars, were assimilated into Carpenter's contribution to the 1957 history of St. Paul's.[28] Carpenter's chapter is the most recent work to deal at length with Colet's attempted reforms of 1518, although Gleason refers briefly to his 'statutes', also repeating several of Carpenter's errors.[29] So what are the misconceptions? Firstly, Carpenter referred to Colet as 'a Reforming Dean';

secondly, he labelled the *Epitome* as 'statutes' and wrongly suggested that Colet had submitted proposals for statute reform to the Bishop of London and the chapter of St. Paul's for consideration;[30] thirdly, Carpenter asserted that Wolsey drew up a body of statutes for the cathedral inspired by, and based upon, Colet's own 1518 *Exhibita*; fourthly, based upon evidence surviving from Alexander Nowell's tenure as dean (1560-1602), Carpenter asserted that Wolsey's statutes had never been in force; and fifthly, Carpenter argued that Colet's failure to bring about liberal, peaceful reform, led to an inevitably more violent reform in the Reformation. Carpenter, his predecessors and his followers, were wrong in each of these five respects.[31] From a reassessment of the documentary evidence, five new conclusions can be drawn.

With regard to his first point, Carpenter followed several previous scholars in describing Colet as 'A Reforming Dean'.[32] In fact, Colet failed, at every attempt, to impose reform upon St. Paul's: one cannot be called a reformer because one attempts reform; one has to achieve it. Moreover, a self-contradictory statement, admitting that Colet achieved no such reform, weakens Carpenter's initial assertion:

> But Colet was to find that it was one thing to make [*sic* i.e. draft] statutes: quite another to secure their acceptance, let alone their enforcement. In neither respect, alas, was the dean successful ... Thus Colet's efforts at reform through statutes were not successful.[33]

Not only did Carpenter falsely claim that Colet effected statute reform, but he also failed to argue convincingly that the dean had been a clerical reformer at any time during his tenure.[34] Carpenter relied upon Foxe, and upon late nineteenth-century scholarship, for his assumptions, including writers such as Milman, who ambitiously described Erasmus and Colet as '... these two great reformers before the Reformation'.[35] Nevertheless, it is a factual inaccuracy to describe Colet as a reformer.

Carpenter's second historical error, following his predecessors,[36] was to brand Colet's *Epitome* and *Exhibita* as 'statutes', which wrongly suggests that his work had been accepted and promulgated as such.[37] Carpenter seems to have inherited a misunderstanding of the dean's activity from Milman: 'He drew up a body of statutes for the church, rigid, but by no means austere or ascetic.'[38] There are two reasons why it is inappropriate to describe the product of Colet's efforts as 'statutes'. Firstly, he produced around 1518 not one, but two documents relating to the cathedral's regulations, the first of which, the *Epitome*, consisted of extracts of the statutes that were already in use and were therefore in no need of further promulgation. Furthermore, close inspection of Colet's commentary suggests that these passages cannot possibly have been proposed as potential new statutes because of their manner of expression. Such phrases as 'O abominable crime! O detestable iniquity!'[39] do not conform to the usual measured language of the statute book, nor do the comments in general advocate an improved standard of behaviour. Therefore, it is implausible to suggest that the *Epitome* was formally offered, as prospective statutes, to the cathedral chapter. Secondly, Carpenter used considerable licence in his story of the supposed submission and rejection of the so-called 'statutes':

> Not surprisingly, the chapter proved openly rebellious, and Bishop Fitzjames was unwilling – such were his relations with Colet – to commend them, nor would he ever confirm them. Thus they remained from the beginning a dead letter.[40]

Carpenter's argument is further weakened by the fact that he offered no evidence for the chapter's rebellion or for Fitzjames's involvement. More recently, Gleason has made the same mistakes:

> Fitzjames never 'commended'[41] the statutes – not necessarily, I think, because he did not approve of them but because he had no wish to get himself embroiled in this kind of controversy ... Wolsey equally judicious, 'witnessed'[42] the statutes but did not sign them.[43]

Thus, Gleason wrongly labels Colet's proposals as statutes; like Carpenter's conjecture, his assertion that Fitzjames rejected them is baseless. Although the *Exhibita* reached Wolsey, who referred to them in two brief passages of his own statutes, there is no evidence to show that they were presented to the cathedral body for consideration as potential statutes.

The third common assumption about Colet's 1518 work is that Wolsey drew up a series of statutes based upon, and inspired by, the dean's *Exhibita*:

> On 1 September 1518, Colet presented a series of *Exhibita* to the Cardinal, these being a digest of the statutes, customs and regulations of the Cathedral; and intended to give the cardinal a picture of the overall situation. Wolsey saw the need for drastic action and himself drew up statutes – they are reproduced in Sparrow Simpson's *Registrum* – based upon those which Colet himself had prepared earlier.[44]

The myth that Wolsey's statutes were based upon the *Exhibita* was handed down from Knight to subsequent scholars, apparently without scrutiny or contradiction.[45] For instance, a year before Carpenter's work was published, Hunt proclaimed that '

... in 1518 he [Colet] presented to the Cardinal a collection of 'Exhibita', which were used by the latter as the basis of his own Statutes'.[46] In fact, a comparison between Wolsey's statutes and the *Exhibita* reveals that they are almost entirely different in content, structure and expression.

A fourth false assumption relates to William Warham's cathedral statutes of 1502, mentioned in both the *Exhibita* and Wolsey's statutes. Knight reproduced some anonymous early sixteenth-century memoranda, possibly written by a member of the cathedral clergy:

> Dean Nowell said to him [perhaps a canon] on his admission, that Warham's and Wolsey's were no Statutes, and that, in taking his oath to observe the Statutes, he must separate the leaves containing these from the rest of the volume ... Colet's *Exhibita* were made, he said, by the Dean alone 'then out with chapter', nor were they true, nor fairly collected. Wolsey's Statutes were made by a stranger, not as the Pope's Legate, but by compromise; the Bishop of London's assent, and that of the Chapter, was not obtained to them; and there was no seal attached, but only the Cardinal's hand.[47]

Carpenter, like several scholars before him,[48] saw this quotation as evidence not only that the Bishop of London and the chapter had rejected the *Exhibita*, but also that they had rejected Wolsey's and Warham's statutes.[49] However, the quotation is problematic in several ways: firstly, Knight's source is not apparently extant; secondly, its authorship and provenance are unknown, which means that its authenticity and validity are questionable; thirdly, the source paraphrases, rather than quotes directly, what Nowell allegedly said, so its accuracy as a representation of what Nowell might have said is obscure – we do not even know when Nowell is supposed to have made these remarks, or when the memoranda were written down; fourthly, even if the passage accurately conveys Nowell's perception of Warham's, Wolsey's and Colet's work, it does not necessarily reveal anything about how their work was received in the early sixteenth century.

On the other hand, four pieces of evidence exist which suggest that Wolsey's and Warham's statutes **were** in force at St. Paul's during the sixteenth century. Firstly, with regard to Warham's 1502 statutes, both Colet and Wolsey referred to them as '*ordinationes*', a term meaning 'statute' and used for the dean's own St. Paul's School statutes of 1518.[50] Writing on the subject of the dean's residence, Colet referred to Warham's statutes as existing law: '... according to Bishop Warham's statutes'.[51] Wolsey mentioned Warham's statutes no fewer than six times in his own rules for St. Paul's.[52] According to Colet and Wolsey, therefore, Warham's statutes were not only in force, but formed a precedent for further statute reform. Secondly, Warham's statutes were composed in 1502, following his primary episcopal visitation of the cathedral.[53] As Bishop of London, Warham possessed the authority to impose statute reform upon the institution.[54] If he possessed the power to promulgate new statutes, then it seems highly unlikely that he would have composed statutes without thereafter using that authority to have them adopted. The memoranda quoted by Simpson may therefore suggest that it was Nowell's personal wish that Warham's statutes should not be considered as legally binding; the evidence suggests that, at least in the early sixteenth century, they were believed to be in force. Thirdly, the quotation suggests that Wolsey's and Warham's statutes were bound up with the rest of the cathedral's statutes in a single volume. Why this should have been the case, if they had not formally been promulgated is not explained. A simple explanation is that they were, in fact, recognized as valid statutes by the chapter, but that Nowell categorically denied their validity.[55] Fourthly, the quotation specifically refers to 'Wolsey's statutes', begging the question of why the writer would use the term if they had not been promulgated. This evidence thus buttresses the argument that both Warham's and Wolsey's statutes had been adopted, contrary to the suppositions of Knight, Milman, Lupton, Hunt and Carpenter.[56]

The fifth false assumption to be challenged, and the most disturbing one, is that Colet was a moderate and liberal man who gently confronted a hard and immoderate clergy:

> The failure of such a liberal man to cleanse the Augean stables was to lead later to the adoption of more violent means ... Had the Church been able to reform itself from within, the story [of the Reformation] might well have been different; but what happened at St. Paul's shows the difficulty confronting moderate men.[57]

Thus, Carpenter represented the dean as a meek reformer. But this is a wholly inaccurate reading of Colet's life and work. Colet was a passionate idealist who continually expressed his hierarchical and perfectionist vision in a blunt and uncompromising manner, whether to the minor clergy in 1506, to the Convocation of 1511/12, to Henry VIII in 1513, or to the canons residentiary in 1518. His denunciations (in the *Epitome*) of alleged iniquities were far from moderate and liberal expressions of his ecclesiological ideals.[58]

In contrast to the foregoing myths concerning Colet's 'reform' activity, I believe that his activities of 1518 were fundamentally ecclesiological. Not only is this fact evident in the ecclesiological content of his written work, but also in his deference to Cardinal Wolsey, which was consistent with his hierarchical understanding of the Church. Relying upon revisionist and post-revisionist insights into Colet's thought, and upon the contentions advanced throughout this book, I suggest that his final reform efforts were motivated by his idealistic ecclesiological vision, and by his political involvement. Two important ecclesiological ingredients in the *Epitome* and the *Exhibita* were the ideas of sacrament and hierarchy. Trapp, Rex, Gleason and MacCulloch observed that the hierarchical and sacramental language of Pseudo-Dionysius heavily influenced Colet;[59] the consequence was his elevated view of the priesthood. Thus, we must interpret the events of 1518 within the context outlined by Rex:

> Much of the evidence cited [concerning Colet] is literary, and such inherently ambivalent evidence has often been crudely interpreted ... Colet himself was anything but anticlerical. He was an avid disciple of the late classical 'Pseudo Dionysius' whose writings on the heavenly and ecclesiastical hierarchies coined the concept of 'hierarchy' (rule by priests) and put it into circulation. Colet regarded ordination as the paramount sacrament of the Church and was unhesitating in his elevation of spiritual authority and dignity over temporal. If he castigated the clergy, he did not spare the laity, assuring them they got the clergy they deserved.[60]

Rex explains that Colet has been misrepresented through the crude interpretation of his written works and that the priesthood was of immense significance for his worldview. Indeed, this is particularly true of Colet's final reform efforts. Furthermore, the *Epitome* and the *Exhibita* must be examined within the context of the 'very high standards' which some clergy, including Colet, set themselves in the late-medieval period.[61] As MacCulloch observes, Colet, following Pseudo-Dionysius, believed that the

> Clergy had a solemn and inescapable duty to be as pure and effective ministers of God as the angels themselves. His apparently anti-clerical outpourings are in fact the highest form of clericalism.[62]

For the dean, the reason that such high standards were required was because the earthly priesthood was a reflection of Christ's priesthood and the celestial hierarchy:

> Priests were entrusted with the awesome power of the divine light of grace ... Colet ... called on the priests of the Church to be no less than the angels in heaven as they ministered to the laity, for their priesthood was a reflection of Christ's priesthood, and the Eucharist that they celebrated was the chief means by which humanity made its encounter with the divine.[63]

Here MacCulloch rightly acknowledges Gleason's cogent analysis of Colet's sacramental theology.[64] However, we can now take MacCulloch's post-revisionist observations a stage further, by examining how Colet's sacramental and hierarchical ecclesiology was applied. Colet's ecclesiological elevation of the clergy was combined with insights inspired by his experience of Wolsey's world of Tudor politics, which rekindled the dean's hope that his perfectionist vision could be made a reality in his cathedral church. It is to this context of recent political involvement to which we now turn.

Political Involvement

In the late-medieval and early-Tudor periods, 'politics' encompassed three main areas: Church, Court and law.[65] Wolsey was a versatile expert of all three spheres.[66] Conversely, for most of his short life, Colet had been a non-political figure, having largely engaged, so far as is discernible, with one of these arenas: the Church;[67] indeed, it remained his chief concern to his death. However, a series of incidents from 1515 to 1518 propelled Colet into the worlds of law and the royal council.[68] The initial reason for this involvement was his reputation as a preacher.[69] By virtue of this homiletic status, and particularly following his November 1515 delivery of a sermon at Wolsey's installation as cardinal, Colet became more deeply involved in the affairs of both Wolsey and Henry VIII.[70] One consequence of the dean's political involvement was a renewed enthusiasm for reform, which manifested itself between 1515 and 1518 in an ongoing dissatisfaction with clerical standards and in proposed statute reform. In order properly to contextualize Colet's last reform efforts, it is necessary to trace his political connections from 1515 onwards.

The roots of Colet's first participation in Tudor politics lay in a long-running dispute concerning the jurisdiction of the Prerogative Court of Canterbury. Kitching noted that

> From the thirteenth century, archbishops of Canterbury had claimed some prerogative authority to grant probate and administration in cases where persons died with property or debts in more than one diocese.[71]

In December 1515, in accordance with the king's request, Convocation appointed a committee consisting of Bishops Nykke of Norwich, Oldham of Exeter and Fisher of Rochester; the Prior of Canterbury; and Dean Colet. The committee's brief was to investigate the Prerogative Court of Canterbury's right to probate jurisdiction for land left in wills that lay outside the deceased person's own diocese.[72] However, with Colet's assistance, Wolsey used the committee for his own ends. As Gleason states,

'It was increasingly clear to Warham both that Colet was Wolsey's man and that Wolsey aimed to oust Warham from the chancellorship'.[73] By sitting on these committees, therefore, the dean had demonstrated his political allegiance to Wolsey. The Tudor chronicler Edward Hall suggested that Wolsey was a menace to Warham's position as chancellor and undermined his power, forcing Warham to resign as Lord Chancellor of England.[74] Unsurprisingly, Wolsey soon became chancellor himself.[75] Moreover, Colet was subsequently rewarded for his part in Wolsey's actions by his appointment to the King's Council. Gleason rightly suggests that the dean's work for Wolsey on the committee was directly linked to Colet's subsequent and swift promotion:

> Though Colet's academic field was theology he was also reasonably well versed in the law ... Colet was thus suited from several points of view for the eminent place to which Wolsey now raised him, nothing less than a seat on the King's ... Council.[76]

In order to understand the nature of Colet's political involvement, it will be helpful briefly to describe the nature and duties of a King's Councillor.[77]

The King's Council was the medieval administrative and judicial body that met regularly in the Star Chamber (or *Camera Stellata*) at the Palace of Westminster, in order to administer justice, and at Court, in order to advise the king in political matters. The council tended to be large and consisted of three levels of councillor. Firstly, there were the principal office holders who attended all council meetings: the Lord Chancellor, the Lord Treasurer and the Keeper of the Privy Seal.[78] Secondly, there were councillors who were professionally qualified to act as judges, such as the Lord Chief Justice, the Chief Baron of the Exchequer and the Solicitor-General.[79] Thirdly, there were the junior councillors, such as the Dean of the Chapel Royal, the King's Almoner, the Abbot of Westminster and the Dean of St. Paul's. Thus, Colet belonged to the third category.[80] He had no professional legal status and there is no record that he sat in the Star Chamber.[81] Wolsey, however, had begun a process of reforming the King's Council after being appointed Lord Chancellor in 1515 and he duly monopolized it,[82] shifting the emphasis of its duties to judicial functions in the Star Chamber, where he presided. Meetings were held almost every day in term from 1515 to 1517.

Between 1517 and 1520, Wolsey created three committees staffed by lesser councillors. These committees did not sit in the Star Chamber, but elsewhere in the Palace of Westminster.[83] The members of the resultant committees included John Islip, Abbot of Westminster; Sir Thomas Neville; Sir Andrew Windsor; Dr. John Clerk; William Roper; and John Colet. They were a mixture of clerics, peers and lawyers. Although the records of council proceedings for the time are fragmentary, they testify that Colet sat on these committees at least three times and probably many more.[84] Moreover, in Dunham's list of individual members of the 'King's Whole Council' in attendance from 1509 to 1527, Colet is recorded as occasionally present on the full council from 25 June to 6 November 1518,[85] indicating that the dean's most intense involvement with Tudor politics was gained in 1518, the same year in which he re-attempted clerical reform at St. Paul's by means of his *Exhibita*. While the dean appears to have played a minor role in executing justice in these committees and on the full council, he was nevertheless part of Wolsey's plan to expand the council's hearing of litigation in order to appease public demand for justice.[86] Why this should have been the case is explained in a letter of 5 March 1518, in which Erasmus thanked Colet for his helpful negotiations with Henry VIII on his behalf, indicating Colet's royal influence at this time:

> I am grateful to you for kindly opening my business with the king, and I beg that you will put it through. For now I need a considerable sum for my journey ...[87]

In a letter to Paolo Bombace in 1518, Erasmus included Colet, as a distinguished preacher, in a list of men who were influential with the king and formed the king's Court, indicating the dean's high social profile as a preacher and influential courtier:

> The men most influential with them [the king and queen] are those who excel in the humanities and in integrity and wisdom. Thomas Linacre is the physician ... Cuthbert Tunstall is his 'Master of the Rolls' ... Thomas More is of the Privy Council ... Pace, almost a brother to him, is secretary. William Mountjoy is head of her majesty's household. John Colet is a select preacher. I have mentioned only the leaders ... This is the kind of man of whom his palace is full, more like an academy than a king's court. What Athens or Stoa or Lyceum could one prefer to a court like that?[88]

Notwithstanding Colet's notoriety, however, his role within Wolsey's administration became influential upon his decanal activity, resulting in his attempt to enlist Wolsey's help in the projected implementation of his perfectionist ideals. Colet's professed unhappiness with standards at St. Paul's, as seen in his *Epitome* and *Exhibita*, was not simply motivated by his idealistic vision for ecclesiastical and sacramental hierarchy; he was also encouraged to act because of his recent contact with Wolsey's political world, which gave him the opportunity to engage powerful assistance in his attempted alteration of the cathedral statutes. However, Colet's political life coincided with another important development, which was responsible for his apparent urgency around 1518: illness.

By 1518, the dean's physical and mental strength had been in decline for several years.[89] As early as 1514, he had been preparing for, and looking forward to, retirement:

> I think daily of retiring and taking refuge among the Carthusians. My nest is nearly finished. When you return to us, as far as I can guess, you will find me there dead to worldly things.[90]

There is evidence that he was ill in 1517: in a letter addressed to Wolsey, dated 18 December 1517, he criticized physicians, of whom he had obviously had bitter experience:

> I trust you always keep as well as possible; and, to preserve your health the better, I trust you have but few dealings with doctors and their art. All they do is make great promises.[91]

Erasmus gave an account of Colet's attacks of illness in his biographical letter of 1521:

> He said that he was preparing an abode for his old age ... But death forestalled him. For having been seized a few years before with the sweating sickness (a disease that is the special scourge of England), he was now for a third time attacked by it; and though he recovered from it to some degree, an internal disorder ensued from what the disease left behind it, of which he died. One physician pronounced him dropsical.[92]

The significance of this ill-health for Colet's ecclesiology was not only that his strength and enthusiasm for reform were limited, but also that his reform efforts were now restricted by lack of time due to impending infirmity, retirement, or even death. His bouts of illness naturally reduced the number of opportunities for him to address Church issues openly. Therefore, the opportunity to gain powerful support from Henry VIII and Wolsey, *via* the political world, was the antidote to his administrative impotence at St. Paul's, an impotence stretching back to 1506. Thus, Colet would have been aware that his personal circumstances had conspired to ensure that 1518 would be the last year in which he had the opportunity to attempt clerical reform.[93]

To conclude: Colet's political involvement, combined with the fear of impending infirmity or death, was the spur to his final effort to implement his ecclesiological vision by means of attempted statute revision at St. Paul's. Ultimately, however, he did not persuade Wolsey to support his prospective statutes. It is now time to examine both men's proposals in more detail.

Wolsey's and Colet's Proposals

Preparing a late nineteenth-century edition of the cathedral statutes, Simpson located various relevant records, predominantly manuscripts found at St. Paul's, in Oxford and Cambridge libraries, and of the British Museum (now the British Library); he also used material printed in Dugdale.[94] Amongst the collection, Simpson reproduced statutes promulgated by Deans Baldock and Lisieux.[95] In his *Epitome*, Colet chose to highlight a number of these statutes, interspersing his own comments – an attempt to distil the moral essence of the cathedral law and to add fresh life to the material. Colet's additions reflected his ecclesiological concern that moral standards should be upheld for the benefit of the entire body of Christ. Consequently, offenders were to be severely punished for the good of the whole.[96] Thus, just as ecclesiastical unity and perfection was the theme of Colet's other works, so it was in his *Epitome*. As in his other works, he wrote that the senior members of the ecclesiastical hierarchy – not least Colet himself – must enforce this strict code of behaviour.[97] Moreover, reflecting the structural pattern of his ecclesiological discourses, the *Epitome* builds up to an angry outburst against the depravity of dissolute clergy.[98] The *Epitome* is therefore typical of Colet's ecclesiological works.

We have seen how Colet's 1506 compilation of old statutes and extra injunctions related only to the cathedral's minor clergy.[99] However, in his *Epitome*, Colet broadened the scope of his efforts, adding material to the pre-existing statutes regarding a wide range of cathedral staff. Although Simpson did not specifically identify Colet's contributions, they are clearly distinguishable from the pre-existent statutes by means of a simple comparison with Baldock's and Lisieux's statutes.[100] Having isolated them, the dean's comments regarding virgers, vicars-choral, minor canons, the grammar master and the residentiary canons can now be discussed.

Colet's statements concerning the virgers[101] related to those laws dealing with idlers and traffickers. The existing statutes decreed that if the traffickers ignored the threat of excommunication, then the virgers were to confiscate the merchandise on sale and throw it onto the pavement outside. Colet also felt strongly about ejecting unsavoury elements from the cathedral. Not only did he leave this particular statute unchanged in his collection of extracts, but he also reiterated the sentiment, in a paraphrased form, in a section written with the virgers in mind: beggars and unsightly objects, or those who interrupted people at prayer, were to be ejected.[102] The virgers were ordered to 'search carefully all the lurking-places of the Cathedral Church, and if there should be anything lurking there which excites suspicion, to throw it out'.[103] Moreover, according to the dean, they were to

> ... drive outside the cathedral notorious persons, especially common prostitutes, people carrying loads through the Cathedral, and beggars, who either lie in the Cathedral asleep in a disgusting manner or rudely importune people who are praying.[104]

In elaborating upon the old statutes, Colet underlined his perfectionist ecclesiological concern that those who were not virtuous and pious should not be allowed to blight the pure and Mystical Body of Christ by their presence. His hierarchical ecclesiology is also evident in his declaration that the dean must 'correct the aberrations of everyone, and chastise with a just chastisement those who are stubborn'.[105] This phrase is reminiscent of his 1506 proposals for the government of the minor clergy, as is the order that the lower clergy should be judged by the chancellor; that regular Saturday morning disciplinary meetings should be held; and that the dean's permission was required for leave of absence.[106] Colet's strict ecclesiology of unity and perfection is manifest in another of his additions:

> Those who are refractory and incorrigible are to be ejected from the choir, and their salary and emoluments taken from them; but all things are to be done with discernment, that each person may be treated for the improvement of his condition, to the edification rather than the destruction of the cathedral.[107]

Hence, he was concerned with the whole cathedral body, not just the individual: once again, a characteristic of his ecclesiology. Under the heading *De Virgiferis*, he wrote that

> ... since the married state is ofttimes one full of business and disturbance, and since married men must needs attend to their wives, as mistresses, and our vergers, distracted by the anxieties of married life, neglect their duty in the Church, or else perforce abandon it (*since no man can serve two masters* well); therefore it is decreed ... that from henceforth none shall be in any wise vergers in St. Paul's, save such as pass their lives in celibacy without wives, and keep continent ... Moreover, let an unmarried man be preferred to this office before a widower, other things being equal; for it is fitting that those who

approach so near to the altar of God, and are present at such great mysteries, should be wholly chaste and undefiled.[108]

Colet believed that, in an ecclesiologically perfected world, carnal marriage could be abolished altogether, being replaced by a spiritual marriage between Christ and the Church.[109] Thus, the foregoing passage reflects Colet's ecclesiology concerning marriage, a subject that he re-addressed with regard to another staff category: the vicars-choral.

Colet was concerned with the number, marital status and discipline of the vicars-choral.[110] After relating that, in former times, the vicars, or vicars-choral, had numbered thirty,[111] he lamented that the number, and behaviour, of the company had changed for the worse. During his tenure, they totalled six, 'and those, too, either married, or capable of being so.'[112] He was perhaps lamenting that, by the early sixteenth century, vicars-choral were more likely to be married professional musicians, rather than celibate priests, thus departing from his marital ideal, as set out in his treatise *De Sacramentis*.[113] Directions of how vicars-choral were to be appointed follow. They shall

> ... above all things, be such as desire to live well, to keep a good character, to show an example of honest dealing, in St. Paul's ... The vicars are not to be proctors, or attorneys, or executors of wills, or to undertake any other office that may draw them away and estrange them from divine service.[114]

This passage is indicative of Colet's ecclesiological emphasis upon the proper execution of one's duties and his strong dislike of legal involvement.[115] The idea is expressed, almost *verbatim*, in his 1518 statutes for the school, where he dictated that a master should not:

> ... take office of sectorshipp (executorship) or proctorship, or any suych besyness whiche shall let theyr dylygence and theyr necessary labour in the Scole.[116]

Likewise, the minor canons came under scrutiny in Colet's *Epitome*:

> Let not a minor canon frequent inns, wineshops, or ale-houses: let him not enter suspected houses; let him not converse with suspected persons; let him preserve his chastity; let him apply himself to his work with all integrity.[117]

Another of Colet's ecclesiological additions to Baldock's and Lisieux's statutes was the stipulation of an additional requirement of the grammar master. In the pre-existent statutes, one section concerned the master of the singing school (*De Magistro Scholae Cantus*) and the master of grammar (*De Magistro Grammatices*); in both the pre-existing statutes and Colet's commentary, the cathedral's chancellor was to make the appointments.[118] However, in the pre-existing statutes, the required qualification for the grammar master was to be the degree of Master of Arts, whereas in the dean's commentary revising this statute, an exemplary moral character was also to be expected.

> The Master of the Grammar School should be an upright and honourable man, and of much and well-attested learning. Let him teach the boys, especially those belonging to the cathedral, grammar, and at the same time show them an example of good living. Let him take great heed that he cause no offence to their tender minds by any pollution of word or deed. Nay more, along with chaste literature, let him imbue them with holy morals, and be to them a master, not of grammar only, but of virtue.[119]

These words express not only Colet's ecclesiological ideals of holy morality and virtue, but also the principles upon which he founded his own school.[120]

We have seen how the dean expressed his ecclesiology by means of his commentary on the cathedral statutes regarding virgers, vicars-choral, minor canons and the grammar master.[121] However, the most extreme example of his ecclesiological passion, in the *Epitome*, is to be found in those passages concerning the residentiary canons. Colet begins by stating the ideal that canons should live 'in obedience, chastity, charity, prayer, fasting, reading, and contemplation'.[122] Even so, his perfectionist hopes were apparently disappointed:

> But alas! How grievous it is that as with everything well begun, so also this institution has gradually, in the course of time, degenerated into an obviously calamitous condition: for the canons began to love the world more than God, and to follow the way of the world rather than the way of heaven ... retaining only the name and title of canon.[123]

Soon, his disappointment turns to rage:

> So deformed are they now in very respect, both in life and in religion, that the Residentiaries themselves at length need reformation no less than the Canons did in days gone by ... They cast aside their care for the Church; they pursue

their own private gains; they convert the common property to their own private use. In these unhappy and disordered times *residence* in the Cathedral is nothing else than seeking one's own advantage, and, to speak more plainly, robbing the Church to enrich oneself. O abominable crime! O detestable iniquity![124]

Colet's disappointment with the Church was nothing new. It was evident in his commentary on the *Ecclesiastical Hierarchy* of Pseudo-Dionysius, written several years before:

Alas! smoke and noisome blackness have now for a long while been exhaling upwards in such dense volume from the vale of benighted men, as well-nigh to overwhelm the light of that city [the Church]; so that now churchmen, shrouded in darkness, not knowing whither they go, have foolishly blinded and confounded themselves with all; so that in the world again there is nothing more confused than the mass of men.[125]

In this commentary, Colet asks Christ to restore 'order and tranquillity' to the Church, the ultimate ambition of his ecclesiology and, indeed, of his life. In his *Epitome*, he suggests the less celestial solution that the canons should reside perpetually in the cathedral precincts.[126] Erasmus stated plainly that Colet was '... too strict about canonical discipline', no doubt leading to the canons' complaint that they were 'being treated as monks'.[127] Thus, Colet's *Epitome* is evidence of his continuing, and unchanging, ecclesiological concern during his latter days as dean.

The *Epitome* cannot be described as an attempt at statute revision, nor did Colet intend his comments to be submitted as prospective alterations to the statutes. Rather, his outbursts, as in his other written works, seem to be a personal reflection upon his colleagues' deficiencies when compared to the ideals, in this case as set forth by Baldock and Lisieux. The *Epitome* is a lament for clerical standards, but hardly a serious proposal for the statute book. His *Exhibita*, however, are a more measured and temperate series of proposals, to which we now turn.

The *Exhibita* are about half the length of the *Epitome* and concern fewer areas of cathedral administration, relating only to the reformation of those with residentiary status at St. Paul's, namely the canons.[128] The *Exhibita* are less dramatic than the *Epitome*. However, Colet's ecclesiological themes are still manifest. He begins, naturally enough, by discussing his own ecclesiastical authority, as set out in the ancient statutes. As in his *Epitome*, he states that, according to these records, the dean has authority over all canons, presbyters and vicars. He is able to correct the delinquent and justly to castigate the obstinately rebellious. Thus, his hierarchical values were not diluted in the *Exhibita*. Having thus established his own authority, Colet turned his attention to the residentiary canons, recommending that they reside permanently in the cathedral precincts, just as he had done in the *Epitome*.[129] He moves on to consider the rules regarding the duties to be performed by the residentiary canons, including officiating at solemn festivals and participating in choral services and processions. He notes various other expectations, including one that the dean must undertake visitations. Colet's suggestions make up forty-seven short sections in total, in contrast to the thirty-three, much longer, sections of the *Epitome*.[130]

As Colet specifically designed the *Exhibita* to be read by Wolsey, the most significant comparisons to be made are not with his *Epitome*, nor with previous St. Paul's statutes, but with Wolsey's subsequent statutes.[131] Such a comparison will reveal how much Wolsey relied upon Colet's proposals; what the two men were attempting to achieve by their different proposals; how they differed in their expression; and how successful they were. The text of Wolsey's statutes appears in Simpson's nineteenth-century compilation of the cathedral statutes.[132] Two short passages in Wolsey's text demonstrate his knowledge of Colet's work: Wolsey's second paragraph contains the phrase '*Nam cum quatuor untaxat praeter Decanum sint Residentes, valde curandum est*'.[133] The same passage appears in the fourth paragraph of the *Exhibita*, entitled '*De aliis quatuor Residentibus*'.[134] Likewise, the fifth paragraph of Wolsey's statutes contain the phrase '*ab aedibus aut domibus suis ad Ecclesiam accedat, non vanitate, non pomposed, sed religiose et graviter, sicut decet professores Canonicae Vitae, studentes placere magis Deo humilitate*'.[135] This sentence is almost identical to a phrase found in the seventh chapter of the *Exhibita*, entitled '*Quid Residentes in Choro*'.[136] Thus Wolsey was aware of Colet's *Exhibita* and indebted to it in a minor way. Nevertheless, there were significant differences between Colet's and Wolsey's work.

Contrary to Victorian ideas, which proclaimed that Wolsey's statutes were 'framed ... on the lines of Colet's presentments',[137] Wolsey's work is almost entirely different to the *Exhibita*. For instance, Wolsey's statutes vary in scope, relating only to the residentiary canons; they are also shorter, being made up of thirteen long sections, rather than the forty-seven short sections of the *Exhibita*.[138] Early on in Wolsey's text, Colet is mentioned by name as being a beloved son: '*dilectos filios Johannem Collet*'.[139] However, this reference betrays no significant reliance by Wolsey upon the *Exhibita*. Indeed, the dean is mentioned only in passing, along with four other residentiary canons: William Harrington, John Smyth, John Downam and Thomas Sewell. In fact, far from using the *Exhibita* as a basis for his statute revisions, Wolsey found Warham's 1502 statutes a more useful reference-point,[140] mentioning Warham's '*ordinationes*' six times in his text.[141] These citations demonstrate that although Wolsey may have been prompted to attempt statute reform by the *Exhibita*, he was not attempting to paraphrase Colet's work; he was concerned with his own interpretation of the existing statutes.

Historians have been silent on the question of why Wolsey became involved in St. Paul's Cathedral statute making. I conjecture two reasons: firstly, because of his receipt of Colet's *Exhibita*; and secondly, because 1518 was a year of intense reform activity for Wolsey, as Lord Chancellor, papal legate *a latere*, Archbishop of York and King's Councillor.[142] Thus, he would have been receptive to the idea of meddling in statute reform at St. Paul's – an idea prompted by Colet's request.

Another significant difference between Wolsey's work and the *Exhibita* is Wolsey's emphasis upon money, compared to Colet's near lack of interest in the matter. Wolsey concerned himself with fourteen separate financial issues in his text, often mentioning specific sums of money either to be paid or received.[143] Wolsey's pragmatic nature is apparent in these specific decrees concerning Church finances. Colet was largely concerned with the moral ideals of the Church, wherein he believed lay its strength. Hence his insistence upon Saturday disciplinary hearings, a proposal absent from Wolsey's statutes.[144] Wolsey, on the other hand, was concerned with the durability of the Church's administrative efficiency. These divergent texts, therefore, portray two very different ecclesiastical ordinaries.

To conclude: the *Epitome*, including its occasional commentary upon selected pre-existent statutes of Baldock and Lisieux, was an ecclesiological statement about the standards of clerical behaviour at St. Paul's that Colet wished to see during his tenure as dean. His additions are so idiosyncratic that they cannot be considered to have been serious proposals for statute reform. What exactly Colet's purpose was in composing them, therefore, is open to conjecture. I suggest that they were a personal, and private, expression of disappointment, perhaps written in preparation for a more considered set of proposals to be structured as *Exhibita*. His *Exhibita* are framed in a more moderate fashion, without the incredulous outbursts of the *Epitome*. Therefore, it is more plausible that these latter proposals were meant for consideration by the cathedral body. However, Wolsey chose not to endorse the *Exhibita*,[145] deciding instead, as an experienced ecclesiastical administrator, to compose his own quite different statutes.

Conclusion

Colet's ecclesiology was the personal context, and motivation, for the composition of his *Epitome* and *Exhibita*. In these texts, he emphasized the need for perfection in the Church in accordance with the celestial and ecclesiastical hierarchy: every cleric's diligent execution of the duties entrusted to him was essential for Church unity; a humble knowledge of one's role and one's position in the clerical ranks was required in order to achieve a unified body capable of ascending the ladder of perfection from humankind to God. The dean's idealism did not necessarily point to any moral failings on the part of the canons, as flagrant breaches of clerical discipline by residentiaries were rare.[146] Nevertheless, he devoted much of his clerical life to promoting the idea of a perfected Church. The *Epitome* and the *Exhibita* represent Colet's last reform efforts. Accounts of his increasing illness, through 1518 and 1519, make it unlikely that he made any further attempts to change the cathedral statutes in his final year.

At the end of his life, Colet was Wolsey's ally and the king's friend, as well as a respected humanist: in 1519, Erasmus wrote to several prominent humanists, including Richard Pace, Thomas Lupset, Lord Mountjoy and John Fisher, expressing his grief at Colet's death.[147] The tone of Erasmus's letters suggests that he expected, perhaps even demanded, that his correspondents should also mourn. However, Erasmus seems to have been mourning the loss of a close personal friend, rather than a great Church reformer. Colet's reform attempts had consistently failed throughout his career as dean – and his attempted statute modifications of 1518 were no exception. During the last few years of his life, he found the St. Paul's clergy shameful, and had attempted to tell them so. Colet's ecclesiological and political activities between 1515 and 1518, combined with increasing illness, resulted in his final attempt to engage with the Church on a practical, rather than a theoretical, level. Like his earlier attempts at reform, they failed, not fundamentally because his ideals were radical, but because his *Epitome* was probably never aired publicly, and because his *Exhibita* were seemingly unacceptable to Wolsey.

Colet's attack on clerical behaviour, whether in 1496 or in 1518, exposed his weakness, which was spiritual pride. He genuinely believed himself to be superior to others in the spiritual life. He lacked, however, the spirit of encouragement and the ability to see good in others. Most of all, his ecclesiology blinded him to what could be realistically expected of the clergy. Requiring the canons to be continuously resident, for instance, could only result in his disappointment. From Oxford scholar to London dean, Colet's ecclesiology never wavered from the unrealistically idealistic. It was this perfectionism that led him to ask the impossible and ignore the meritorious. Thus, at the end of 1518, it was St. Paul's School for which Colet could justly be proud. As for statute reform, his ideals for the Church remained an unrealized vision of perfection.

CONCLUSION

John Colet was a visionary. As a clerical reformer, however, he failed: he could not implement his idealistic and unrealistic ecclesiology, although he attempted clerical reform by various means: cathedral administration; proposed new statutes; preaching; education; and political networking. Thus, he cannot be called a reformer, or a proto-Protestant; nor did he belong to a circle of humanist reformers, either in Oxford or in London. Colet's ecclesiology, which he developed whilst resident in Oxford, was characteristic to him alone and was the dominant force behind his activity as Dean of St. Paul's Cathedral. The basis for his ecclesiology was his engagement with Christian humanism as well as with a wide variety of writers, such as St. Paul, Pseudo-Dionysius, Plato, the Neoplatonists, St. Augustine and representatives of the Franciscan tradition. Consequently, his ecclesiology was a hierarchical, perfectionist, morally strict and ascetic code, the aim of which was to promote unity, and therefore order and beauty, within the Church, thereby facilitating a communal ascent towards union with God. This book was written in response to omissions within existing scholarship. Historians writing from the Victorian era to the mid-twentieth century portrayed Colet as an active reformer and a Protestant before Protestantism, who heralded the English Reformation. Thereafter, revisionist scholars presented him as a minor humanist celebrity and part of a group of pre-Reformation Catholic reformers including Fisher, More, Erasmus and Melton. Colet's ecclesiology, however, had largely been ignored until the recent past and has only been of passing interest to historians. Thus, a detailed post-revisionist reassessment of Colet's thought and activity was needed. Specifically, there remained two gaps to be filled: firstly, the question of Colet's intellectual and spiritual relationship to the Church; and secondly, the question of his activity as dean. I decided that the most effective way of examining these two areas would be to re-evaluate his ecclesiastical significance by investigating his life and works generally, in order to determine what his vision was, as well as when, where and why it was developed, and how it revealed itself during his administration of the cathedral and his London life. Thus, Colet's distinctive qualities could be established by means of an examination of his written works and by an analysis of several episodes from his life.

In the light of existing scholarship, I have attempted four main tasks: firstly, to acknowledge Colet's ecclesiology as the primary focus of his life and work; secondly, to offer a detailed and lengthy examination of that ecclesiology; thirdly, to give a substantial discussion of Colet's ecclesiastical career; and fourthly, to reassess Colet's significance within the late-medieval Church and society by examining his work and thought.

Findings

Colet was devoted to the service of the Church. His tracts and correspondence, as well as accounts of his life, suggest that he thought about very little else. In essaying a fresh appraisal of Colet's life, we find that Colet's ideal Church was a hierarchical and Christocentric institution reconciled to God by a process of corporate cleansing, illumination and perfection.[148] The Church, for Colet, consisted of Christ at the head of a celestial and ecclesiastical hierarchy. The diffusion of God's love throughout the Church was achieved through the hierarchical order. Humanity conformed to the divine will and was thereby reformed from disorder to union with God. The Church was thus transformed from multiplicity to unity for the single purpose of attaining perfection. Hence, his ecclesiology was otherworldly, celestial and absolutist in its concern for an institutional, rather than individual, relationship with God. He elevated the role of human will above intellect and thus departed from scholastic, and even humanist, notions of the potential achievements of reason. His scheme was highly clericalist and restricted to a secular ecclesiastical hierarchical structure of priesthood and laity.[149] The maintenance of this hierarchical order was essential for the attainment of perfection.

Colet assembled an eclectic theology and ecclesiology. He inherited his Christocentricity, as well as his emphasis upon love and unity, from Paul;[150] he took ideas of order, hierarchy, cleansing, illumination and perfection from the works of Pseudo-Dionysius;[151] he extracted notions of the emanations of God's love, through which humanity (for Colet, the Church) returns to God (or the One) from the Platonists and Neoplatonists;[152] he adopted an anti-Pelagian soteriological stance by emphasizing the Augustinian notions of the depravity of humanity and its utter dependency upon God's grace;[153] and he accepted the Franciscan idea of the primacy of the loving will over intellect.[154] To the aforementioned elements he added his characteristic obsession with order and beauty, as well as with the cosmic nature, or otherworldliness, of that order. His perfectionism fostered unrealistic expectations of the clergy and contributed to the thwarting of his attempted reforms. Nevertheless, Colet's thought was a unique contribution to the late-medieval Church, being distinct from that of his humanist contemporaries, Erasmus, Fisher, Ficino and Lefèvre d'Etaples.

Although Colet's works demonstrate that his relationship with the Church was passionate, it was mostly an unworkable partnership. The root cause of this failure was the development of his ecclesiology within an academic, rather than an ecclesiastical, environment. Arguably, most, if not all, of Colet's extant texts were composed during his time at Oxford, between 1496 and 1505, before his preferment to the deanery of St. Paul's. Thus, Colet's vision for the Church was not influenced by a ministerial context.[155] Rather, his cerebral theology was a conceptual ideal, which he then attempted to impose upon the clergy and other staff at the cathedral. However, Colet never questioned its appropriateness for the Church. Hence, his vision was an unworkable theory of reform, rather than a practical programme for change. If Colet's ministerial experience at St. Paul's had influenced his ecclesiology, and had he been adaptable enough in nature to accommodate that experience, then one might expect his cathedral ministry to have developed during his tenure as dean so as to suit the needs of that community. However, as is borne out by the evidence of his life and works, Colet's ideas were rigid – his persistent attempts at cathedral reform were remarkable for their lack of variation. As long as Colet remained an aloof abstract theorist, rather than a pragmatic realist, his ideals would be unusable.

Thus, my second general conclusion, which concerns the nature of Colet's cathedral administration and London ministry between 1505 and 1518, is that his ecclesiastical career was characterized by various attempts to implement his perfectionist values in London – through his proposed statute reform of 1506; his Convocation sermon of 1511/12; his preaching between 1512 and 1515; his use of political connections; and his final reform efforts of 1518.

The attempted implementation of Colet's ideals was repeatedly impeded by his inappropriate approach to it, as manifested in his first entanglement with the cathedral administration in 1506. That episode – his attempt to reform the minor clergy at St. Paul's – demonstrated how little he understood practical ecclesiastical life. His vision of ecclesiastical unity contrasted with his view of the Church as a diseased and dysfunctional institution. In fact, neither extreme was the reality. Colet possessed a fervently idealistic ecclesiology, but had little notion of how to apply it, or of what could realistically be achieved.

During his career as dean, Colet gained a reputation as a preacher.[156] His attempts to exhort the English clergy towards greater piety and unity were evident in his sermon delivered to the Convocation of the Province of Canterbury in 1511/12.[157] Colet's sermon was new in that he combined the ancient and modern sermon forms, expanding them to include his ecclesiological emphasis. He used a plain style for effective communication, but used Latin only, in order to maintain theological and ecclesiastical credibility with his clerical congregation. Moreover, Colet's sermon was characteristic, in that he ignored live issues of sin, repentance, penance, purgatory and hell, instead focusing on the need for more Church councils and diligent clergy. Thus, the dean sought a renewal of people's minds rather than of their hearts: he wished for an obedient institution, not just penitent individuals.

Erasmus, Colet's great friend, portrayed him as a prolific, but excitable and arrogant, preacher.[158] Colet's vision, as expressed in his sermons from 1512-15, produced extreme reactions and was responsible for the rise and fall of his political and ecclesiastical fortunes in this period. Nevertheless, his sermons remained undiluted over these years, regardless of a royal reprimand and an episcopal attack.

Colet's entry into political life encouraged him to seek Wolsey's support for a further attempt at clerical reform at St. Paul's in 1518. Thus, the dean judged his political connections to be potentially useful in the prospective implementation of his ideals. However, Colet's 1518 reform efforts were a failure compared to those of his predecessors (Deans Baldock and Lisieux) and to those of his contemporaries (Wolsey and Warham).[159] Due to the controversies of his middle tenure, caused by the friction between his inflexible ecclesiological vision and the genuinely difficult situation with which he was faced, Colet was ineffective as a reformer.

To summarize these two main conclusions: Colet's intellectual and spiritual relationship with the Church was an all-consuming passion, to which he devoted his entire life. It was his only real concern: even his school was an attempt to build up the future Mystical Body of Christ through education.[160] Colet's activity was driven by his ecclesiological values, which were formed in Oxford and which he attempted to implement in London. He was an idealist and a perfectionist; for these reasons, his attempts at reform failed.

Colet's impact upon late-medieval Church and society can be explained in both negative and positive terms. With regard to the negative, we have seen that, contrary to various misconceptions, Colet was not a reformer, nor a statute maker, nor a proto-Protestant, nor part of a humanist reform circle. Moreover, many of his potential achievements remained unfulfilled. In fact, Colet was inferior to many of his contemporaries: he was not as influential a humanist as Erasmus; he was not as great a preacher as Fisher; he was not as successful a clerical reformer as Wolsey; he was not a bishop, although, given his ecclesiological emphasis upon the episcopate, he would surely have liked to have been; and he was not a monk, although his ascetic character and intention to retire to a Carthusian house suggests sympathy with the monastic life. Furthermore, Colet was not as successful a dean as his contemporaries, or his decanal predecessors, in the fields of statute reform and cathedral administration. Therefore, with so much negative evidence, can it be concluded that Colet has any positive significance for our understanding the late-medieval Church? I conclude that he does, by virtue of his ecclesiology, as expressed in his life and works.

Thus, a more positive interpretation is that Colet was an example of independent creative thought in the late-medieval Church. Englishmen like Fisher, Melton and More, as well as Continental theologians such as Johann Geiler von Kaysersberg, Savonarola and Lefèvre d'Etaples, sought Church reform by means of renewal of the individual heart. Such men pursued the reformation of unrepentant sinners. Colet, however, was concerned with the obedient priest and the renewal of people's minds. For him, reform was only possible through **corporate** obedience to the celestial and ecclesiastical hierarchy, which in turn brought unity, order and beauty to the Mystical Body and enabled it to ascend to God. Ultimately, those who knew Colet found this idiosyncratic and perfectionist ecclesiology an unworkable basis for self-improvement – not because, as members of the late-medieval Church, they were necessarily dissolute and depraved, but because they possessed a spirit of discernment and self-preservation that did not allow Colet's spiritually proud approach to interfere with the smooth administration of Church life. Therefore, Colet's passion for the Church tell us not only that Catholic reformers were working hard for the regeneration of the pre-Reformation Church, for we already know this from revisionist scholarship, but also that Colet attempted to reform the Church in his characteristic way. Colet was a significant humanist, educationalist, social commentator, exegete, preacher and even a politician. Colet's vision was the thread linking all these areas of his life. Evidence concerning Colet's ecclesiological life and work, therefore, offers the modern historian a new perspective into the many aspects of pre-Reformation life in England upon which Colet attempted to impose his ecclesiological values. His ecclesiastical ideals may not have been well received during his lifetime, but they did point, in a prophetic way, to the need for unity and purity within the Church, in order for it to grow, as a body, closer to God. Therefore Colet's place as a key figure within late-medieval English society as a whole is not to be underestimated.

Further Study

This work inevitably raises fresh questions and leaves some existing issues unexamined. The past thirty years has witnessed a welcome return to the scrutiny of Colet's life and thought. For instance, the significance of Gleason's biography cannot be underestimated, and the work of revisionist scholars since its publication has opened up further possibilities for Colet studies. However, nearly five hundred years after Colet's appointment to the deanery of St. Paul's, it is clear that a vast amount of research remains to be done. There are at least three main areas requiring attention: firstly, the search for lost sources by, or relating to, Colet; secondly, the huge task of producing modern editions of Colet's surviving works – new translations supplied with detailed commentaries; and thirdly, the examination of other aspects of Colet's work – especially his involvement with the Mercers' Company. These are all important avenues for future research because the recovery of source material, the execution of scholarly editions, and the extension of research into other areas of Colet's life, such as his activities as a mercer, would greatly enrich our understanding of pre-Reformation London life.

England is fortunate in possessing several Colet manuscripts, which are relatively easily accessible in Cambridge, Oxford and London.[161] However, there are some sources, extant at the end of the nineteenth century, which have subsequently disappeared. One example is a lost manuscript of 1506, which ostensibly contains Colet's compilation of existing statutes, and his proposed fresh injunctions, for the discipline of chantry priests and minor clergy. Although Simpson's 1890 edition of this document gives an account of its contents, the rediscovery of the original manuscript itself would permit a more thorough and reliable examination of the text, which has significance for our understanding of pre-Reformation statute reform and cathedral administration.[162] Similarly, the discovery of one of the little books, or *libelli*, that Colet apparently commissioned in 1506 would demonstrate that his orders had been enacted. It would also show what material Colet chose to include in these reference books, and therefore reveal, more precisely, his chief ecclesiological concerns with regard to chantry priests and minor clergy.

Two other important lost Colet manuscripts are the *Epitome*, his collection of pre-existent cathedral statutes with commentary, and the *Exhibita*, his 1518 statement of reform proposals addressed to Wolsey.[163] These manuscripts were extant when Simpson was preparing his 1873 edition of the St. Paul's Cathedral statutes. Their re-emergence would bring fresh opportunities for scholars to study Colet's work. It would be particularly advantageous to compare the manuscripts with contemporaneous statutes relating to other cathedrals, in order to ascertain precisely the distinctive qualities of Colet's work. By comparing the 1506 manuscript and the original manuscripts of the *Epitome* and the *Exhibita*, it may be possible to determine whether or not Colet's ideals had developed in the intervening twelve years and, if so, then to what extent. Moreover, the re-discovery of these three manuscripts would also permit an examination of the folios, watermarks and handwriting, thereby making it possible to determine the method of their compilation; to identify any material excluded from, and any errors in, Simpson's transcriptions; and clearly to distinguish Colet's prospective injunctions from the pre-existing statutes.[164]

Erasmus related that Colet lectured in Oxford on all of St. Paul's epistles.[165] Therefore, the rediscovery of Colet's lost Oxford lectures, and of the texts attributed to him by Pitts and Bale, would considerably assist the analysis of late-medieval exegesis, theology and ecclesiology. Equally, the recovery of any of Colet's sermon texts would greatly benefit the study of Colet as a preacher, particularly the question of his homiletic style.

Progress in Colet studies would also be helped by the production of further modern editions of his works. Two relatively recent editions have proved invaluable in Colet scholarship and have been used throughout this book: Gleason's translation of *De Sacramentis* and the translation of Colet's commentary on 1 Corinthians by O'Kelly and Jarrott.[166] These two excellent works, both provided with illuminating introductions, have proved how valuable modern editions can be. However, these 1980s translations are the exception rather than the rule. For the most part, scholars must rely upon Lupton's nineteenth-century editions of the texts. Precious though they are, being the only translations in existence, they are nevertheless not without inaccuracies – and the editor's introductions give a dated Victorian Protestant perspective. Fresh translations are therefore needed of Colet's lectures on Romans; his treatise on the Mystical Body of Christ; his letter to Richard Kidderminster; his commentaries on the *Ecclesiastical Hierarchy* and the *Celestial Hierarchy* of Pseudo-Dionysius; his exposition of Romans, chapters one to five; and his letters to Radulphus on the Mosaic account of creation.[167] As far as Colet's other correspondence is concerned, letters to and from Erasmus have been translated. However, an edition of all Colet's extant letters, to various recipients, would make a welcome addition to scholarship.

One work, in particular, deserves a full translation and close critical analysis. This is Colet's vigorous debate with Erasmus over Christ's agony in the garden of Gethsemane, which was undertaken in epistolary form in 1499, and was so intriguing to the latter that he published a version of the correspondence during Colet's lifetime under the title *Disputatiuncula*.[168] Although Gleason provides an excellent summary of the debate, no full translation of it – the *Disputatiuncula* version – has been made.[169] Erasmus's text is rich in evidence of Colet's theological and Christological thought. A translation of the *Disputatiuncula*, with commentary, would be fascinating not only on a biographical level, as a dispute between two friends, but also on a theological level, as a debate between two late-medieval humanists with opposing views on the nature of Christ.

The third main area in need of scholarly attention is the question of how Colet's thought on various issues, as expressed in his written works, related to his life as a London citizen. It would be equally possible to expand this study into other areas of Colet's thought and practice: for instance, the relationship between Colet's written work on canon law and his legal jurisdiction at St. Paul's. Moreover, scholarship could be advanced by the study of Colet's attitude to prayer, monasticism, marriage and the laity. With regard to the latter category, one area requiring further attention is Colet's work with the Mercers' Company of London. Here, one could build upon Gleason's, and this work's, demonstration of how the mercers were influential in the foundation and administration of Colet's school.[170] Indeed, scholarship would benefit from a detailed study of how the Mercers' Company influenced Colet's activity in general and of how much he influenced the company.

There is so much still to be done that it is unlikely that these tasks can be undertaken by a single person, or even in a single generation. I hope that by revealing something of Colet's life and work, I may have encouraged scholars to investigate the dean and thus enable us to gain a deeper understanding of the significance of this intriguing figure in English and European history.

ABBREVIATIONS

Add.   Additional.

fol(s).   folio(s).

MS   manuscript.

n.   note.

no.   number.

r.   *recto.*

STC   *A Short-Title Catalogue of Books Printed in England, Scotland and Ireland and of English Books Printed Abroad, 1475-1640,* first compiled in 1926 by A.W. Pollard and G.R. Redgrave, 2nd edition revised and enlarged by W.A. Jackson, 1976-86, and F.S. Ferguson, completed by K.F. Pantzer, The Bibliographical Society, I: A-H; II: I-Z; III: printers and publishers index, indices and appendices, Bibliographical Society, London, 1976-91.

v.   *verso.*

vol.   volume.

NOTES

Introduction
1 J.B. Gleason, 'The Birth Dates of John Colet and Erasmus of Rotterdam: Fresh Documentary Evidence', *Renaissance Quarterly*, 32, 1979, pp. 73-6.
2 J.B. Gleason, *John Colet*, University of California Press, Berkeley, California, 1989 [hereafter Gleason], pp. 39-43. It has been plausibly suggested that his humanist reform ideals were nurtured in Cambridge, with men such as John Fisher (later Bishop of Rochester) and William Melton (later Chancellor of York): R. Rex, *The Theology of John Fisher*, Cambridge University Press, Cambridge [hereafter CUP], 1991 [hereafter Rex, *Fisher*], pp. 22-6.
3 W.R. Godfrey, 'John Colet of Cambridge', *Archiv für Reformationsgeschichte*, 65, 1974, pp. 6-17 [hereafter Godfrey].
4 Colet transcribed certain letters, written between himself and Ficino, into the flyleaves of his copy of Ficino's *Epistolae*, Venice, 1495: now preserved as All Souls' College Library, Oxford [hereafter AS], h. infra 1.5. See S. Jayne, *John Colet and Marsilio Ficino*, Oxford University Press, Oxford [hereafter OUP], 1963 [hereafter Jayne], pp. 81-3.
5 D. Erasmus, D., *Opus Epistolarum Desiderii Erasmi Roterdami*, I-IV, edited by P.S. Allen and H.M. Allen, OUP, 1906-22 [hereafter Allen], IV, p. 514; D. Erasmus, *Christian Humanism and the Reformation: Selected Writings of Erasmus with The Life of Erasmus by Beatus Rhenanus*, edited and translated by J.C. Olin, 1st edition, Fordham University Press, New York, 1965; 2nd edition, 1975 [hereafter Olin], p. 177.
6 Cambridge University Library [hereafter CUL], MS Gg.iv.26, fols. 2r-61v (Romans) and 75r-153r (1 Corinthians).
7 Gleason, pp. 67 and 121-2; Jayne, *passim*; J.B. Trapp, 'John Colet' in P. Bietenholz and T.B. Deutscher (eds.), *Contemporaries of Erasmus: A Biographical Register of the Renaissance and Reformation*, I, University of Toronto Press, Toronto, 1985, pp. 324-8 [hereafter Trapp, 'Colet'], p. 238; Allen, IV, p. 514; Olin, p. 177.
8 Lupton and Gleason mysteriously considered Dennington to be situated between Oxford and Cambridge: J.H. Lupton, *A Life of John Colet, D.D.*, 1st edition, George Bell and Sons, London, 1887; 2nd edition, Bell, London, 1909 [hereafter Lupton], pp. 116-7; Gleason, p. 43. However, Lupton also asserts that Dennington is north of Framlingham in Suffolk: Lupton, pp. 116-7 and 145 (n. 2). Dennington is, in fact, in Suffolk and, therefore, not between Oxford and Cambridge.
9 See list of benefices in F. Seebohm, *The Oxford Reformers of 1498: Being a History of the Fellow-Work of John Colet, Erasmus, and Thomas More*, 1st edition, Longmans, Green, London, 1867; 3rd Longmans, Green, edition, London 1896 [hereafter Seebohm], p. 529.

[10] J. Le Neve, *Fasti Ecclesiae Anglicanae, 1300-1541, VI: Northern Province*, edited by B. Jones, Institute of Historical Research, London, 1963, p. 38; J. Le Neve, *Fasti Ecclesiae Anglicanae, 1300-1541, III: Salisbury Diocese*, edited by J.M. Horn, Institute of Historical Research, London, 1962, p. 48; Lupton, pp. 122-3; and Seebohm, p. 529.

[11] For Colet's appointment, see Guildhall Library, London [hereafter GL], MS 25187 (Colet's Visitation Expenses, 1506), fol. 1v and A.B. Emden, *A Biographical Register of the University of Oxford to A.D. 1500*, I, Clarendon, Oxford, 1957 [hereafter Emden], p. 463.

[12] Seebohm, pp. 208-10; Gleason, pp. 217-22. The school was more than just a re-foundation of the ancient grammar school. See C.M. Barron, *London in the Later Middle Ages: Government and People, 1200-1500*, OUP, 2004, p. 226 and *idem*, 'The Expansion of Education in Fifteenth-Century London' in J. Blair and B. Golding (eds.), *The Cloister and the World: Essays in Medieval History in Honour of Barbara Harvey*, OUP, 1996, pp. 219-45, especially pp. 236-7.

[13] Seebohm, p. 503; Gleason, p. 261.

[14] Contrary to the claims of Kennett, Knight and Seebohm: British Library [hereafter BL], Lansdowne MS 1030, fol. 2r; S. Knight, *The Life of Dr. John Colet, Dean of St. Paul's, in the Reigns of K. Henry VII and K. Henry VIII and Founder of St. Paul's School: With an Appendix Containing Some Account of the Masters and More Eminent Scholars of that Foundation, and Several Original Papers Relating to the Said Life*, 1st edition, J. Downing, London, 1724; 2nd edition, Clarendon, Oxford, 1823 [hereafter Knight], pp. 181-99; Seebohm, pp. 222-55. Proto-Protestant, within this context, means a forerunner of, and contributor to, English Protestantism.

[15] Contrary to the claims of Rex, *Fisher*, p. 26; S. Brigden, *London and the Reformation*, OUP, 1989, [hereafter Brigden, *London*], p. 71; C. Harper-Bill, C., *The Pre-Reformation Church in England, 1400-1530*, Boydell Press, Woodbridge, 1989 [hereafter Harper-Bill, *Church*], p. 26; C. Harper-Bill, 'Dean Colet's Convocation Sermon and the Pre-Reformation Church in England', *History*, 73, 1988, pp. 191-210 [hereafter Harper-Bill, 'Sermon'], pp. 191-5; and C. Haigh, *English Reformations: Religion, Politics, and Society under the Tudors*, Clarendon, Oxford, 1993 [hereafter Haigh, *Reformations*], p. 9.

[16] See W.S. Simpson, 'A Newly Discovered Manuscript Containing Statutes Compiled by Dean Colet for the Government of Chantry Priests and Other Clergy in St. Paul's Cathedral', *Archaeologia*, 52, 1890, pp. 145-74 [hereafter Simpson].

[17] Allen, IV, pp. 507-528; Olin, pp. 164-91; Seebohm, p. 160; and Rex, *Fisher*, pp. 22-6.

[18] Gleason, pp. 138-41.

[19] M. Dowling, *Fisher of Men: A Life of John Fisher, 1469-1535*, Macmillan, Basingstoke, 1999 [hereafter Dowling, *Fisher*], p. 31; N. Mann, 'The Origins of Humanism' in J. Kraye (ed.), *The Cambridge Companion to Renaissance Humanism*, CUP, 1996 [hereafter Kraye], p. 1.

[20] A. Hamilton, 'Humanists and the Bible' in J. Kraye (ed.), *The Cambridge Companion to Renaissance Humanism*, CUP, 1996, pp. 100-117 [hereafter Hamilton], p. 100.

[21] Dowling, *Fisher*, p. 30; R. Rex, 'Humanism' [hereafter Rex, 'Humanism'] in A. Pettegree (ed.), *The Reformation World*, Routledge, London, 2000 [hereafter Pettegree, *Reformation*], pp. 56-60 and 65.

[22] J. Colet, *John Colet's Commentary on First Corinthians: A New Edition of the Latin Text, with Translation, Annotations, and Introduction*, edited and translated by B. O'Kelly and C.A.L. Jarrott, Medieval and Early Renaissance Studies, vol. 21, Binghamton, New York, 1985 [hereafter *Corinthians*] and J. Colet, *Joannis Coleti Enarratio In Epistolam S. Pauli ad Romanos: An Exposition of St. Paul's Epistle to the Romans, delivered as Lectures in the University of Oxford about the year 1497, by John Colet D.D.*, translated by J.H. Lupton, Bell, London, 1873 [hereafter *Romans*], *passim*.

[23] J. Colet, *Joannes Coletus Super Opera Dionysii: Two Treatises on the Hierarchies of Dionysius, by John Colet D.D.*, translated and edited by J.H. Lupton, George Bell and Sons, London, 1869 [hereafter *Hierarchies*], *passim*.

[24] CUL, MS Gg.iv.26, fols. 67r-74v; J. Colet, *Joannis Coleti Opuscula Quaedam Theologica: Letters to Radulphus on the Mosaic Account of Creation; On Christ's Mystical Body the Church; Exposition of St. Paul's Epistle to the Romans (chapters I-V) by John Colet, D.D.*, translated by J.H. Lupton, Bell, London, 1876 [hereafter *Opuscula*], pp. 31-45/Latin, pp. 185-95 for Colet on humanity's fallen nature.
[25] AS, h. infra 1.5: Colet's marginalia on Ficino's *Epistolae*; Gleason, pp. 46 and 194-5; Jayne, pp. 47-55; L. Miles, *John Colet and the Platonic Tradition*, Allen and Unwin, London, 1962 [hereafter Miles], *passim*; *idem*, 'Platonism and Christian Doctrine: The Revival of Interest in John Colet', *Philosophical Forum*, 21, 1964, pp. 87-103 [hereafter Miles, 'Platonism'].
[26] E.A. Livingstone (ed.), *The Concise Dictionary of the Christian Church*, OUP, 1977, pp. 405-6.
[27] For instance, CUL, MS Gg.iv.26, fol. 34v; *Romans*, p. 74/Latin, p. 186.
[28] K.L. Flannery, SJ, 'Plato and Platonism' in A. Hastings, A. Mason and H. Pyper (eds.), *The Oxford Companion to Christian Thought*, OUP, 2000, pp. 542-4.
[29] BL, Add. MS 63853, fol. 34v; *Hierarchies*, p. 51/Latin, p. 199.
[30] He was an honorary Doctor of Divinity, friend of Wolsey and Henry VIII, as well as Dean of St. Paul's: Allen, IV, pp. 515-21; Olin, pp. 177-82; Emden, p. 463. See W.F. Hook, *The Lives of the Archbishops of Canterbury*, VI, Richard Bentley, London, 1868 [hereafter Hook], pp. 288-289 for an assessment of Colet's inappropriate manner.
[31] C. Schwarz, *et al.* (eds.), *Chambers English Dictionary*, Chambers, Edinburgh, 1990, p. 448.
[32] H.C. Porter, 'The Gloomy Dean and the Law' in G.V. Bennett and J.D. Walsh (eds.), *Essays in Modern English Church History in Memory of Norman Sykes*, Black, London, 1966, pp. 18-43 [hereafter Porter], pp. 27-9; P.I. Kaufman, 'John Colet's *Opus de Sacramentis* and Clerical Anticlericalism: The Limitations of 'Ordinary Wayes'', *The Journal of British Studies*, 22, 1982, pp. 1-22 [hereafter Kaufman, 'Anticlericalism']; E.F. Rice Jr., 'John Colet and the Annihilation of the Natural', *The Harvard Theological Review*, 45, 1952, pp. 141-63 [hereafter Rice, 'Annihilation'], pp. 141-50; R. Rex, *Henry VIII and the English Reformation*, Macmillan, Basingstoke, 1993 [hereafter Rex, *Henry VIII*], pp. 51-2; J.B. Trapp, 'An English Late Medieval Cleric and Italian Thought: The Case of John Colet, Dean of St. Paul's (1467-1519)' in G. Kratzmann and J. Simpson (eds.), *Medieval English Religious and Ethical Literature: Essays in Honour of G.H. Russell*, CUP, 1986, pp. 233-50 [hereafter Trapp, 'English Cleric'], pp. 237-40; D. Erasmus, *The Collected Works of Erasmus*, I-VIII, translated and edited by R.A.B. Mynors and D.F.S. Thomson; annotated by P.G. Bietenholz, W.K. Ferguson and J.K. McConica, University of Toronto Press, 1974-88 [hereafter *Erasmus*], p. 135; Gleason, p. 213; Haigh, *Reformations*, pp. 9-10; W.J. Hankey, 'Augustinian Immediacy and Dionysian Mediation in John Colet, Edmund Spenser, Richard Hooker and the Cardinal de Bérulle' in D. de Courcelles (ed.), *Augustinus in Der Neuzeit: Colloque de la Herzog August Bibliotek de Wolfenbüttel, 14-17 Octobre, 1996*, Brepols, Paris, 1998, pp. 125-60 [hereafter Hankey], pp. 131, 134 and 139; and D. MacCulloch, *Reformation: Europe's House Divided, 1490-1700*, Allen Lane, London, 2003 [hereafter MacCulloch *Reformation*], p. 34.
[33] BL, Lansdowne MS 1030, fol. 2r; J. Foxe, *John Foxe's Book of Martyrs 1583: Acts and Monuments of Matters Most Speciall and Memorable* [STC 11225]: Facsimile edition for CD ROM by D.G. Newcombe and M. Pidd, OUP, 2001 [hereafter Foxe], vol. II, book VII, p. 838.
[34] *Ibid.*, p. 839. Although Gleason points out that the ill disposition of some clergy against Colet was mere idle talk rather than genuine heresy allegations: Gleason, p. 241; Foxe, vol. II, book VII, p. 839.
[35] Allen, IV, pp. 507-28; Olin, pp. 164-91; BL, Lansdowne MS 1030, fols. 2r-181v; Knight, *passim*; C. Wordsworth, 'The Life of Dean Colet, from the Phoenix' in *idem*, *Ecclesiastical Biography: Lives of Eminent Men, Connected with the Religion of England*, I, London, 1853, pp. 433-57; Seebohm, pp. 1-5, 29-92, 137-42, 206-67, 343-6, 461-9 and 503-5; J.A.R. Marriott, *The Life*

of John Colet, Methuen, London, 1933 [hereafter Marriott], pp. 185-91; L. Miles, 'Protestant Colet and Catholic More', *The Anglican Theological Review* [hereafter *ATR*], 33, 1951, pp. 29-42 [hereafter Miles, 'Protestant Colet']; W.A. Clebsch, 'John Colet and the Reformation', *ATR*, 37, 1955, pp. 167-77 [hereafter Clebsch]; D.J. Parsons, 'John Colet's Stature as an Exegete', *ATR*, 40, 1958, pp. 38-42 [hereafter Parsons]; S. Dark, *Five Deans: John Colet, John Donne, Jonathan Swift, Arthur Penrhyn Stanley, William Ralph Inge*, 1st edition, London, 1928; 2nd edition, London, 1960, pp. 1-20; and R. Peters, 'John Colet's Knowledge and Use of Patristics', *Moreana*, 22, 1964, pp. 45-59 [hereafter Peters].

[36] Lupton, pp. 154-77; H.H. Milman, *The Annals of St. Paul's Cathedral*, 1st edition, John Murray, London, 1868; 2nd edition, Murray, London, 1869 [hereafter Milman], pp. 110-28; E.F. Carpenter, 'Reformation, 1485-1660' in W.R. Matthews and W.M. Atkins (eds.), *A History of St. Paul's Cathedral and the Men Associated With It*, J. Baker, London, 1957, pp. 100-71 [hereafter Carpenter], pp. 106-16; E.W. Hunt, *Dean Colet and his Theology*, SPCK, London, 1956 [hereafter Hunt], pp. 103-30; Miles, *passim*; Rice, 'Annihilation', pp. 141-63; and Jayne, pp. 38-78.

[37] R. Hutton, 'Revisionism in Britain' in M. Bentley (ed.), *A Companion to Historiography*, Routledge, London, 1997, p. 386. For revisionists, see P.I. Kaufman, 'John Colet and Erasmus's *Enchiridion*', *Church History*, 46, 1977, pp. 296-312 [hereafter Kaufman, '*Enchiridion*']; J.B. Trapp, 'John Colet and the *Hierarchies* of the Ps-Dionysius' in K. Robbins (ed.), *Religion and Humanism*, Studies in Church History, 17, Blackwell, Oxford, 1981, pp. 127-48 [hereafter Trapp, 'Pseudo-Dionysius']; Kaufman, 'Anticlericalism', pp. 1-22; *idem*, *Augustinian Piety and Catholic Reform: Augustine, Colet, and Erasmus*, Macon, Georgia, 1982, *passim*; Trapp, 'Colet'; Trapp, 'English Cleric'; P.I. Kaufman, *The 'Polytyque Churche': Religion and Early Tudor Political Culture, 1485-1516*, Mercer University Press, Macon, Georgia, 1986 [hereafter Kaufman, *Churche*], pp. 67-74, 79-84, 89-90 and 102-4; Harper-Bill, 'Sermon', pp. 191-210; Gleason, pp. 235-69; Harper-Bill, *Church*, pp. 26, 44, 46 and 52; and Haigh, *Reformations*, pp. 8-11.

[38] Allen, IV, pp. 513-27; Olin, pp. 176-91. Vitrier was Warden of the Franciscan Convent at St. Omer in France.

[39] Gleason, p.4.

[40] MacCulloch, *Reformation*, p. 103.

[41] Allen, IV, p. 513; Olin, p. 176.

[42] Allen, IV, pp. 513-4; Olin, pp. 176-7.

[43] Allen, IV, pp. 515 and 519; Olin, pp. 177 and 179-80.

[44] W. Tyndale, *Answer to Sir Thomas More's Dialogue: The Supper of the Lord after the True Meaning of John VI and 1 Corinthians XI; and W. Tracy's Testament Expounded*, edited by H. Walter, Parker Society, 38, Cambridge, 1850 [hereafter Tyndale, *Answer*], p. 168. In the 1530s, Polydore Vergil expressed 'admiration [for Colet] in a passage on the foundation of St. Paul's School': D.E. Greenway, 'Historical Writing at St. Paul's' in D. Keene, A. Burns and A. Saint (eds.), *St. Paul's: The Cathedral Church of London, 604-2004*, Yale University Press, New Haven, Connecticut, and London, 2004 [hereafter Keene *et al.*], p. 156.

[45] J. Bale, *Index Britannicae Scriptorum: John Bale's Index of British and Other Writers*, edited by R.L. Poole and M. Bateson, OUP, 1902, p. 395.

[46] Hamilton, p. 109; Seebohm, pp. 1-5 and 29-90.

[47] H. Latimer, *The Sermons of Hugh Latimer*, I, edited by G.E. Corrie, Parker Society, 33, Cambridge, 1844 [hereafter Latimer], p. 440.

[48] T. Harding, *A Reioindre to M. Jewels Replie. By Perusing Whereof the Reader May See the Answers to Parte of his Chalenge Iustified*, Ex Officina Ioannis Foaleri, Antwerp, 1566 [*STC* 12769] p. 44.

[49] M. Parker, *De Antiquitate Britannicae Ecclesiae Cantuariensis, cum Archiepiscopis Euisdem*, J. Daye, London, 1572 [*STC* 19292] [hereafter Parker], p. 353.

50 For the first edition to include an account of Colet, see J. Foxe, *The Eccesiasticall History, Conteynyng the Actes and Monumentes of Martyrs*, J. Daye, London, 1570 [*STC* 11223], vol. II, book VII, pp. 964-5 (Bodleian Library copy, shelfmark Mason F. 143, consulted). The text relating to Colet remained unchanged in Foxe's 1576 and 1583 editions. The latter edition has been used for the purposes of this book.
51 Foxe, vol. II, book VII, p. 838.
52 *Ibid.* The heretical Lollards, from the Dutch word to 'mumble' (prayers), were extremely critical of the doctrines and practices of the late-medieval Church and were associated with the works of the fourteenth-century Oxford theologian John Wycliffe (*c.*1330-84): R. Rex, *The Lollards*, Macmillan, Basingstoke, 2002 [hereafter Rex, *Lollards*], *passim*; S. Lahey, 'Wyclif and Lollardy' in G.R. Evans (ed.), *The Medieval Theologians: An Introduction to the Theology in the Medieval Period*, Blackwell, Oxford, 2001 [hereafter Evans], pp. 334-56.
53 P.M. Dawley, *John Whitgift and the English Reformation*, New York, 1954; British edition, Adam and Charles Black, London, 1955, p. 194.
54 J. Pitts, *Ioannis Pitsei, Angli S. Theologiae Doctoris, Liverduni in Lotharingia, Decani. Revelationum Historicarum de Rebus Anglicis Tomus Unus*, Paris, 1619, p. 692. Works listed that are no longer extant are: *In Proverbia Salomonis*; *In Evangelium S. Mattaei*; *Breviloquium Dictorum Christi*; *Exceptiones Doctorum*; *Conciones Ordinariae*; *Conciones Extraordinariae*; *Epistolae ad Tailerum*; *Ortolanus*; and *Abbreviationes*. Jayne suggests that the last two works may be the apophthegms and abstracts of St. Paul's epistles contained in Trinity College Library, Cambridge, Gale Collection MS 0.4.44: Jayne, p. 152. However, I do not agree with this assessment: see my Ph.D. thesis, 'In Search of Perfection: Ecclesiology in the Life and Works of John Colet, Dean of St. Paul's Cathedral, 1505-19', Unpublished Ph.D. Thesis, University of London, 2004, chapter I.
55 D. Lupton, *The History of Protestant Divines*, London, 1637, republished by Jacobus Verheiden, Amsterdam, 1979, pp. 209-10.
56 W. Dugdale, *A History of St Paul's Cathedral in London, from its Foundation Until These Times*, Thomas Warren, London, 1658 [hereafter Dugdale], pp. 257-68.
57 H. Wharton, *Historia de Episcopis et Decanis Londinensibus et Assavensibus*, London, 1695, pp. 238-41.
58 BL, Lansdowne MS 1030, fols. 2r-181r.
59 *Ibid.*, fols. 2r and 12r.
60 *Ibid.*, fol. 2r; B. Mansfield, *Phoenix of His Age: Interpretations of Erasmus, c.1550-1750*, University of Toronto Press, Toronto, 1979, p. 269; Knight, 1st edition, 1724.
61 Knight, 2nd edition, 1823.
62 Seebohm, *passim*.
63 Gleason, p. 8.
64 Seebohm begins his work with Colet's return from Italy: Seebohm, pp. 1-5.
65 J.R. Green, *A Short History of the English People*, London, 1874, p. 5, quoted by Lupton in the preface to *Opuscula*, p. x and in Gleason, p. 9.
66 Seebohm, pp. 29-90.
67 Gleason, pp. 8 and 93-184.
68 Lupton, *passim.*, pp. 14, 20, 167 (n. 1) and 260 (Erasmus); 144 (n. 1) (Foxe); 186, 202 (n. 3) and 285 (Kennett); 12 (n. 2), 15 (n. 1), 122 (n. 3) and 202 (n. 3) (Knight); 33 (n. 1) *et passim* (Seebohm).
69 Lupton, pp. 59-87.
70 *Ibid.*, pp. 199-214, based on Erasmus: Allen, IV, pp. 513-27.

[71] J. Colet, *Joannis Coleti Enarratio In Primam Epistolam S. Pauli ad Corinthios: An Exposition of St. Paul's First Epistle to the Corinthians, by John Colet*, translated by J.H. Lupton, Bell, London, 1876; *Romans, Opuscula, Hierarchies, passim.*

[72] Lupton, pp. 56, 71, 79-80, 84, 88, 106, 134, 140, 197, 255 and 263.

[73] *Ibid.*, pp. 178-98 and 154-77.

[74] At the beginning of the twentieth century, Colet was known as a literary giant, as Dean Inge (1911-34) testified in his diary: 'Asquith, I am told, wishes me to revive the tradition of the Deanery as the most literary post in the Church - the tradition of Colet, Donne, Tillotson, Milman, Mansell and Church', quoted in A. Burns, 'From 1830 to the Present' in Keene *et al*, p. 94.

[75] Marriott, p. 189.

[76] P.S. Allen, 'Dean Colet and Archbishop Warham', *EHR*, 17, 1902, pp. 303-6.

[77] Allen, I-IV, Oxford, 1906-22.

[78] Rice, 'Annihilation', pp. 141-63.

[79] *Ibid.*, p.141.

[80] See CUL, MS Gg.iv.26, fol. 67r; *Opuscula*, p.31/Latin, p. 185.

[81] Miles, 'Protestant Colet'; P.A. Duhamel, 'The Oxford Lectures of John Colet: An Essay in Defining the English Renaissance', *The Journal of the History of Ideas*, 14, 1953, pp. 493-510 [hereafter Duhamel]; Clebsch; Carpenter; and Parsons.

[82] Hunt, pp. 1-130, *passim*.

[83] *Ibid.*, pp. 18-72 (reformer), 73-87 (preacher), 88-103 (exegete).

[84] *Ibid.*, pp. 103-30.

[85] *Ibid.*, pp. 103-30; *Pseudo-Dionysius: The Complete Works*, translated and edited by C. Luibheid, Paulist Press, New York, 1987 [hereafter *Pseudo-Dionysius*], p. 200-59; BL, Add. MS 63853, fols. 1r-4r; *Hierarchies*, pp. 2-7/Latin, pp. 165-9.

[86] R.P. Adams, *The Better Part of Valour: More, Erasmus, Colet, and Vives on Humanism, War, and Peace, 1496-1535*, Seattle, Washington State, 1962; C.A. Patrides, 'Renaissance Views on the 'Unconfused Orders Angellick'', *Journal of the History of Ideas* [hereafter *JHI*], 23, 1962, pp. 265-7; J.H. Rieger, 'Erasmus, Colet and the Schoolboy Jesus', *Studies in the Renaissance*, 9, 1962, pp. 187-94; C.S. Meyer, 'John Colet's Significance for the English Reformation', *Concordia Theological Monthly*, 34, 1963, pp. 410-19; Peters; and E.E. Reynolds, *Thomas More and Erasmus*, New York, 1965, pp. 24-33 and 75-86.

[87] Miles, *passim*; Jayne, *passim*; AS, h. infra 1.5.

[88] Jayne, pp. 39-55.

[89] *Ibid.*, pp. 39-40.

[90] Creating a further fictitious group of 'Oxford Hellenists': *ibid.*, p. 41.

[91] Porter.

[92] *Ibid.*, pp. 24-5.

[93] *Ibid.*, p. 26.

[94] CUL, MS Gg.iv.26, fol. 93v: '... non esse Christianorum quaquumque de re vel externa ...'; *Corinthians*, p. 127/Latin, p. 126; Porter, p. 33.

[95] *Ibid.*, p. 36; C. Haigh, 'Anticlericalism and the English Reformation', *History*, 68, 1983, pp. 391-407, reprinted in C. Haigh (ed.), *The English Reformation Revised*, CUP, 1987, pp. 56-74 [hereafter Haigh, 'Anticlericalism'], pp. 56-74.

[96] Gleason, pp. 179-84 and 199.

[97] Trapp, 'Colet'; J.B. Trapp, 'Pieter Meghen, 1466/7-1540: Scribe and Courier', *Erasmus in English*, 11, 1981-2, pp. 28-35 [hereafter Trapp, 'Meghen']; J.B. Trapp, 'John Colet, His Manuscripts and the Pseudo-Dionysius' in R.R. Bolgar (ed.), *Classical Influences on European*

Culture, 1500-1700: Proceedings of an International Conference held at King's College, Cambridge, April 1974, CUP, 1976, pp. 205-22 [hereafter Trapp, 'Manuscripts'], p. 208.
[98] Trapp, 'Colet'; Trapp, 'Pseudo-Dionysius'; and Trapp, 'English Cleric'.
[99] Kaufman, *'Enchiridion'*, pp. 296-312; E.H. Harbison, *The Christian Scholar in the Age of the Reformation*, Charles Scribner and Sons, New York, 1956, p. 70. This mistaken view was also taken by Marriott and Duhamel: Marriott, pp. 82-96; Duhamel, p. 506.
[100] Kaufman, *'Enchiridion'*, pp. 296-301 and 312.
[101] C.A.L. Jarrott, 'Erasmus's Annotations and Colet's Commentaries on Paul: A Comparison of Some Theological Themes' in R.L. De Molen (ed.), *Essays on the Works of Erasmus*, Yale University Press, New Haven, Connecticut, 1978, pp. 125-44 [hereafter Jarrott], pp. 125 and 137-8: a reference to Porter, p. 18.
[102] See, for example, E. Duffy, *The Stripping of the Altars: Traditional Religion in England, c.1400-c.1580*, Yale University Press, New Haven, Connecticut, and London, 1992 [hereafter Duffy]; Haigh, *Reformations*; Dowling, *Fisher*; and Rex, *Fisher, passim*.
[103] By Seebohm, pp. 224-32 and Lupton, pp. 124-32, in the nineteenth century.
[104] Rex, *Henry VIII*, p. 52; Rex, *Fisher*, pp. 22-6. Colet's humanist credentials are recognized by Dowling: M. Dowling, *Humanism in the Age of Henry VIII*, Croom Helm, London, 1986 [hereafter Dowling, *Humanism*], pp.5 and 113-19; M. Dowling, 'John Fisher and the Preaching Ministry', *Archiv für Reformationsgeschichte*, 82, 1991, pp. 287-309; [hereafter Dowling, 'Preaching']; Dowling, *Fisher*, p. 32. However, Dowling doubts the existence of a Fisher circle as such: Dowling, *Fisher*, p. 47.
[105] Brigden, *London*, p. 71; S. Brigden, *New Worlds, Lost Worlds: The Rule of the Tudors, 1485-1603*, Allen Lane, London, 2000 [hereafter Brigden *New Worlds*], p. 89.
[106] Harper-Bill, *Church*, p. 26; Harper-Bill, 'Sermon', pp. 191-5; Haigh, *Reformations*, p. 9 and Kaufman, 'Anticlericalism', p. 22.
[107] R. Faith, 'Estates and Income, 1066-1540' in Keene *et al.*, p. 150; C.M. Barron and M. Rousseau, 'Cathedral, City and State, 1300-1540' in Keene *et al.*, pp. 33-44 [hereafter Barron and Rousseau], p. 40.
[108] J.B. Trapp, 'John Colet' in H.C.G. Matthew and B. Harrison (eds.), *The Oxford Dictionary of National Biography in Association with the British Academy: From the Earliest Times to the Year 2000*, XII, OUP, 2004, pp. 601-9 [hereafter Trapp, *New DNB*]. Professor Trapp allowed me the privilege of a preview of his article before its publication, for which I was very grateful.
[109] Gleason, pp. 15-66 (education), 67-92 (dating), 93-216 (intellectual life), 217-34 (school) and 235-69 (politics).
[110] *Ibid.*, pp. 3-14.
[111] *Ibid.*, pp. 8-10, 67 and 217-69.
[112] *Ibid.*, pp. 185-269, *passim*.
[113] *Ibid.*, p. 213.
[114] *Ibid.*, pp. 67-92.
[115] In his biblical commentaries: *Corinthians, Romans*; his commentaries on the works of Pseudo-Dionysius: *Hierarchies*; his treatises, especially on the Church: *De Compositione Sancti Corporis Christi Mystici* in *Opuscula*, pp. 31-45/Latin, pp. 185-95; and his sermon to the Convocation of the Province of Canterbury: *Sermon*.
[116] Simpson, pp. 145-74.
[117] *Letters and Papers, Foreign and Domestic, of the Reign of Henry VIII, 1509-47, Preserved in the Public Record Office, The British Museum, and Elsewhere in England, Arranged and Catalogued by J.S. Brewer, M.A., Under the Direction of the Master of the Rolls, and with the sanction of Her Majesty's Secretaries of State*, Volume I, Parts i and ii; Volume II, Parts i and ii, 1st edition, Longman and Co.,

London, 1862; 2nd edition, Longman, London, 1920 [hereafter *LP*], II, ii, pp. 1360, 1365 and 1370.
[118] Rex, *Fisher*, pp. 22-6.

Chapter One

[1] This examination of Colet's early years is intended to serve as a complimentary study to Gleason's existing one.
[2] Knight, p. 1.
[3] Lupton, p. 2. Henry was more likely to have been the third son: Lupton, p. 311. Henry's two older brothers were Thomas and William. A monument to William found in Blythborough Church in Suffolk, declaimed that he died in January 1503-4.
[4] Lupton, p. 3; Gleason puts Henry Colet's birth date at 1430, on the basis that he Henry finished his apprenticeship in 1456-7, having been in the livery company for five years: see *Acts of Court of the Mercers' Company, 1453-1527*, edited by L. Lyell and F.D. Watney, CUP, 1936 [hereafter *Mercers*], p. 47 (4 February 1461)
[5] Lupton, p. 3, citing Weever's 'Funeral Monuments', p.761.
[6] *Ibid.*, p. 312 for the Colet family tree.
[7] *Mercers*, p. 88 (11 September 1475, when eight out of twenty-five eligible mercers did not ride).
[8] *Mercers*, p. 47.
[9] *Ibid.*, pp. 58-9 (23 July 1463).
[10] BL, Cotton MS., Vittell A. 16, leaf 135; Lupton, p. 9, n. 3.
[11] Alfred B. Beaven, *The Aldermen of the City of London, Temp. Henry III-1908*, 2 Volumes, London: Eden Fisher, 1908-1913 [hereafter Beaven], II, p. 15.
[12] Beaven, I, p. 90.
[13] *Mercers*, p. 95 (18 December 1476); Beaven, I, p. 154; Lupton, p. 9; Gleason, p. 24.
[14] Beaven, I, pp. 278 and 324. He allegedly even ranked as an Earl: Gleason, p. 25; B. Varley, *The History of Stockport Grammar School*, Manchester University Press, Manchester, 1946, p. 10.
[15] Gleason, p. 22; *Mercers*, pp. 188-9.
[16] By 12 June 1461 Henry gave 33*s* 4*d* – well above average for a loan 'for the spede of therle of Warwick'. In 1477, he was one of the highest mercer contributors to the rebuilding of the city walls: *Mercers*, pp. 51-2.
[17] BL, Add. MS 19540; Lupton, p. 10.
[18] Knight, pp. 4-5.
[19] Lupton, p. 12; Knight, p. 277: 'At the requeste and commaundment of my said sovereigne lorde', 1 May 1496. He gave, under his seal, 'the pledge of his entire fortune present and to come for the faithful observance of the treaty'; Gleason, p. 32.
[20] Knight, p. 6
[21] Or Homerton in Huntungdinshire according to Trapp, *New DNB*, p. 601.
[22] Mary L. Mackenzie, *Dame Christian Colet: Her Life and Family*, Privately Printed, Cambridge, 1923, p. 58.
[23] Gleason, p. 24. In letters dated 1521 and 1532 to Bonifacius Amerbach, Erasmus speaks of Christian Knevet/Colet as 'a matron of singular piety': Knight, pp. 8-9.
[24] Trapp, *New DNB*, p. 601.
[25] *Ibid.*, Christian bequeathed two silver-gilt standing cups and covers to the Mercers' Company, held at the Mercers' Hall today.
[26] One child, Thomas, was buried in New Buckingham Church: '*Hic iacet Thomas filius Henrici Collet, civis et aldermanni Civitatis London., qui obiit die Nativitatis Sce Maree* [sic] *1479*': Lupton, p. 14.

27 Will dated 13 January 1523 and proved 2 November 1523: Trapp, *New DNB*, p. 601
28 Gleason, p. 36. He would have attended such a school from the age of six to around fourteen years.
29 Knight, p. 8.
30 For an assessment of schools at this time, see Gleason, pp. 35-8.
31 Lupton, p. 17 citing Brewer, *Rotuli Parliamentorum*, vol. V, p. 137.
32 These buildings were next to the Mercer's Hall but destroyed in the great fire of 1666.
33 Lupton, pp. 17-18.
34 He is mentioned in Longland's *Vision of Piers the Plowman*: 'Than drave I me among drapers my donet to lerne.'; Lupton, p. 23.
35 Trapp, *New DNB*, p. 602.
36 Lupton, pp. 27-44.
37 *Ibid.*, p. 27.
38 Godfrey, pp. 6-17.
39 'A Questionist was the scholar who was engaging in those exercises that accompanied his admissionto the bachelors' degree': John M. Fletcher, 'The Teaching of Arts in Oxford, 1400-1520', *Paedagogica Historica*, 7, 1967, p. 440; Gleason, p. 39 and p. 350, n. 33.
40 Rex, *Fisher*; Gleason, *passim*.
41 For a view on Cambridge University during this time, see Gleason, pp. 38-41.
42 Lupton, p. 43.
43 *Ibid.*, pp. 39-40.
44 Not situated between Oxford and Cambridge, as Gleason suggests (Gleason, p. 43).
45 Allen, II, pp. 268-70.
46 '… *in transmarinis Academemiis*': Parker, p. 306.
47 Letter from Francis Deloine to Erasmus (Erasmi Eptistolae). Deloine expresses his pleasure at Colet having recalled the time when they spent time together at Orleans.
48 Colet to Erasmus, dated Oxford 1497. 'From 1494 the city [Paris] had an active circle of devotees of Ficino': Gleason, p. 60.
49 Hook, p. 285.
50 Gleason mistakenly suggests that Linacre studied only in Padua from 1487-92 (Gleason, p. 44).
51 Jayne, pp. 16-17; G.B. Parks, *The English Traveller to Italy*, Stanford, 1954, I, pp. 423-94 and Appendix, pp. 621-40.
52 Lupton, p. 46 citing Johnson's *Life of Linacre*, pp. 141-6 and 151.
53 See Gleason, pp. 58-9 on Colet's lack of Greek: 'Though he could give a hearing to reformist sentiment, Colet apparently saw no connection between it and the study of the Greek New Testament, for while he was in Italy he showed no interest at all in studying Greek.': Gleason, p. 58.
54 W.K. Ferguson, 'An Unpublished Letter of John Colet', *The American Historical Review* [hereafter *AHR*], 34, 1934, pp. 696-9 [hereafter Ferguson]. Here at p. 699.
55 Jayne, p.17; Ferguson, pp. 696-9; Trapp, J.B., 'Christopher Urswick and his Books: the Reading of Henry VII's Almoner', *Renaissance Studies*, I, 1987, pp. 48-71. Here at p. 50.
56 Colet was not enrolled for the following year; there is only one entry for him: Gleason, p. 45.
57 Cosmo de' Medici appointed Ficino to preside over the Academy. It was dissolved in 1521 on the grounds that some of its members were involved in a plot against the life of Cardinal Giulio de' Medici: Lupton, p. 52, n. 3.
58 In his lectures on Romans, Colet quotes a long passage from Ficino's *Theologica Platonica* and declaims that 'there can be nothing finer in philosophy' than Ficino's writing: *Romans*, p. 32.

[59] Jayne, pp. 17 and 70-5.
[60] Lupton, pp. 53-6; Marriott, *passim*; Ferguson, pp. 696-9.
[61] Trapp, *New DNB*, p. 602.
[62] Jayne, *passim*; Gleason, pp. 47-52. Gleason believes Colet may have been in Florence but missed meeting Ficino, who was then in exile: ' ... by the time he was settled there [Florence], Ficino was off to a self-imposed exile of indeterminate duration ... Thus , there is no need to doubt that Colet passed in Florence at least a good part of the two years or more after he is last heard of in Rome', Gleason, p. 52.
[63] Lupton, pp. 55-6.
[64] *Ibid.*, p. 61.
[65] Gleason, p. 64.
[66] Lupton, p. 61.
[67] When he was elected Dean of St. Paul's on 2 June 1505 he was referred to as 'Professor of Sacred Theology', which meant that he had a D.D. by this time: Gleason, p. 43.
[68] And following the author of the letter to the Hebrews, 11:4.
[69] Trapp, *New DNB*, p. 602.
[70] AS infra. 1.5
[71] Trapp, *New DNB*, p. 606.
[72] John Bale mentions many more Colet texts extant at the end of the sixteenth century: J. Bale, *Index Britannicae Scriptorum: John Bale's Index of British and Other Writers*, edited by R.L. Poole and M. Bateson, Oxford, 1902, p. 602.
[73] Exposition of Romans 1-5, p. 81
[74] Lupton, p. 68.
[75] Exposition on Romans, p. 162.
[76] *Hierarchies*, p. 123.
[77] Lupton, p. 76; *Corinthians*, p. 110.
[78] *Ibid.*
[79] *Corinthians*, p. 90 and J. Colet, *Opus De Sacramentis Ecclesiae: A Treatise on the Sacraments by John Colet*, translated in Gleason, pp. 270-333 [hereafter *De Sacramentis*].
[80] Lupton, p. 78.
[81] Lupton, p. 80.
[82] Three orders: Bishops, Priests and Deacons; three sacraments: baptism, Holy Communion and Chrism; three classes: baptized, communicants and monks.
[83] *Opuscula*, p. 40.
[84] *Corinthians*, p. 125.
[85] *Romans*, p. 127.
[86] *Ibid.*
[87] *Romans*, p. 86.

Chapter Two

[1] BL, Add. MS 63853, fols. 33v and 87r; *Hierarchies*, pp. 50 and 133/Latin, pp. 198 and 253; *Pseudo-Dionysius*, pp. 155, 163 (n. 75) and 235-9; for the origins of the triad, see A. Louth, *The Origins of the Christian Mystical Tradition*, Clarendon, Oxford, 1981 [hereafter Louth, *Origins*], pp. 57-9.

[2] It is the hierarchy of priesthood over laity that concerned Colet. Monks were ranked highest amongst the laity, but were not of priestly status: *Hierarchies*, p. 133/Latin, p. 253.

[3] *Romans*; *Corinthians*, *passim*.

[4] *Hierarchies*, *passim*.

5 For instance, *Romans*, p. 146 for Plotinus and p. 186 for Plato. Pico della Mirandola is specifically mentioned in *Corinthians*, p. 258; *Romans*, pp. 138 and 185-6; *Opuscula*, pp. 170-1; and *Hierarchies*, pp. 236-8. For Ficino's Neoplatonic influence, see Jayne, *passim*; Trapp, 'English Cleric', pp. 237-40.
6 St. Augustine argued against Pelagius's heresy, which was that humans could take the initial steps towards salvation by their own efforts. There are numerous references to St. Augustine throughout Colet's works. See Gleason, p. 335.
7 *Ibid.*, pp. 47 and 198-9.
8 See *ibid.*, pp. 138-41.
9 On his exegesis, see, for instance, Seebohm, pp. 29-42 and 78-90; Lupton, pp. 59-115; and Duhamel, pp. 493-510. Gleason also focused mainly on Colet's exegetical thought: Gleason, pp. 126-84.
10 Porter, pp. 27-9.
11 J.J.W. Alden, 'An Examination of the Thought of John Colet (1467?-1519): A Catholic Humanist Reformer at the Eve of the Protestant Reformation, Unpublished Ph.D. Thesis, Yale University, 1969. [hereafter Alden], pp. 157-90. The idea that Colet influenced the English Reformation has rightly been dismissed: Gleason, pp. 3-14.
12 Trapp, 'Manuscripts', p. 220. Other inferences have come from Rice, 'Annihilation', pp. 141-63; Haigh, *Reformations*, p. 9; and J.B. Trapp, *Erasmus, Colet and More: The Early Tudor Humanists and Their Books*, British Library, London, 1991 [hereafter Trapp, *Erasmus*], p. 135. *De Sacramentis* is discussed in Kaufman, 'Anticlericalism', pp. 1-22 and Gleason, pp. 210-13. Rex and MacCulloch have, in passing, succinctly summarized the hierarchical aspect of Colet's thought: Rex, *Henry VIII*, pp. 51-2; MacCulloch, *Reformation*, p. 34. However, much more remains to be said on this topic. The nature in which Colet's ecclesiology departs from contemporaneous humanism, by virtue of its Augustinianism, has been persuasively argued in Hankey, p. 131 and Trapp, 'English Cleric', pp. 237-40.
13 Rice, 'Annihilation', pp. 141-63.
14 As anticlerical: Kaufman, 'Anticlericalism', pp. 1-22; as clerical: Haigh, *Reformations*, p. 9 and MacCulloch, *Reformation*, p. 34.
15 Rice, 'Annihilation', p. 141.
16 Gleason, p. 265.
17 Trapp, *Erasmus*, p. 135. See also Trapp, 'English Cleric', p. 239: Colet meditates upon 'heavenly love and heavenly beauty and their relation to earthly varieties ... all faculties of the soul are employed in listening to the music of the spheres'.
18 *Corinthians*, p. 178/Latin, p. 177: '*et quidam Christi*'; Gleason, p. 209.
19 Rice, 'Annihilation', pp. 160-3; Gleason, p. 213.
20 Kaufman, 'Anticlericalism', p. 1.
21 *Ibid.*, p. 22.
22 W.R. Cooper, 'Richard Hunne', *Reformation*, 1, 1996, pp. 221-51.
23 See pp. 46-55; Gleason, p. 38.
24 Kaufman, 'Anticlericalism', p. 14.
25 Gleason, pp. 253 and 265.
26 Kaufman, 'Anticlericalism', p. 13.
27 Haigh, 'Anticlericalism', pp. 56-74; Haigh, *Reformations*, p. 9.
28 *Ibid.*, p. 10.
29 MacCulloch, *Reformation*, p. 34.
30 Rex, *Henry VIII*, pp. 51-2.
31 *Ibid.*, p. 54.

³² See pp. 51-5; *Hierarchies*, pp. 48, 53, 56, 128-30, 132, 150 and 203; J. Colet, (translated by [T. Lupset]), *The Sermon of Doctor Colete, made to the Conuocation at Paulis*, London, 1530 [*STC* 5550], reprinted in Lupton, pp. 293-304 [hereafter *Sermon*], p.294.

³³ Gleason, p. 273/Latin, p. 272: '... *opus iustissimum*'. Like Plato, Colet saw justice as central to any decent society or virtuous soul: D. Forrester, 'Justice' in A. Hastings, A. Mason and H. Pyper (eds.), *The Oxford Companion to Christian Thought: Intellectual, Spiritual, and Moral Horizons of Christianity*, OUP, 2000, p. 360.

³⁴ Gleason, pp. 211-3.

³⁵ J. Rist, 'Augustine of Hippo' in Evans, p. 13; G.R. Evans, 'Anselm of Canterbury' *ibid.*, p. 97; M. Robson, 'Saint Bonaventure' *ibid.*, p. 191; A. Broadie, 'Duns Scotus and William Ockham' *ibid.*, pp. 251, 253 and 257.

³⁶ *De Sacramentis*, in Gleason, pp. 271-3.

³⁷ Gleason, p. 213.

³⁸ *Ibid.*, p. 265.

³⁹ *Ibid.*

⁴⁰ Allen, IV, p. 520; Olin, p. 181. Trapp, 'English Cleric', p. 240; Jayne, p. 99. However, he retained his ideology that the priesthood was superior to the rest of creation.

⁴¹ MacCulloch, *Reformation*, p. 34.

⁴² Hankey, p. 131.

⁴³ See pp. 60-63; However, Hankey concludes too much from Colet's Augustinianism by suggesting that Colet was a misanthrope and 'in no sense a humanist': Hankey, p. 141.

⁴⁴ *Ibid.*, p. 139.

⁴⁵ *Corinthians*, p. 89/Latin, p. 88; Gleason, p. 153; Acts 17:34.

⁴⁶ *Pseudo-Dionysius*, pp. 47-290, *passim*.

⁴⁷ K. Froehlich, 'Pseudo-Dionysius and the Reformation of the Sixteenth Century' in *Pseudo-Dionysius: The Complete Works*, translated and edited by C. Luibheid, Paulist Press, New York, 1987, pp. 33-46 [hereafter Froehlich], p. 34.

⁴⁸ Trapp, *Erasmus*, p. 28; Colet was also familiar with Hugh's theology: Gleason, p. 206.

⁴⁹ Richard of St. Victor, *The Twelve Patriarchs, The Mystical Ark, Book Three of the Trinity*, translated by G.A. Zinn, University of Toronto Press, Toronto, 1979 [hereafter Zinn].

⁵⁰ *Ibid.*, p. 7.

⁵¹ *Ibid.*, p. 305.

⁵² See pp. 44-6; B. McGinn, 'Love, Knowledge, and Mystical Union in Western Christianity: Twelfth to Sixteenth Centuries', *Church History*, 56, 1987, pp. 10-12.

⁵³ Gleason, p. 197: The Franciscans 'asserted the primacy of will, and therefore of love, over intellect'.

⁵⁴ See Jayne, pp. 56-76; Gleason, pp. 47 and 198-9.

⁵⁵ BL, Add. MS 63853, fol. 34r; *Hierarchies*, p. 51/Latin, pp. 199-200. See also *Hierarchies*, pp. 223, 244, 249-59 and 270; *Romans*, pp. 190 and 208-13; *Opuscula*, pp. 187 and 194; Gleason, pp. 208-9.

⁵⁶ CUL, MS Gg.iv.26, fol. 82r: '*mali, insipientes, impuri, nihil*'; *Corinthians*, p. 87/Latin, p. 86.

⁵⁷ CUL, MS Gg.iv.26, fol. 82r-v: '*Is a nobis omni amore amandus et excolendus Iesus Chrsitus*'; *Corinthians*, p. 87/Latin, p. 86.

⁵⁸ M.S. Kempshall, 'Ecclesiology and Politics' in Evans, pp. 303-33 [hereafter Kempshall], p. 303.

⁵⁹ *Ibid.*, p. 304.

⁶⁰ BL, Add. MS 63853, fols. 95r-97v; *Hierarchies*, pp. 147-50/Latin, pp. 262-5.

⁶¹ Hence Colet's emphasis upon standards of episcopal preaching.

⁶² Alongside Pauline theology.

63 *Corinthians*, pp. 88-9; Gleason, p. 153.
64 BL, Add. MS 63853, fol. 32r; *Hierarchies*, pp. 49-50/Latin, p. 198.
65 J. Leclercq, 'The Influence and Non-Influence of Dionysius in the Western Middle Ages' in *Pseudo-Dionysius: The Complete Works*, translated and edited by C. Luibheid, Paulist Press, New York, 1987, pp. 25-32 [hereafter Leclercq], p. 30.
66 Although he did in BL, Add. MS 63853, fol. 32v; *Hierarchies*, p. 49/Latin, p. 198.
67 BL, Add. MS 63853, fol. 31r; *Hierarchies*, p. 48/Latin, p. 197.
68 BL, Add. MS 63853, fol. 32r; *Hierarchies*, p. 49/Latin, p. 198.
69 BL, Add. MS 63853, fol. 36r-v, *Hierarchies*, p. 53/Latin, p. 201.
70 See pp. 46-55.
71 Colet referred to thirty-one theologians in his written works: Gleason, pp. 334-9.
72 According to Erasmus, Colet expounded all of Paul's epistles: Allen, IV, p. 514; Olin, p. 177; most of these expositions are now lost.
73 Romans 12:2; Lupton, p. 294/Latin in Knight, p. 240.
74 CUL, MS Gg.iv.26, fol. 28r; *Romans*, pp. 58-9/Latin, pp. 175-6.
75 CUL, MS Gg.iv.26, fol. 35v:; *Romans*, pp. 74-5/Latin, p. 187.
76 Although Hankey, again, concludes too much in asserting that, for Colet, 'Platonism is simply Paul's philosophy': Hankey, p. 134.
77 Gleason, pp. 138-41.
78 Olin, p. 176; Allen, IV, p. 514; Froehlich, p. 36.
79 Hankey, p. 134.
80 Jayne, pp. 12, 28-9, 36, 43 and 67-8.
81 Trapp, 'English Cleric', pp. 237-8; Jayne, pp. 60-5, 70-75 and 104-9.
82 See p. 61; Gleason, pp. 198-9; and MacCulloch, *Reformation*, p. 113.
83 AS, h. infra 1.5: Colet's marginalia in a copy of Marsilio Ficino's *Epistolae* (Venice, 1495) and Colet's transcription of some correspondence with Ficino; Jayne, *passim*.
84 CUL, MS Gg.iv.26, fol. 86v; *Corinthians*, pp. 99 and 101/Latin, pp. 98 and 100.
85 Jayne, pp. 58-68; Trapp, 'English Cleric', p. 243.
86 Froehlich, pp. 41-4.
87 *Ibid.*, p. 44.
88 Carroll has recently correctly suggested that Pseudo-Dionysius's work was, in fact, 'a Christianized version of the philosophy of the fifth-century Neoplatonist Proclus': C. Carroll, 'Humanism and English Literature in the Fifteenth and Sixteenth Centuries' in Kraye, p. 250.
89 See BL, Add. MS 63853, fols. 10r-36v; *Hierarchies*, pp. 18-53/Latin, pp. 176-201; CUL, MS Gg.iv.26, fols. 76v, 79v and 86v-87r; *Corinthians*, pp. 71, 81, 101 and 105/Latin, pp. 70, 80, 100 and 104; CUL, MS Gg.iv.26, fols. 7r, 13r-v, 20v, 21r and 31r-v; *Romans*, pp. 16, 29, 44 and 65/Latin, pp. 146, 155, 165 and 180 and many other passages.
90 BL, Add. MS 63853, fol. 8r; *Hierarchies*, p. 15/Latin, p. 173. See also letters to Radulphus: Corpus Christi College Library, Cambridge [hereafter CCC], MS 355, p. 214; *Opuscula*, p. 18/Latin, p. 176.
91 'Outside this house, that is, outside the Church, no one is saved': Origen, '*Homilia In Iesu Nave*', quoted in A.E. McGrath (ed.), *The Christian Theology Reader*, OUP, 1995, p. 301.
92 CUL, MS Gg.iv.26, fols. 67r-74v; *Opuscula*, pp. 31-45/Latin, pp. 185-95.
93 Gleason, pp. 63 and 334-9: Appendix 2: list of writers referred to by Colet.
94 P. Rorem, 'Augustine, the Medieval Theologians, and the Reformation' in Evans, pp. 365-72 [hereafter Rorem, 'Augustine'].
95 CUL, MS Gg.iv.26, fol. 87r; *Corinthians*, p. 105/Latin, p. 104; CUL, MS Gg.iv.26, fol. 17r; *Romans*, p. 35/Latin, p. 160.

[96] H.A. Oberman, *Forerunners of the Reformation: The Shape of Late Medieval Thought*, Lutterworth Press, London, 1967 [hereafter Oberman], p. 127.
[97] Rorem, 'Augustine', p. 365.
[98] CUL, MS Gg.iv.26, fol. 67r; *Opuscula*, p. 31/Latin, p. 183.
[99] CUL, MS Gg.iv.26, fol. 70r; *Opuscula*, p. 38/Latin, p. 189; CUL, MS Gg.iv.26, fol. 28r.; *Romans*, pp. 58-9/Latin, p. 176.
[100] Kempshall, p. 303.
[101] Allen, IV, pp. 514 and 521; Olin, pp. 177 and 183.
[102] *Corinthians*, p. 239/Latin, p. 238; MacCulloch, *Reformation*, pp. 112-3.
[103] Hankey, p. 133
[104] *Romans*, p. 166; translation in Hankey, p. 140.
[105] *Ibid.*, p. 141.
[106] Gleason, p. 198.
[107] *Ibid.*, pp. 203 and 205.
[108] St. Bonaventure, *The Journey of the Mind to God*, translated by P. Boehner and edited by S.F. Brown, Indianapolis, Indiana, 1990 [hereafter Bonaventure], p. xii.
[109] CUL, MS Gg.iv.26, fol. 67r; *Opuscula*, p. 31/Latin, p. 185.
[110] CUL, MS Gg.iv.26, fol. 76r; *Corinthians*, pp. 69 and 71/Latin, pp. 68 and 70.
[111] Bonaventure, p. xiii.
[112] St. Bonaventure, *Sabbato Sancto Sermo I*, in Bonaventure, p. xii.
[113] *Ibid.*, p. xvi.
[114] *Ibid.*, p. xvii. The six levels are reflected upon in Colet's third letter to Radulphus: CCC, MS 355, p. 219; *Opuscula*, p. 23/Latin, p. 179.
[115] Bonaventure, p. xvii.
[116] *Ibid.*, p. xviii: introduction by S. Brown.
[117] BL, Add. MS 63853, fol. 34r.; *Hierarchies*, p. 51: 'In this mutual love consists all order, duty and office in the Church'/Latin, p. 199.
[118] Gleason, p. 198. For evidence, see *Hierarchies*, pp. 145-9/Latin, pp. 262-5.
[119] BL, Add. MS 63853, fol. 2v; *Hierarchies*, p. 4/Latin, p. 167.
[120] BL, Add. MS 63853, fol. 32r; *Hierarchies*, p. 49/Latin, p. 198.
[121] BL, Add. MS 63853, fol. 3r; *Hierarchies*, p. 5/Latin, p. 167.
[122] 'For colour consists of darkness and light': BL, Add. MS 63853, fol. 3v; *Hierarchies*, p. 5/Latin, p. 168: BL, Add. MS 63853, fol. 34v: *Hierarchies*, p. 52/Latin, p. 199. See also CUL, MS Gg.iv.26, fol. 36v; *Romans*, p. 78/Latin, p. 189 for the term 'colour' or '*colores*'.
[123] *Pseudo-Dionysius*, pp. 195-200.
[124] BL, Add. MS 63853, fol. 34v; *Hierarchies*, p. 51/Latin, p. 199.
[125] Miles, p. 97.
[126] BL, Add. MS 63853, fol. 73v; *Hierarchies*, pp. 114-5/Latin, pp. 239-40.
[127] BL, Add. MS 63853, fol. 75v; *Hierarchies*, p. 116/Latin, p. 241.
[128] BL, Add. MS 63853, fol. 76r; *Hierarchies*, p. 117/Latin, p. 242; MacCulloch, *Reformation*, p. 34.
[129] BL, Add. MS 63853, fol. 33v; *Hierarchies*, p. 50/Latin, p. 198.
[130] BL, Add. MS 63853, fol. 33v; *Hierarchies*, p. 50/Latin, p. 198.
[131] BL, Add. MS 63853, fol. 36r-v; *Hierarchies*, p. 53/Latin, p. 201.
[132] BL, Add. MS 63853, fol. 36v; *Hierarchies*, p. 54/Latin, p. 201.
[133] BL, Add. MS 63853, fol. 87r; *Hierarchies*, p. 133/Latin, p. 253.
[134] BL, Add. MS 63853, fol. 38v; *Hierarchies*, p. 57/Latin, p. 203.
[135] *Sermon*, p. 294; Knight, p. 240.
[136] MacCulloch, *Reformation*, p. 103.

137 BL, Add. MS 63853, fol. 41r; *Hierarchies*, pp. 61-2/Latin, p. 206.
138 BL, Add. MS 63853, fol. 41v; *Hierarchies*, p. 63/Latin, p. 206.
139 BL, Add. MS 63853, fol. 42r; *Hierarchies*, pp. 63-4/Latin, p. 207.
140 Allen, IV, p. 525; Olin, p. 188.
141 Foxe, vol. II, book VII, p. 838.
142 Allen, IV, pp. 507-27, Epistle 1211.
143 BL, Add. MS 63853, fol. 42r-v; *Hierarchies*, p. 64/Latin, p. 207.
144 BL, Add. MS 63853, fols. 42v-43r; *Hierarchies*, p. 64/Latin, p. 208.
145 BL, Add. MS 63853, fol. 46v; *Hierarchies*, pp. 70-71/Latin, p. 212.
146 BL, Add. MS 63853, fol. 51v; *Hierarchies*, p .77/Latin, p. 216.
147 Simpson, pp. 145-74.
148 Lupton, p. 178; College of Arms, London [hereafter CA], MS WC, fols. 219r-220v.
149 Dugdale, pp. 257-68; *Registrum Statutorum et Consuetudinum Ecclesiae Cathedralis Sancti Pauli Londinensis*, edited by W.S. Simpson, London, 1873 [hereafter *Registrum*], pp. 237-48.
150 BL, Add. MS 63853, fols. 54v-55r; *Hierarchies*, pp. 83-4/Latin, p. 220.
151 Allen, IV, p. 525; Olin, p. 188.
152 BL, Add. MS 63853, fol. 59v; *Hierarchies*, pp. 90-1/ Latin, p. 225.
153 Lupton, p. 298: 'O pristes, by the whiche we are conformable to this worlde, by the whiche the face of churche is made euyll fauored'/Latin in Knight, p. 244.
154 Hook, p. 295.
155 BL, Add. MS 63853, fol. 80r-v; *Hierarchies*, pp. 123-4/Latin, pp. 246-7.
156 Gleason, p. 44.
157 *Ibid.*, p. 32; Lupton, p. 12.
158 Allen, IV, p. 514; Olin, p. 177.
159 BL, Add. MS 63853, fol. 98v; *Hierarchies*, p. 142/Latin, p. 258.
160 BL, Add. MS 63853, fol. 98v; *Hierarchies*, p. 142/Latin, p. 258.
161 BL, Add. MS 63853, fol. 95r; *Hierarchies*, p. 147/Latin, p. 262.
162 BL, Add. MS 63853, fol. 97r-v; *Hierarchies*, p. 150/Latin, p. 264.
163 BL, Add. MS 63853, fol. 97v; *Hierarchies*, p. 150/Latin, p. 264.
164 *Sermon*, pp. 299-304, section on canon law.
165 BL, Add. MS 63853, fol. 98r; *Hierarchies*, p. 151/Latin, pp. 264-5.
166 BL, Add. MS 63853, fol. 104v; *Hierarchies*, p. 162/Latin, p. 272.
167 These subjects became significant in Colet's administration of the cathedral.
168 CUL, MS Gg.iv.26, fol. 77v; *Corinthians*, p. 75/Latin, p. 74.
169 CUL, MS Gg.iv.26, fol. 77r; *Corinthians*, p. 73/Latin, p. 72.
170 CUL, MS Gg.iv.26, fol. 67r; *Opuscula*, pp. 31-2/Latin, p. 185.
171 CUL, MS Gg.iv.26, fol. 70r; *Opuscula*, p. 38/Latin, pp. 189-90.
172 CUL, MS Gg.iv.26, fol. 67v; *Opuscula*, pp. 32-3/Latin, p. 186.
173 CCC, MS 355, p. 87; *Opuscula*, p. 97/Latin, p. 233. Colet also adhered to the doctrine of double predestination (to damnation as well as salvation): MacCulloch, *Reformation*, p. 112; Gleason, p. 70.
174 MacCulloch, *Reformation*, p. 113.
175 CCC, MS 355, p. 48; *Opuscula*, p. 75/Latin, p. 218.
176 Trapp, 'English Cleric', p. 248.
177 St. Augustine, *City of God*, translated by H. Bettenson, Penguin, Harmondsworth, 1972.
178 CUL, MS Gg.iv.26, fol. 70r; *Opuscula*, p. 38/Latin, p. 189.
179 CUL, MS Gg.iv.26, fol. 70v; *Opuscula*, p. 40/Latin, p. 190.
180 BL, Add. MS 63853, fol. 40r; *Hierarchies*, p. 61/Latin, p. 205.
181 CUL, MS Gg.iv.26, fol. 73r; *Opuscula*, p. 45/Latin, p. 195.

[182] Although Hankey's assertion that 'Colet thinks entirely in terms of that [divine] law [*lex divinitatis*]' is an overstatement: Hankey, p. 136.
[183] Lupton, p. 300; Latin in Knight, p. 246.
[184] CUL, MS Gg.iv.26, fols. 90v-91r; *Corinthians*, pp. 121-3/Latin, pp. 120-2. Church courts were often distrusted: Haigh, *Reformations*, pp. 49-50.
[185] CUL, MS Gg.iv.26, fol. 55r-v; *Romans*, p. 118/Latin, p. 218.
[186] CCC, MS 355, p. 192; *Opuscula*, p. 162/Latin, pp. 279-80.
[187] CCC, MS 355, p. 193; *Opuscula*, p. 162/Latin, p. 280.
[188] CCC, MS 355, p. 193; *Opuscula*, p. 163/Latin, p. 280.
[189] CCC, MS 355, p. 194; *Opuscula*, p. 163/Latin, p. 281.
[190] CUL, MS Gg.iv.26, fol. 93r; *Corinthians*, p. 127/Latin, p. 126.
[191] For Colet's austere character see Gleason, pp. 64-5 and 264-7.
[192] *Ibid.*, p. 193.
[193] CCC, MS 355, p. 155; *Opuscula*, p. 139/Latin, p. 263.
[194] CCC, MS 355, p. 156; *Opuscula*, p. 140/Latin, p. 264.
[195] Like Origen: Gleason, p. 201.
[196] *Ibid.*, p. 198.
[197] CUL, MS Gg.iv.26, fol. 91v:; *Corinthians*, pp. 121 and 123/Latin, pp. 120 and 122.
[198] CUP, MS Gg.iv.26, fol. 55r; *Romans*, p. 118/ Latin, p. 218.
[199] Rice, 'Annihilation', pp. 141-63. For Colet's meanness with money and great wealth, see Gleason, pp. 64, 264 and Knight, pp. 400-3 (a transcription of Colet's final will).
[200] Allen, IV, p. 518; Olin, p. 179.
[201] Gleason, p. 210.
[202] Jayne, pp. 38-76; Trapp, 'English Cleric', pp. 237-40.
[203] J.L. Carrington, 'Desiderius Erasmus (1460-1536)' in C. Lindberg (ed.), *The Reformation Theologians: An Introduction to Theology in the Early Modern Period*, Blackwell, Oxford, 2002 [hereafter Lindberg], pp. 35-6; Gleason, pp. 63-4.
[204] A.G. Dickens and W.R.D. Jones, *Erasmus the Reformer*, Methuen, London, 1994 [hereafter Dickens and Jones], pp. 21 and 24-5. Colet considered monks to be the 'purest portion' of the laity, but not of priestly rank: *Hierarchies*, p. 134.
[205] MacCulloch, *Reformation*, p. 103.
[206] For Erasmus' views, see MacCulloch, *Reformation*, pp. 112-5.
[207] *Ibid.*, p. 112.
[208] Dowling, *Humanism*, pp. 1, 100 and 167.
[209] G. Bedouelle, 'Jacques Lefèvre d'Etaples (*c.*1460-1536)' in Lindberg, pp. 19-33 [hereafter Bedouelle].
[210] Books ascribed to Hermes Trismegisthus, *c.*1st to 3rd centuries.
[211] CUL, MS Gg.iv.26, fols. 2r-61v.
[212] Bedouelle, p. 19.
[213] E.F. Rice Jr., 'The Humanist Idea of Christian Antiquity: Lefèvre d'Étaples and his Circle', *Studies in the Renaissance*, 9, 1962, pp. 126-60; reprinted in W.L. Gundersheimer (ed.), *French Humanism, 1470-1600*, Macmillan, London, 1969, pp. 163-80 [hereafter Rice, 'Lefèvre'], p. 175.
[214] The preface to which is printed in Lefèvre d'Etaples, *The Prefatory Epistles of Lefèvre d'Etaples and Related Texts*, edited by E.F. Rice, Jr., Columbia University Press, New York, 1972, pp. 60-6.
[215] Bedouelle, p. 24
[216] Published in 1498/9.
[217] *Ibid.*, i.e. the Christian does not merely imitate Christ, but is called to take the form of Christ: Bedouelle, p. 30.

218 *Ibid.*; BL, Add. MS 63853, fol. 12r-v; *Hierarchies*, pp. 22-3/Latin, pp. 178-9.
219 E.F. Rice, Jr., 'Humanist Aristotelianism in France: Jacques Lefèvre and his Circle' in A.H.T. Levi (ed.), *Humanism in France at the End of the Middle Ages and in the Early Renaissance*, Manchester University Press, 1970, pp.132-49; Rice, 'Lefèvre', p. 163; Gleason, p. 192.
220 Rice, 'Lefèvre', p. 179; Gleason, pp. 141-4.
221 BL, Add. MS 63853, fol. 110v; Gleason, p. 279/Latin, p. 278.
222 Rice, 'Lefèvre', pp. 177-8.
223 *Ibid.*; Jayne, p. 70.
224 Gleason, p. 138.
225 BL, Add. MS 63853, fol. 110v; *De Sacramentis*, p. 279/Latin, p. 278.
226 CUL, MS Gg.iv.26, fol. 136v; *Corinthians*, p. 243/Latin, p. 242.
227 *Pseudo-Dionysius*, p. 155.
228 *Ibid.*, p. 154, commented upon by Colet in BL, Add. MS 63853, fol. 8r-v; *Hierarchies*, p. 15/Latin, p. 173.
229 See chapter entitled 'Issues of Hierarchy and Authority' in P. Rorem, *Pseudo-Dionysius: A Commentary on the Texts and an Introduction to Their Influence*, OUP, 1993, pp. 18-24.
230 BL, Add. MS 63853, fol. 22r; *Hierarchies*, p. 40/Latin, p. 190.
231 *Hierarchies*, pp. 145-9/Latin, pp. 262-5.
232 Allen, IV, p. 520; Olin, p. 181.

Chapter Three

1 CUL, MS Gg.iv.26, fol. 129r.; *Corinthians*, p. 221/Latin, p. 220.
2 This passage was written as part of Colet's Oxford lectures on St. Paul, *c.*1496-1505.
3 Simpson, pp. 145-74.
4 Hook, pp. 288-9.
5 Colet was appointed in June 1505: Gleason, pp. 32 and 348 (n. 111); GL, MS 25187, fol. 1v for Colet's appointment and fols. 1v-2r for Colet's visitation expenses, July 1506.
6 Simpson rediscovered the manuscript in 1890, when it was in the possession of Mr. Richard C. Jackson of Camberwell, who died in 1923. It has been missing ever since. Simpson describes it as composed of twenty-three vellum leaves, 12 ⅛ inches high and 8 inches wide. The writing occupies 7 ¼ inches by 4 ¼ inches. Entirely in Latin, the handwriting is clear and in Roman style, common to St. Paul's at that time, with fourteen lines to a page. Some capital letters are ornamented with red and blue: Simpson, p. 145.
7 *Ibid.*, pp. 161-7.
8 Pre-existing statutes by Deans Baldock and Lisieux: *Registrum*, pp. 1-177.
99 Simpson, p. 161.
10 *Ibid.*, pp. 156-167.
11 And bishops' reforms, including Braybroke: Simpson, p. 171.
12 *Ibid.*, pp. 145-6.
13 Carpenter, p. 117; Trapp, 'Manuscripts', p. 212.
14 *Ibid.*
15 See pp. 72, 29-82.
16 V. Davis, 'The Lesser Clergy in the Later Middle Ages' in Keene *et al.*, pp. 157-61 [hereafter Davis, 'Lesser Clergy'], p. 161.
17 Keene *et al.*, p. 474 (n. 32) cites both Simpson's edition of Colet's 1518 statute proposals (*Registrum*, pp. 217-48) and Simpson's edition of the 1506 proposals for minor clergy: Simpson, *passim*. Trapp mistakenly states that '... he [Colet] framed statutes for the Chapter, accepted by them after 20 June 1506, and exhibited [them] to Wolsey in 1518. Conventional in

their nature, they do not in themselves justify reports of the chapter's resentment ...': Trapp, *New DNB*, p. 603.

[18] See pp. 157-77.

[19] As opposed to monastic foundations (the so-called 'Cathedral Priories') staffed by 'regular' clergy and unordained monks, such as Gloucester Cathedral. The secular cathedrals were Bangor, Chichester, Exeter, Hereford, Lichfield, Lincoln, Salisbury, St. Paul's, Wells and York.

[20] K. Edwards, *The English Secular Cathedral in the Middle Ages*, 1st edition, Manchester University Press, 1949; 2nd edition, Manchester University Press, 1967 [hereafter Edwards], pp. 20, 26, 57, 251, 259 and 322.

[21] S.E. Lehmberg, 'The Reformation of Choirs: Cathedral Musical Establishments in Tudor England' in D.J. Guth and J.W. McKenna (eds.), *Tudor Rule and Revolution: Essays for G.R. Elton from his American Friends*, CUP, 1982 [hereafter Lehmberg, 'Reformation of Choirs'], p. 46.

[22] *Ibid.*, p. 47.

[23] Edwards, p. 322.

[24] A.R.B. Fuller, 'The Minor Corporations of the Secular Cathedrals of the Province of Canterbury Excluding the Welsh Sees Between the Thirteenth-Century and 1585 with Special Reference to the Minor Canons of St. Paul's Cathedral from their Origin in the Fourteenth Century to the Visitation of Bishop Gibson in 1724', Unpublished M.A. Thesis, University of London, 1947 [hereafter Fuller], p. 120.

[25] GL, MS 25526, fols. 1v-2r: a list of chantries at the Dissolution; N. Gear, 'The Chantries of St. Paul's Cathedral', Unpublished M.A. Thesis, London University, 1996 [hereafter Gear]; C.M. Barron, 'The Parish Fraternities of Medieval London' in C.M. Barron and C. Harper-Bill (eds.), *The Church in Pre-Reformation Society: Essays in Honour of F.R.H. Du Boulay*, Boydell Press, Woodbridge, 1985, pp. 13-37 [hereafter Barron, 'Parish Fraternities'], pp. 34-5; Simpson, p. 171 for a list of chantries rationalized by Bishop Braybroke in 1391.

[26] M. Bowker, *The Secular Clergy in the Diocese of Lincoln, 1495-1520*, Cambridge Studies in Life and Thought, New Series, 13, CUP, 1968 [hereafter Bowker], p. 163.

[27] *Ibid.*, p. 165.

[28] Lehmberg, 'Reformation of Choirs', p. 17.

[29] Fuller, p. 124; similarly at other secular cathedrals: N. Orme, *The Minor Clergy of Exeter Cathedral, 1300-1548*, Exeter University Press, Exeter, 1980 [hereafter Orme, *Minor Clergy*], p. xviii.

[30] Fuller, p. 124.

[31] D. Lepine, *A Brotherhood of Canons Serving God: English Secular Cathedrals in the Later Middle Ages*, Boydell Press, Woodbridge, 1995 [hereafter Lepine], p. 130.

[32] Fuller, p. 124

[33] *Registrum*, p. 67.

[34] Fuller, p. 124, quoting BL, Lansdowne MS 364, fol. 6v.

[35] F. Harrison, *Life in a Medieval College: The Story of the Vicars-Choral of York Minster*, John Murray, London, 1952 [hereafter Harrison], p. 24.

[36] Lepine, pp. 130-1.

[37] Harrison, p. 24.

[38] S.E. Lehmberg, *The Reformation of Cathedrals: Cathedrals in English Society from 1485-1603*, Princeton University Press, New Jersey, 1988 [hereafter Lehmberg, *Cathedrals*], p. 182.

[39] C. Dyer, *Standards of Living in the Later Middle Ages: Social Change in England, c.1200-1520*, CUP, 1989 [hereafter Dyer], p. 84; R.B. Dobson, 'The Residentiary Canons of York in the Fifteenth Century', *The Journal of Ecclesiastical History* [hereafter *JEH*], 30 (1979) pp. 145-74 [hereafter Dobson]; R.B. Dobson, 'Cathedral Chapter and Cathedral Cities: York, Durham and Carlisle in the Fifteenth Century', *Northern History*, 19, 1983, pp. 15-44 [hereafter Dobson,

'Cathedral Chapters']; and R.B. Dobson, 'Urban Decline in Late Medieval England', *Transactions of the Royal Historical Society* [hereafter *TRHS*], 5th Series, 27, 1977, pp. 1-22.

[40] Harrison, p. 24.

[41] R.B. Dobson, 'The Later Middle Ages, 1215-1500' in G.E. Aylmer and R. Cant (eds.), *A History of York Minster*, Clarendon, Oxford, 1977, p. 93.

[42] Edwards, p. 282.

[43] According to the will of Thomas Fitzwarren, Mayor of London, which was proved 14 June 1499: Scott, p. 9.

[44] K.L. Wood-Legh, *Perpetual Chantries in Britain*, CUP, 1965 [hereafter Wood-Legh], p. 1.

[45] Barron, 'Parish Fraternities', pp. 34-5; Gear, p. 68; Simpson, p. 171; and C. Burgess, ' 'For the Increase of Divine Service': Chantries in the Parish in Late Medieval Bristol', *JEH*, 36, 1985, pp. 46-65.

[46] Wood-Legh, p. 113.

[47] *Ibid.*; Simpson, p. 171.

[48] Fuller, p. 127.

[49] Lepine, p. 8; A. Gransden, 'A History of Wells Cathedral, *c.*1090-1547' in L.S. Colchester (ed.), *Wells Cathedral: A History*, Open Books, Shepton Mallet, 1982, p. 38.

[50] Duffy, pp. 368-70.

[51] Such as John of Gaunt: Wood-Legh, p. 85.

[52] R. Rex and C.D.C. Armstrong, 'Henry VIII's Ecclesiastical and Collegiate Foundations', *Historical Research*, 75 (2002) pp. 390-407 [hereafter Rex and Armstrong]; C. Burgess and B. Kümin, 'Penitential Bequests and Parish Regimes in Late Medieval England', *JEH*, 44, 1993, pp. 610-30.

[53] Edwards, p. 286.

[54] Fuller, p. 121.

[55] *Registrum*, p. 67.

[56] Gear, p. 86.

[57] Fuller, p. 123.

[58] *Ibid.*, pp. 158-9.

[59] *Ibid.*, p. 125.

[60] This title does not mean a cardinal in the ordinary sense. It was strictly a minor clerical position within the college. The senior and junior cardinals were immediately junior to the sub-dean.

[61] Fuller, p. 122.

[62] There was also a college of minor canons at St. George's Chapel, Windsor, constituted in 1352: see E.H. Fellowes, *The Vicars or Minor Canons of His Majesty's Free Chapel of St. George*, Oxley, Windsor, 1945 [hereafter Fellowes], p. 7.

[63] *Registrum*, p. 16.

[64] *Ibid.*, p. 19.

[65] Lehmberg, 'Reformation of Choirs', p. 47.

[66] Simpson, p. 161.

[67] Haigh, *Reformations*, pp. 5, 10, 17, 41-3, 48-50 and 176-9.

[68] *Ibid.*, pp. 18, 129-30, 134, 150-1 and 156-7.

[69] Simpson, p. 161.

[70] GL, MS 25187, fols. 1v-2r.

[71] GL, MS 25184: a single parchment roll, brought to my attention by Dr. David Crankshaw, for which I am very grateful.

[72] *Ibid.*, lines 1-7 at the head of the roll.

[73] *Ibid.*, lines 13, 15, 20 and 21.

[74] This cannot be the same document as GL, MS 25187, which comprises only two folios, and therefore cannot be called a book (*Liber*).
[75] Simpson, p. 161.
[76] Allen, IV, p. 518; Olin, p. 179.
[77] Simpson, p. 161.
[78] Harrison, pp. 1-24; Edwards, pp. 22-8, 35-6, 80 and 115-9.
[79] *Ibid.*, pp. 80 and 115-9.
[80] Davis, 'Lesser Clergy', p. 160, citing *Registrum*, pp. 142-58.
[81] H.F. Westlake, *The Parish Guilds of Medieval England*, SPCK, London, 1919 [hereafter Westlake], p. 48.
[82] Harrison, pp. 1-10 and 20.
[83] *Ibid.*, pp. 44-5.
[84] *Ibid.*, p. 47; Simpson, p. 156.
[85] Lupton, p. 119; Colet was also connected to York through William Melton: Rex, *Fisher*, pp. 22-6.
[86] Rex, *Henry VIII*, p. 47; see also Lehmberg, *Cathedrals*, pp. 218-23 and 264-5; M. Bowker, *The Henrician Reformation: The Diocese of Lincoln under John Longland, 1521-1547*, CUP, 1981, pp. 34-7.
[87] Harrison, pp. 62-4.
[88] Bowker, p. 172.
[89] *Ibid.*, p. 173.
[90] *Ibid.*; Scott, p. 9.
[91] Harrison, p. 63.
[92] *Ibid.*, pp. 64, 70 and 71.
[93] Bowker, p. 171.
[94] A.J. Kettle, 'City and Close: Lichfield in the Century before the Reformation' in C.M. Barron and C. Harper-Bill (eds.), *The Church in Pre-Reformation Society: Essays in Honour of F.R.H. Du Boulay*, Boydell Press, Woodbridge, 1985 [hereafter Barron and Harper-Bill], pp. 158-70 [hereafter Kettle], pp. 160-7.
[95] *Ibid.*, pp. 161 and 167.
[96] Allen, IV, p. 524; Olin, p. 187.
[97] Kettle, p. 167.
[98] *Ibid.*, p. 163.
[99] T.N. Cooper, 'Children, the Liturgy and the Reformation: The Evidence of the Lichfield Cathedral Choristers' in D. Wood (ed.), *Church and Childhood*, Studies in Church History, 31, Blackwell, Oxford, 1994, p. 265.
[100] Lepine, pp. 5-6.
[101] *Registrum*, pp. 137-8.
[102] *Ibid.*, pp. 67-9.
[103] Lupton, p. 293.
[104] Haigh, *Reformations*, p. 9.
[105] Perhaps every three years.
[106] Simpson, pp. 166-7.
[107] Lepine, p. 108.
[108] Like Melton: see A.G. Dickens and D. Carr (eds.), *The Reformation in England to the Accession of Elizabeth I*, Documents of Modern History, Edward Arnold, London, 1967 [hereafter Dickens and Carr], pp. 15-6.
[109] C. Burgess, 'Late Medieval Wills and Pious Convention: Testamentary Evidence Reconsidered' in M. Hicks (ed.), *Profit, Piety and the Professions in Later Medieval England*, Sutton, Gloucester, 1990, pp. 14-33; Gear, p. 68.

110 Fuller, p. 133.
111 Wood-Legh, p. 269.
112 P. Marshall, *The Catholic Priesthood and the English Reformation*, Clarendon, Oxford, 1994, pp. 50-5; Westlake, p. 48.
113 A. Kreider, *English Chantries: The Road to Dissolution*, Harvard University Press, Cambridge, Massachusetts, and London, 1979, p. 75.
114 Lepine, p. 90.
115 *Registrum*, pp. 1-177, *passim*.
116 Fuller, p. 7.
117 Kettle, p. 162.
118 Allen, IV, p. 515; Olin, p. 178.
119 Simpson, p. 161.
120 Olin, p. 182; Allen, IV, p. 521.
121 Olin, p. 180; Allen, IV, p. 519.
122 Olin, p. 176; Allen, IV, p. 513.
123 MacCulloch, *Reformation*, p. 103.
124 Simpson, p. 162.
125 *Ibid.*
126 Gleason, pp. 334-9.
127 Olin, pp. 176-7; Allen, IV, p. 514.
128 CUL, MS Gg.iv.26, fol. 128r; *Corinthians*, p. 217/Latin, p. 216.
129 Gleason, p. 138; Allen, IV, p. 514; Olin, p. 176.
130 CUL, MS Gg.iv.26, fol. 128r-v; *Corinthians*, p. 217/Latin, pp. 216 and 218.
131 Lupton, p. 296 and Knight, p. 242 for the sermon; Lupton, pp. 116-23 and Seebohm, p. 529 for his preferments.
132 Gleason, p. 44.
133 CUL, MS Gg.iv.26, fol. 128v; *Corinthians*, p. 219/Latin, p. 218.
134 CUL, MS Gg.iv.26, fol. 128v; *Corinthians*, p. 219/Latin, p. 218.
135 CUL, MS Gg.iv.26, fol. 135r; *Corinthians*, p. 241/Latin, p. 240.
136 CUL, MS Gg.iv.26, fol. 57r-v; *Romans*, p. 123/Latin, p. 221.
137 CUL, MS Gg.iv.26, fol. 47v; *Romans*, p. 103/Latin, p. 207.
138 CUL, MS Gg.iv.26, fol. 57r; *Romans*, p. 123/Latin, p. 221.
139 BL. Add. MS 63853, fol. 34r:; *Hierarchies*, p. 51/Latin, p. 199.
140 Olin, pp. 178-9; Allen, IV, pp. 515 and 518.
141 Olin, p. 179; Allen, IV, p. 518.
142 Gleason, pp. 138-41.
143 CUL, MS Gg.iv.26, fol. 130v; *Corinthians*, p. 225/Latin, p. 224.
144 CUL, MS Gg.iv.26, fol. 132v; *Corinthians*, p. 231/Latin, p. 230.
145 CCC, MS 355, p. 155; *Opuscula*, p. 139/Latin, p. 263.
146 Gleason, pp. 141-4.
147 Therefore the intellect was inferior to the will for Colet, for the will was love: CUL, MS Gg.iv.26, fol. 79v; *Corinthians*, pp. 79 and 81/Latin, pp. 78 and 80.
148 CCC, MS 355, p. 159; *Opuscula*, pp. 141-2/Latin, p. 264.
149 Gleason, p. 138.
150 Or canon law: Lupton, p. 300: 'There are no trespaces, but that there be lawes against them in the body of the Canon lawe'; Knight, p. 246.
151 CUL, MS Gg.iv.26, fol. 127v; *Corinthians*, p. 215/Latin, p. 214.
152 Allen, IV, p. 518; Olin, p. 179; MacCulloch, *Reformation*, p. 103.

[153] H. Kleineke and S. Hovland, 'The Household and Daily Life of the Dean in the Fifteenth Century' in Keene *et al.* [hereafter Kleineke and Hovland], p. 168; J. Pound, 'Clerical Poverty in Early Sixteenth-Century England: Some East Anglian Evidence', *JEH*, 37, 1986, pp. 389-96.
[154] W.G. Hoskins, *The Age of Plunder: King Henry's England, 1500-1547*, Longman, London, 1976 [hereafter Hoskins], p. 23.
[155] *Ibid.*, p. 31.
[156] Colet's wills of 1514 and 1519, reproduced in Knight, pp. 201 and 400-9.
[157] Hoskins, p. 37.
[158] Dyer, p. 55.
[159] *Ibid.*, p. 71.
[160] A.R. Bridbury, 'English Provincial Towns in the Later Middle Ages', *The Economic History Review*, 2nd Series, 34, 1981, pp. 10-24; J. Cornwall, 'English Country Towns in the Fifteen Twenties', *ibid.*, 2nd Series, 15, 1962, pp. 54-69.
[161] Dyer, p. 84.
[162] Orme, *Minor Clergy*, p. xviii-xv.
[163] F. Heal, *Hospitality in Early Modern England*, Clarendon, Oxford, 1990 [hereafter Heal], p. 9.
[164] Lepine, p. 132.
[165] Heal, p. 223.
[166] J. Shillingford, *Letters and Papers of John Shillingford*, edited by S.A. Moore, Camden Society, New Series, 2, London, 1871, p. 57.
[167] Lepine, p. 131.
[168] Heal, p. 246.
[169] GL, MS 25166, fols. 1r-9v.
[170] Dyer, p. 70, Table 5.
[171] Olin, p. 182; Allen, IV, p. 521.
[172] Lupton, p. 148.
[173] Olin, p. 178; Allen, IV, p. 515.
[174] Olin, pp. 178-9; Allen, IV, pp. 515 and 518.
[175] GL, MS 25166, fols. 1v-9v.
[176] See Kleineke and Hovland, pp. 167-8.
[177] Olin, p. 179; Allen, IV, p. 518.
[178] Olin, p. 182; Allen, IV, p. 521.
[179] Lepine, p. 124.
[180] GL, MS 25166, fols. 1v and 4v.
[181] Allen, IV, p. 518; Olin, p. 179; Simpson, p. 170.
[182] Foxe, vol. II, book VII, p. 838.
[183] Allen, IV, p. 525; Olin, p. 188.
[184] Olin, p. 188; Allen, IV, p. 525.
[185] Olin, p. 187; Allen, IV, p. 524.
[186] Seebohm, p. 529 and Lupton, pp. 116-23. In fact, Colet was not ordained deacon until 17 December 1497, and priest on 25 March 1498, yet he held the majority of his benefices before this time. Even the deanery of St. Paul's was, in a sense, a gift from Henry VII.
[187] Lupton, p. 131. Lupton uses the term 'New Learning' incorrectly. It was, in fact, a pejorative term to describe evangelical theology, not humanism: R. Rex, 'The New Learning', *JEH*, 44, 1993, pp. 26-43 [hereafter Rex, 'New Learning']; MacCulloch, *Reformation*, pp. 76-7.
[188] *Registrum*, pp. 1-177, *passim*.
[189] Haigh, *Reformations*, p. 9.
[190] Harper-Bill, p. 51.

[191] *Ibid.*, p. 27.
[192] CUL, MS Gg.iv.26, fol. 129r; *Corinthians*, p. 221/Latin, p. 220.

Chapter Four

[1] Anne F. Sutton, *The Mercery of London: Trade, Goods and People, 1130-1578*, Ashgate, Aldershot, 2005 [hereafter Sutton].
[2] *Ibid.*, p. 171.
[3] *Ibid.*, p. 193.
[4] *Ibid.*, p. 313.
[5] *Ibid.*, pp. 216 and 274.
[6] *Ibid.*, pp. 221-2.
[7] *Ibid.*, p. 234.
[8] *Ibid.*, pp. 326-8.
[9] Sutton, p. 361.
[10] The most useful manuscript source for information concerning the guild is Bodleian, MS Tanner 221. Folios 48v-52v (1517-8) give a good indication of the high quality of the ritual and liturgy.
[11] Sutton, p. 381, n. 9.
[12] E.A. New, 'The Cult of the Holy Name of Jesus, with Special Reference to the Fraternity in St. Paul's Cathedral, London, c.1450-1558', Unpublished Ph.D. Thesis, University of London, 1999 [hereafert New], ch. 1.
[13] These bequests were from John Alen (1534-45); Nicholas Alwyn (d.1505); Thomas Baldry (1507-34); Thomas Batail (d.1455); William Baily (1515-34/5); William Botry (1520-35); William Bromwell (1506-36); William Brown (d.1518); William Dauntsey (1530/1); Benjamin Digby (1527/8); Richard Haddon (d.1516); John Hosier (1507-16/7); Thomas Hynd (1507-34/5); William Ipswell (d.1508); John Isham (d.1517); Nicholas Lathell of the Exchequer (1471-1500); William Statham (1519/20); John Stile (d.1517); Richard Vaughan (1514-17/18); Thomas Wyndout (d.1500). Sutton, p. 381, n. 7 quoting New, pp. 394-402.
[14] Sutton, p. 381 and n.10.
[15] Sutton, p. 381.
[16] Colet was concerned with restoring high liturgical standards, as usual: *Ibid.*, n. 11; New, pp. 108-13.
[17] Sutton, p. 381, n.11.
[18] *Ibid.*, p. 382; New p. 133.
[19] Reduced to eighteen years in 1518: MS Tanner 221, fol. 13v and New, p. 149.
[20] Sutton, p. 382.
[21] *Ibid.*, p. 381.
[22] Sutton, p. 382; New, pp. 114-5, 142-7.
[23] On this basis New argues (New, pp. 125-6) that the guild of the Holy Name formed an 'unofficial' religious fraternity for the Mercers' Company. However, Sutton suggests this is not tenable as other livery companies were also prominent within the guild, apart from thirty clerical members. Unfortunately, there is no extant record of the entire membership.
[24] Brigden, *London*, pp. 38-9; New, pp. 415-6; Sutton, p. 382.
[25] *Ibid.*, p. 361; *Mercers*, pp. 429-30, 487-8.
[26] Sutton, pp. 361-5.
[27] M. McDonnell, *A History of St. Paul's School*, Chapman and Hall, London, 1909 [hereafter McDonnell, *History*], p. 1; BL, Harleian MS 6956.
[28] *Registrum*, p. 22; Lupton, p. 156.
[29] *Ibid.*, p. 2.

[30] Reprinted in McDonnell, *History*, p. 3.
[31] *Ibid.*, pp. 5-6.
[32] McDonnell, *History*, p. 6, quoting Strype, vol. I, p. 182.
[33] McDonnell, *History*, p. 7.
[34] Sir Michael McDonnell, *The Annals of St. Paul's School*, Chapman and Hall, London, 1959 [Hereafter McDonnell, *Annals*], p. 31.
[35] Lupton, pp. 156-60.
[36] Gleason, p. 221; McDonnell, *Annals*, p. 48.
[37] The Cathedral Choir School is now a modern building situated adjacent to Wren's cathedral on the east side; Colet's St. Paul's School has moved to new premises in Barnes, West London.
[38] Gleason, p. 217.
[39] *Ibid.*, p. 219.
[40] Kenneth Charlton, *Education in Renaissance England*, Routledge, London and University of Toronto Press, Toronto, 1965 [hereafter Charlton], p. 92.
[41] *Ibid.*, p. 93.
[42] Knight, p. 402.
[43] According to Gleason, p. 218.
[44] Thomas Lupset, *An Exhortation to Yonge Men, Perswadinge Them to Walke in the Pathe Way That Leadeth to Honeste and Goodnes* [STC 16936], London, 1535.
[45] Gleason, p. 220.
[46] McDonnell, *History*, pp. 13-4 quoting Appendix to *The Third Report of Commissioners on Charities*, 1820, p. 164.
[47] *Mercers*, p. 360.
[48] *Ibid.*, p. 361.
[49] *Ibid.*, pp. 360-4.
[50] McDonnell, *Annals*, p. 41.
[51] *Mercers*, p. 393.
[52] Gleason, p. 221; McDonnell, *Annals*, pp. 44-5.
[53] Knight, p. 284.
[54] *Mercers*, p. 401.
[55] *Ibid.*, p. 404.
[56] McDonnell, *History*, p. 18, quoting Brewer, vol. I, p. 3900.
[57] McDonnell, *History*, p. 19.
[58] William Herbert, *The History of the Twelve Great Livery Companies of London*, 2 Volumes, David and Charles, Newton Abbot, 1834-1837; reprinted, New York, 1968 [hereafter Herbert], I, p. 273.
[59] *Ibid.*
[60] Gleason, p.219; Arthur F. Leach, *VCH, Lancaster*, II, 1908, p.590. In 1402-3 a school in Stratford-on-Avon was administered by a guild. Lay trustees were also employed at schools in Macclesfield (1502-3) and Bridgenorth in Shropshire, 1503: Arthur F. Leach, 'St. Paul's School before Colet', *Archaeologia*, 62, I, 1910 [hereafter Leach, 'St. Paul's School'], p. 207; Charlton, p. 92.
[61] Herbert, I, p. 235; *Mercers*, pp. 59, 116, 141, 230-3, 244; Leach 'St. Paul's School', p. 208.
[62] Allen, II, pp. 366-70; translated in Gleason, p. 219.
[63] Colet gave the Mercers' free reign to interpret his school statutes as they wished: Lupton, 'Statutes', pp. 281-2.
[64] Gleason, p. 220.
[65] Lupton, pp. 170-1.

66 Double that paid to the high master of Magdalen College School at Oxford: Gleason, p. 222. Lupton suggests that the highmaster was paid over £34 a year: Lupton, p. 177.
67 McDonnell, *Annals*, p. 60.
68 The only such occurrence until the nineteenth century: Jean M. Imray, *The Charity of Richard Whittington: A History of the Trust Administered by the Mercers' Company, 1424-1966*, Athlone, London, 1968, p. 75, n. 1.
69 *Mercers*, p.403.
70 *Ibid.* pp. 3 and 572. According to Gleason, Newbold's death was not in 1540 as McDonnell suggested: McDonnell, *Annals*, p. 56.
71 Lupton, pp. 167-8 quoting 'Report of the Charity Commisioners', May, 1820, vol. III, p. 230.
72 From Colet's School Statutes, reprinted in Lupton, pp. 279-80.
73 McDonnell, *History*, p. 44.
74 Knight, p. 373; translation in Gleason, pp. 222-3.
75 Lupton, p. 166.
76 Gleason, p. 223; Robert M. Grant, 'One Hundred and Fifty-Three Large Fish (John 21:11)', *HTR*, 42, 1949 [hereafter Grant], pp. 273-5.
77 Gleason, p. 223. Augustine also saw the base number seventeen as the sum of the commandments in the Decalogue and the sevenfold Spirit of God: Grant, pp. 273-5.
78 Sir Cyril Picciotto, *St. Paul's School*, London and Glasgow, 1939, p.7.
79 Colet's School Statutes in Lupton, p. 277.
80 Letter from Erasmus to John Botzheim, 30 January 1523, in Allen, I, p. 6.
81 Gleason, p. 225.
82 An issue which had been raised by Giovanni Dominici over a hundred years earlier in 1405, in his book *Lucula Noctis*, in which he argued that Christian writing illuminated the darkness of pagan ignorance: Gleason, p. 225; Iohannes Dominici, *Lucula Noctis*, ed. Edmund Hunt, Notre Dame University Press, Indiana, 1940, p. xiv.
83 Colet's Statutes in Lupton, p. 279.
84 Baptista Mantuana was a Carmelite poet and theologian whose works were taught at the schools of the Brethren of the Common Life and early Jesuit colleges: Gleason, p. 227.
85 Lupton, pp. 279-80.
86 *Ibid.*, p. 280.
87 Macdonnel, *History*, pp. 45 and 53.
88 Macdonnel, *Annals*, pp. 75-6.
89 Gleason, p. 228.
90 Charlton, p. 117.
91 *Ibid.*
92 *The Poems of Erasmus*, ed. C. Reedijk, Leiden; Brill, The Netherlands, 1956, pp. 297-300.
93 The Latin text of which in printed in Knight, pp. 285-302.
94 For instance, in chapter 33, Erasmus demonstrates 194 different ways of saying 'I was pleased to get your letter': Gleason, p. 229.
95 *Ibid.*
96 *Ibid.*, p. 230.
97 John Colet, *Coleti Catechismus*, W. de Worde, London, 1534 [*STC* 5543]. Only five pages long, it is reprinted in Lupton, pp. 285-9.
98 McDonnell, *History*, p. 51.
99 It may also have given its name to the English *Institution of a Christian Man* of 1537: Gleason, p. 231.
100 The first printed edition is 1527.

[101] John Colet, *Rudimenta Grammatices et Docendi Methodus, non tam Scholae Gypsuychianae*. [Colet's *Aeditio* with Lily's 'Rudimenta' with the Latin text of Cardinal Wolsey's rules for the teaching of Latin at Ipswich School prefixed], M. de Keysere, Antwerp, 1536 [*STC* 5543a].
[102] McDonnell, *History*, p. 50.
[103] *Ibid.*
[104] Charlton, p. 108.
[105] McDonnell, *History*, p. 61, translation by Knight.
[106] McDonnell, *History*, p. 62.
[107] McDonnell, *History*, p. 33. Likewise the Eton statutes were copied from those of Winchester College.
[108] They are reprinted in Lupton, pp. 271-84.
[109] Lupton, p. 272.
[110] McDonnell, *History*, p. 35.
[111] *Ibid.*; Lupton, p. 272.
[112] *Ibid.*, p. 276.
[113] McDonnell, *History*, p. 36.
[114] *Ibid.*
[115] Lupton, p. 278.
[116] *Ibid.*, pp. 279-80.
[117] Charlton, pp. 55-6.

Chapter Five

[1] P. Marshall, *Reformation England, 1480-1642*, Arnold, London, 2003 [hereafter Marshall, *Reformation*], p. 11; MacCulloch, *Reformation*, p. 88; S. Wabuda, *Preaching During the English Reformation*, CUP, 2002 [hereafter Wabuda], pp. 4, 28-9, 64-5 and 67; Brigden, *New Worlds*, pp. 89-91; J.A. Guy, *Politics, Law and Counsel in Tudor and Early Stuart England*, Ashgate, Aldershot, 2000 [hereafter Guy, *Politics*], p. 32; Dickens and Jones, p. 32; Gleason, p. 184; W.J. Sheils, *The English Reformation, 1530-1570*, Longman, London, 1989 [hereafter Sheils], pp. 2-3, 33 and 71; Rex, *Henry VIII*, p. 51; Kaufman, *Church*, pp. 67-9, Alden, pp. 191-260; W.A. Clebsch, *England's Earliest Protestants, 1520-1535*, Yale University Press, New Haven, Connecticut, 1964 [hereafter Clebsch, *Protestants*], p. 258; Porter, pp. 29-30; Carpenter, p. 108; and J. Brown, 'John Colet and the Preachers of the Reformation' in *idem* (ed.), *Puritan Preaching in England: A Study of Past and Present*, Hodder and Stoughton, London and New York, 1900, pp. 35-63.
[2] For this claim, see Haigh, *Reformations*, pp. 9-11.
[3] On conciliarism in England, see F. Oakley, 'Almain and Major: Conciliar Theory on the Eve of the Reformation', *The American Historical Review* [hereafter *AHR*], 70, 1965, pp. 673-90 [hereafter Oakley, 'Almain and Major'], p. 673, reprinted in *idem*, *Natural Law, Conciliarism and Consent in the Middle Ages: Studies in Ecclesiastical and Intellectual History*, Variorum, London, 1984 (Article X in the reprint) [hereafter Oakley, *Natural Law*]; *idem*, 'Conciliarism in the Sixteenth Century: Jacques Almain Again', *Archiv für Reformationsgeschichte*, 68, 1977, pp. 111-32, reprinted in Oakley, *Natural Law* (Article XII in the reprint); A. Black., *Council and Commune: The Conciliar Movement and the Fifteenth-Century Heritage*, Burns and Oates, London, 1979 [hereafter Black], p. 38; F. Oakley, *The Conciliarist Tradition: Constitutionalism in the Catholic Church, 1300-1870*, OUP, 2003 [hereafter Oakley, *Conciliarist Tradition*], pp. 129-40; MacCulloch, *Reformation*, pp. 38-42.
[4] Statutes were drawn up for the guild, of which Colet was rector, in 1507: *Registrum*, pp. 445-57; Bodleian Library, Oxford, MS Tanner 221, fols. 3r-8v: Records for the Guild of Jesus in the Crowds, St. Paul's Cathedral, 1507, with a preface by Colet, including his autograph signature. See also E. New, 'Fraternities: A Case Study of the Jesus Guild' in Keene *et al.*, p. 162: 'Dean John Colet supervized a reorganization of the fraternity in 1507 ... Colet may also

have seen the fraternity as a way to improve liturgical and musical standards in St. Paul's, and to encourage the laity to use the cathedral.' New attributes this latter idea to Professor Caroline Barron. On the guild, see also Barron and Rousseau, p. 43 and Wabuda, p. 147.

[5] *Mercers*, pp. 363-77.

[6] Lupton, pp. 154-78; Gleason, p. 220; Mercers' Company, Mercers' Hall, London, unnumbered MS entitled 'Colet's Ordinances', containing Colet's *Statuta Paulinae Scholae: Statutes of St. Paul's School*, dated 18 June 1518, reprinted in Lupton, pp. 271-92; *Mercers*, p. 361.

[7] Convocation was a provincial synod of higher and representative lower clergy, which met contemporaneously with parliament, in order to discuss administrative and legislative issues concerning the government of the province: G. Baskerville, 'Elections to Convocation in the Diocese of Gloucester Under Bishop Hooper', *The English Historical Review* [hereafter *EHR*], 44, 1929, pp. 1-32, especially appendix, pp. 17-31, which demonstrates that many parish priests (but only a few for each diocese) were elected as proctors to Convocation; M.A.R. Graves, *Early Tudor Parliaments, 1485-1558*, Longman, London, 1990. There are two Convocations at which the sermon could have been preached: one beginning in January 1509/10 and the other in February 1511/12 (see E.B. Fryde, D.E. Greenway, S. Porter, and I. Roy (eds.), *The Handbook of British Chronology*, Royal Historical Society, 1st edition, London, 1946; 3rd edition, London, 1986 [hereafter *Chronology*], p. 603. It has been argued, based on internal evidence, that the earlier date is more plausible (M.J. Kelly, 'Canterbury Jurisdiction and Influence during the Episcopate of William Warham, 1503-1532', Unpublished Ph.D. Thesis, Cambridge University, 1963 p. 112 (n. 2) and Gleason, pp. 181 and 370 (n. 33)). However, on the grounds that the earliest extant printed Latin edition of the sermon bears the date '1511' (J. Colet, *Oratio Habita a D. Joanne Colet ad Clerum in Convocatione. Anno. M.D.xj* (London, [1511-12?]) [STC 5545], reproduced in S. Knight, *The Life of Dr. John Colet, Dean of St. Paul's, in the Reigns of K. Henry VII and K. Henry VIII and Founder of St. Paul's School: With an Appendix Containing Some Account of the Masters and More Eminent Scholars of that Foundation, and Several Original Papers Relating to the Said Life*, 1st edition, J. Downing, London, 1724; 2nd edition, Clarendon, Oxford, 1823, pp. 239-50 [hereafter *Oratio*], title page). I favour a date of 1511/12 for its delivery. The exact dating of the sermon is not crucial for my argument.

[8] Lupton, p. 294; Knight, p. 240; P. S. Allen, 'Dean Colet and Archbishop Warham', *EHR*, 17, 1902, pp. 303-6.

[9] Romans 12:2: 'Be you nat conformable to this worlde, but be ye reformed': Lupton, p. 294; Knight, p. 240: '*Nolite conformari ...*'; Romans, passim.

[10] Carpenter, p. 108, following Lupton, pp. 178-88.

[11] Porter, p. 29.

[12] Quotation from R.N. Swanson, 'Problems of the Priesthood in pre-Reformation England', *EHR*, 105, 1990, [hereafter Swanson] p. 869; Sheils, p. 2; Dickens and Jones, p. 32: 'Colet's notorious sermon to Convocation (1512) never ceases to astonish by its violent and daring denunciation of the shortcomings of the English Clergy'.

[13] Swanson, p. 869.

[14] Kaufman, *Churche*, p. 69.

[15] Guy, *Politics*, p. 32.

[16] Haigh, *Reformations*, pp. 9-11; Rex, *Henry VIII*, p. 51; C. Harper-Bill, 'Archbishop John Morton and the Province of Canterbury, 1486-1500', *JEH*, 29 (1978) pp. 1-21 [hereafter Harper-Bill, 'Morton'], pp. 1-7; Harper-Bill, 'Sermon', p. 210; Gleason, pp. 72 and 184; Brown, pp. 35-61; Clebsch, *Protestants*, p. 258; and Alden, pp. 191-260.

[17] Brigden, *New Worlds*, p. 89.

[18] Haigh, *Reformations*, p. 9.

[19] Rex, *Henry VIII*, p. 51.

[20] Harper-Bill, 'Morton', pp. 1-7.
[21] Sheils, p. 2: apparently Colet's sermon reflects the ideas of Thomas Bourgchier, Archbishop of Canterbury (1455), but which ideas he does not say.
[22] Harper-Bill, 'Sermon', p. 210.
[23] Haigh, *Reformations*, p. 9; Harper-Bill, 'Sermon', pp. 191-210.
[24] Gleason, p. 184.
[25] Wabuda, pp. 4, 38-9, 64-5 and 67; MacCulloch, *Reformation*, p. 88; Marshall, *Reformation*, p. 11; Barron and Rousseau, p. 40; and Davis, 'Lesser Clergy', p. 161.
[26] Wabuda, p. 9, arguing against Harper-Bill, 'Sermon', p. 210; Duffy, pp. 11 and 377-593; and Haigh, *Reformations*, pp. 236-7.
[27] Wabuda, pp. 28-9; quotation from Lupton, p. 297.
[28] Wabuda, pp. 64-5.
[29] *Ibid.*, pp. 6, 10, 16, 28, 56, 64-80, 81-2 and 90-9.
[30] *Ibid.*, p. 67.
[31] MacCulloch, *Reformation*, p. 88.
[32] *Ibid.*
[33] N.P. Tanner (ed.), *Kent Heresy Proceedings, 1511-12*, Kent Archaeological Society, 26, Maidstone, 1997 [hereafter Tanner], pp. 43 and 50.
[34] Lupton, p. 298; Knight, p. 244.
[35] Lupton, p. 294; Knight, p. 240.
[36] Marshall, *Reformation*, p. 11; Lupton, pp. 293-304.
[37] Barron and Rousseau, p. 40.
[38] Davis, 'Lesser Clergy', p. 161.
[39] Just as one can be a socialist without being a member of the Labour Party.
[40] Lupton, pp. 293-304; Knight, pp. 239-50.
[41] Lupton, p. 293; Knight, p. 239.
[42] Lupton, p. 293; Knight, p. 239.
[43] Lupton, p. 294; Knight, p. 239.
[44] Lupton, p. 294; Knight, p. 240. It was usual practice to say the *Pater Noster* at this point in a sermon: Wabuda, p. 53; J. Fisher, *The English Works of John Fisher*, I, edited by J.E.B. Mayor, Early English Text Society [hereafter EETS], 27, London, 1935 [hereafter *Fisher*], pp. 302-3.
[45] Lupton, pp. 295-7; Knight, pp. 240-43.
[46] Seebohm, p. 529; Lupton, pp. 116-22.
[47] Lupton, p. 297; Knight, p. 243.
[48] Lupton, pp. 297-8; Knight, pp. 243-4.
[49] Lupton, pp. 297-8; Knight, pp. 243-4.
[50] Lupton, pp. 298-9; Knight, pp. 244-5.
[51] Lupton, pp. 298-9; Knight, pp. 244-5.
[52] Lupton, p. 299; Knight, p. 245.
[53] Lupton, p. 299; Knight, p. 245.
[54] CUL, MS Gg.iv.26, fol. 136r.; *Corinthians*, p. 241/Latin, p. 240.
[55] Even though the calibre of ordinands was reasonably high: R.L. Storey, 'Ordinations of Secular Priests in Early Tudor London', *Nottingham Medieval Studies*, 33, 1989, pp. 122-33.
[56] There is evidence of monastic apostasy: C. Harper-Bill, 'Monastic Apostasy in Late Medieval England', *JEH*, 32, 1981, pp. 1-18; Lupton, pp. 300-2; Knight, pp. 246-8.
[57] Lupton, pp. 300-2; Knight, pp. 246-8; and Dowling, *Fisher*, p. 58.
[58] Lupton, p. 302; Knight, p. 248.
[59] Lupton, pp. 302-3; Knight, pp. 248-9.
[60] Lupton, pp. 303-4; Knight, pp. 249-50.

61 A message appealing to Wolsey: K. Brown, 'Wolsey and Ecclesiastical Order: The Case of the Franciscan Observants' in S.J. Gunn and P. G. Lindley (eds.), *Cardinal Wolsey's Church, State and Art*, CUP, 1991, pp. 219-38.
62 Lupton, pp. 302-3; Knight, p. 249.
63 Lupton, p. 303; Knight, pp. 249-50.
64 Duffy, p. 54.
65 *Ibid.*; Wabuda, p. 34: Bishop Grosseteste of Lincoln (d.1253) required priests in his diocese to know and expound the Ten Commandments, the Creed, the Our Father and *Ave Maria*.
66 L. Boyle, 'The *Oculus Sacerdotis* and Some Other Works of William of Pagula', *TRHS*, 5th Series, 5, 1955, pp. 81-110.
67 J. Mirk, *Instructions for Parish Priests by John Myrc*, edited by E. Peacock, EETS, 31, London, 1902.
68 J. Mirk, *Mirk's Festial: A Collection of Homilies by Joannes Mirkus (John Mirk)*, edited by T. Erbe, EETS, Extra Series, 46, London, 1905.
69 Allen, IV, p. 514; Olin, p. 178.
70 Allen, IV, p. 525; Olin, p. 188.
71 Blench, p. 71.
72 *Ibid.*, pp. 71-4.
73 Lupton, p. 294; Knight, p. 240.
74 Gleason, p. 184.
75 Blench, p. 113.
76 *Ibid.*, p. 229, and in previous centuries: Haigh, *Reformations*, p. 9.
77 Blench, p. 229, quoting *Fisher*, pp. 145-6.
78 J. Huizinga, *The Waning of the Middle Ages: A Study of the Forms of Life, Thought and Art in France and the Netherlands in the XIVth and XVth Centuries*, 1st Dutch edition, 1919; 2nd Dutch edition, 1921; English edition, London, 1924 [hereafter Huizinga] p. 22.
79 *Ibid.*, p. 28
80 G.M. Trevelyan, *English Social History*, Longmans, Green, London, 1944, p. 25.
81 Blench, pp. 242-6.
82 *Ibid.*, p. 246; Dowling, *Fisher*, pp. 77-85.
83 A.T. Thayer, 'Judge and Doctor: Images of the Confessor in Printed Model Sermon Collections, 1450-1520' in K.J. Lualdi and A.T. Thayer (eds.), *Penitence in the Age of Reformations*, Ashgate, Aldershot and Burlington, Vermont, 2000, pp. 10-29.
84 BL, Add. MS 63853, fol. 113r; *De Sacramentis*, p. 283/Latin, p. 282.
85 BL, Add. MS 63853, fol. 134v; *De Sacramentis*, p. 323/Latin, p. 322.
86 BL, Add. MS 63853, fol. 134r; *De Sacramentis*, pp. 321-3/Latin, pp. 320-2.
87 *De Sacramentis*, pp. 321-7.
88 BL, Add. MS 63853, fol. 133r; *De Sacramentis*, p. 321/Latin, p. 320.
89 Dowling, *Fisher*, pp. 77-85.
90 CUL, MS Gg.iv.26, fol. 3r; *Romans*, pp. 34-5/Latin, p. 159; CUL, MS Gg.iv.26, fol. 139v; *Corinthians*, p. 249/Latin, p. 248.
91 Such as Fisher and Longland: *Fisher*, pp. 145-6; Blench, p. 232; and Dowling, *Fisher*, pp. 73-6.
92 Lupton, pp. 300-3; Knight, pp. 246-8.
93 Dowling, 'Preaching'.
94 M.K. Jones and M.G. Underwood, *The King's Mother: Lady Margaret Beaufort, Countess of Richmond and Derby*, CUP, 1992, pp. 202-27.

[95] T. Swynnerton, *A Reformation Rhetoric: Thomas Swynnerton's The Tropes and Figures of Scripture*, Renaissance Texts from Manuscript, I, edited by R. Rex, CUP, 1999 [hereafter Swynnerton], p. 27.
[96] Although Colet's attempt to learn Greek failed: Gleason, pp. 58-9.
[97] Reuchlin was a German humanist who espoused Hebrew philosophy known as the Cabbala, in which Colet had a brief interest: Hamilton, p. 106; Gleason, pp. 145-6; and Dowling, *Fisher*, p. 5.
[98] B. Bradshaw, 'Bishop John Fisher, 1469-1535: The Man and His Work' in B. Bradshaw and E. Duffy (eds.), *Humanism, Reform and the Reformation: The Career of Bishop John Fisher*, CUP, 1989, pp. 1-24 [hereafter Bradshaw], pp. 1-2.
[99] Erasmus, II, no. 278.
[100] GL Jones, *The Discovery of Hebrew in Tudor England: A Third Language*, Manchester University Press, Manchester, 1983 [hereafter Jones, *Hebrew*] p. 89. Christian cabbalism sought to integrate all religious wisdom in order to convert the Jews.
[101] Erasmus, IV, no. 471.
[102] Dowling, *Fisher*, p. 38, quoting a letter from Colet to Erasmus, reprinted in Erasmus, V, no. 593.
[103] Dowling, *Fisher*, pp. 50-60.
[104] Dowling, 'Preaching', p. 294.
[105] Dowling, *Fisher*, pp. 76-7.
[106] When Colet preached on war at court: Allen, IV, p. 526; Olin, p. 190.
[107] Dowling, *Fisher*, p. 85.
[108] Blench, p. 239, quoting *Fisher*, p. 181.
[109] Dowling, 'Preaching', pp. 290-300.
[110] Dowling, *Fisher*, pp. 77-85.
[111] *Ibid.*, p. 78, quoting *Fisher*, pp. 17-18.
[112] Lupton, p. 295; Knight, p. 241; and Dowling, *Fisher*, p. 78.
[113] *Fisher*, p. 26 (preached at Henry VII's funeral in 1509), quoted in Wabuda, p. 8. See Duffy, pp. 58-63 for the late-medieval doctrine of purgatory.
[114] Lupton, pp. 293-304; Knight, pp. 239-50; and Dowling, 'Preaching', pp. 287-309.
[115] *Ibid.*, p. 309.
[116] D. Erasmus, *Desiderius Erasmus Roterodamus: Ausgewählte Werke*, edited by H. Holborn and A. Holborn, Munich, 1933, p. 55: an idea also used by More: P. I. Kaufman, 'Humanist Spirituality and Ecclesial Reaction: Thomas More's *Monstra*', Church History, 56, 1987, pp. 25-38 [hereafter Kaufman, 'More'].
[117] Lupton, pp. 293-304; Knight, pp. 239-50.
[118] Lupton, p. 294; Knight, p. 240.
[119] Huizinga, p. 28.
[120] Oberman, p. 56.
[121] Thomas à Kempis, *The Imitation of Christ*, translated and edited by L. Shirley-Price, Penguin, Harmondsworth, 1952 [hereafter Kempis] *passim*.
[122] J.C. Olin, 'Introduction' in *idem* (ed.), *The Catholic Reformation: Savonarola to Ignatius Loyola: Reform in the Church, 1495-1540*, 1st edition, Westminster, Maryland, 1969; 2nd edition, London, 1978 [hereafter Olin, *Catholic Reformation*] pp. i-xxii.
[123] Huizinga, p. 29.
[124] Dickens and Jones, p. 32.
[125] Kaufman, 'More', p. 29. My emphasis.
[126] The opposite is true in both cases.
[127] Harper-Bill, 'Sermon', p. 192; Lupton, p. 299.

[128] J.C. Olin, 'Introduction' in Olin, *Catholic Reformation*, p. xxii; Oberman, p. 3.
[129] Allen, IV, p. 513; Olin, p. 177; P. M.J. McNair, 'The Reformation of the Sixteenth Century in Renaissance Italy' in K. Robbins (ed.), *Religion and Humanism*, Studies in Church History, 17, Blackwell, Oxford, 1981, p. 153. See also R. Rex, 'Humanism' in Pettegree, *Reformation*, p. 55.
[130] Dickens and Jones, p. 32; Swynnerton, p. 27.
[131] For instance, CUL, MS Gg.iv.26, fol. 102v. The *Heptaplus* is quoted in *Corinthians*, p. 258 and *Romans*, pp. 185-6.
[132] Probably on his return to England; Jayne, *passim*; Gleason, p. 45.
[133] Jones, *Hebrew*, p. 89.
[134] Seebohm, pp. 17-22.
[135] It was immediately printed in pamphlet form: Oberman, p. 3.
[136] *Ibid.*, pp. 5-6.
[137] *Ibid.*, pp. 14-15.
[138] Lupton, pp. 298 and 296.
[139] Oberman, pp. 7-14.
[140] *Chronology*, p. 603.
[141] D.C. Steinmetz, *Reformers in the Wings: From Geiler von Kaysersberg to Theodore Beza*, 2nd edition, OUP, 2001 [hereafter Steinmetz], pp. 9-10.
[142] E.J.D. Douglass, *Justification in Late Medieval Preaching: A Study of John Geiler of Keisersberg*, Leiden, Brill, The Netherlands, 1966 [hereafter cited as Douglass], p. 6. Geiler was a preacher at Strasbourg Cathedral from 1478 until his death in 1510. See M.U. Chrisman, *Lay Culture, Learned Culture: Books and Social Change in Strasbourg, 1480-1599*, Yale University Press, New Haven, Connecticut, and London, 1982 [hereafter Chrisman], p. 82.
[143] Douglass, p. 6
[144] E. Rummel, 'Voices of Reform from Hus to Erasmus' [hereafter Rummel] in T.A. Brady Jr., H.A. Oberman, J.D. Tracy (eds.), *Handbook of European History, 1400-1600: Late Middle Ages, Renaissance and Reformation. Volume II: Visions, Programs and Outcomes*, Leiden, Brill, The Netherlands, 1995, p. 77.
[145] *Ibid.*, p. 78
[146] Trevelyan, p. 89.
[147] Chrisman, pp. 34 and 205-6.
[148] L.J. Abray, *The People's Reformation: Magistrates, Clergy, and Commons in Strasbourg, 1500-1598*, Cornell University Press, New York, 1985, pp. 28-9.
[149] *De Sacramentis*, pp. 271-3.
[150] Also known as Faber Stapulensis: Steinmetz, pp. 32-7.
[151] J. Lefèvre d'Etaples, *Preface to His Commentaries on the Four Gospels*, Strasbourg, 1521, p. 1, reprinted in Olin, *Catholic Reformation*, p. 111.
[152] *Ibid.*, p. 112. There is no evidence that Lefèvre had seen an edition of Colet's sermon, nor have Lefèvre scholars explored this possibility.
[153] *Ibid.*, pp. 109 and 113-4.
[154] Bedouelle, p. 30.
[155] Olin, *Catholic Reformation*, p. 115. Colet, of course, did write commentaries on the works of Pseudo-Dionysius, presumably unknown to Lefèvre at this time (1497).
[156] *Ibid.*
[157] Rice, 'Review', p. 108.
[158] M.C. Boulding, 'Jacobus Faber Stapulensis, c.1460-1536, Forerunner of Vatican II' in A. Bellenger (ed.), *Opening the Scrolls: Essays in Catholic History in Honour of Godfrey Anstruther*, Downside Abbey, Somerset, 1987, p. 34.
[159] Bedouelle, p. 23.

[160] Lupton, p. 302; Knight, p. 248
[161] Oakley, 'Almain and Major', p. 673.
[162] C.M. Bellitto, 'The Spirituality of Reform in the Late Medieval Church: The Example of Nicholas de Clamanges', *Church History*, 68, 1999, p. 2.
[163] Black, p. 38.
[164] M.A. Mullett, *The Catholic Reformation*, Routledge, London, 1999, p. 2.
[165] B. Gordon, 'Conciliarism in Late Medieval Europe' in Pettegree, *Reformation*, p. 45: 'In January 1497 King Charles VIII of France asked the theological faculty at Paris whether the decree *Frequens* was still valid, and the answer was an unequivocal yes'.
[166] Although, without further evidence, this possibility must remain a conjecture.
[167] Oakley, *Conciliarist Tradition*, pp. 111-32.
[168] *Ibid.*, p. 125.
[169] *Ibid.*; J. Wicks, 'Thomas de Vio Cajetan (1469-1534)' in Lindberg, pp. 269-80 [hereafter Wicks], p. 273.
[170] Oakley, *Conciliarist Tradition*, pp. 127-8.
[171] MacCulloch, *Reformation*, p. 88.
[172] Oakley, *Conciliarist Tradition*, p. 132.
[173] *Ibid.*, pp. 129-40.
[174] Dionysius Carthusianus, *Opera Minora*, I, Cologne, 1532, pp. 43-4. According to Lupton: 'The name of this Carthusian was Dionysius Rykel, or De Leuwis, of Ruremonde, in Belgium ... he died in 1471. His expositions may thus be fairly compared, in respect of time, with Colet's': Lupton, p. 64 (n. 1).
[175] MacCulloch, *Reformation*, pp. 40-1. MacCulloch uses the spelling 'Konstanz'.
[176] Lupton, p. 302; Knight, p. 248.
[177] See Colet's treatise: '*De Compositione Sancti Corporis Christi Mystici*' in CUL, MS Gg.iv.26, fols. 67r-73v; *Opuscula*, pp. 29-48/Latin, pp. 183-96.
[178] Lupton, p. 294; Knight, p. 240: '*S. D. nostri papae*'; *Hierarchies*, pp. 48-50 and *passim*.
[179] Black, p. 74; MacCulloch, *Reformation*, p. 41.
[180] Although an English translation was produced after his death: J. Colet (translated by [T. Lupset]), *The Sermon of Doctor Colete, made to the Conuocation at Paulis*, London, 1530 [*STC* 5550].
[181] S. Lander, 'Church Courts and the Reformation in the Diocese of Chichester, 1500-58' in F. Heal and R. O'Day (eds.), *Continuity and Change: Personnel and Administration of the Church in England, 1500-1642*, Leicester Univeristy Press, Leicester, 1976, pp. 215-37, reprinted in C. Haigh (ed.), *The English Reformation Revised*, CUP, 1987, pp. 34-55 [hereafter Lander].
[182] Haigh, *Reformations*, pp. 10-11.
[183] Foxe, vol. II, book VII, p. 838.

Chapter Six

[1] For Colet's vexation, see Allen, I, pp. 525-8 and II, pp. 36-7; Erasmus, II, nos. 270 and 314.
[2] J.A. Guy, *The Cardinal's Court: The Impact of Thomas Wolsey in Star Chamber*, Harvester Press, Hassocks, Sussex, 1977 [hereafter Guy, *Cardinal's Court*], pp. 41-2; W.H. Dunham Jr., 'The Members of Henry VIII's Whole Council, 1509-1527', *EHR*, 59, 1944, pp. 187-210 [hereafter Dunham, 'Council'], p. 208.
[3] Colet normally confined his affairs to the ecclesiastical sphere.
[4] *Oratio*; *Sermon*; CA, MS WC, fols. 219r-220v; Allen, IV, pp. 523-8; Olin, pp. 185-90; Foxe, vol. II, book VII, p. 838; *LP*, II, ii, pp. 1445, 1450, 1460, 1467, 1470 and 1474: Colet preached many sermons to the king at Greenwich, several of which were given on Good Friday.

5 Erasmus, II, no. 260; Allen, I, pp. 510-12; Allen, IV, pp. 525-6; Olin, pp. 188-9; Erasmus, II, no. 270; Allen, I, p. 527; Erasmus II, nos. 278 and 314; Allen, II, pp. 36-7; Foxe, vol. II, book VII, pp. 838-9; Tyndale, *Answer*, p. 168; Latimer, p. 440.
6 On the king, see Seebohm, pp. 258-67; Lupton, pp. 189-93; Hunt, pp. 76-9; Olin, p. 189; M. Aston, *Lollards and Reformers: Images and Literacy in Late Medieval Religion*, Hambledon, London, 1984 [hereafter Aston], p. 213; Gleason, pp. 257-60; Dickens and Jones, p. 39; Brigden, *New Worlds*, p. 91; and Rex and Armstrong, pp. 390-407. On Fitzjames, see Lupton, pp. 202-5; S. Lee, 'John Colet', in L. Stephens (ed.), *The Dictionary of National Biography*, XI, OUP, 1887, p. 321 [hereafter Lee]; Kaufman, *Churche*, pp. 66-9; Gleason, pp. 235-60; P. Gwyn, *The King's Cardinal: The Rise and Fall of Thomas Wolsey*, Barrie and Jenkins, London, 1990 [hereafter Gwyn], pp. 37 and 339-40; Dickens and Jones, p. 39; and Guy, *Politics*, p. 32. On the Church, see Porter, pp. 29-36; Harper-Bill, *Church*, pp. 26, 44, 46 and 52; Gwyn, pp. 45, 278 and 338; Dickens and Jones, p. 39; and Brigden, *New Worlds*, p. 91. On Wolsey, see Lupton, pp. 193-8; Hunt, p. 76; Gwyn, pp. 56-7; Gleason, pp. 236-42; and Brigden, *New Worlds*, p. 91.
7 On the king, see Lupton, pp. 188-93. On Fitzjames, see *ibid.*, pp. 201-5. On the chapter, see *ibid.*, pp. 124-32. On the Lollards, see *ibid.*, p. 144. On Wolsey, see *ibid.*, pp. 193-8.
8 Gleason, pp. 236-41 and 235-60, *passim*.
9 *Ibid.*, pp. 241 and 253.
10 *LP*, II, ii, pp. 1440, 1445, 1450, 1455, 1460, 1467, 1470 and 1474.
11 Olin, p. 188; Allen, IV, p. 525.
12 Olin, pp. 188-9; Allen, IV, p. 526.
13 A.F. Pollard, *Wolsey*, Longmans, Green, London, 1929 [hereafter Pollard], p. 17; Hunt, p. 76.
14 Allen, IV, p. 526; Olin, p. 189; *L.P.*, II, ii, p. 1460.
15 Allen, IV, p. 526; Olin, p. 189.
16 CUL, MS Gg.iv.26, fol. 40r; *Romans*, pp. 85-6/Latin, p. 194.
17 CUL, MS Gg.iv.26, fol. 39v; *Romans*, p. 84/Latin, p. 193.
18 Seebohm, p. 264.
19 Olin, p. 190; Latin in Allen, IV, p. 526.
20 Olin, p. 190; Allen, IV, p. 527.
21 Olin, p. 190; Allen, IV, p. 527.
22 Allen, II, pp. 613-4 and Allen, IV, p. 527, quoted in Gleason, p. 259.
23 Erasmus was aware of Colet's vexations.
24 Lupton, pp. 189-93; Hunt, p. 79; and Gleason, pp. 256-60.
25 Allen, IV, p. 526; Olin, p. 189; and Brigden, *New Worlds*, p. 91
26 Dickens and Jones, p. 39.
27 Harper-Bill, *Church*, p. 10.
28 Henry VIII claimed, in 1515, that 'Kings in England in past time have never had any superior but God alone': F. Heal, *Of Prelates and Princes: A Study of the Economic and Social Position of the Tudor Episcopate*, CUP, 1980 [hereafter Heal, *Prelates*], p. 2.
29 Harper-Bill, *Church*, p. 11.
30 *Ibid*.
31 Gwyn, pp. 49-50.
32 See pp. 151-4.
33 Erasmus, II, no. 270; Allen, I, p. 527 (on Colet's suspension); Erasmus, II, no. 314; Allen, II, p. 37 (on Colet's continued vexation on 20 October 1514).
34 Allen, IV, p. 525; Olin, p. 188.
35 *Ibid.*, pp. 187-8; Latin in Allen, IV, p. 525.
36 Olin, p. 188; Allen, IV, p. 525: '*pasce oves meas*'; Foxe, vol. II, book VII, p. 839.

[37] Allen, IV, pp. 525-8; Olin, pp. 188-91.
[38] By the introduction of Erasmus's *Novum Instrumentum* in 1516.
[39] *Revised Standard Version Interlinear Greek-English New Testament:* The Nestle Greek Text with a Literal English Translation by A. Marshall, Macmillan, Basingstoke, 1968, p. 460.
[40] Allen, IV, p. 525; Olin, p. 188.
[41] Foxe, vol. II, book VII, p. 838.
[42] Lupton, pp. 178-205; Porter, pp. 29-36; Kaufman, *Churche*, pp. 66-9; and Guy, *Politics*, p. 32.
[43] Lee, p. 321; Lupton, pp. 202-5; Kaufman, *Churche*, p. 67; Gleason, pp. 237-41; Gwyn, pp. 37 and 340; Dickens and Jones, p. 39; Guy, *Politics*, p. 32; and Brigden, *New Worlds*, p. 91.
[44] Lee, p. 321.
[45] Kaufman, *Churche*, p. 67.
[46] Gwyn, p. 340.
[47] Gleason, p. 240.
[48] Dickens and Jones, pp. 34-40 for their suspicion of Gleason, and p. 39 for the quotation.
[49] Brigden, *New Worlds*, p. 91.
[50] Erasmus, II, no. 270; Latin in Allen, I, p. 527.
[51] Gleason, pp. 240-1.
[52] Gleason, pp. 237-41.
[53] Erasmus, II, no. 314; Latin in Allen, II, p. 37. The 'nest' refers to Colet's lodgings, set aside for him at the Carthusian monastery at Sheen.
[54] Foxe also reported Warham's friendship with Colet: 'The Archbishop more wisely weying the matter, and being well acquainted with Colet, so tooke hys part against his accusers, that he at that time was rid out of trouble': Foxe, vol. II, book VII, p. 838.
[55] Gleason, p. 236.
[56] Olin, p. 184; Latin in Allen, IV, p. 522.
[57] A heresy compared to the 'veneration' of images: see Gleason, p. 236.
[58] *Ibid.*, p. 236; Knight, p. 402.
[59] Gleason, p. 236.
[60] Heal, *Prelates*, p. 7.
[61] *Ibid.*, quoting T. Becon, *The Early Works of Thomas Becon*, edited by J. Ayre, Parker Society, 2, Cambridge, 1843, p. 24.
[62] CUL, MS Gg.iv.26, fol. 41v:; *Romans*, pp. 88-9/Latin, pp. 196-7.
[63] CUL, MS Gg.iv.26, fol. 149v; *Corinthians*, p. 275/Latin, p. 274.
[64] CUL, MS Gg.iv.26, fol. 59v:; *Romans*, p. 128/Latin, p. 224.
[65] BL, Add. MS 63853 fol. 42r; *Hierarchies*, p. 64/Latin, p. 207.
[66] Foxe, vol. II, book VII, p. 838; N. Tanner, 'Penances Imposed on Kentish Lollards by Archbishop Warham, 1511-12' in M. Aston and C. Richmond (eds.), *Lollardy and the Gentry in the Later Middle Ages*, Sutton, Stroud, 1997, pp. 229-49 [hereafter Tanner, 'Penances'].
[67] According to Foxe, Fitzjames preached from pre-written, or 'bosome' sermons from books, 'declaring nothing els to the people, but as they bring theyr prayers with them': Foxe, vol. II, book VII, p. 838.
[68] Erasmus, II, no. 260; Allen, I, pp. 510-12; Erasmus, II, no. 270; Allen, I, p. 527; Erasmus, II, no. 278; Erasmus, II, no. 314; Allen, II, p. 37; Allen, IV, pp. 525-6; Olin, pp. 188-9.
[69] G.R. Elton, *Reform and Reformation: England, 1509-1558*, Edward Arnold, London, 1977, p. 57.
[70] Foxe, vol. II, book VII, pp. 838-9. See also J. Fines, 'Heresy Trials in the Diocese of Coventry and Lichfield, 1511-12', *JEH*, 14, 1963, pp. 160-74 [hereafter Fines], p. 160; J.A.F. Thomson, *The Early Tudor Church and Society, 1485-1529*, Longman, London, 1993, [hereafter Thomson] p. 238.

71 Erasmus, II, nos. 189 and 192; Allen, I, pp. 412 and 425.
72 Foxe, vol. II, book VII, p. 839; see also Aston, p. 213, quoting Tyndale, *Answer*, p. 168. Tyndale does not give a source for his assertion.
73 Lupton, p. 204, quoting Latimer, p. 440.
74 CUL, MS Gg.iv.26, fol. 73r; *Opuscula*, p. 45 ('Where there is schism and separation, there is no one common feeling')/Latin, p. 194.
75 During the debate on benefit of clergy and the Hunne case: Gwyn, pp. 34-57.
76 Lupton, pp. 128-32; Porter, pp. 29-36; Harper-Bill, *Church*, pp. 26, 44, 46 and 52; and Gleason, pp. 235-43.
77 Brigden, *New Worlds*, p. 91.
78 Lupton, pp. 128-32; Porter, pp. 25-6; Harper-Bill, *Church*, p. 52; Gleason, p. 244.
79 Dickens and Jones, p. 39, referring to Allen, IV, p. 515; Olin, p. 178.
80 CUL, MS Gg.iv.26, fol. 31r; *Romans*, p. 65/Latin, p. 180.
81 CUL, MS Gg.iv.26, fol. 33r; *Romans*, p. 70/Latin, p. 183.
82 His problems with the Church were not dissimilar to those of Archbishop Morton: Harper-Bill, 'Morton', pp. 1-21.
83 Dennington, Thurning, Stepney and prebendal preferments in York, Salisbury and Chichester: Seebohm, p. 529; Lupton, pp. 116-20.
84 Rex, 'New Learning', pp. 26-43; Harper-Bill, *Church*, p. 52.
85 *Ibid.*, p. 46.
86 Colet's sermon was preached on 6 February 1511/12. The next meeting of the Convocation of the Province of Canterbury to be held at St. Paul's took place on 22 June 1514: *Chronology*, p. 603; John Taylor preached on that occasion in similar terms to Colet's 1511/12 Convocation sermon: BL , Cotton MS Vitellius B. ii, fol. 80r; W. Melton, *Sermo Exhortatorius Cancelarii Ebor[acensis]*, W. de Worde, London, *c*.1510 [*STC* 17806], extracts of which are printed in Dickens and Carr, pp. 15-6, translated by Dickens.
87 CUL, MS Gg.iv.26, fol. 39v; *Romans*, p. 84/Latin, p. 193.
88 Olin, p. 178; Latin in Allen, IV, p. 515.
89 Olin, p. 187; Allen, IV, p. 524.
90 Dobson, pp. 145-74; A.H. Thompson, *The English Clergy and their Organization in the Later Middle Ages*, Clarendon, Oxford, 1947, pp. 72-100.
91 Harper-Bill, *Church*, p. 81; Rex, *Lollards*, p. 101; and J.F. Davis, *Heresy and Reformation in the South-East of England, 1520-1559*, Royal Historical Society, London, 1983, pp. 1-5.
92 Rex, *Lollards, passim*.
93 Harper-Bill, *Church*, p. 82.
94 Gwyn, p. 37.
95 Lupton, p. 298; Knight, p. 244; CUL, MS Gg.iv.26, fol. 39v; *Romans*, p. 84/Latin, p. 193; Tanner, pp. 43 and 50.
96 CUL, MS Gg.iv.26, fol. 130v; *Corinthians*, p. 225/Latin, p. 224.
97 CUL, MS Gg.iv.26, fol. 130v; *Corinthians*, p. 225/Latin, p. 224.
98 Foxe, vol. II, book VII, p. 838.
99 Allen, IV, p. 522; Olin, p. 184; quotation from A. Hope, 'Lollardy: The Stone the Builders Rejected?' in P. Lake and M. Dowling (eds.), *Protestantism and the National Church in Sixteenth Century England*, Croom Helm, London, 1987, pp. 1-35 [hereafter Hope], p. 20. This concept of the poor reflecting the image of God was a well-established idea in the late medieval period: Aston, pp. 155-61.
100 A. Hudson, *The Premature Reformation: Wycliffite Texts and Lollard History*, Clarendon, Oxford, 1988, p. 466; Foxe, vol. II, book VII, p. 838.
101 Hope, p. 2.

[102] Lupton, p. 144. No date is given for the visit; C. Cross, *Church and People: England 1450-1660*, Blackwell, Oxford, 1999, pp. 21-41.
[103] Foxe, vol. II, book VII, p. 838.
[104] CUL, MS Gg.iv.26, fol. 39r; *Romans*, p. 84/Latin, p. 193.
[105] See Gleason, pp. 254-5 for Colet's dislike of pilgrimages.
[106] Tanner, pp. 43 and 50.
[107] Lupton, p. 298; Knight, p. 244.
[108] Gwyn, pp. 52-3 and 239-40; Pollard, p. 50.
[109] CA, MS WC, fols. 219r-220v.
[110] Lupton, pp. 194-8; Hunt, p. 76; Gwyn, pp. 56-7; Gleason, pp. 244-6; and Brigden, *New Worlds*, p. 91.
[111] Lupton, p. 198; Brigden, *New Worlds*, p. 91; and p. 245.
[112] Gwyn, p. 57.
[113] *Ibid.*, pp. 56-7.
[114] *Hierarchies*, p. 42.
[115] Bishop Hugh Oldham.
[116] CA, MS WC, fol. 219r.
[117] The CA, MS WC is dated 1664 (fol. 1r). The date of the original account is unknown, although the paraphrased extracts suggest that the earliest source was an eyewitness account.
[118] Lupton, p. 195.
[119] CA, MS WC, fol. 219r.
[120] Colet's sentiments probably relate to the struggles, in the fifteenth century, over papal appointments to higher benefices in the English Church, a struggle effectively won by the kings of England in the statute of *Provisors*. Although the position of 'cardinal' was not a benefice in the same category as the others, the Pope had little influence over such appointments without royal approbation. See Harper-Bill, *Church*, pp. 3, 15 and 25.
[121] CA, MS WC,, fol. 219v.
[122] Gwyn, p. 49.
[123] CA, MS WC, fol. 219v; Lupton, p. 196.
[124] Gwyn, p. 53.
[125] CA, MS WC, fol. 219v.
[126] CUL, MS Gg.iv.26, fol. 163r; *Hierarchies*, p. 16/Latin, p. 174.
[127] CA, MS WC, fol. 220r.
[128] *Ibid.*; AS, h infra 1.5; Jayne, *passim*.
[129] Allen, IV, pp. 525-6; Olin, pp. 188-90.
[130] Gwyn, pp. 52-3.
[131] A place on the King's Council: Dunham, 'Council', p. 208.
[132] If not preaching, this 'holy instruction' could possibly have been individual spiritual direction.
[133] Erasmus, II, no. 260; Latin in Allen, I, pp. 510-12.
[134] Although Erasmus was mistaken in his belief that Colet did not financially benefit from preaching, unless he was referring only to Colet's preaching at St. Paul's. Colet was paid twenty shillings for each sermon preached: *LP*, II, ii, pp. 1445, 1450, 1455, 1460, 1467 and 1470.
[135] D. Erasmus, *The Colloquies of Erasmus*, translated by C.R. Thompson, University of Chicago Press, Chicago, 1965, p. 305.
[136] For Colet's vexation in 1513, see Erasmus, II, no. 260; Allen, I, pp. 510-12 (29 April 1512); Allen, IV, pp. 525-6; Olin, pp. 188-9. For the Good Friday sermon, see *LP*, II, ii, p. 1460. For Colet's apparent absence from Court, see *ibid.*, II, ii, pp. 1460-7. On further harassment, see

Erasmus, II, no. 314; Allen, II, p. 37. On his sermon preached before Wolsey, see CA, MS WC, fols. 219r-220v.
[137] Allen, IV, 526; Olin, p. 190; Aston, p. 213.
[138] Allen, IV, p. 525; Olin, p. 190; Foxe, vol. II, book VII, p. 838.
[139] CA, MS WC, fols. 219r-220v.
[140] Erasmus, VI, no. 855.

Chapter Seven

[1] Guy, *Cardinal's Court*, pp. 36-7; *Mercers*, pp. 440, 441, 454, 466, 486, 495, 519-21 and 527. McConica's argument that English humanists influenced Henrician reform policy has been persuasively refuted by Elton, Dickens and Fox: see J.K. McConica, *English Humanists and Reformation Politics Under Henry VIII and Edward VI*, 1st edition, Clarendon, Oxford, 1965; 2nd edition, 1967, *passim*; G.R. Elton's review of McConica's book in *The Historical Journal*, 10, 1967, pp. 137-8; A.G. Dickens's review of the same in *History*, 52, 1967, pp. 77-8; and A. Fox, 'English Humanism and the Body Politic' in A. Fox and J. Guy, *Reassessing the Henrician Age: Humanism, Politics and Reform, 1500-1550*, Blackwell, Oxford, 1986, pp. 34-51.
[2] *Registrum*, pp. 217-48: Colet's statute amendments, labelled *Epitome*, occupy pp. 217-36; his 1518 proposals, named *Exhibita*, occupy pp. 237-48.
[3] Allen, IV, p. 517; Olin, p. 178; Foxe, vol. II, book VII, pp. 838-9; Knight, pp. 199-207; Seebohm, pp. 1-43; Milman, pp. 112-24; Dean Mansell, see *Registrum*, p. xlvii (n. 1); Lupton, pp. 132-9; Marriott, p. 119; H. Maynard Smith, *Pre-Reformation England*, Macmillan, London, 1938 [hereafter Maynard Smith] p. 108; Hunt, pp. 50-6; Carpenter, pp. 106-15; and Gleason, p. 241.
[4] As described by Carpenter, pp. 114-5.
[5] *Hierarchies*, pp. 42-53.
[6] *Registrum*, pp. 217-48. Neither text includes Colet's lost 1506 injunctions for minor clergy and chantry priests: see Simpson, pp. 145-74.
[7] By Simpson in *Registrum*, p. 217.
[8] *Ibid.*, pp. 237-48.
[9] Dugdale, pp. 237-68; *Registrum*, pp. 217-48. For simplicity's sake, only the *Registrum* will be cited hereafter.
[10] *Registrum*, pp. 220-2.
[11] Allen, IV, p. 520; Olin, p. 181.
[12] Allen, IV, p. 527; Olin, p. 190; Seebohm, pp. 461-70 and 503-5.
[13] Milman, p. 124; Lupton, p. 137; Hunt, p. 55; and Gleason, p. 241.
[14] Allen, IV, p. 517; Olin, p. 178; Gleason, p. 241.
[15] Seebohm, pp. 1-43; Milman, pp. 112-24; Lupton, pp. 132-9; Hunt, pp. 50-6; Carpenter, pp. 106-16; and Gleason, p. 241.
[16] Lupton, pp. 132-3 and 137.
[17] Marriott, p. 119.
[18] Hunt, p. 51, quoting Lupton, p. 132; Allen, IV, p. 515: '*collegii sui collapsam disciplinam sarsit*'.
[19] Gleason, p. 241, quoting respectively from Carpenter, p. 114 for 'commended' and *Registrum*, pp. 418-9 for 'witnessed'.
[20] Gleason, p. 241.
[21] Hunt, pp. 51-6; *Registrum*, pp. 217-36.
[22] Presumably soon after his appointment in 1505: Emden, p. 63; Hunt, p. 51.
[23] Gleason, p. 242.
[24] Trapp, *New DNB*, p. 603; Davis, 'Lesser Clergy', p. 161; Barron and Rousseau, p. 40.
[25] Lupton, p. 132.

NOTES TO CHAPTER SEVEN

[26] For instance, the phrase '*Is Omnes causas ad Capitulum spectantes audit*' appears in the *Epitome* and in the *Exhibita Registrum*, pp. 220 and 237.
[27] For instance, those passages concerning rules for the grammar master. See *Registrum*, p. 225: '*Magister Scholae vir probus et honestus debet esse, atque, multae et laudatae literaturae*', compared with BL, Add. MS 6274, fol.1v: the grammar master should be a man 'hoole in body honest and vertuouse and lernyd in ... good and clene laten litterature'; reprinted in Lupton, p. 272.
[28] Foxe, vol. II, book VII, pp. 838-9; Carpenter, pp. 106-16.
[29] Gleason, p. 241, within the space of a single paragraph.
[30] As does Gleason, *ibid*.
[31] Knight, pp. 199-207 and 226-41; Seebohm, p. 389; Milman, pp. 112-24; Lupton, p. 133; Hunt, pp. 50-6; and Gleason, p. 241.
[32] Allen, IV, p. 517; Olin, p. 178; Foxe, vol. II, book VII, pp. 838-9; Knight, pp. 200-7; Seebohm, pp. 1-43; Milman, pp. 112-24; Lupton, pp. 132-9; Maynard Smith, p. 108; Hunt, pp. 50-6; Carpenter, p. 106.
[33] Carpenter, p. 114.
[34] *Ibid.*, pp. 106-16. Another example of self-contradictory scholarship is found in Hunt, who asserted that Colet's reform efforts were 'unavailing' (Hunt, p. 55), but nevertheless devoted an entire chapter of his book to Colet 'The Reformer': Hunt, pp. 18-72.
[35] Foxe, vol. II, book VII, p. 838; Milman, p. 112.
[36] Particularly Knight, pp. 200-1 and Milman, p. 124.
[37] Carpenter, p. 112.
[38] Milman, p. 124.
[39] '*O scelus nefandum! O detestanda iniquitas!*': *Registrum*, p. 230.
[40] Carpenter, p. 114.
[41] Carpenter's word: see Carpenter, p. 114.
[42] According to *Registrum*, pp. 418-9.
[43] Gleason, p. 241.
[44] Carpenter, p. 114.
[45] Knight, pp. 199-207; Lupton, p. 133.
[46] Hunt, p. 56, following Lupton, p. 133.
[47] Knight, p. 200, reprinted in Lupton, p. 133 and Hunt, p. 55.
[48] Knight, pp. 199-207; Seebohm, p. 389; Milman, p. 124; Lupton, p. 133; and Hunt, p. 56.
[49] Carpenter, p. 114.
[50] *Registrum*, pp. 251-3, 260 and 262. For the school statutes, see BL, Add. MS 6274, fols.1r-11v.
[51] *Registrum*, p. 238: '... *secundum ordinationem Domini Warham Episcopi*'.
[52] *Ibid.*, pp. 251, 252, 253 (twice), 260 and 262 ('*juxta ordinationes dicti Domini Warham*').
[53] Warham's statutes are printed in *ibid*, pp. 206-14; Wolsey stated that Warham promulgated them following his episcopal visitation: '... *Domini Willielmi Warham nuper ejusdem Ecclesiae Episcopi in sua visitatione ordinaria ...*': *ibid*, p. 251.
[54] *Ibid.*, p. 19.
[55] For some reason now obscure.
[56] Knight, p. 207; Milman, p. 124; Lupton, p. 133; Hunt, p. 56; and Carpenter, p. 114.
[57] *Ibid.*, pp. 114-5.
[58] His recourse to Wolsey, as archbishop, and a legate *a latere*, was entirely consistent with his emphasis on hierarchy and Episcopal authority.
[59] Trapp, 'Manuscripts'; Trapp, 'Colet'; Trapp, 'Pseudo-Dionysius'; and Gleason, pp. 185-213.
[60] Rex, *Henry VIII*, pp. 51-2.
[61] MacCulloch, *Reformation*, p. 33.

62 *Ibid.*, p. 34.
63 *Ibid.*, p. 477.
64 Gleason, pp. 185-213.
65 Guy, *Cardinal's Court*, pp. 28-9 for a list of clerics, knights and justices involved in politics.
66 Pollard, p. 57; Gwyn, pp. 58-68.
67 Except for his sermon on war in 1513: Allen, IV, p. 526; Olin, p. 190.
68 Gleason, pp. 246-66.
69 Allen, IV, pp. 523-8; Olin, pp. 185-90; Foxe, vol. II, book VII, p. 838; *LP*, II, ii, pp. 1445, 1450, 1460, 1467, 1470 and 1474: Colet preached many sermons to the king.
70 His sermons on war had drawn the king's attention to him, as had his sermon preached before Wolsey in 1515; CA, MS WC, fols.219r-220v; Gleason, pp. 246-66.
71 C. Kitching, 'The Prerogative Court of Canterbury from Warham to Whitgift' in F. Heal and R. O'Day (eds.), *Continuity and Change: Personnel and Administration of the Church in England, 1500-1642*, Leicester University Press, 1976, pp. 191-214 [hereafter Kitching], pp. 191-2.
72 Lupton, pp. 226-7.
73 *Ibid.*
74 Pollard, p. 57; J.D. Mackie, *The Early Tudors, 1485-1558*, Allen Lane, London, 1976, p. 295; Gleason, p. 256.
75 As soon as nine days after Warham's resignation, on 24 December 1515 at the earliest: *ibid.*, p. 247.
76 *Ibid.*
77 Dunham, 'Council', pp. 187-210; J.A. Guy,, 'The Privy Council: Revolution or Evolution?' in C. Coleman and D. Starkey (eds.), *Revolution Reassessed: Revisions in the History of Tudor Government and Administration*, Clarendon, Oxford, 1986, pp. 59-85 [hereafter Guy, 'Privy Council'], p. 64; Gleason, p. 266.
78 Guy, 'Privy Council', pp. 59-60.
79 *Ibid.*, pp. 60-2.
80 *Ibid.*, pp. 62-3.
81 Although the records for Star Chamber are patchy for this period: Guy, *Cardinal's Court*, pp. 36-7.
82 Dunham, 'Council', pp. 204 and 187; Guy, 'Privy Council', p. 63.
83 *Ibid.*, p. 65.
84 Gleason, p. 247.
85 Dunham, 'Council', p. 208.
86 Guy, *Cardinal's Court*, p. 36.
87 Erasmus, V, no. 786; Allen, III, p. 241.
88 Erasmus, VI, no. 855; Allen, III, p. 355.
89 Allen, IV, p. 527; Olin, p. 190.
90 Erasmus, II, no. 314. The 'nest' probably refers to Colet's lodgings, set aside for him at the Carthusian monastery at Sheen.
91 Lupton, p. 227; Latin in *Opuscula*, p. 313.
92 Olin, p. 181; Allen, IV, p. 520.
93 1518 was a particularly bad year for 'the Sweat': Gwyn, pp. 58-9 and 440.
94 *Registrum*, pp. iv-xlix.
95 *Ibid.*, pp. 1-177, *passim*; see particularly *ibid.*, p. 3: 'Statutes and Customs of the Cathedral Church of St. Paul, extracted from the Ancient Books and Muniments of the Cathedral by Deans Ralph de Baldock and Thomas Lisieux'.
96 *Registrum.*, pp. 217-8.
97 *Hierarchies*, pp. 42-55; *Registrum*, pp. 221-5.

[98] BL, Add. MS 63853, fols.81v-82r; *Hierarchies*, p. 126/Latin, p. 248; *Registrum*, pp. 228-30.
[99] See chapter 3.
[100] Between the *Epitome* and the pre-existing statutes: *Registrum*, pp. 1-177, *passim*.
[101] St. Paul's was, and is, the only cathedral to use the spelling 'virger' rather than 'verger'.
[102] *Registrum*, pp. 224-5, compared with p. 72.
[103] *Ibid.*, p. 224; translation in Hunt, p. 51.
[104] *Registrum*, pp. 224-5; Hunt, p. 52.
[105] *Registrum*, p. 225; Hunt, p. 52.
[106] *Registrum*, pp. 222-5.
[107] *Registrum*, p. 221; Hunt, p. 52.
[108] Lupton, p. 135; *Registrum*, p. 225.
[109] *De Sacramentis*, pp. 277-9; Gleason, p. 211.
[110] *Registrum*, p. 234.
[111] *Ibid.*, pp. 67 and 104.
[112] Lupton, p. 136; *Registrum*, p. 234. Perhaps suggesting that they were only in minor orders and thus able to marry.
[113] *De Sacramentis*, pp. 277-9; Gleason, p. 211.
[114] Lupton, p. 136; *Registrum*, p. 234.
[115] CUL, MS Gg.iv.26, fol.90r-v.
[116] Lupton, p. 136. Lupton's parentheses.
[117] Hunt, p. 54; *Registrum*, p. 235.
[118] *Registrum*, p. 23 for the pre-existing statutes and p. 226 for Colet's words.
[119] Lupton, pp. 136-7; *Registrum*, pp. 226-7.
[120] Perhaps indicating that the *Epitome* and the school statutes were composed at a similar time: BL, Add. MS 6274, fols.1r-11v. The manuscript is dated 18 June 1518: fol.1r.
[121] See pp. 68-82 and 105.
[122] Hunt, p. 53; *Registrum*, p. 228.
[123] Hunt, p. 53; *Registrum*, p. 229.
[124] Lupton, p. 134; *Registrum*, pp. 229-30.
[125] Hunt, p. 20; BL, Add. MS 63853, fols.81v-82r.
[126] *Registrum*, p. 233.
[127] Olin, p. 187; Allen, IV, p. 524.
[128] *Registrum*, p. 237.
[129] *Ibid.*, p. 238: from '*De Residentia Decani*' and '*De Loco-tenente Decani*' to '*Residentia solum in Ecclesia S. Pauli*'.
[130] *Ibid.*, pp. 239: '*De Officio Residenciariorum in Divino Cultu*'; '*Quid Residentes in Choro*' and '*Ceremoniae in Choro*'; and 247: '*Visitatio Decani*'. The entire *Exhibita* occupies *ibid.*, pp. 237-48; *Epitome*, pp. 217-36.
[131] Colet's *Exhibita* are headed thus: '*Exhibita a Johanne Collet Decano, reverendissimo Patri et Domino Cardinali Eboracensi ac Apostolico Legato a latere* [Wolsey], *pro Reformatione Status Residenciariorum in Ecclesia Sancti Pauli, primo Septembris, Anno Domini 1518*': *Registrum*, p. 237.
[132] *Ibid.*, p. 249; full statutes, pp. 249-63. Simpson's source for the *Exhibita* is now lost.
[133] *Registrum*, p. 253. The section is entitled: '*De Exoneratione Ecclesiae ab aere alieno, et dignioribus ad futuram Residentiam praeferendis, cum provisione pro Residentia Decani, et de numero Residentium*'; *Registrum*, p. 251.
[134] *Ibid.*, p. 238; Colet wrote: '*Nam quum quatuor duntaxat sint Residentes, valde currandum est, ut hii boni viri et sapientes sint...*'.
[135] *Ibid.*, p. 239.
[136] *Ibid.*

[137] Lupton, p. 132 (n. 2); Carpenter, p. 112. 'Presentments' is a curious choice of word, given that documents submitted in visitations were called 'bills of presentment' or just 'presentments' for short. Such documents contained answers to the visitation articles, or generally drew attention to faults needing remedy. There is, however, no record that Colet made a visitation around this time.
[138] *Registrum*, pp. 237-48, compared with pp. 249-63.
[139] *Ibid.*, p. 249.
[140] *Ibid.*, p. 206: '*Statuta Domini Willielmi Warham Episcopi London facta cum consensu Decani et Capituli*.' Warham was consecrated Bishop of London on 5 October 1502 and translated to Canterbury on 29 November 1502. The statutes occupy pp. 206-14 in *Registrum*.
[141] *Ibid.*, pp. 251, 252, 253 (twice), 260 and 262.
[142] Gleason, pp. 240-4.
[143] For example, *Registrum*, p. 250: '*880 libras inter eosdemnovellos Stagiarios*'; other references are on pp. 251, 253, 254 and 262.
[144] *Ibid.*, p. 241. Colet's *Exhibita* give much more emphasis to the choir than Wolsey's statutes.
[145] *Ibid.*, pp. 418-9.
[146] Lepine, p. 155.
[147] Erasmus, VII, no. 1023, dated 15 October 1519, was addressed to Guillaume Budé; nos. 1025, 1026, 1027 and 1028, dated 16 October 1519, were addressed to Richard Pace, Thomas Lupset, William Dancaster and William Blount (Lord Mountjoy) respectively. No. 1030, dated 17 October 1519, was written to Bishop John Fisher. All these letters express profound loss at Colet's demise.

Conclusion

[148] BL, Add. MS 63853, fols. 33v and 87r; *Hierarchies*, pp. 50 and 133/Latin, pp. 198 and 253; *Pseudo-Dionysius*, pp. 155, 163 (n. 75) and 235-9. For the origins of the triad, see Louth, *Origins*, pp. 57-9.
[149] *Hierarchies*, p. 133/Latin, p. 253.
[150] *Romans* and *Corinthians, passim*.
[151] *Hierarchies, passim*.
[152] For instance, *Romans*, p. 146 for Plotinus and p. 186 for Plato. Pico della Mirandola is specifically mentioned in *Corinthians*, p. 258; *Romans*, pp. 138 and 185-6; *Opuscula*, pp. 170-1; and *Hierarchies*, pp. 236-8. For Ficino's Neoplatonic influence, see Jayne, *passim* and Trapp, 'English Cleric', pp. 237-40.
[153] Gleason, p. 335.
[154] *Ibid.*, pp. 47 and 198-9.
[155] He was not resident in any of his benefices except St. Paul's: Lupton, p. 183; Seebohm, p. 529.
[156] Erasmus, II, no. 278; Allen, IV, p. 515; Olin, p. 178; CA, MS WC, fols. 219r-220v; *LP*, II, ii, pp. 1440, 1445, 1450, 1455, 1460, 1467, 1470 and 1474.
[157] *Sermon*, pp. 293-304.
[158] Erasmus, II, no. 260.
[159] The statutes of Deans Lisieux and Baldock: *Registrum*, pp. 1-117.
[160] BL, Add. MS 6274, fols. 1r-11v.
[161] CUL, MS Gg.iv.26; CCC MS 355; Emmanuel College Library, Cambridge, MS 245; AS, h infra 1.5; Bodleian Library, Oxford, MS Tanner 221; BL, Add. MSS 6274 and 63853.
[162] Simpson, pp. 145-74.
[163] *Registrum*, pp. 217-48.

[164] Further discussion of the 1506 manuscript can be found in J. Arnold, 'John Colet and a Lost Manuscript of 1506', *History*, 89, April, 2004, pp. 174-92.//
[165] Allen, IV, p. 514; Olin, p. 177.
[166] Gleason, pp. 270-333; *Corinthians, passim*.
[167] CUL, MS Gg.iv.26, fols. 2r-74v; BL, Add. MS 63853, fols. 1r-104v; and CCC, MS 355, pp. 1-226.
[168] Erasmus, I, nos. 106-11; Erasmus's version was published in a volume of shorter works, entitled *Lucubratiunculae*, dated February 1503; Gleason, p. 94.
[169] Although the original correspondence has been translated: Erasmus, I, nos. 106-11; Gleason, pp. 93-125.
[170] Gleason, pp. 19-24 and 64.

BIBLIOGRAPHY

MANUSCRIPTS

ALL SOULS' COLLEGE, OXFORD, THE CODRINGTON LIBRARY

h. infra l.5: Colet's marginalia in a copy of Marsilio Ficino's *Epistolae* (Venice, 1495) and Colet's transcription of some correspondence with Ficino.

BODLEIAN LIBRARY, OXFORD

Tanner 221: Records for the Guild of Jesus in the Crowds, St. Paul's Cathedral, re-founded by Colet in 1507, with a preface written by Colet, which includes his signature.

BORTHWICK INSTITUTE OF HISTORICAL RESEARCH, YORK

DY.4.6d: Letters patent sent from Colet to York Minster, dated 1503.

BRITISH LIBRARY, LONDON

Additional Manuscripts
6274: Colet's Statutes for St. Paul's School, dated 18 June 1518.

29549: Finch-Hatton Papers. Folio 7r-v is a letter from Thomas Lupset to Richard Pace, c.1530.

63853: Colet's commentary on the *Celestial Hierarchy* of Dionysius; his commentary on the *Ecclesiastical Hierarchy* of Dionysius; and *De Sacramentis*. Colet's treatise on the sacraments, copied c.1504-1510 by Pieter Meghen of Bois-le-Duc (The Netherlands).

Cotton Manuscripts

> Vitellius B. ii, folios 80r-81v: an account of John Taylor's sermon preached to Convocation in 1514.

Lansdowne Manuscripts

> 1030: folios 2v-182r: notes for a biography of Colet and others by White Kennett.

Sloane Manuscripts

> 1207: A Letter to Anne Bolyn from T. Alwaye. Folios 42v–53v contain a copy of Colet's Convocation Sermon (c.1531).

CAMBRIDGE UNIVERSITY LIBRARY

> Dd.vii.3: Latin transcriptions, from the Vulgate, of St. Matthew and St. Mark's Gospels, by Pieter Meghen, commissioned by Colet.

> Ee.v.21: Register of Statutes and Customs of St. Paul's Cathedral by Thomas Lisieux, c.1450.

> Gg.iv.26: Colet's lectures on Romans; letter to the Abbot of Wynchcombe; treatise on the Mystical Body of Christ; commentary on 1 Corinthians; and commentary on the *Celestial Hierarchy* of Dionysius.

COLLEGE OF ARMS, LONDON

> WC: Folios 219r-220v contain an account of Wolsey's installation as Cardinal at Westminster Abbey, in 1518, including a sermon preached by Colet.

CORPUS CHRISTI COLLEGE, CAMBRIDGE, THE PARKER LIBRARY

> 355: Exposition on Romans (chapters 1-5); letters to Radulphus on the Mosaic account of creation.

EMMANUEL COLLEGE LIBRARY, CAMBRIDGE

> 245 (formerly MS 3.3.12): Transcript of Colet's commentary on 1 Corinthians by Pieter Meghen from Cambridge University Library, MS Gg.iv.26.

GUILDHALL LIBRARY, LONDON

> 9531/9: *Registrum Reverendi Ricardi Fitzjames.*

> 9537/9: Call book for Bishop Bancroft's Visitation of 1598.

25166/1-9: Account books of William Worsley, Dean of St. Paul's Cathedral, 1479/80-1496/7.

25184: A single roll, dated 1559, listing works pertaining to St. Paul's Cathedral including several by Colet, now lost.

25187: An account of moneys found in, and added to, the chest in the vestibule of St. Paul's Cathedral, 1505-8, with an account of Dean Colet's visitation expenses, 1506.

25526: A list of St. Paul's Cathedral chantries at the dissolution n 1547.

29410: Charter of incorporation of the college of minor canons at St. Paul's Cathedral, 1394.

29414: Charter of *Inspeximus* of Henry VIII, 1511.

29416: A 1395 ratification of the constitution of the college of minor canons as set out in the foundation charter of 1394 by Robert Braybroke, Bishop of London (1382-1404).

29418: A 1525 transcript of the statutes of the college of minor canons of 18 March 1396/7, with additional statutes from 1519-21.

LAMBETH PALACE LIBRARY, LONDON

DCI: Register of the entries of Doctors of Law in the College of Advocates in Doctors' Commons, autographed by Colet.

Registrum Warham, 1503-1532.

MERCERS' COMPANY, LONDON

Unnumbered MS: Colet's Ordinances of St. Paul's School, dated 18 June 1518.

Unnumbered MS: Colet's Charter of Manors given to the Mercers, dated 12 July 1511.

Unnumbered MS: Colet's last will dated 22 August 1519.

ST. PAUL'S SCHOOL, LONDON

Unnumbered MS: *Super Opera Dionysii, De Sacramentis*: a copy of British Library, Additional MS 63853.

TRINITY COLLEGE LIBRARY, CAMBRIDGE, THE GALE COLLECTION

MS 0.4.44: Short summaries of the New Testament epistles in order and a commentary on 1 Peter.

PRINTED PRIMARY SOURCES

Acts of Court of the Mercers' Company, 1453-1527, edited by L. Lyell and F.D. Watney, Cambridge University Press, Cambridge, 1936.

Acts of the Dean and Chapter of the Cathedral Church of Chichester, 1545-1642, edited by W.D. Peckham, Sussex Record Society, 58, Sussex Record Society, Lewes, Sussex, 1960.

Bale, J., *Index Britannicae Scriptorum: John Bale's Index of British and Other Writers*, edited by R.L. Poole and M. Bateson, Oxford University Press, Oxford, 1902.

Bayne, C.G. and Dunham, W.H. (eds.), *Select Cases in the Council of Henry VII*, Selden Society, 75, Selden Society, London, 1958.

Becon, T., *The Early Works of Thomas Becon*, edited by J. Ayre, Parker Society, 2, Cambridge, 1843.

Boyle, L., 'The *Oculus Sacerdotis* and Some Other Works of William of Pagula', *Transactions of the Royal Historical Society*, 5th Series, 5, 1955, pp. 81-110.

Carley, J.P. (ed.), *The Libraries of King Henry VIII*, British Library, London, 2000.

Colet, J., *A Right Fruitfull Admonition*, G. Cawood, London, 1577 [*STC* 5549].

Colet, J., *A Ryght Frutefull Monycion, Co[n]cerning the Ordre of a Good Chrysten Mannes Lyfe*, J. Bydell, Salisbury, 1534 [*STC* 5547].

Colet, J., *Coleti Catechismus*, W. de Worde, London, 1534 [*STC* 5543].

Colet, J., *Daily Devotions, or, The Christian's Morning and Evening Sacrifice with Some Short Directions for a Godly Life*, E. G[riffin], F.J. Benson, London, 1641 [*STC* 5549.7].

Colet, J., *Joannes Coletus Super Opera Dionysii: Two Treatises on the Hierarchies of Dionysius, by John Colet D.D.*, translated by J.H. Lupton, George Bell and Sons, London, 1869.

Colet, J., *Ioannis Coleti Opus De Sacramentis Ecclesiae: A Treatise on the Sacraments of the Church, by John Colet, D.D.*, with introduction and notes by J.H. Lupton, George Bell and Sons, London, 1867.

Colet, J., *Joannis Coleti Enarratio In Epistolam S. Pauli ad Romanos: An Exposition of St. Paul's Epistle to the Romans, delivered as Lectures in the University of Oxford about the year 1497, by John Colet D.D.*, translated by J.H. Lupton, George Bell and Sons, London, 1873.

Colet, J., *Joannis Coleti Enarratio In Primam Epistolam S. Pauli ad Corinthios: An Exposition of St. Paul's First Epistle to the Corinthians, by John Colet*, translated by J.H. Lupton, George Bell and Sons, London, 1876.

Colet, J., *Joannis Coleti Opuscula Quaedam Theologica: Letters to Radulphus on the Mosaic Account of Creation; On Christ's Mystical Body the Church; Exposition of St. Paul's Epistle to the Romans (Chapters I-V) by John Colet, D.D.*, translated by J.H. Lupton, George Bell and Sons, London, 1876.

Colet, J., *John Colet's Commentary on First Corinthians: A New Edition of the Latin Text, with Translation, Annotations, and Introduction*, edited and translated by B. O'Kelly and C.A.L. Jarrott, Medieval and Early Renaissance Studies, vol. 21, Binghamton, New York, 1985.

Colet, J., *Opus De Sacramentis Ecclesiae: A Treatise on the Sacraments by John Colet*, translated in J.B. Gleason, *John Colet*, University of California Press, Berkeley, California, 1989, pp. 270-333.

Colet, J., *Oratio Habita a D. Joanne Colet ad Clerum in Convocatione. Anno. M.D.xi*, London, [1511-12?]) [*STC* 5545], reproduced in S. Knight, *The Life of Dr. John Colet, Dean of St. Paul's, in the Reigns of K. Henry VII and K. Henry VIII and Founder of St. Paul's School: With an Appendix Containing Some Account of the Masters and More Eminent Scholars of that Foundation, and Several Original Papers Relating to the Said Life*, 1st edition, J. Downing, London, 1724; 2nd edition, Oxford University Press, Oxford, 1823, pp. 239-50.

Colet, J., *Rudimenta Grammatices et Docendi Methodus, non tam Scholae Gypsuychianae*. [Colet's 'Aeditio' with Lily's 'Rudimenta' with the Latin text of Cardinal Wolsey's rules for the teaching of Latin at Ipswich School prefixed], M. de Keysere, Antwerp, 1536 [*STC* 5543a].

Colet, J., (translated by [T. Lupset]) *The Sermon of Doctor Colete, made to the Conuocation at Paulis*, London, 1530 [*STC* 5550], reprinted in J.H. Lupton, *A Life of John Colet, D.D.*, 1st edition, George Bell and Sons, London, 1887; 2nd edition, George Bell and Sons, London, 1909, pp. 293-304.

Colet, J., *The vij Petycions of the Pater Noster bu Jhon [sic] Collet, Deane of Powels*, T. Bethelet, London, [1531?] [*STC* 5550.5].

Dickens, A.G. and Carr, D. (eds.), *The Reformation in England to the Accession of Elizabeth I*, Documents of Modern History, Edward Arnold, London, 1967.

Dionysius Carthusianus, *Opera Minora*, I, Cologne, 1532.

Dugdale, W., *A History of St. Paul's Cathedral in London, from its Foundation Until these Times*, Thomas Warren, London, 1658.

Edgeworth, R., *Sermons Very Fruitfull, Godly and Learned by Roger Edgeworth: Preaching in the Reformation, c.1535-1553*, edited by J. Wilson, Boydell Press, Woodbridge, 1993.

Erasmus, D., *Christian Humanism and the Reformation: Selected Writings of Erasmus with The Life of Erasmus by Beatus Rhenanus*, edited and translated by J.C. Olin, 1st edition, Harper and Row, New York, 1965; 2nd edition, Fordham University Press, New York, 1987.

Erasmus, D., *Desiderius Erasmus Roterodamus: Ausgewählte Werke*, edited by H. Holborn and A. Holborn, Munich, 1933.

Erasmus, D., *Erasmi Opera Omnia*, edited by J. Clericus, III, Lugduni Batavorum, Amsterdam, The Netherlands, 10 volumes, 1703-6.

BIBLIOGRAPHY

Erasmus, D., *Opus Epistolarum Desiderii Erasmi Roterdami*, I-IV, edited by P.S. Allen and H.M. Allen, Oxford University Press, Oxford, 1906-22.

Erasmus, D., *Pilgrimages to Saint Mary of Walsingham and Saint Thomas of Canterbury, with the Colloquy on Rash Vows, and the Characters of Archbishop Warham and Dean Colet*, translated and edited by J.G. Nichols, London, 1849.

Erasmus, D., *The Colloquies of Erasmus*, translated by C.R. Thompson, University of Chicago Press, Chicago, 1965.

Erasmus, D., *The Collected Works of Erasmus*, I-VIII, translated and edited by R.A.B. Mynors and D.F.S. Thomson; annotated by P.G. Bietnholz, W.K. Ferguson and J.K. McConica, University of Toronto Press, Toronto, 1974-1988.

Erasmus, D., *The Lives of Jehan Vitrier, Warden of the Franciscan Convent at St. Omer, and John Colet, Dean of St. Paul's, London. Written in Latin, by Erasmus of Rotterdam, in a Letter to Justus Jonas*, translated with notes and appendices by J.H. Lupton, George Bell and Sons, London, 1883.

Erasmus, D., *The Poems of Erasmus*, ed. C. Reedijk, Leiden, Brill, The Netherlands, 1956.

Ferguson, W.K., 'An Unpublished Letter of John Colet', *The American Historical Review*, 34, 1934, pp. 696-9.

Fisher, J., *The English Works of John Fisher*, I, edited by J.E.B. Mayor, The Early English Text Society, 27, London, 1935.

Foxe, J., *Acts and Monuments of Matters Happening in the Church*, I-VIII, edited by J. Pratt, 1st edition, G. Seeley, London, 1853; 2nd edition, The Religious Tract Society, London, 1877.

Foxe, J., *Actes and Monuments of these Latter and Perillous Dayes, Touching Matters of the Church*, J. Daye, London, 1563 [*STC*, 11222].

Foxe, J., *John Foxe's Book of Martyrs 1583: Acts and Monuments of Matters Most Speciall and Memorable* [*STC* 11225]: Facsimile edition for C.D. R.O.M., edited by D.G. Newcombe and M. Pidd, Oxford University Press, Oxford, 2001.

Foxe, J., *The Eccesiasticall History, Conteynyng the Actes and Monumentes of Martyrs*, J. Daye, London, 1570 [*STC*, 11223].

Foxe, J., *The Second Volume of the Ecclesiasticall History, Contaynyng the Actes and Monumentes of Matyrs, with a generall discourse of these latter persecutions …*, J. Daye, London, 1576 [*STC*, 11224].

Gibbs, M. (ed.), *Early Charters of St. Paul's Cathedral*, Camden Society, 3rd Series, 58, Royal Historical Society, London, 1938.

Harding, T., *A Reioindre to M. Jewels Replie: By Perusing Whereof the Reader May See the Answers to Parte of his Chalenge Iustified*, Ex Officina Ioannis Foaleri, Antwerp, 1566 [*STC* 12769].

Hilton, W., *The Ladder of Perfection*, translated by L. Shirley-Price, Penguin, Harmondsworth, 1957.

John of Paris, *De Regia Potestate et Papali*, edited by F. Bleienstein, Ernst Klett Verlag, Stuttgart, 1969.

Kempis, Thomas à, *The Imitation of Christ*, translated by L. Shirley-Price, Penguin, Harmondsworth, 1952.

Latimer, H., *The Sermons of Hugh Latimer*, I, edited by G.E. Corrie, Parker Society, 33, Cambridge University Press, Cambridge, 1844.

Lefèvre d'Etaples, J., *Preface to His Commentaries on the Four Gospels* (Strasbourg, 1521), reprinted in J.C. Olin (ed.), *The Catholic Reformation: Savonarola to Ignatius Loyola: Reform in the Church, 1495-1540*, 1st edition, Harper and Row, New York, 1969, pp. 107-17.

Lefèvre d'Etaples, *The Prefatory Epistles of Jacques Lefèvre d'Etaples and Related Texts*, edited by E.F. Rice, Jr., Columbia University Press, New York, 1972.

Letters and Papers, Foreign and Domestic, of the Reign of Henry VIII, 1509-47, Preserved in the Public Record Office, The British Museum, and Elsewhere in England, Arranged and Catalogued by J.S. Brewer, M.A., Under the Direction of the Master of the Rolls, and with the sanction of Her Majesty's Secretaries of State, Volume I, Parts i and ii; Volume II, Parts i and ii, 1st edition, Longman and Co., London, 1862; 2nd edition, Longman, London, 1920.

Lupset, T., *An Exhortation to Yonge Men, Perswadinge Them to Walke in the Pathe Way That Leadeth to Honeste and Goodnes* [STC 16936], T. Berthelet, London, 1535.

Lupton, D., *The History of Protestant Divines*, N and J Oakes, London, 1637, republished by Jacobus Verheiden, Theatrum Orbis Terrarum, Amsterdam, 1979.

Luther, M., *The Babylonian Captivity of the Church* in A.R. Wentz (ed.), *Word and Sacrament, Luther's Works*, 37, Fortress Press, Philadelphia, New York State, 1961, pp. 115-204.

Luther, M., *Three Treatises*, edited by J.M. Jacobs, 1st edition, Fortress Press, Philadelphia, New York State, 1957; 2nd edition, Fortress Press, Philadelphia, New York State, 1966. [Contains the treatises *To the Christian Nobility of the German Nation, The Babylonian Captivity of the Church* and *The Freedom of a Christian*].

McGrath, A.E. (ed.), *The Christian Theology Reader*, Oxford University Press, Oxford, 1995.

Melton, W., *Sermo Exhortatorius Cancelarii Ebor[acensis]*, W. de Worde, London, c.1510 [STC 17806].

Mirk, J., *Instructions for Parish Priests by John Myrc*, edited by E. Peacock, The Early English Text Society, Extra Series, 31, London, 1902.

Mirk, J., *Mirk's Festial: A Collection of Homilies by Joannes Mirkus (John Mirk)*, edited by T. Erbe, The Early English Text Society, Extra Series, 46, London, 1905.

More, T., *A Dialogue Concerning Heresies* in T. More, *The Complete Works of Thomas More*, 6, edited by T.M.C. Lawler, G. Marc'hadour and R. Marius, Yale University Press, New Haven, Connecticut, and London, 1981.

BIBLIOGRAPHY

More, T., *The Apology*, reprinted in T. More, *The Complete Works of Thomas More*, 9, edited by J.B. Trapp, Yale University Press, New Haven, Connecticut, and London, 1979.

More, T., *The Correspondence of Sir Thomas More*, edited by E.F. Rogers, Princeton University Press, Princeton, New Jersey, 1947.

Parker, M., *De Antiquitate Britannicae Ecclesiae Cantuariensis, cum Archiepiscopis Euisdem*, John Daye, London, 1572 [STC 19292].

Pits. J., *Ioannis Pitsei, Angli S. Theologiae Doctoris, Liverduni in Lotharingia, Decani. Revelationum Historicarum de Rebus Anglicis Tomus Unus*, R. Thierry and S. Cramorsy, Paris, 1619.

Pseudo-Dionysius: The Complete Works, translated and edited by C. Luibheid, Paulist Press, New York, 1987.

Registrum Statutorum et Consuetudinum Ecclesiae Cathedralis Sancti Pauli Londinensis, edited by W.S. Simpson, London, 1873.

Revised Standard Version Interlinear Greek-English New Testament: The Nestle Greek Text with a Literal English Translation by A. Marshall, Macmillan, Basingstoke, 1968.

Richard of St. Victor, *The Twelve Patriarchs, The Mystical Ark, Book Three of the Trinity*, translated by G.A. Zinn, University of Toronto Press, Toronto, 1979.

Shillingford, J., *Letters and Papers of John Shillingford*, edited by S.A. Moore, Camden Society, New Series, 2, London, 1871.

Simpson, W.S., 'A Newly Discovered Manuscript Containing Statutes Compiled by Dean Colet for the Government of Chantry Priests and Other Clergy in St. Paul's Cathedral', *Archaeologia*, 52, 1890, pp. 145-74.

Simpson, W.S., 'The Charter and Statutes of the College of Minor Canons in St. Paul's Cathedral, London', *Archaeologia*, 43, 1871, pp. 165-200.

St. Augustine, *City of God*, translated by H. Bettenson, Penguin, Harmondsworth, 1972.

St. Augustine, *Confessions*, translated by R.S. Pine-Coffin, Penguin, Harmondsworth, 1961.

St. Bonaventure, *The Journey of the Mind to God*, translated by P. Boehner and edited by S.F. Brown, Hackett, Indianapolis, Indiana, 1993.

Swynnerton, T., *A Reformation Rhetoric: Thomas Swynnerton's The Tropes and Figures of Scripture*, Renaissance Texts from Manuscript, I, edited by R. Rex, Cambridge University Press, Cambridge, 1999.

Synodalia: A Collection of Articles of Religion, Canons, and Proceedings of Convocations in the Province of Canterbury, from the Year 1547 to the Year 1717, edited by E. Cardwell, I, Oxford University Press, Oxford, 1842.

Tanner, N.P. (ed.), *Kent Heresy Proceedings, 1511-12*, Kent Archaeological Society, 26, Maidstone, 1997.

The Doctrinal of Sapyence, W. Caxton, London, 1489 [*STC* 21431].

Tyndale, W., *An Answer to Sir Thomas More's Dialogue: The Supper of the Lord after the True Meaning of John VI and 1 Corinthians XI; and W. Tracy's Testament Expounded*, edited by H. Walter, Parker Society, 38, Cambridge, 1850.

Vergil, P., *Anglia Historia of Polydore Vergil, A.D. 1485-1537*, edited by D. Hay, Camden Society, 3rd Series, 74, London, 1950.

Wharton, H., *Historia de Episcopis et Decanis Londinensibus et Assavensibus*, London, 1695.

Wood, A., *Athenae Oxonienses*, edited by PP. Bliss, 4 volumes, F.C. and J Rivington, London, 1813-1820.

Wycliffe, J., *Iohannes Wyclif Opera Minora*, edited by I. Loserth, Wyclif Society, London, 1913.

SECONDARY SOURCES

Abray, L.J., *The People's Reformation: Magistrates, Clergy, and Commons in Strasbourg, 1500-1598*, Cornell University Press, Ithaca, New York, 1985.

Adams, R.PP., *The Better Part of Valour: More, Erasmus, Colet, and Vives on Humanism, War, and Peace, 1496-1535*, University of Washington Press, Seattle, Washington State, 1962.

Alden, J.J.W., 'An Examination of the Thought of John Colet (1467?-1519): A Catholic Humanist Reformer at the Eve of the Protestant Reformation, Unpublished PhD Thesis, Yale University, 1969.

Allen, P.S., 'Dean Colet and Archbishop Warham', *The English Historical Review*, 17, 1902, pp. 303-6.

Allen, P.S., *The Age of Erasmus*, Clarendon Press, Oxford, 1914.

Amos, N. Scott, 'New Learning, Old Theology: Renaissance Biblical Humanism, Scripture, and the Question of Theological Method', *Renaissance Studies*, 17, 2003, pp. 47-54.

Arnold, J., 'Colet, Wolsey and the Poltics of Reform: St. Paul's Cathedral in 1518', *The English Historical Review*, 121, September, 2006.

Arnold, J., 'In Search of Perfection: Ecclesiology in the Life and Works of John Colet, Dean of St. Paul's Cathedral, 1505-19', Unpublished Ph.D. Thesis, King's College, London University, 2004.

Arnold, J., 'John Colet and a Lost Manuscript of 1506', *History*, 89, 2004, pp. 174-92.

Arnold, J., 'John Colet, Preaching and Reform at St. Paul's Cathedral, 1505-19', *Historical Research*, 76, 2003, pp. 450-68.

BIBLIOGRAPHY

A Short-Title Catalogue of Books Printed in England, Scotland and Ireland and of English Books Printed Abroad, 1475-1640, first compiled in 1926 by A.W. Pollard and G.R. Redgrave, 2nd edition revised and enlarged by W.A. Jackson, 1976-86, and F.S. Ferguson, completed by K.F. Pantzer, The Bibliographical Society, I: A-H; II: I-Z; III: printers and publishers index, indices and appendices, Bibliographical Society, London, 1976-91.

Aston, M., *Lollards and Reformers: Images and Literacy in Late Medieval Religion*, Hambledon Press, London, 1984.

Baker, D., 'Old Wine in New Bottles: Attitudes to Reform in Fifteenth-Century England' in D. Baker (ed.), *Renaissance and Renewal in Christian History: Papers Read at the Fifteenth Summer Meeting and the Sixteenth Winter Meeting of the Ecclesiastical History Society*, Blackwell, Oxford, 1977, pp. 193-212.

Beaven, A.B., *The Aldermen of the City of London, Temp. Henry III-1908*, 2 Volumes, London: Eden Fisher, 1908-1913.

Barron, C.M., *London in the Later Middle Ages: Government and People, 1200-1500*, Oxford University Press, Oxford, 2004.

Barron, C.M., 'The Expansion of Education in Fifteenth-Century London' in J. Blair and B. Golding (eds.), *The Cloister and the World: Essays in Medieval History in Honour of Barbara Harvey*, Clarendon Press, Oxford, 1996, pp. 219-45.

Barron, C.M., 'The Parish Fraternities of Medieval London' in C.M. Barron and C. Harper-Bill (eds.), *The Church in Pre-Reformation Society: Essays in Honour of F.R.H. Du Boulay*, Boydell Press, Woodbridge, 1985, pp. 13-37.

Barron, C.M. and Harper-Bill, C. (eds.), *The Church in Pre-Reformation Society: Essays in Honour of F.R.H. Du Boulay*, Boydell Press, Woodbridge, 1985.

Barron, C.M. and Rousseau, M., 'Cathedral, City and State, 1300-1540' in D. Keene, A. Burns and A. Saint (eds.), *St. Paul's: The Cathedral Church of London, 604-2004*, Yale University Press, New Haven, Connecticut, and London, 2004, pp. 33-44.

Baskerville, G., 'Elections to Convocation in the Diocese of Gloucester under Bishop Hooper', *The English Historical Review*, 44 (1929) pp. 1-32.

Bedouelle, G., 'Jacques Lefèvre d'Etaples (c.1460-1536)' in C. Lindberg (ed.), *The Reformation Theologians: An Introduction to Theology in the Early Modern Period*, Blackwell, Oxford, 2002, pp. 19-33.

Black, A., *Council and Commune: The Conciliar Movement and the Fifteenth-Century Heritage*, Burns and Oates, London, 1979.

Blench, J.W., *Preaching in England in the Late Fifteenth and Sixteenth Centuries: A Study of English Sermons, 1450-c.1600*, Blackwell, Oxford, 1964.

Boulding, C., 'Jacobus Faber Stapulensis, c.1460-1536, Forerunner of Vatican II' in A. Bellenger (ed.), *Opening the Scrolls: Essays in Catholic History in Honour of Godfrey Anstruther*, Downside Abbey, Stratton on the Fosse, Somerset, 1987, pp. 27-49.

Bowker, M., *The Henrician Reformation: The Diocese of Lincoln under John Longland, 1521-1547*, Cambridge University Press, Cambridge, 1981.

Boyle, L., 'The *Oculus Sacerdotis* and Some Other Works of William of Pagula', *Transactions of the Royal Historical Society*, 5th Series, 5, 1955, pp. 81-110.

Bradshaw, B., 'Bishop John Fisher, 1469-1535: The Man and His Work' in B. Bradshaw and E. Duffy (eds.), *Humanism, Reform and the Reformation: The Career of Bishop John Fisher*, Cambridge University Press, Cambridge, 1989, pp. 1-24.

Bridbury, A.R., 'English Provincial Towns in the Later Middle Ages', *The Economic History Review*, 2nd Series, 34, 1981, pp. 1-24.

Brigden, S., *London and the Reformation*, Clarendon Press, Oxford, 1989.

Brigden, S., *New Worlds, Lost Worlds: The Rule of the Tudors, 1485-1603*, Allen Lane, London, 2000.

Briquet, C.M., *Les Filigranes: Dictionaire Historique des Marques du Papier des leur Apparition vers 1282 Jusqu'en 1600 avec 39 Figures dans le Texte et 16,112 Fac-similes de Filigranes*. 4 Volumes, 1st edition, A, Picard et fils; A, Jullien, Geneva, 1907; 2nd edition, Hiersemann, Leipzig, 1923.

Brown, J., 'John Colet and the Preachers of the Reformation' in J. Brown (ed.), *Puritan Preaching in England: A Study of Past and Present*, Hodder and Stoughton, London and New York, 1900, pp. 35-63.

Brown, K., 'Wolsey and Ecclesiastical Order: The Case of the Franciscan Observants' in S.J. Gunn and PP. G. Lindley (eds.), *Cardinal Wolsey: Church, State and Art*, Cambridge University Press, Cambridge, 1991, pp. 219-38.

Burgess, C., "For the Increase of Divine Service': Chantries in the Parish in Late Medieval Bristol', *The Journal of Ecclesiastical History*, 36, 1985, pp. 46-65.

Burgess, C., 'Late Medieval Wills and Pious Convention: Testamentary Evidence Reconsidered' in M. Hicks (ed.), *Profit, Piety and the Professions in Late Medieval England*, Sutton, Gloucester, 1990, pp. 14-33.

Burgess, C. and Kümin, B., 'Penitential Bequests and Parish Regimes in Late Medieval England', *The Journal of Ecclesiastical History*, 44, 1993, pp. 610-30.

Burns, A., 'From 1830 to the Present' in D. Keene, A. Burns and A. Saint (eds.), *St. Paul's: The Cathedral Church of London, 604-2004*, Yale University Press, New Haven, Connecticut, and London, 2004, pp. 84-110.

Campbell, W.E., 'John Colet, Dean of St. Paul's', *The Dublin Review*, 218, 1946, pp. 97-107.

Carpenter, E.F., 'Reformation 1485-1660' in W.R. Matthews and W.M. Atkins (eds.), *A History of St. Paul's Cathedral and the Men Associated With It*, J. Baker, London, 1957, pp. 100-71.

Carrington, J.L., 'Desiderius Erasmus (1460-1536)' in C. Lindberg (ed.), *The Reformation Theologians: An Introduction to Theology in the Early Modern Period*, Blackwell, Oxford, 2002, pp. 34-48.

Carroll, C., 'Humanism and English Literature in the Fifteenth and Sixteenth Centuries' in J. Kraye (ed.), *The Cambridge Companion to Renaissance Humanism*, Cambridge University Press, Cambridge, 1996, pp. 246-68.

Charlton, K., *Education in Renaissance England*, Routledge and Kegan Paul, London and University of Toronto Press, 1965

Chrisman, M.U., *Lay Culture, Learned Culture: Books and Social Change in Strasbourg, 1480-1599*, Yale University Press, New Haven, Connecticut, and London, 1982.

Clebsch, W.A., *England's Earliest Protestants, 1520-1535*, Yale University Press, New Haven, Connecticut, 1964.

Clebsch, W.A., 'John Colet and the Reformation', *The Anglican Theological Review*, 37, 1955, pp. 167-77.

Cooper, T.N., 'Children, the Liturgy and the Reformation: The Evidence of the Lichfield Cathedral Choristers' in D. Wood (ed.), *Church and Childhood*, Studies in Church History, 31, Blackwell, Oxford, 1994, pp. 261-74.

Cooper, W.R., 'Richard Hunne', *Reformation*, 1, 1996, pp. 221-51.

Cornwall, J., 'English Country Towns in the Fifteen Twenties', *The Economic History Review*, 2nd Series, 15, 1962, pp. 54-69.

Cross, C., *Church and People: England 1450-1660*, 1st edition, Fontana, London, 1976; 2nd edition, Blackwell, Oxford, 1999.

Cross, F.L. and Livingstone E.A. (eds.), *The Oxford Dictionary of the Christian Church*, 1st edition, Oxford University Press, Oxford, 1957; 3rd edition, Oxford University Press, Oxford, 1997.

Daniell, D., *William Tyndale: A Biography*, Yale University Press, New Haven, Connecticut, and London, 1994.

Dark, S., *Five Deans: John Colet, John Donne, Jonathan Swift, Arthur Penrhyn Stanley, William Ralph Inge*, Jonathan Cape, London 1928.

Davis, J.F., *Heresy and Reformation in the South-East of England, 1520-1559*, Royal Historical Society, London, 1983.

Davis, V., 'The Lesser Clergy in the Later Middle Ages' in D. Keene, A. Burns and A. Saint (eds.), *St. Paul's: The Cathedral Church of London*, Yale University Press, New Haven, Connecticut, and London, 2004, pp. 157-61.

Dawley, P.M., *John Whitgift and the Reformation*, Adam and Charles Black, London, 1955.

Dickens, A.G., *The English Reformation*, 1st edition, B.T. Batsford, London, 1964; 2nd edition, Batsford, London, 1989.

Dickens, A.G. and Jones, W.R.D., *Erasmus the Reformer*, Methuen, London, 1994.

Dobson, R.B., 'Cathedral Chapter and Cathedral Cities: York, Durham and Carlisle in the Fifteenth Century', *Northern History*, 19, 1983, pp. 15-44.

Dobson, R.B., 'The Later Middle Ages, 1215-1500' in G.E. Aylmer and R. Cant (eds.), *A History of York Minster*, Clarendon Press, Oxford, 1977, pp. 44-111.

Dobson, R.B., 'The Residentiary Canons of York in the Fifteenth Century', *The Journal of Ecclesiastical History*, 30, 1979, pp. 145-74.

Dobson, R.B., 'Urban Decline in Late Medieval England', *Transactions of the Royal Historical Society*, 5th Series, 27, 1977, pp. 1-22.

Douglass, E.J.D., *Justification in Late Medieval Preaching: A Study of John Geiler of Keisersberg*, Leiden, Brill, The Netherlands, 1966.

Dowling, M., *Humanism in the Age of Henry VIII*, Croom Helm, London, 1986.

Dowling, M., 'John Fisher and the Preaching Ministry', *Archiv für Reformationsgeschichte*, 82, 1991, pp. 287-309.

Dowling, M., *Fisher of Men: A Life of John Fisher, 1469-1535*, Macmillan, Basingstoke, 1999.

Duffy, E., 'Continuity and Divergence in Tudor Religion' in R.N. Swanson (ed.), *Unity and Diversity in the Church*, Studies in Church History, 32, Blackwell, Oxford, 1996, pp. 171-205.

Duffy, E., *The Stripping of the Altars: Traditional Religion in England, c.1400-c.1580*, Yale University Press, New Haven, Connecticut, and London, 1992.

Duhamel, P.A., 'The Oxford Lectures of John Colet: An Essay in Defining the English Renaissance', *The Journal of the History of Ideas*, 14, 1953, pp. 493-510.

Dunham, W.H. Jr., 'The Members of Henry VIII's Whole Council, 1509-1527', *The English Historical Review*, 59, 1944, pp. 187-210.

Dyer, C., *Standards of Living in the Later Middle Ages: Social Change in England, c.1200-1520*, Cambridge University Press, Cambridge, 1989.

Edwards, K., *The English Secular Cathedral in the Middle Ages*, 1st edition, Manchester University Press, 1949; 2nd edition, 1967.

Elton, G.R., 'A Review of J.K. McConica, *English Humanists and Reformation Politics Under Henry VIII and Edward VI*, 1st edition, Clarendon Press, Oxford, 1965; 2nd edition, Oxford, 1967', *The Historical Journal*, 10, 1967, pp. 137-8.

Elton, G.R., *Reform and Reformation: England, 1509-1558*, Edward Arnold, London, 1977.

Emden, A.B., *A Biographical Register of the University of Oxford to A.D. 1500*, I, Clarendon Press, Oxford, 1957.

Evans, G.R., 'Anselm of Canterbury' in G.R. Evans (ed.), *The Medieval Theologians: An Introduction to Theology in the Medieval Period*, Blackwell, Oxford, 2001, pp. 94-101.

Faith, R., 'Estates and Income, 1066-1540' in D. Keene, A. Burns and A. Saint (eds.), *St. Paul's: The Cathedral Church of London, 604-2004*, Yale University Press, New Haven, Connecticut, and London, 2004, pp. 143-50.

Fellowes, E.H., *The Vicars or Minor Canons of His Majesty's Free Chapel of St. George*, Oxley, Windsor, 1945.

Fines, J., 'Heresy Trials in the Diocese of Coventry and Lichfield, 1511-12', *The Journal of Ecclesiastical History*, 14, 1963, pp. 160-74.

Fines, J., 'The Post-Mortem Condemnation for Heresy of Richard Hunne', *The English Historical Review*, 78, 1963, pp. 523-31.

Flannery, K.L. SJ, 'Plato and Platonism' in A. Hastings, A. Mason and H. Pyper (eds.), *The Oxford Companion to Christian Thought: Intellectual, Spiritual and Moral Horizons of Christianity*, Oxford University Press, Oxford, 2000, pp. 542-4.

Fletcher, J.M., 'The Teaching of Arts in Oxford, 1400-1520', *Paedagogica Historica*, 7, 1967, p. 440.

Forrester, D., 'Justice' in A. Hastings, A. Mason and H. Pyper (eds.), *The Oxford Companion to Christian Thought: Intellectual, Spiritual and Moral Horizons of Christianity*, Oxford University Press, Oxford, 2000, pp. 360-2.

Fox, A., 'English Humanism and the Body Politic' in A. Fox and J. Guy, *Reassessing the Henrician Age: Humanism, Politics and Reform, 1500-1550*, Blackwell, Oxford, 1986, pp. 34-51.

Fox, A., 'Facts and Fallacies: Interpreting English Humanism' in A. Fox and J. Guy, *Reassessing the Henrician Age: Humanism, Politics and Reform, 1500-1550*, Blackwell, Oxford, 1986, pp. 9-25.

Froehlich, K., 'Pseudo-Dionysius and the Reformation of the Sixteenth Century' in *Pseudo-Dionysius: The Complete Works*, translated and edited by C. Luibheid, Paulist Press, New York, 1987, pp. 33-46.

Fryde, E.B., Greenway, D.E., Porter, S., and Roy, I. (eds.), *The Handbook of British Chronology*, Royal Historical Society, 1st edition, London, 1946; 3rd edition, London, 1986.

Fuller, A.R.B., 'The Minor Corporations of the Secular Cathedrals of the Province of Canterbury Excluding the Welsh Sees Between the Thirteenth-Century and 1585 with Special Reference to the Minor Canons of St. Paul's Cathedral from their Origin in the Fourteenth Century to the Visitation of Bishop Gibson in 1724', Unpublished M.A. Thesis, London University, 1947.

Gear, N., 'The Chantries of St. Paul's Cathedral', Unpublished M.A. Thesis, London University, 1996.

Gleason, J.B., *John Colet*, University of California Press, Berkeley, California, 1989.

Gleason, J.B., 'The Birth Dates of John Colet and Erasmus of Rotterdam: Fresh Documentary Evidence', *Renaissance Quarterly*, 32, 1979, pp. 73-6.

Godfrey, W.R., 'John Colet of Cambridge', *Archiv für Reformationsgeschichte*, 65, 1974, pp. 6-17.

Gordon, B., 'Conciliarism in Late Medieval Europe' in A. Pettegree (ed.), *The Reformation World*, Routledge, London, 2000, pp. 31-50.

Gransden, A., 'The History of Wells Cathedral, c.1090-1547' in L.S. Colchester (ed.), *Wells Cathedral: A History*, Open Books, Shepton Mallet, 1982, pp. 24-51.

Grant, R.M., 'One Hundred and Fifty-Three Large Fish (John 21:11)', *The Harvard Theological Review*, 42, 1949, pp. 273-5.

Graves, M.A.R., *Early Tudor Parliaments, 1485-1558*, Longman, London, 1990.

Greenway, D.E., 'Historical Writing at St. Paul's' in D. Keene, A. Burns and A. Saint (eds.), *St. Paul's: The Cathedral Church of London, 604-2004*, Yale University Press, New Haven, Connecticut, and London, 2004, pp. 151-6.

Gunn, S.J., *Early Tudor Government, 1485-1558*, Palgrave Macmillan, Basingstoke, 1995.

Guy, J.A., 'Henry VIII and the Praemunire Manoeuvres of 1530-1531', *The English Historical Review*, 97, 1982, pp. 497-507.

Guy, J.A., 'The Privy Council: Revolution or Evolution?' in C. Coleman and D. Starkey (eds.), *Revolution Reassessed: Revisions in the History of Tudor Government and Administration*, Clarendon Press, Oxford, 1986, pp. 59-85.

Guy, J.A., *The Cardinal's Court: The Impact of Thomas Wolsey in Star Chamber*, Harvester Press, Hassocks, Sussex, 1977.

Guy, J.A., *Politics, Law and Counsel in Tudor and Early Stuart England*, Ashgate, Aldershot, 2000.

Gwyn, P., *The King's Cardinal: The Rise and Fall of Thomas Wolsey*, Barrie and Jenkins, London, 1990.

Haigh, C. 'Anticlericalism and the English Reformation', *History*, 68, 1983, pp. 391-407, reprinted in C. Haigh (ed.), *The English Reformation Revised*, Cambridge University Press, Cambridge, 1987, pp. 56-74.

Haigh, C., *English Reformations: Religion, Politics and Society under the Tudors*, Clarendon, Oxford, 1993.

Hamilton, A., 'Humanists and the Bible' in J. Kraye (ed.), *The Cambridge Companion to Renaissance Humanism*, Cambridge University Press, Cambridge, 1996, pp. 100-17.

Hankey, W.J., 'Augustinian Immediacy and Dionysian Mediation in John Colet, Edmund Spenser, Richard Hooker and the Cardinal de Bérulle' in D. de Courcelles (ed.), *Augustinas in Der Neuzeit: Colloque de la Herzog August Bibliotek de Wolfenbüttel, 14-17 Octobre, 1996*, Brepols, Paris, 1998, pp. 125-60.

Harbison, E.H., *The Christian Scholar in the Age of Reformation*, Charles Scribner and Sons, New York, 1956.

Harper-Bill, C., 'Archbishop John Morton and the Province of Canterbury, 1486-1500', *The Journal of Ecclesiastical History*, 29, 1978, pp. 1-21.

Harper-Bill, C., 'Dean Colet's Convocation Sermon and the Pre-Reformation Church in England', *History*, 73, 1988, pp. 191-210.

Harper-Bill, C., 'Monastic Apostasy in Late Medieval England', *The Journal of Ecclesiastical History*, 32, 1981, pp. 1-18.

Harper-Bill, C., *Religious Belief and Ecclesiastical Careers in Late Medieval England*, Boydell Press, Woodbridge, 1991.

Harper-Bill, C., *The Pre-Reformation Church in England, 1400-1530*, Boydell Press, Woodbridge, 1989.

Harrison, F., *Life in a Medieval College: The Story of the Vicars-Choral of York Minster*, John Murray, London, 1952.

Harvey, P. and Drabble, M. (eds.), *The Oxford Companion to English Literature*, (1st edition, Clarendon, Oxford, 1932; 5th edition, Oxford University Press, Oxford, 1987.

Hay, D., 'Scholarship, Religion and the Church' in K. Robbins (ed.), *Religion and Humanism*, Studies in Church History, 17, Blackwell, Oxford, 1981, pp. 1-18.

Heal, F., *Hospitality in Early Modern England*, Clarendon Press, Oxford, 1990.

Heal, F., *Of Prelates and Princes: A Study of the Economic and Social Position of the Tudor Episcopate*, Cambridge University Press, Cambridge, 1980.

Heath, P., *English Parish Clergy on the Eve of the Reformation*, Cambridge University Press, Cambridge, 1969.

Hellinga, L., 'Importation of Books Printed on the Continent into England and Scotland before *c*.1520' in S. Hindman (ed.), *Printing the Written Word: The Social History of Books, c.1450-1520*, Cornell University Press, Ithaca, New York State, 1991, pp. 205-24.

Hennessy, G. (ed.), *Novum Repertorium Ecclesiasticum Parochiale Londinense, or London Diocesan Clergy Succession from the Earliest Time to the Year 1898*, Swan Sonnenschein & Co., London, 1898.

Herbert, W., *The History of the Twelve Great Livery Companies of London*, 2 Volumes, David and Charles, Newton Abbot, 1834

Hook, W.F., *The Lives of the Archbishops of Canterbury*, VI, Richard Bentley, London, 1868.

Hope, A., 'Lollardy: The Stone the Builders Rejected?' in P. Lake and M. Dowling (eds.), *Protestantism and the National Church in Sixteenth Century England*, Croom Helm, London, 1987, pp. 1-35.

Hoskins, W.G., *The Age of Plunder: King Henry's England, 1500-1547*, Longman, London, 1976.

Hudson, A., *The Premature Reformation: Wycliffite Texts and Lollard History*, Clarendon Press, Oxford, 1988.

Huizinga, J., *The Waning of the Middle Ages: A Study of the Forms of Life, Thought and Art in France and the Netherlands in the XIVth and XVth Centuries*, Arnold, London, 1924.

Hunt, E.W., *Dean Colet and His Theology*, SPCK, London, 1956.

Hutton, R., 'Revisionism in Britain' in M. Bentley (ed.), *A Companion to Historiography*, Routledge, London, 1997, pp. 377-91.

Hyma, A., 'Erasmus and the Oxford Reformers (1503-1519)', *Nederlands Archief voor Kerkgeschiedenis*, 38, 1951, pp. 65-85.

Imray, J.M., *The Charity of Richard Whittington: A History of the Trust Administered by the Mercers' Company, 1424-1966*, Athlone, London, 1968.

Jarrott, C.A.L., 'Erasmus's Annotations and Colet's Commentaries on Paul: A Comparison of Some Theological Themes' in R.L. De Molen (ed.), *Essays on the Works of Erasmus*, Yale University Press, New Haven, Connecticut, 1978, pp. 125-44.

Jayne, S., *John Colet and Marsilio Ficino*, Oxford University Press, Oxford, 1963.

Jones, G.L., *The Discovery of Hebrew in Tudor England: A Third Language*, Manchester University Press, Manchester, 1983.

Jones, M.K. and Underwood, M.G., *The King's Mother: Lady Margaret Beaufort, Countess of Richmond and Derby*, Cambridge University Press, Cambridge, 1992.

Joyce, J.W., *England's Sacred Synods*, Rivingtons, London, 1855.

Kaufman, P.I., *Augustinian Piety and Catholic Reform: Augustine, Colet, and Erasmus*, Mercer University Press, Macon, Georgia, 1982.

Kaufman, P.I., 'Humanist Spirituality and Ecclesial Reaction: Thomas More's *Monstra*', *Church History*, 56, 1987, pp. 25-38.

Kaufman, P.I., 'John Colet and Erasmus's *Enchiridion*', *Church History*, 46, 1977, pp. 296-312.

Kaufman, P.I., 'John Colet's *Opus de Sacramentis* and Clerical Anticlericalism: The Limitations of 'Ordinary Wayes'', *The Journal of British Studies*, 22, 1982, pp. 1-22.

Kaufman, P.I., *The 'Polytyque Churche': Religion and Early Tudor Political Culture, 1485-1516*, Mercer University Press, Macon, Georgia, 1986.

Kelly, M.J., 'Canterbury Jurisdiction and Influence during the Episcopate of William Warham, 1503-1532', Unpublished Ph.D. Thesis, Cambridge University, 1963.

Kempshall, M.S., 'Ecclesiology and Politics' in G.R. Evans (ed.), *The Medieval Theologians: An Introduction to the Theology of the Medieval Period*, Blackwell, Oxford, 2001, pp. 303-33.

Kermode, J.I., 'Urban Decline? The Flight from Office in Late Medieval York', *The Economic History Review*, 2nd Series, 34, 1982, pp. 179-98.

Kettle, A.J, 'City and Close: Lichfield in the Century Before the Reformation' in C.M Barron and C. Harper-Bill (eds.), *The Church in Pre-Reformation Society: Essays in Honour of F.R.H. Du Boulay*, Boydell Press, Woodbridge, 1985, pp. 158-70.

Kitching, C., 'The Prerogative Court of Canterbury from Warham to Whitgift' in F. Heal and R. O'Day (eds.), *Continuity and Change: Personnel and Administration of the Church in England, 1500-1642*, Leicester University Press, Leicester, 1976, pp. 191-214.

Kleineke, H. and Hovland, S., 'The Household and Daily Life of the Dean in the Fifteenth Century' in D. Keene, A. Burns and A. Saint (eds.), *St. Paul's: The Cathedral Church of London, 604-2004*, Yale University Press, New Haven, Connecticut, and London, 2004, pp. 167-8.

Knight, S., *The Life of Dr. John Colet, Dean of St. Paul's, in the Reigns of K. Henry VII and K. Henry VIII and Founder of St. Paul's School: With an Appendix Containing Some Account of the Masters and More Eminent Scholars of that Foundation, and Several Original Papers Relating to the Said Life*, 1st edition, J. Downing, London, 1724; 2nd edition, Clarendon, Oxford, 1823.

Kreider, A., *English Chantries: The Road to Dissolution*, Harvard University Press, Cambridge, Massachusetts, and London, 1979.

Kümin, B., 'Voluntary Religion and Reformation Change in Eight Urban Parishes' in P. Collinson and J. Craig (eds.), *The Reformation in English Towns, 1500-1640*, Palgrave Macmillan, Basingstoke, 1998, pp. 175-89.

Lahey, S., 'Wyclif and Lollardy' in G.R. Evans (ed.), *The Medieval Theologians: An Introduction to Theology in the Medieval Period*, Blackwell, Oxford, 2001, pp. 334-56.

Lander, J.R., *Crown and Nobility, 1450-1509*, Edward Arnold, London, 1976.

Lander, S., 'Church Courts and the Reformation in the Diocese of Chichester, 1500-58' in F. Heal and R. O'Day (eds.), *Continuity and Change: Personnel and Administration of the Church in England, 1500-1642*, Leicester University Press, Leicester, 1976, pp. 215-237, reprinted in C. Haigh (ed.), *The English Reformation Revised*, Cambridge University Press, Cambridge, 1987, pp. 34-55.

Leach, A.F., 'St. Paul's School before Colet', *Archaeologia*, 62, I, 1910, pp. 207-20.

Leclercq, J., 'The Influence and Non-Influence of Dionysius in the Western Middle Ages' in *Pseudo-Dionysius: The Complete Works*, translated and edited by C. Luibheid, Paulist Press, New York, 1987, pp. 25-32.

Lee, S., 'John Colet', in L. Stephens, (ed.), *The Dictionary of National Biography*, XI, Spottiswoode & Co., London, 1887, pp. 321-8.

Lehmberg, S.E., 'The Reformation of Choirs: Cathedral Musical Establishments in Tudor England' in D.J. Guth and J.W. McKenna (eds.), *Tudor Rule and Revolution: Essays for G.R. Elton from his American Friends*, Cambridge University Press, Cambridge, 1982, pp. 45-69.

Lehmberg, S.E., *The Reformation of Cathedrals: Cathedrals in English Society, 1486-1603*, University of Princeton Press, Princeton, New Jersey, 1988.

Le Neve, J., *Fasti Ecclesiae Anglicanae, 1300-1541, III: Salisbury Diocese*, edited by J.M. Horn, Institute of Historical Research, London, 1962.

Le Neve, J., *Fasti Ecclesiae Anglicanae, 1300-1541, V: St. Paul's, London*, edited by J.M. Horn, Institute of Historical Research, London, 1963.

Le Neve, J., *Fasti Ecclesiae Anglicanae, 1300-1541, VI: Northern Province*, edited by B. Jones, Institute of Historical Research, London, 1963.

Lepine, D., *A Brotherhood of Canons Serving God: English Secular Cathedrals in the Later Middle Ages*, Boydell Press, Woodbridge, 1995.

Livingstone, E.A. (ed.), *The Concise Dictionary of the Christian Church*, Oxford University Press, Oxford, 1977.

Louth, A., *Denys the Areopagite*, Geoffrey Chapman, London, 1989.

Louth, A., *The Origins of the Christian Mystical Tradition*, Clarendon Press, Oxford, 1981.

Lupton, J.H., *A Life of John Colet, D.D.*, 1st edition, George Bell and Sons, London, 1887; 2nd edition, George Bell, London, 1909.

Lupton, J.H., *The Influence of Dean Colet upon the Reformation of the English Church*, George Bell, London, 1893.

MacCulloch, D., *Reformation: Europe's House Divided, 1490-1700*, Allen Lane, London, 2003.

Mackenzie, M.L., *Dame Christian Colet: Her Life and Family*, Privately Printed, Cambridge, 1923.

Mackie, J.D., *The Early Tudors, 1485-1558*, Allen Lane, London, 1976.

Mann, N., 'The Origins of Humanism' in J. Kraye (ed.), *The Cambridge Companion to Renaissance Humanism*, Cambridge University Press, Cambridge, 1996, pp. 1-19.

Mansfield, B., *Phoenix of His Age: Interpretations of Erasmus, c.1550-1750*, University of Toronto Press, Toronto, 1979.

Marriott, J.A.R., *The Life of John Colet*, Methuen, London, 1933.

Marius, R., *Thomas More: A Biography*, Knopf, New York, 1985.

Marshall, PP., *Reformation England, 1480-1642*, Arnold, London, 2003.

Marshall, PP., *The Catholic Priesthood and the English Reformation*, Clarendon, Oxford, 1994.

McConica, J.K., *English Humanists and Reformation Politics Under Henry VIII and Edward VI*, 1st edition, Clarendon Press, Oxford, 1965; 2nd edition, 1967.

McDonnell, M., *A History of St. Paul's School*, Chapman and Hall, London, 1909.

McDonnell, M., *The Annals of St. Paul's School*, Privately printed, London, 1959.

McGinn, B., 'Love, Knowledge, and Mystical Union in Western Christianity: Twelfth to Sixteenth Centuries', *Church History*, 56, 1987, pp. 7-24.

McNair, PP. M.J., 'The Reformation of the Sixteenth Century in Renaissance Italy' in K. Robbins (ed.), *Religion and Humanism*, Studies in Church History, 17, Blackwell, Oxford, 1981, pp. 149-66.

Meyer, C.S., 'John Colet's Significance for the English Reformation', *Concordia Theological Monthly*, 34, 1963, pp. 410-19.

Miles, L., 'Protestant Colet and Catholic More', *The Anglican Theological Review*, 33, 1951, pp. 29-42.

Miles, L., *John Colet and the Platonic Tradition*, Allen and Unwin, London, 1962.

Miles, J., 'Platonism and Christian Doctrine: The Revival of Interest in John Colet', *Philosophical Forum*, 21, 1964, pp. 87-103.

Milman, H.H., *The Annals of St. Paul's Cathedral*, 1st edition, John Murray, London 1868; 2nd edition, Murray, London, 1869.

Milsom, S.F.C., 'Richard Hunne's 'Praemunire'', *The English Historical Review*, 76, 1961, pp. 80-82.

Nauert, C.G., 'Humanism as Method: Roots of Conflict with the Scholastics', *The Sixteenth Century Journal*, 29, 1998, pp. 427-38.

New, E.A., 'Fraternities: A Case Study of the Jesus Guild' in D. Keene, A. Burns and A. Saint (eds.), *St. Paul's: The Cathedral Church of London, 604-2004*, Yale University Press, New Haven, Connecticut, and London, 2004, pp. 162-3.

New, E.A., 'The Cult of the Holy Name of Jesus, with Special Reference to the Fraternity in St. Paul's Cathedral, London, c.1450-1558', Unpublished Ph.D. Thesis, University of London, 1999.

Oakley, F., 'Almain and Major: Conciliar Theory on the Eve of the Reformation', *The American Historical Review*, 70, 1965, pp. 673-690.

Oakley, F., 'Conciliarism in the Sixteenth Century: Jacques Almain Again', *Archiv für Reformationsgeschichte*, 68, 1977, pp. 111-32.

Oakley, F., *Natural Law, Conciliarism and Consent in the Middle Ages: Studies in Ecclesiastical And Intellectual History*, Variorum Reprints, London, 1984.

Oakley, F., *The Conciliarist Tradition: Constitutionalism in the Catholic Church, 1300-1870*, Oxford University Press, Oxford, 2003.

Oberman, H.A., *Forerunners of the Reformation: The Shape of Late Medieval Thought*, Lutterworth Press, London, 1967.

Oberman, H.A., *Masters of the Reformation: The Emergence of a New Intellectual Climate in Europe*, translated by D. Martin, Tübingen, 1977; 1st British edition, Cambridge University Press, Cambridge, 1981.

Ogle, A., *The Tragedy of Lollards' Tower*, Pen-in-Hand, London, 1949.

Olin, J.C., 'Introduction' in J.C. Olin (ed.), *The Catholic Reformation: Savonarola to Ignatius Loyola: Reform in the Church, 1495-1540*, 1st edition, Westminster, Maryland, 1969; 2nd edition, Harper and Row, London, 1969, pp. i-xxiii.

Olin, J.C., *Six Essays on Erasmus and a Translation of Erasmus' Letter to Corondelet, 1523*, Fordham University Press, New York, 1979.

Orme, N., *The Minor Clergy of Exeter Cathedral, 1300-1548*, University of Exeter Press, Exeter, 1980.

Owst, G.R., *Preaching in Medieval England*, Cambridge University Press, Cambridge, 1926.

Parks, G.B., *The English Traveller to Italy*, Stanford, 1954, I.

Parsons, D.J., 'John Colet's Stature as an Exegete', *The Anglican Theological Review*, 40, 1958, pp. 38-42.

Patrides, C.A., 'Renaissance Views on the 'Unconfused Orders Angellick'', *The Journal of the History of Ideas*, 23, 1962, pp. 265-7.

Peckham, W.D., 'The Vicars-Choral of Chichester Cathedral', *Sussex Archaeological Collections*, 78, 1937, pp. 126-59.

Peters, R., 'John Colet's Knowledge and Use of Patristics', *Moreana*, 22, 1964, pp. 45-59.

Pettegree, A., 'Humanism and the Reformation in Britain and the Netherlands' in N.S. Amos, A. Pettegree and H. van Nierop (eds.), *The Education of a Christian Society: Humanism and the Reformation in Britain and the Netherlands*, Ashagte, Aldershot, 1999, pp. 1-18.

Phythian-Adams, C., 'Urban Decay in Late Medieval England' in PP. Abrams and E.A. Wrigley (eds.), *Towns in Societies: Essays in Economic History and Historical Sociology*, Cambridge University Press, Cambridge, 1978, pp. 159-85.

Pollard, A.F., 'Council, Star Chamber, and Privy Council Under the Tudors, I: The Council', *The English Historical Review*, 17, 1922, pp. 337-60.

Pollard, A.F., 'Council, Star Chamber, and Privy Council Under the Tudors, II: The Star Chamber', *The English Historical Review*, 17, 1922, pp. 516-39.

Pollard, A.F., *Henry VIII*, Longmans, Green, London, 1951.

Pollard, A.F., *Wolsey*, Longmans, Green, London, 1929.

Porter, H.C., 'The Gloomy Dean and the Law' in G.V. Bennett and J.D. Walsh (eds.), *Essays in Modern Church History in Memory of Norman Sykes*, Black, London, 1966, pp. 18-43.

Porter, H.C., *Reformation and Reaction in Tudor Cambridge*, Cambridge University Press, Cambridge, 1958.

Pound, J., 'Clerical Poverty in Early Sixteenth-Century England: Some East Anglian Evidence', *The Journal of Ecclesiastical History*, 37, 1986, pp. 389-96.

Rex, R., *Henry VIII and the English Reformation*, Macmillan, Basingstoke, 1993.

Rex, R., 'Humanism' in A. Pettegree (ed.), *The Reformation World*, Routledge, London, 2000, pp. 51-70.

Rex, R., 'The Early Impact of Reformation Theology at Cambridge University, 1521-1547', *Reformation and Renaissance Review*, 4, 2001, pp. 38-71.

Rex, R., *The Lollards*, Macmillan, Basingstoke, 2002.

Rex, R., 'The New Learning', *The Journal of Ecclesiastical History*, 44, 1993, pp. 26-43.

Rex, R., 'The Role of English Humanists in the Reformation up to 1559' in N.S. Amos, A. Pettegree and H. van Nierop (eds.), *The Education of a Christian Society: Humanism and the Reformation in Britain and the Netherlands*, Ashgate, Aldershot, 1999, pp. 19-40.

Rex, R., *The Theology of John Fisher*, Cambridge University Press, Cambridge, 1991.

Rex, R. and Armstrong, C.D.C., 'Henry VIII's Ecclesiastical and Collegiate Foundations', *Historical Research*, 75, 2002, pp. 390-407.

Reynolds, E.E., *Thomas More and Erasmus*, Longmans, Green, London, 1965.

Rice, E.F. Jr., 'Humanist Aristotelianism in France: Jacques Lefèvre d'Etaples and his Circle' in A.H.T. Levi (ed.), *Humanism in France at the End of the Middle Ages and in the Early Renaissance*, Manchester University Press, 1970, pp. 132-49.

Rice, E.F. Jr., 'John Colet and the Annihilation of the Natural', *The Harvard Theological Review*, 45, 1952, pp. 141-63.

Rice, E.F. Jr., 'The Humanist Idea of Christian Antiquity: Lefèvre d'Etaples and his Circle' in *Studies in the Renaissance*, 9, 1962, pp. 126-60, reprinted in W.L. Gundersheimer (ed.), *French Humanism, 1470-1600*, Macmillan, London, 1969, pp. 163-80.

Rieger, J.H., 'Erasmus, Colet and the Schoolboy Jesus', *Studies in the Renaissance*, 9, 1962, pp. 187-94.

Rist, J., 'Augustine of Hippo' in G.R. Evans (ed.), *The Medieval Theologians: An Introduction to Theology in the Medieval Period*, Blackwell, Oxford, 2001, pp. 3-23.

Robson, M., 'Saint Bonaventure' in G.R. Evans (ed.), *The Medieval Theologians: An Introduction to Theology in the Medieval Period*, Blackwell, Oxford, 2001, pp. 187-200.

Rorem, P.P., 'Augustine, the Medieval Theologians, and the Reformation' in G.R. Evans (ed.), *The Medieval Theologians: An Introduction to Theology in the Medieval Period*, Blackwell, Oxford, 2001, pp. 365-72.

Rorem, P.P., *Pseudo-Dionysius: A Commentary on the Texts and an Introduction to Their Influence*, Oxford University Press, Oxford, 1993.

Rummel, E., 'Voices of Reform from Hus to Erasmus' in T.A. Brady Jr., H.A. Oberman and J.D. Tracy (eds.), *Handbook of European History, 1400-1600: Late Middle Ages, Renaissance and Reformation. Volume II: Visions, Programs and Outcomes*, Leiden, Brill, The Netherlands, 1995, pp. 61-92.

Rycraft, A., 'The Arrival of Humanistic Script in York?' in D. Wood (ed.), *Life and Thought in the Northern Church, c.1100-c.1700: Essays in Honour of Claire Cross*, Studies in Church History, Subsidia 12, Boydell Press, Woodbridge, 1999, pp. 170-81.

Schwarz, C., Davidson, G., Seaton, A., Tebbit, V. (eds.), *Chambers English Dictionary*, Chambers, Edinburgh, 1990.

Seebohm, F., *The Oxford Reformers of 1498: Being a History of the Fellow-Work of John Colet, Erasmus and Thomas More*, 1st edition, Longmans, Green, London, 1867; 3rd edition, Longmans, London, 1896.

Sheils, W.J., *The English Reformation, 1530-1570*, Longman, London, 1989.

Smith, H. Maynard, *Pre-Reformation England*, Macmillan, London, 1938.

Steinmetz, D.C., *Reformers in the Wings: From Geiler von Kaysersberg to Theodore Beza*, 1st edition, Fortress Press, Philadelphia; 2nd edition, Oxford University Press, Oxford, 2001.

Stephens, L. (ed.), *The Dictionary of National Biography*, XI and XIX, Oxford University Press, London, 1887 and 1889.

Storey, R.L., 'Ordinations of Secular Priests in Early Tudor London', *Nottingham Medieval Studies*, 33, 1989, pp. 122-33.

Sutton, A.F., *The Mercery of London: Trade, Goods and People, 1130-1578*, Ashgate, Aldershot, 2005.

Swanson, R.N., 'Problems of the Priesthood in Pre-Reformation England', *The English Historical Review*, 105 (1990) pp. 845-69.

Tanner, N., 'Penances Imposed on Kentish Lollards by Archbishop Warham, 1511-12' in M. Aston and C. Richmond (eds.), *Lollardy and the Gentry in the Later Middle Ages*, Sutton, Stroud, 1997, pp. 229-49.

Thayer, A.T., 'Judge and Doctor: Images of the Confessor in Printed Model Sermon Collections, 1450-1520' in K.J. Lualdi and A.T. Thayer (eds.), *Penitence in the Age of Reformations*, Ashgate, Aldershot, 2000, pp. 10-29.

Thompson, A.H., 'Notes on Colleges of Secular Canons in England', *The Archaeological Journal*, 74, 1917, pp. 139-85.

Thompson, A.H., *The English Clergy and their Organization in the Later Middle Ages*, Clarendon, Oxford, 1947.

Thomson, J.A.F., *The Early Tudor Church and Society, 1485-1529*, Longman, London, 1993.

Thomson, J.A.F., *The Later Lollards, 1414-1520*, Oxford University Press, Oxford, 1965.

Tillyard, E.M.W., *The Elizabethan World Picture*, 1st edition, Chatto and Windus, London, 1943.

Trapp, J.B., 'An English Late Medieval Cleric and Italian Thought: The Case of John Colet, Dean of St. Paul's (1467-1519)' in G. Kratzmann and J. Simpson (eds.), *Medieval English Religious and Ethical Literature: Essays in Honour of G. H. Russell*, Cambridge University Press, Cambridge, 1986, pp. 233-50.

Trapp, J.B., 'Christopher Urswick and his Books: the Reading of Henry VII's Almoner', *Renaissance Studies*, I, 1987, pp. 48-71.

Trapp, J.B., 'Dame Christian Colet and Thomas More', *Moreana*, 16 (Festschrift for E. F. Rogers), 1967, pp. 103-114.

Trapp, J.B., *Erasmus, Colet and More: The Early Tudor Humanists and Their Books*, British Library, London, 1991.

Trapp, J.B., 'Erasmus on William Grocyn and Ps-Dionysius: A Re-examination', *The Journal of the Warburg and Courtauld Institutes*, 59, 1996, pp. 294-303.

Trapp, J.B., 'John Colet' in H.C.G. Matthew and B. Harrison (eds.), *The Oxford Dictionary of National Biography in Association with the British Academy: From the Earliest Times to the Year 2000*, XII, Oxford University Press, Oxford, 2004, pp. 601-9.

Trapp, J.B., 'John Colet' in PP. Bietenholz and T.B. Deutscher (eds.), *Contemporaries of Erasmus: A Biographical Register of the Renaissance and Reformation*, I, University of Toronto Press, Toronto, 1985, pp. 324-8.

Trapp, J.B., 'John Colet and the *Hierarchies* of the Ps-Dionysius' in K. Robbins (ed.), *Religion and Humanism*, Studies in Church History, 17, Blackwell, Oxford, 1981, pp. 127-48.

Trapp, J.B., 'John Colet, His Manuscripts and the Pseudo-Dionysius' in R.R. Bolgar (ed.), *Classical Influences on European Culture, 1500-1700: Proceedings of an International Conference held at King's College, Cambridge, April 1974*, Cambridge University Press, Cambridge, 1976, pp. 205-22.

Trapp, J.B., 'Notes on Manuscripts Written by Peter Meghen', *The Book Collector*, 24, 1975, pp. 80-96.

Trapp, J.B., 'Pieter Meghen, 1466/7-1540: Scribe and Courier', *Erasmus in English*, 11, 1981-2, pp. 28-35.

Trapp, J.B., 'Pieter Meghen, Yet Again' in J.B. Trapp (ed.), *Manuscripts in the Fifty Years After the Invention of Printing*, Warburg Institute, London, 1983, pp. 23-8.

Trevelyan, G.M., *English Social History*, 1st edition, Longmans, Green, London, 1944.

Varley, B., *The History of Stockport Grammar School*, Manchester University Press, Manchester, 1946.

Wabuda, S., *Preaching During the English Reformation*, Cambridge University Press, Cambridge, 2002.

Walker, G., 'The Renaissance in Britain' in PP. Collinson (ed.), *The Short Oxford History of the British Isles: The Sixteenth Century, 1485-1603*, Oxford University Press, Oxford, 2002, pp. 145-87.

Westlake, H.F., *The Parish Guilds of Medieval England*, SPCK, London, 1919.

Wicks, J., 'Thomas de Vio Cajetan (1469-1534)' in C. Lindberg (ed.), *The Reformation Theologians: An Introduction to Theology in the Early Modern Period*, Blackwell, Oxford, 2002, pp. 269-80.

Wood-Legh, K.L., *Perpetual Chantries in Britain*, Cambridge University Press, Cambridge, 1965.

Wordsworth, C., 'The Life of Dean Colet, from the Phoenix' in C. Wordsworth, *Ecclesiastical Biography: Lives of Eminent Men, Connected with the Religion of England*, I , Rivington, London, 1853, pp. 433-57.

INDEX

Accidence 100, 104
Accusations 50, 51, 142, 146, 151, 159
Acts and Monuments 5
Aeditio 20, 104
Aldermen 17, 18
Alexander VI 138
Almain, Jacques 132
Ambrose 23, 78, 100, 102
Amersham 150
Angels 28, 30, 33, 35, 36, 37, 44, 46, 47, 58, 62, 63, 64, 75, 120, 165
Annihilation of the Natural 8
Annotationes 10
Anstell, John 69
Anticlericalism 9, 10, 33, 34, 35, 109, 147, 152, 154,
Apostles 49, 50, 51, 59, 85, 103, 111, 128, 141, 153
Aquinas 25, 26, 31, 43, 44, 62, 63, 123, 128
Archbishops 8, 21, 51, 94, 108, 110, 112, 113, 141, 143, 152, 153, 157, 166, 176
Areopagite, see Pseudo-Dionysius
Aristotle 21, 39, 43, 62, 63
Aristotelian 9, 31, 43, 62
Asceticism 27, 66, 68, 84, 86, 96, 115, 123, 144, 145, 149, 161, 178, 181
Augustine 23, 25, 29, 31, 39, 42-4, 54, 60, 61, 101, 102, 178
Augustinian 2, 8, 9, 13, 24, 31, 37, 38, 41, 43, 44, 46, 47, 49, 56, 61, 179
Authority, Ecclesiastical 23, 33, 34, 38, 40, 42, 43, 51, 64, 75, 78, 87, 94, 95, 114, 115, 128, 130, 131, 132, 135, 136, 139, 140, 146, 149, 151, 152, 153, 156,

Authority, *cont.*, 157, 160, 164, 165, 166, 174, 175

Bale, John 5, 184
Baldock, Ralph de 77, 87, 94, 157, 159, 170, 173, 174, 176, 181
Baldry, Thomas 90, 97
Baptism 50
Baptista Mantuanus 10, 102
Beaufort, Lady Margaret 90, 121, 122
Beauty and Order 27, 30, 31, 34, 40, 49, 55, 56, 57, 60, 64, 110, 115, 116, 120, 124, 134, 178, 179, 182, 185
Bernard of Clairvaux 38, 76, 114, 123, 126
Bible, in English 26, 91, 128
Biblical Interpretation 5, 6, 7, 24, 26, 43, 117, 149
Biel, Gabriel 125
Biography of Colet (Erasmus) 4-10, 13, 19, 143, 146, 148, 151, 182
Bishop of Exeter 83, 152, 166
Bishop of Lincoln 109, 117, 152
Bishop of London – see Fitzjames
Bishop of Salisbury 5
Bishops, Authority of 32, 39, 40, 47-56
Blasphemy 119
Body of Christ 25, 30, 31, 33, 34, 39, 44, 46, 54, 55, 57, 59, 61, 133, 170, 171, 178, 181, 184
Bombace, Paolo 156, 168
Bonaventure 39, 44-5
Book of Martyrs 5
Botevant, Prebend of 21, 74
Braybroke, Bishop 70, 73, 77, 87

Brethren of the Common Life 125
Bricot 145
Bridport, Parish of 83, 84
Buckenham, Norfolk 18
Buckingham 17, 18, 89, 98, 149
Butler, John 150

Cabbala 25, 122 130
Cambridge 1, 13, 18, 20, 25, 26, 87, 121, 122, 146, 170, 183
Camera Stellata 167
Campeggio, Cardinal 92
Canon Law 9, 57, 58, 81, 108, 113, 115, 120, 124, 128, 134, 185
Canons, Cathedral 5, 38, 48, 51, 65, 68-71, 75, 76, 77, 84-7, 115, 125, 149, 156, 157, 158, 164, 170, 172, 173, 174, 175, 177
Canterbury 5, 7, 12, 14, 19, 22, 94, 108, 141, 143, 152, 166, 180
Capellanos 66, 71
Cardinals, Role of 151-7
Carthusians 38, 61, 136, 143, 169, 181
Carthusianus, Dionysius 132, 133
Catechism 103-5
Cathedral Clergy 2, 5, 13, 14, 15, 19, 27, 31, 33, 34, 36, 41, 45-87, 90, 91, 96, 99, 108-117, 121-129, 133, 134, 135, 137, 142, 143, 144, 147, 149, 151-163, 164, 165, 170, 171, 177, 180, 181, 183
Catholic 1-11, 90, 91, 108-13, 116, 149-53, 178,182
Celestial Hierarchy, the Treatise 25, 28, 38, 40, 47, 62-4, 114, 165, 184
Chancellor, Cambridge University 121
Chancellor, Cathedral 70, 93, 94, 95, 171, 173
Chancellor, of England 167, 176,
Chancellor, Paris University 133
Chantries/Chantry Priests 13, 48, 51, 66-80, 83, 84, 85, 87, 89, 90, 93, 96, 98, 99, 183
Chapel Royal 69, 75, 167
Chaplain, School 99, 100, 105-7, 115
Chapter, Cathedral 136, 137-56, 158-64, 175
Cheapside 93
Cherubim 62, 153
Choir 53, 66-87, 93, 171
Choristers 70, 75, 84, 87, 95, 101, 104
Christian Humanism 2-16, 23, 27, 33,

Christian Humanism, *cont.*, 36, 37, 49, 61, 62, 121, 126, 148, 178
Christian Knyvet 1, 18
Christocentricity 31, 41, 42, 179
Chrodegang, Rule of 74
Cicero 2, 20, 21, 25, 42, 157
City of God, Augustine 39, 41, 43
Classical Authors 2, 27, 28, 31, 34, 42, 61, 81, 100, 101, 102, 103, 106, 165
Clergy, Minor 13, 14, 48, 65-87, 90, 115, 157, 164, 170, 171, 172, 173, 180, 183
Clericalism 34, 165
Colet, Henry 1, 13, 17, 19, 52, 88-92, 94, 95, 97
Colet, Robert 17
Colet, William 17
Commentaries 6, 10, 25-9, 31, 32, 38, 39, 41, 42, 46, 48, 51, 54, 55, 56, 62, 63, 126, 129, 130, 145, 153, 154, 157, 160, 161, 173, 174, 176, 183
Conciliarism 14, 40, 108, 112, 113, 130-34
Continental Preachers 125-31
Continental Thought 12, 14, 22, 23, 63, 108, 113, 119, 125-31, 132, 134, 171, 182
Conversation 14, 78, 62, 68, 78, 80, 81, 82, 85
Convocation 5, 6, 7, 9, 12, 14, 41, 48, 49, 51, 57, 76, 79, 81, 108-35, 137, 142, 148, 149, 152, 153, 164, 166, 180
Corinthians 1, 25, 26, 27, 28, 55, 56, 63, 184
Corporation of London 18
Cottingham Church 70
Courts, of Law 9, 58, 96, 114, 124, 166
Court, Royal 15, 122, 136, 137, 138, 149, 166, 168
Cranmer, Thomas 6
Crown 18, 136, 140, 154
Curriculum, School 100-06
Customs, of St. Paul's 158, 162
Cyprian 23, 78

De Copia 103, 106
De Sacramentis 10, 11, 25, 33-6, 63, 172, 184
Deacon 21, 47, 49, 69, 85, 115
Dean of Lichfield 75, 76, 77, 87
Demiurge 2
Dennington, Suffolk 1, 21, 52
Diligence 27, 74, 82, 87

INDEX

Dionysius, see Pseudo-Dionysius
Discipline, Clerical 14, 55, 57, 60, 67, 73, 74, 76, 82, 86, 87, 89, 90, 92, 96, 112, 119, 121, 125, 128, 129, 149, 158, 159, 172, 174, 177, 183
Disputatiuncula 24, 184
Diversity, in the Church 53, 57, 60
Divinity Lecturer, St. Paul's 71
Doctorate in Theology/Divinity 23, 87
Downam, John 175
Dress, Clerical 69, 71, 119
Dugdale, William 6, 93, 158, 170
Duke of Lancaster 70
Durnford, Prebend of 21

Ecclesiastical Hierarchy,
  the Treatise 13, 25, 32, 38, 40, 46-55, 145, 174, 184
Ecclesiastical Hierarchy,
  Subject of 30, 33, 108, 110, 115, 118, 120, 129, 133, 134, 153, 156, 170, 176, 179, 182
Ecclesiology, Introduction to 1-16,
  in Colet's Works 30-65
Ecclesiology, in Practice 66-87, 108-86
Edward IV 17, 85
Emanations 28, 31, 39, 43, 46, 49, 179
Enchiridion Militis Christiani 10, 25, 124
English Hospice in Rome 22, 126
English Reformation 1, 3, 4, 10, 11, 12, 33, 178
English Secular Cathedrals 14, 67, 68, 73, 74, 76
Episcopate 39, 46, 51, 109, 181, see also Bishops
Epistolae, of Ficino 9, 23, 25, 42, 154
Epitome 157-77
Erasmus:
  Biography of Colet 1-25, 26, 42, 43, 44, 50, 78, 80, 81, 82, 84, 85, 86, 95, 96, 101, 104, 137, 138, 139, 140, 141, 143, 144, 145, 146, 147, 148, 149, 155, 156, 158, 168, 169, 174, 177, 181, 184
  Influence of 24-9, 103, 106, 168
  First meeting 24-5
  The humanist 39, 42, 61, 100, 107, 109, 121, 122, 124, 125, 161, 178, 180
Eton 19, 32, 36, 49, 62-3, 94, 101-7
Eucharist 35, 51, 69, 120, 165

Exegesis 5, 7, 8, 26, 29, 32, 62, 110, 184, see also Biblical Interpretation
Exempla 4, 44, 118, 173
Exeter 77, 83, 84, 85, 152, 166
Exhibita 157-77
Exordium 117

Faith 4, 24, 27, 43, 47, 56, 79, 101-3, 106, 116, 121, 123, 127, 128, 150, 151
Ferdinand of Aragon 138
Festial, John Mirk's 117
Ficino, Marsilio 1, 2, 9, 10, 22-8, 32, 39, 42, 49, 60, 61, 62, 126, 154, 180
Fisher, John 14-5, 32, 61-3, 119-25, 134, 166, 177, 178, 180, 181, 182
Fitzjames, Bishop Richard 5, 15, 50, 54, 85, 92, 96, 135, 136-151, 155-6, 159, 162
Florence 22, 23, 127, 132
Fox, Richard 134
Foxe, John 3-7, 137, 141, 145, 146, 150, 161
France 13, 21, 62, 138, 140, 154
Francis of Assisi 123
Franciscans 2, 13, 31, 37, 39, 41, 44, 45, 46, 54, 61, 178, 179
Frequens 131-2

Gascoigne, Thomas 76, 110
Geiler, Johann 14, 113, 125-9, 130, 182
Geoffrey, Thomas 150
Gerson, Jean 133
Gleason, John 4, 7, 9-12, 17, 20, 23, 33, 35-7, 44, 45, 59, 79, 95, 99, 101, 102, 103, 109, 110, 118, 137, 140, 142, 143, 144, 147, 158, 159, 160, 162, 165, 166, 167, 182, 185
Godly Conversation, see Conversation
Good Friday, 1513 136-40
Gospels 59, 129, 149
Grace 27, 28, 30, 31, 41, 43, 44, 45, 46, 49, 54, 56-8, 61-3, 79, 81, 120, 125, 128, 152, 153, 165, 179
Grace Books 1, 20
Grammar, Learning of 20, 21, 27, 75, 93-5
Grammar Master(s) 93-5, 170, 173
Grammar Schools 12, 93-108
Greek 2, 7, 9, 22-7, 38, 102, 103, 106, 107, 122, 141
Greenwich 137, 139

Grocyn, William 22, 23, 99, 107, 121
Grosseteste, Bishop 76, 109
Guild of the Holy Name of Jesus 14, 88-95, 97, 100, 108

Harding, Thomas 5
Hall, Edward 167
Harrington, William 175
Heaven 28, 34, 36, 41, 44, 47, 48, 49, 53, 64, 71, 129-31, 153-4, 165, 173
Henry VII 1, 18, 52, 87, 89, 95, 122
Henry VIII 97, 112, 136, 137, 138, 140, 154, 156, 164, 166, 168, 169
Heptaplus 25, 126
Heresy 3, 16, 81, 109, 112, 114, 122, 124, 137, 143, 145, 147, 149, 150
Heretics 5, 22, 112, 114, 122, 124, 136, 144, 146, 147, 149, 150, 151, 155, 156
Hermetic Corpus 25, 62
Heywood, Thomas 75, 76, 77, 87, see also Dean of Lichfield
Hierarchy, Church 13, 24, 30-64, 65, 71, 80, 108, 110, 111, 112, 114, 115, 118, 120, 129, 133, 134-5, 136, 142, 145, 146, 153, 154, 156, 157, 165, 168, 170, 174, 176, 179, 182, 184
Highmaster, of St. Paul's School 22, 99, 100, 102, 104, 105, 106
Higher Clergy 46, 55, 64
Hilduin, Abbot of St. Denis 38
Holiness 26, 48, 55, 107
Holy Orders 27-8, 52
Holy Spirit 47-8, 55, 57, 79, 132
Homiletic Style 14, 24, 26, 113, 116-21, 123, 124, 139, 156, 166, 184
Hospitality 14, 50, 68, 69, 83-7, 116, 119, 135, 136, 141, 142, 144, 145, 146, 147, 154, 159
Hostility to Colet 75, 156
Humanism 1-12, 23, 27, 33, 36, 37, 49, 61, 62, 121, 126, 148, 178, see also Christian Humanism
Humanity 2, 8-10, 15, 26-9, 30, 31-47, 55-65, 96, 101, 111, 116, 120, 125, 134, 179
Hunne, Richard 33, 109

Idealism, Colet's 2, 3, 8, 10, 11, 12, 14, 15, 16, 26, 28, 48, 59, 60, 63, 65, 66, 67, 68, 77, 78, 85, 86, 92, 96, 101 102, 103, 109, 111, 113, 119, 121, 124

Idealism, *cont.*, 125, 128, 133, 134, 136, 139, 140, 141, 147, 148, 149, 151, 152, 155, 164, 165, 168, 172, 173, 174, 176, 177, 178, 179, 180, 181, 182, 183
Ideology 9, 12, 14, 15, 16, 35, 49, 61
Ignatius 25, 43
Illumination (Purification and Perfection) 27, 30, 31, 35, 47, 49, 50, 54, 63, 120, 130, 179
Incarnation 28, 41, 55, 57
Individuality 14, 30, 38, 40, 57, 59, 60, 119, 120, 123, 125, 126, 127, 128, 129, 134, 171, 179
Injunctions, for Minor Clergy 13, 51, 65-87, 159, 170, 183
Injunctions, Papal 93
Injunctions, Royal 104
Institutum Christiani Hominis 100, 104
Intellect (and Will) 30, 31, 39, 42, 44, 46, 54, 60-62
Intellectual Life, Colet's 1-12, 16, 22, 32, 41, 43, 66, 77, 78, 79, 81, 109, 121, 178, 179, 181
Ipswich 102
Italy 1, 2, 7, 13, 21, 22, 62, 96, 100, 107, 126-8
Itinerarium, of Bonaventure 44

Jerome 20, 23, 25, 43, 78, 100, 102
Jewel, Bishop John 5, 6
John of Salisbury 38
John Scotus Erigena 38
Jonas, Jodicus 4, 78, 104, 107
Julius II, Pope 95, 138
Julius Caesar 138
Justice 35, 44, 45, 48, 59, 167, 168

Katherine of Aragon 122
King's Council 136, 156, 167, 176
Knight, Samuel 6, 7, 18, 19, 162, 163, 164
Knyvet, Christian 1, 18

Lady Margaret Beaufort, see Beaufort
Laity 30, 33-5, 53, 54, 58, 64, 92, 96, 99, 107, 109, 114, 115, 116, 121, 126, 128, 129, 134, 142, 148, 165, 179, 185
Lambourn, Rector of 21
Lancaster College 70
Langland, William 76, 109
Lateran Councils 93, 111, 116
Latimer, Hugh 5, 22, 137, 146

Latin authors 102-8, see Classical Authors
Lefèvre d'Etaples 14, 25, 32, 61, 62, 63, 113, 116, 125, 129, 130, 180, 182
Legate *a Latere* 92, 157, 163, 176, 182
Libelli 72-86, 183
Lichfield, William 19
Lily, William 22, 23, 99, 100, 102, 104, 107
Linacre, Thomas 22, 23, 103, 107, 121, 168
Lisieux, Dean 77, 87, 157, 159, 170, 173, 174, 176, 181, 182, 188
Literature, Godly 78, 79, 81, 101, 102, 103, 105, 106, 107, 173
Litigation 27, 55, 58, 154, 168
Liturgy 71, 89, 91
Lollardy 109, 112, 137, 144, 147, 149, 150, 151, 155, 156
London 1, 3, 5, 7, 10, 12, 13, 14, 17, 18, 19, 20, 24, 25, 49, 50, 72, 77, 83, 87-108, 137, 142, 143, 145, 146, 147, 150, 161, 163 164, 176, 177, 178, 179, 180, 181, 183, 184, 185
Longland, John 117, 119, 120, 149
Lord Mayor 18
Low Countries 52, 89
Lucubratiunculae 24-5
Lupset, Thomas 96, 177
Lupton, Joseph 7, 11, 20, 23, 24, 27, 87, 95, 100, 109, 137, 140, 147, 151, 158, 159, 160, 164, 184
Luther, Martin 4, 42, 43, 119, 122, 123

Magdalen College 20, 99
Magnus Intercursus 18, 52, 89
Mankind 45, 49, 55, 62, 147, 177
Manuscripts 10, 26, 42, 66, 67, 73, 78, 79, 82, 151, 170, 183
Manuscript, Lost 65-87
Master of the Mercers' Company 18, 89, 91, 92, 99, 100
Matrimony 28, 35
Medieval Sermons 116-35
Meghen, Peter 67
Melton, William 16, 148, 178, 182,
Mercers 17-20, 48, 88, 108
Mirk, John 117
Monks 36, 38, 53, 61, 86, 115, 149, 174, 181
Mora, Prebend of 21
Morality 2, 9, 10, 13, 14, 20, 21, 27, 42

Morality, *cont.*, 61, 66, 68, 70, 74, 76, 78, 81, 82, 95, 96, 99, 105, 110, 111, 114, 125, 126, 138, 140, 147, 151, 154, 155, 156, 170, 173, 176, 177, 178
More, Thomas 2, 7, 91, 109, 121, 168
Mosaic Account of Creation 25, 184
Moses 47, 79
Mountjoy, Lord 168, 177
Multiplicity 30, 36, 39, 64, 124, 179
Music 66, 69, 74, 75, 76, 87, 101, 172
Mystical Body of Christ 25, 30, 33, 34, 39, 44, 46, 54, 55, 59, 61, 133, 171, 181, 184
Mysticism 29, 61

Neoplatonism 2, 9, 10, 13, 20, 23, 25, 37, 41-3
New Learning 87
New Testament 26, 79, 141
Nichomachean Ethics 39
Nowell, Dean Alexander 161, 163, 164
Nykke, Bishop of Norwich 166

Obedience 31, 50, 55, 66, 79, 87, 108, 110, 113, 114, 115, 116, 118, 119, 120-37, 142, 173, 182
Obits 71, 74
Oculus Sacerdotis 117, 122
Old Testament 84
Oldham, Hugh, Bishop of Exeter 83, 166
Opus Dei 68, 74, 78, 82, 86
Order, see Beauty
Ordinances 89, 101, 105, 158
Origen 23, 25, 43, 56, 60, 61, 78
Orleans 21
Otherworldliness 23, 31, 33, 41, 46, 59, 63, 64, 179
Oxford 1, 4, 5, 7, 10, 11, 12, 13, 16, 20, 21, 22, 23, 24, 25, 26, 27, 41, 65, 66, 67, 87, 94, 96, 99, 105, 107, 122, 151, 154, 170, 177, 178, 180, 181, 183, 184
Oxford Reformers 7, 10, 16

Pace, Richard 107, 168, 177
Pagan Authors, see Classical Authors
Paris 22, 62, 131, 132, 133
Parishes 19, 21, 71, 76, 87, 98, 99, 117, 148, 154
Parker, Matthew 5, 21
Pater Noster 5, 114, 146
Pauline Theology 2, 10, 13, 21, 24, 26, 31

Pauline Theology, *cont.*, 41-3, 47, 61, 130
Pelagian Heresy 31, 43, 46, 120, 179
Penance 29, 14, 41, 42, 59, 61, 63, 113, 119, 120, 124, 125, 127, 131, 149, 181
Penitence, see Penance
Penitential Psalms 117, 119
Perfection 1, 2, 14, 16, 26, 27, 28, 30, 31, 33, 34, 35, 36, 45, 46, 47, 48, 53, 54, 55, 60, 63, 64, 65, 79, 80, 82, 86, 87, 96, 99, 107, 108, 111, 114, 116, 118, 120, 121, 124, 126, 130, 131, 132, 134, 135, 136, 139, 147, 154, 156, 164, 166, 168, 170, 171, 173, 176, 177, 178, 179, 180, 181, 182
Perfectionist Ideals, see Perfection
Philosophy 20, 23, 28, 29, 43, 62, 78, 101, 106, 122
Pico della Mirandola 9, 23, 25, 28, 49, 62, 122, 126, 131
Piers Plowman 110
Pitts, John 6, 184
Plainsong 75
Platonic Academy 2, 23, 42
Plato/Platonism 1, 2, 5, 8, 9, 10, 13, 20, 21, 22, 23, 24, 25, 26, 28, 29, 31, 33, 37, 39, 41, 42, 43, 46, 49, 54, 60, 61, 62, 101, 111, 178, 179
Plotinus 2, 20, 25, 26, 28, 42
Pluralism 52, 70, 79, 122, 148
Politian 22
Polticial Theology, see Politics
Politics 1, 4, 11, 12, 15, 38, 39, 40, 43, 46, 60, 62, 88, 99, 125, 136, 140, 143, 151, 157-77, 178, 180, 181, 182
Poor Clerks 68, 69, 75, 83
Pope Julius II 95, 138
Pope Sixtus IV 52
Post-revisionism 4, 164, 166, 178
Prayer 7, 45, 53, 68, 69, 70, 71, 79, 90, 91, 114, 117, 119, 125, 126, 142, 146, 171, 173, 185
Preaching, see Chapters 5 and 7
Pre-Reformation 3, 4, 8, 10, 11, 15, 16, 116, 118, 119, 125, 182, 183
Prevenient Grace 61
Pricksong 75
Priesthood 10, 30, 33, 34, 35, 36, 37, 48, 51, 60, 69, 82, 111, 114, 120, 121, 126, 128, 134, 165, 179
Privy Council 168
Proto-Protestant 1, 3, 4, 5, 6, 7, 11, 16,

Proto-Protestant, *cont.*, 109, 110, 147, 178, 181
Psalm Singing 70, 74
Pseudo-Dionysius 5, 7, 8, 9, 10, 13, 25, 26, 28, 31, 32, 34, 36, 38, 39, 40, 42, 43, 46, 47, 49, 54, 57, 62, 63, 64, 78, 130, 133, 144, 145, 165, 174, 178, 179, 184
Punishment 58, 75
Purification, see Illumination

Radulphus, Letter to 25, 55, 184
Rank 10, 33, 35, 39, 51, 52, 53, 59, 69, 85, 153, 176, see also Hierarchy
Reconciliation 59, 62, 120, 148
Reform 1-18, 30, 31, 33, 35, 41, 49, 51, 54, 62, 63, 64, 65-87, 88, 90, 91, 92, 93, 97, 99, 108, 109, 110, 111, 112, 113, 115, 116, 118, 119, 124, 125, 126, 128, 130, 131, 132, 133, 134, 137, 147, 148, 149, 151, 156, 157-77, 178, 179, 180, 181, 182, 183
Reformation 1-16, 35, 41, 54, 67, 71, 74, 76, 96, 99, 109, 111, 112, 115, 116, 119, 125, 127, 131, 133, 134, 161, 164, 173, 174, 178, 182, 183
Registrum Statutorum 162
Repentance 14, 50, 113, 119, 120, 121, 123, 125, 126, 127, 128, 129, 131, 134, 181
Residentiary Canons 68, 69, 84, 85, 86, 149, 157, 158, 164, 170, 173, 174, 175, 177, 178
Reuchlin, Johannes 25, 122
Revisionism 4, 10, 11, 20, 160, 164, 166, 170, 174, 175, 178, 182
Richard III 70, 94
Richard of Kidderminster 26, 184
Richard of St. Victor 38
Ritwise, John 100
Romans 1, 25, 26, 36, 41, 44, 49, 56, 58, 60, 62, 96, 144, 184
Rome 22, 91, 126, 132
Royal Council 15, 166

Sacrament 10, 11, 25, 28, 33, 34, 35, 36, 48, 52, 54, 61, 63, 64, 82, 89, 103, 110, 114, 119, 120, 124, 149, 151, 165, 166, 168, 172, 184
Salisbury 69, 70, 76, 84
Salust 100, 102

INDEX

Savonarola 14, 23, 113, 126, 127, 182
Saymer, Thomas 97
Scholasticism 24, 30, 38, 43, 61, 81, 124, 132, 179
Schooling 17-21
Seebohm, Frederick 7-11, 139
Seraphim 62, 152, 153, 154
Simplicity 36, 46, 61, 64, 128
Sin 49, 60, 61, 114, 121, 123, 128, 151,
Slovenliness 73
St. Anthony's School 19, 20, 94
St. John Chrysostom 25, 43
St. Paul's Cathedral, see Chapters 3 to 7 esp. 1, 4, 12, 19, 21, 23, 31, 36, 66, 69, 84, 89, 95, 98, 108, 136, 151, 157, 176, 178, 183
St. Paul's School 88-107, 108, 160, 163, 177
St. Peter's College 70
St. Thomas Becket 93
St. Thomas of Acre (Acon) 14, 19, 20, 21, 88, 91, 92, 93
Stafford, George 146
Stafford, Humphrey 18
Standish, Henry 145
Star Chamber 167
Statutes, see Chapters 3 and 7
Stepney 1, 19, 21
Stratford, Henry 19
Surmaster, St. Paul's School 7, 100, 105, 106

Taylor, John 148
Terence 100, 102
Theologia Platonica 25, 42
Threadneedle Street 19, 94
Thrones, Angelic 62, 153
Thurning 1, 21
Tully 100, 102
Tunstall, Cuthbert 168
Tyndale, William 5, 137, 146

Unity, Church 27, 30, 31, 34, 39, 41, 55, 57, 80, 82, 86, 87, 116, 118, 120, 124, 134, 148, 150, 170, 171, 176, 178, 179, 180, 182
Unpopularity, Colet's 53, 82, 87
Urswick, Christopher 22
Utopia, of Thomas More 36

Valla, Laurentia 25, 125, 126

Vicars 13, 68, 69, 70, 74, 75, 76, 77, 87, 157-70, 172, 173, 174
Vicars-Choral, see Vicars
Victorian Scholarship 7, 11, 19, 32, 110, 147, 175, 178, 184
Virgil 21, 100, 102
Vision, Colet's 1-16, 27, 31, 32, 36, 38, 41, 47, 49, 55, 57, 60, 63, 64, 77, 86, 108, 109, 111, 112, 113, 116, 119, 121, 124, 125, 127, 132, 133, 134, 151, 152, 153, 155, 156, 164, 165, 166, 168, 170, 177, 178, 180, 181, 182
Visitations 13, 72, 76, 84, 127, 164, 175
Vitrier, Jean 4

War 14, 137-40, 151-5
Warham, William 8, 51, 112, 113, 142, 143, 146, 153, 163, 157, 163, 164, 167, 175, 181
Wells Cathedral 69, 70, 76, 135
Wendover 17
Westminster Abbey 19, 136, 151
Westminster Palace 167
Westminster School 19
White Kennett, Bishop 6, 7
Will, see Intellect
Winchester 93, 101, 102, 107, 134
Wolsey, Thomas 15, 40, 51, 92, 99, 102, 136, 137, 141, 142, 151-77, 181, 183
Worsley, Dean 84, 85
Wycliffe, John 109, 149, 155

York 1, 21, 69, 70, 74, 85, 143, 176

Zeal, Colet's Reforming 9, 49, 112, 114, 126, 153

Lightning Source UK Ltd.
Milton Keynes UK
UKHW020625220720
366952UK00004B/78